The Man
from Porlock

Princeton Series of Collected Essays

This series was initiated in response to requests from students and teachers who want the best essays of leading scholars available in a convenient format. Each book in this series serves scholarship by gathering in one place previously published articles representing the valuable contribution of a noted authority to his field. The format allows for the addition of a preface or introduction and an index to enhance the collection's usefulness. Photoreproduction of the essays keeps costs to a minimum and thus makes possible publication in a relatively inexpensive form.

The Man
from Porlock

*Engagements
1944-1981*

Theodore Weiss

Princeton University Press, Princeton, New Jersey

Copyright © 1982 by Princeton University Press
Published by Princeton University Press, 41 William Street, Princeton,
New Jersey
In the United Kingdom: Princeton University Press, Guildford, Surrey

ALL RIGHTS RESERVED

Library of Congress Cataloging in Publication Data will be
found on the last printed page of this book

Publication of this book has been aided by a grant from the Paul
Mellon Fund of Princeton University Press

Clothbound editions of Princeton University Press books
are printed on acid-free paper, and binding materials are
chosen for strength and durability

Printed in the United States of America by Princeton
University Press, Princeton, New Jersey

Acknowledgments

I owe thanks to many people, especially helpful editors like Herbert Leibowitz, John Gross, John Palmer, and Stephen Berg who, by requesting some of these essays, in a sense inspired them. This is also a good place to thank my friends William Humphrey, M. L. Rosenthal, Joseph Frank, Marjorie Perloff, Robert Fagles, and Edmund Keeley for years-long encouragement. I am particularly grateful to my editor Marjorie Sherwood for her patient kindness, her sympathy for this volume's welfare.

"Poetry from Porlock," *Times Literary Supplement*, September 26, 1980, London. "E.P.: The Man Who Cared Too Much," *Parnassus*, Fall-Winter 1976, Vol. 5, No. 1, New York. "Wallace Stevens: Lunching with Hoon," *The American Poetry Review*, September-October 1978, Vol. 7, No. 5, Philadelphia. "Retrospecting the Retrospective," *Quarterly Review of Literature*, 1977, Vol. XX, 3-4, Princeton. "The Blight of Modernism and Philip Larkin's Antidote," *The American Poetry Review*, January-February 1977, Philadelphia. "The Many-sidedness of Modernism," *The Times Literary Supplement*, February 1, 1980, London. "The Nonsense of Yvor Winters' *Anatomy*," *Quarterly Review of Literature*, Spring 1944, Vol. 1, No. 3; Summer 1944, Vol. 1, No. 4, Chapel Hill, N.C. "Donald Davie: Between Two Worlds or on the Move," *Parnassus*, Fall-Winter 1974, Vol. 3, No. 1, New York. "T. S. Eliot and the Courtyard Revolution," *The Sewanee Review*, April-June 1946, Vol. LIX, No. 2, Sewanee. "How to End the Renaissance," *The Sewanee Review*, October-December 1965, Vol. LXXIII, No. 4, Sewanee. "Franz Kafka and the Economy of Chaos," *The Kafka Problem*, ed. Angel Flores, 1946, New Directions, New York. "Giacomo Leopardi, Pioneer Among Exiles," *Quarterly Review of Literature*, 1955, Vol. VIII,´ No. 1, Annandale-on-Hudson, New York. "As the Wind Sits: The Poetics of *King Lear*," *On King Lear*, 1981, Princeton University Press, Princeton, N.J. "Lucretius: The Imagination of the Literal," *Salmagundi*, Fall 1976, No. 35, Saratoga Springs, N.Y.

Also by Theodore Weiss

Selections from the Note-Books of Gerard Manley Hopkins (1945)

The Catch (poems, 1951)

Outlanders (poems, 1960)

Gunsight (a long poem, 1962)

The Medium (poems, 1965)

The Last Day and the First (poems, 1968)

The World before Us: Poems, 1950-1970 (1970)

The Breath of Clowns and Kings: Shakespeare's Early Comedies and Histories (1971)

Fireweeds (poems, 1976)

Views & Spectacles: Selected Shorter Poems (1978)

Views & Spectacles: New and Selected Shorter Poems (1979)

Recoveries (a long poem, 1982)

Contents

The Man
from Porlock

The Man from Porlock
(in lieu of a preface)

He woke intending to write a long poem. For during a profound, three-hour sleep, brought on by a prescribed anodyne, he had "the most vivid confidence that he could not have composed less than from two to three hundred lines; if that indeed can be called composition in which all the images rose up before him as *things*. . . ." He did manage to get the poem's setting onto the page, but only fifty-four verses in all. Dissatisfied, he prefaced them with a prose gloss to assure the reader that he published the fragment only at a great poet's urging since he himself considered it "a psychological curiosity" rather than a work possessed of "*poetic* merits." A conclusion one might be inclined to agree with. That is, unless one feels with Swinburne that the poem is "the supreme example of music" in English and that analyzing it would be tantamount to "trying to unravel a rainbow." Or if, like Borges, one considers it "a page of undisputed splendor."

Whatever demurs one might have before such opinions, those opening verses and the prose gloss, describing their history, constitute one of Coleridge's most fascinating compositions. Together they resemble something like, if in little, Dante's *Vita Nuova*, a format Dante employed before he got onto a poetic medium that could accommodate everything. So too the amalgam in "Kubla Khan," not only of poetry and prose but of disparate levels of discourse—the matter-of-fact, focusing on the personal, with the ultra-poetic—anticipates something of the texture of modern works, *The Cantos* and *Paterson*, say. And the poem itself anticipates those works' disjunctures as well.

A basic part of "Kubla Khan's" charm, in fact, resides precisely in its fragmentariness. Being, in Coleridge's words, "a plank from the wreck of Paradise" insures it a power of suggestiveness that, completed, it might not have enjoyed. So I suspect that the fragments of Sappho are especially resonant for us, at least in part, because fragments, beyond themselves realizing in our imaginations the condition of Keats' sweetest ''unheard music.'' What would happen to the torso of Apollo and to Rilke's poem about it, to their glamor, had Apollo kept his head? Here the Dionysian has even succeeded in suffusing its opposite! Children of the atomistic age, skeptical before wholeness and finish, many of us prefer open-ended poems; we think them closer to things as they are.

But though our poem is indeed open-ended, we tend to find compositions as high-toned as ''Kubla Khan'' hard to take. Contrary attitudes seem to be at work on us here. Through the influence of science and our respect for fact we subscribe to the idea of poems as a kind of reportage or mimesis. But by way of Freud we are occupied with the unconscious even as it leads to surrealism and a variety of extreme positions in behalf of the intuitive and the spontaneous. These latter seem much truer than businesslike, meddling, middle-class reason. Such preference should prompt sympathy for a work like ''Kubla Khan'' with its images rising up as things. But the modern attitude toward the unconscious tends to the descendental rather than the transcendental. Thus, whatever odd stirrings, by no means exclusively lofty, ''Kubla Khan'' contains, many of us heave a sigh of relief before the poem's brevity.

Beyond ''Kubla Khan's'' interest of itself, it deserves attention for its bearing on the problems that beset the arts, particularly poetry, in the modern world. The headnote tells us that Coleridge had retired, in ill health, to a lonely farmhouse between two provincial English towns, Porlock and Linton. A likely place and moment under a drug's stimulus for the dream of a poem, an ambiguous vision of paradise. Even more likely since, just before falling asleep, Coleridge had been reading in ''Purchas's Pilgrimage'' about the Khan Kubla and the palace and garden the Khan had bade be built, ''and thus ten miles of fertile ground were enclosed with a wall.'' Coleridge, given his physical and mental condition, must have appreciated that wall. Like the Khan, he dreamt of would-be practical utopias, the establishing of a paradise. But poetry finally was his principal garden, palace, and lofty if fragile wall against the oppressive world at large.

Late in the poem Coleridge interrupts his dream with another—a vision. Thus ''Kubla Khan'' is a fragment of a vision interrupted by a fragment of a vision. What, after all, does Abyssinia have to do with Xanadu or a damsel and her dulcimer with the Khan Kubla? The connection must lie in the miscellaneous literary plunder secreted in the Ali Baba recesses of the poet's mind and in the saltancy of his imagination. Such juxtaposings seem precursive of the often feverishly ranging, rearranging mind of a Pound. Had "Kubla Khan" continued, it might have consisted of an extended series of such interruptions and couplings, fragments yoked to fragments, a veritable imagist poem. Or the exuberantly free associations of a richly furnished mind, moving from the objective and the remote to the subjective, if not the immediate, and back again.

With the dream's objectivity abruptly broken, this brief passage of a vision recollected occurs, for the first time, in the first person. Now Coleridge experiences yearning and distress. He would revive the maiden's song, and out of delighting in it he would with music "build that dome in air." It would resemble other literary domes, Troy and Camelot, Milton's Pandemonium. However, this pleasure-dome would be reared in air of air alone. But it turns out ambiguous and dangerous like the song. Though sunny, its shadow "Floated midway on the waves," it was erected over "caves of ice." And all those hearing the poet's song, so "enchanting" would it be, would see those caves, so cry "Beware! Beware! / His flashing eyes, his floating hair!" They would further urge, "Weave a circle round him thrice, / And close your eyes with holy dread." Having fed on honeydew "And drunk the milk of Paradise," the singer must be bewitched and capable of bewitching in turn. Lovely though the dream was, Coleridge apparently recognized its ominousness. Or perhaps he recognized it from the viewpoint of those fearful of vision and the imagination. In Stevens' words, "Political man ordained / Imagination as the fateful sin." Like the Khan and Coleridge, public men also desire a wall, but one against the frightening, demonic forces in us.

In Stevens' "Anecdote of the Prince of Peacocks," the Prince, wandering in the moonlight on a "bushy plain," meets no other than Berserk. "Sun-colored," Berserk warns the Prince that those like the Prince who wander on this plain "forget so soon / But I set my traps / In the midst of dreams." At once the Prince realizes that "the blue ground / Was full of blocks / And blocking steel." But though he now knows the plain's "dread," he also knows "the beauty of the moonlight. . . . Falling as sleep falls / In the innocent air." Dread, it would seem, the ensnaring reality, best set in dreams, enhances—perhaps even makes possible—the beauty.

Unfortunately, just as Coleridge fell to work on the poem, with a sense of "having a distinct recollection of the whole," an illusion common enough immediately after dreams, a man from Porlock "on business," breaking in on Coleridge, detained him "above an hour." When Coleridge returned much of the rest of the poem had "passed away like the images of a stream [the waves of the poem's sacred river?]

into which a stone had been cast, but, alas, without the after restoration of the latter.'' Yet, even though we say alas with Coleridge, we may wonder whether such interruptions were not fortunate, rescuing him from his persistent temptation to fantasy, a land, given its traps, one might disappear in forever. However, may the interruption not have been, in fact, the flagging of Coleridge's inspiration? Perhaps the occasion resembled Pound's ''the film breaks,'' said to D. D. Paige in St. Elizabeth's to explain Pound's losing the thread of his thought. (It is tempting to propose that *The Cantos* are often like that, splicings of disparate films.) If the man from Porlock was a fabrication on Coleridge's part, what happier invention, what apter sympathy-provoking excuse? Even a delicious revenge on Porlock in general: swearing the enemy in as witness, ally, collaborator! Or an inspired way of explaining one's failure and of enhancing what would otherwise have been a slight fragment.

It is tantalizing that a mind like Coleridge's, with its intensely speculative cast, should take off to its opposite, also in its way abstracted: fantasy, enchantment, other-worldliness, and that the latter's images should rise up before him as things. At least for the moment of possession he found a realm which eliminated the vexing distance between thought and thing, word and the world, desire and reality. Almost a preliminary rehearsal of ''no ideas but in things'' or imagism. But how far-fetched Coleridge's things had to be! As far, given the oppression of the modern world, as those Pound ransacked from remote times and places. And things Coleridge's images are, because they occurred in the self-contained dominion of the mind. Or dream with its all-lit, fluent movement. Yet images fragile as those in a stream. Till human voices wake us, and we drown.

Supposedly the stone that shattered the dream was, in the person of a Porlockian, daily reality with its insistent demands. Whatever Coleridge's inclination to exotic poems and their world, the normal, daylit world constantly clamored around him. Moreover, very present was the reality, always more urgent (in his paradoxical words, ''Reality's dark dream''), of his incapacity to cope with that world, its clamant bills, his domestic discord and guilt, as well as his physical or psychosomatic illnesses. In addition, his own trenchantly critical mind, no less insistent, may have amounted to a considerable portion of a Porlockian.

However, perhaps more accurately, none other might be nominated for that Porlockian role than Coleridge's dear friend, William Wordsworth. At first sight, great poet and collaborator that Wordsworth was, such nomination must seem absurd. But Coleridge's admiration for Wordsworth led Coleridge to depreciate his own gifts. He could write to Godwin, ". . . by showing him [Coleridge] what true poetry was, he [Wordsworth] made him know that he himself was no Poet." Despite his playing Pound to Wordsworth's Eliot, Coleridge could say, "Wordsworth is a very great man, the only man to whom *at all times* and *in all modes of excellence* I feel myself inferior." Little wonder he felt interrupted and increasingly incapable of writing poetry. Beyond Wordsworth's larger competence with life's daily problems, prominent in his superiority was his ability to turn the immediate, seemingly commonplace world into genuine, highly original poetry. He was proving—the lesson modern poetry has most taken to heart—that simple speech, informed with the passions, could produce powerful, fresh work, little deferential to the best poetry of the past. Beside this accomplishment Coleridge's gift for evoking remote times and outlandish places must have seemed inconsequential to him and hardly worth pursuing.

At the same time Coleridge could write other kinds of poems, occasional pieces, meditative lyrics, which he himself called Conversation Poems. These illustrate his talent for composing forthrightly colloquial verse, the talk of an educated man, very possibly a model for Wordsworth. But they were usually poems of dejection. Appropriately for the mundane and the personal, they focused on intimate fears and failures, including Coleridge's melancholy before the waning of his poetic powers and his response to nature. Wordsworth, when he forgot his resolution to write emphatically simple speech, often at his best as in "Tintern Abbey"—its language, like Coleridge's, that of a cultivated, meditative man—also made poems primarily out of the prevailing of the light of common day, the dwindling of his perceptions, the loss of poetry. In fact, after his first great flourishing, a prosaicism overtook the bulk of his long life's work to confirm the sad truth of his awareness in "Tintern Abbey." The Porlockian in him triumphed.

Such waning with the coming-on of age is normal enough. Yet, a major theme of romantic and post-romantic poetry, this waning and the struggle against it have produced some of the most moving poems we have. Certainly with the speedy growth of the practical and the political the tug-of-war between the poetic and the prosaic has never raged more earnestly than in recent times. The struggle may have been present from the start. But since initially poetry was the official medium, all matters beyond mere lists were expressed in it. Furthermore, since poetry in the West was, except for folk songs, an aristocratic enterprise, lofty, noble subjects comprised its chief content. But already a materialistic world like Rome had little patience with the imagination. Yet, amazingly enough, as though to prove that poetry must willy-nilly out, by embracing his country's prosaic position with all his heart and mind, by insisting on the anti-poetic and cramming his work with materials that should have resisted all reclaiming, so banished poetry forever, Lucretius produced a magnificent poem—one that stressed the commonplace to the point at which it became fantastical. Any modern poet might envy Lucretius his poem's comprehensiveness, its burly integrity out of atomic bits and pieces. It was Lucretius' enthusiasm for his subject, his all-out commitment to it, that made the work possible, made it splendid.

By the nineteenth century, with the prominence of prose, especially in the newspaper and the novel, and with the exertions of the then science, poets were a generally embattled lot. However many forays they made into the long, ambitious poem, for the most part they defiantly retreated to, and are appreciated for, the shorter personal lyric, the isolated outcry. Wordsworth, it is true, advocating the speech of men and women in their daily lives, recovered some of poetry's basic force, the feeling that quickens folk poems. Yet his work was chiefly restricted to rural conditions; the city and the challenge of turning its turmoil into poetry defied or eluded him. In his reasserting the importance of nature before the inevitable headlong growth of industry and technology, valuable though his reassertion was, he was not far from being a nostalgic. That involvement in nature's freshness soon wore out for him. Thus, not long after, because of Hardy's doubts before the encroachments of science and the modern world, his poetry was a saddened, diminished, if still at times splendid, thing, especially moving in its sadness.

Even so in England as in America common speech has won the day. The man from Porlock and Porlock itself, steadily expanding, have been sworn in as an intrinsic part of poetry. In his crucial essay, "The American Scholar," Emerson called for local news, the daily world that Lucretius long ago enjoyed, the meal in the firkin, the gait in the street. At the same time Emerson insisted that these be seen with such depth (many recent poets have lost sight of this latter half of Emerson's pronouncement) that the eternal laws shine through. As for Lucretius his beloved atoms. Whitman, setting out to satisfy Emerson's prescription, did so to overflow. With Lucretian verve and delicacy Whitman's poetry leaps from the minute and the near to the sun and the stars, the flaming outer ramparts of the universe, then back again. He reveled in the chain of being, the gleaming, individual links of it, even if it no longer hung securely or in one piece from anything or anyone other than himself. His ardor was the magnetism that ran through all things and made them more or less cohere. And he insisted that this wholeness, possible for him, was possible for all. He strove to enthrone the man and all men from Porlock even if he had to make mighty claims for them.

Pace-setters that Pound and Eliot were, their championing of colloquial speech sped the democratic cause in poetry. And the modern urban world supplied a good deal of their subject matter. But they insisted on the highest standards for art and, as internationalists, were impatient with the merely local. Their commitment to their own time, to making it new, notwithstanding, they refused to relinquish Xanadu. Their work abundantly reflects their devotion to the accomplishments of ancient, distant countries. They believed it their responsibility to recall, preserve, and promote the irreplaceable, easily-lost riches of earlier literature and art. Beyond his passion for things Greek and Mediterranean, Pound undertook direct acquisition of the Oriental. And he attempted the noble, quixotic experiment of educating the man from Porlock (and I do not mean his friend William Carlos Williams alone), of persuading him to spice his American-accented speech and mind with far-off realms and times, to rid himself of at least some of his provincialism. In this ambition Pound was not so far from Whitman as is assumed. Actually, whatever Eliot's interest in Eastern philosophy and religion, Whitman was much more receptive to the mystical elements in Oriental and Indian art and thought than was Pound.

Through his empiricism, his would-be hardheadedness, Pound, in his overriding desire to improve the lot of the impoverished poet and artist, discovered, almost to his surprise, that the economic and cultural fate of artists was inextricably bound up with that of all men. Thus he became increasingly democratic even if he decided, out of his great irascibility, that fascism was the only way to ensure democracy. He could not resist his belief in great men and great leaders, and in his impatience for results he eagerly mistook Mussolini for such a leader. Also, with a burning desire to save America, always more ideology-ridden and dogmatic, he loaded the *Cantos* increasingly with reports, documents, historical texts (he was always fundamentally a pedagogue) or Porlockian materials. It must be emphasized, however, that since for him these texts, pedestrian-seeming to nonbelievers, were true, they were in their acute pertinency inevitably beautiful. The question here is whether his imaginary garden—he was bent on building his dream into a reality at least as much as the Khan Kubla or Coleridge—could support so many toads or whether they finally overran the garden. But intent on reasserting the whole man, Pound and Eliot also sought to recover for poetry resources that prose had arrogated to itself.

It was their concern for far-off times and places that William Carlos

Williams balked at. Yet he had lived in Europe and he knew its art movements well. And in writing his *Paterson* he did not hesitate, in the manner of Pound, to employ the American past. But he felt that Pound and most of all Eliot with *The Waste Land* had sold out the modern by capitulating to bookishness and slavish Anglophilism. Like Wordsworth and Whitman, Williams plumped for the here and now, in his case a modern drab town, Rutherford, near New York. Settling in with the town's poor, he became medical pastor to this flock, possibly not so different from Wordsworth's rustics. Relatedly, Williams was convinced that the present man from Porlock or Rutherford—bills, business, daily troubles and all—could and must be made to sing.

Similarly Marianne Moore, also sticking fast to the United States, in her poetic definition of "Poetry" urges "the genuine," "the useful," what we can "understand." Moreover, taking issue with Tolstoy's "Poetry is verse: prose is not verse. Or else poetry is everything with the exception of business documents and school books," she would, like Pound, open poetry to everything. In her words, ". . . nor is it valid / to discriminate against 'business documents and / school-books'; all these phenomena are important." Of course she insisted that these materials must be used by real poets, "literalists of / the imagination" who can produce " 'imaginary gardens with real toads in them.' " Her own poems sport quotations from assorted magazines, pamphlets, schoolbooks, and other prosaic, toad-spotted sources.

Except for *Paterson* Williams disdained quotations unless, even more practically and toad-like than Moore's, they were overheard snatches of the city's daily speech, its slang's tangy, urgent idiom. He strove for what might seem the impossible: to find the poetic in drab and tarnished places, people, objects, ones that would appear to be (in the phrase Stevens used on Williams, aptly suggesting that it was romantic) anti-poetic, or Porlockian. Yet Williams was also a great pastoral poet; at times he could wrest natural purity and power, let us say piety, the sacramental, out of the mid-city. Like Whitman, Williams expected the gods, whoever they might be, to be everywhere, not least of all in the bustling as well as the dusty streets of the USA. And for this expectation alone he became a hero and a model to many young poets.

Meantime, throughout this introduction as throughout his life another figure has kept his luxurious, amused distance. If there has ever been a modern who could consider himself the rightful heir of the Khan Kubla, and of Coleridge with his speculative interests, it is the Khan Hoon, Wallace Stevens. He had little to do with Pound and Eliot, and he also felt at odds with his friend Williams in the latter's insistence on "style" as the principal quality of a poem, on the way a thing is said rather than on the thing itself. This has its share of irony since Williams usually worked in a plain, stripped diction, whereas Stevens enjoyed an ornamental one, befitting a mandarin. Occupied by business and plain days in Hartford much more than Coleridge was by Porlock, Stevens in privacy and weekend solitude obeyed his own floribund muse. Despite occasional demurs, he carried on his double life with little sense of conflict or deprivation. On the contrary, he delighted in both prospering parts, delighted in keeping them completely separate. As though to say the pies that Emily Dickinson won second prize for in the local fair pleased her as much as her poems. And why not? Like a good American puritan, having taken successful care of his daily business, Stevens could give himself to his Sunday baths unstintingly.

Now in recent American poetry we witness the bewilderingly rich ramifyings of the efforts of the poets I have been describing. The poetry of speech has prevailed. However, Stevens has been enthroned in the academy, particularly among its literary critics, who love his complexities, his lifelong speculations on the prospects of sublimity in an antisublime age. With the university a principal center of interest in poetry, understandably Stevens' voluminous mandarin sleeve has issued a remarkable litter. Thus, while plain poems are being written en masse, often with little sense of what their putative godfather Williams meant by form, measure, style, other poets are carrying on their antipodes in an almost priestly fashion. For these latter rhetoric, whether of the Eastern variety, the Californian, the Southern, flourishes. (However, despite the frequent strenuous denials of rhetoric and the countless attempts at its disguise, I do not mean to imply that any poetry, if it is still poetry, is possible without rhetoric.) In that Stevens' example has helped to encourage the grand, the witty, the engagingly intellectual among his heirs we must be thankful. The risk here is a redoubtable ornateness that threatens to overwhelm the poem and the reader. With the notion broadcast among literary theorists that poetry, like language itself, is no more than a game, that we can know nothing beyond ourselves and that language, it should not surprise us that some poets have concentrated on their language's resources, antics, private life. Prodigiously enough, a number have produced long poems. The dream that Coleridge lost they have doughtily persevered in finding.

The common-speech and free-versifying poets (free often altogether of verse) are also waylaid by hazards, most seriously that of the prosaic, of falling into such anonymity that many of their poems seem written by a single, slack hand, little interfered with by the mind. The man from Porlock, it would seem, has finally come into his own. As he has among many of the post-Hardy, post-Georgian, post-Auden British poets.

Readers have remarked this work's unmemorability. Given the poets' determination to shun all earmarks of rhetoric, their desire to appear natural, casual as passing speech itself, with no designs on the reader, how can it be otherwise? Especially if the work lacks any recognizable form or cadence. One could be awed by how little some poets seem to think sufficient to outfit a poem. But once a style takes hold, like blue jeans or any other uniform or habit (formalism for that matter), usually adopted in the name of freedom, it tends to become a general hand-me-down, a tyrannically required hand-me-round. And bodies, fitting or not, are stuffed into it.

Ironically enough, a portion of this plainness has taken a course quite the reverse of the popular academic notion that only previous poetry produces poetry—namely, an attempt, common in all the arts, to wipe out the line between life and art. The wish to draw the word and the deed closer together is obviously commendable. But in a would-be faithfulness to the world carried too far, words and expression are bound to suffer and therefore—whatever one's passion for immediacy and verisimilitude—the insight, the wisdom that one would relay about that world as well. This trend, pushed to its ultimate, seems to me a suicidal one, at least for anything like art. But there is now a crowd of practitioners who have no truck with such elitist, decadent nonsense as art. They produce poems devoted to the details of daily life, kept pristinely drab, as though there were something sacred about drabness simply because it happens. Dullness, since they find so much of it in and around them, preoccupies them, dullness and boredom. Since few artists in the past set out to produce boredom, it may seem the one subject still to be explored. Boredom on the grand scale a Leopardi grapples with is one thing; the niggling, sluggish, squalid variety, quite another. And it is even less attractive when tarted up in poems with surrealistic touches.

Often this work amounts to a kind of confessional poetry with little to confess beyond the self-indulgent confusion of the poet or the reportage I mentioned earlier. In 1965 Lowell could already say, "You see, I have a feeling that the arts are in a very funny position now—that we are free to say what we want to, and somehow what we want to say is the confusion and sadness and incoherence of the human condition." Except for the comfort of company most of us do not need poets to tell us about confusion and sadness and incoherence. In the past a good deal more seems to have been expected of artists. The present attitude produces a poetry engrossed with process, the automatic, which, believing itself the only reality, dismisses the mind and its hardwon disciplines and accomplishments. Accomplishment, from such a view, becomes a falsehood, a flouting of things as they are.

One would suspect that there is not enough in such work to detain a mature, serious audience very long. To quote Stevens, "From oriole to crow, note the decline / In music. Crow is realist. But, then, / oriole, also, may be realist." It may be revealing to trace the career of the image poets have had of themselves as birds, from high-flying, full-throated creatures, the eagle, the nightingale, the skylark, daring the very empyrean, or at least Hopkins' plucky little windhover, to Baudelaire's albatross, that "vast sea-bird" with a pipe stuck in his beak. Baudelaire concludes of him, now the poet, "Exiled in earth, amidst its hooting crowds, / He cannot walk, borne down by his giant wings." This is a bird and a condition Coleridge might have sympathized with, even as he employed it in "The Ancient Mariner." And down we go to Williams (Keats before him) with his sparrows as they "hop ingenuously / about the pavement." To that taxidermist's botch, Ted Hughes' Crow, and the latest, scrawny, non-flying, barnyard fowl, clucking, fluttering, pecking at the dirt. At last that seemingly unlikeliest flock, a feathered oxymoron, birds of one feather, awoke one morning, the Porlockians, to find that they en masse were, mirabile dictu, mumbling poems of a sort.

However, looking at all these works more objectively, we should be grateful even for the extremes, for the enrichments they may in very martyrdom make available. Poets of genuine ambition for poetry will be desiring and seeking what they lack. Stevens, we recall, yearned now and then for "normal life, insight into the commonplace, reconciliation with everyday reality. The thing that it makes me most happy to do are things of this sort." But then he admits, "However, it is not possible to get away from one's own nature." So too he could applaud the savage, the lion raging in the lute. It is, as Eliot and Pound saw it, the whole human being that one hopes for in poetry, not the commonplace or the daily alone and not the grand and the lofty. Nonetheless, we had better acknowledge and be pleased by our age's diversity of talents, the ways in which together they keep a many-sided poetry thriving. For Coleridge the poet "in *ideal* perfection, brings the whole soul of man into activity." But most sensibly, as with Stevens' oriole and crow, he warned, "Do not let us introduce an Act of Uniformity against Poets." Or in the ecology of poetry let us try to be hospitable to as many species as possible. In the Lord's mansion of poetry, all the houses—even the outhouses—are no doubt necessary.

Meantime, it is a startling development that, in a giant, ultra-materialistic country like the United States, a spate of poetry-writing is going on which surpasses, as far as this writer can tell, anything gone before. So great is the abundance that some of those aware of it are dismayed, if not overwhelmed. Finding one's way in this flood, arriving at satisfactory judgments of this poetry's worth, is a problem. In answer to the question now frequently asked, usually by people more concerned with reputations than poems, "Are there any major poets today?" or "Why has no new Pound or Eliot emerged?" one might reply, "Mainly because we have had Pound and Eliot and their peers." The discoverers and first explorers, by their work they made masses of poets possible. They prepared not only the way but the climate and the materials as well.

So we have gone from an arduous golden age to an impressive silver one, with large numbers of poets ensconced in the university, busily producing their work and, in proliferating workshops, additional poets. Through their efforts a degree of skill has developed among the young generally far exceeding that of a few decades ago. With so many poets working at the top of their bent, still developing some part or other of that which their pioneering predecessors uncovered, obvious major emergences are not likely. Nor, for that matter, with such sophistication among these poets (as Eliot said of himself and his contemporaries, we know more than the dead great writers; "they are that which we know."), is it likely that they would listen long to new pronouncements—unless they be adequately exotic as from Latin America, say, or Iron Curtain poets—of the Pound and Eliot variety. As against several lonely eminences we may have to be content with a plethora of good poets and poems, and of course put up with a growing swarm of bad ones. That is, until some poets convince us that they are fusing the best lessons of the diverse schools in an updated version of the ambition of Pound and Eliot: the visionary combined with the commonplace, the noble out of the democratic and the colloquial. Like Titania and Bottom, these seemingly antipodal qualities must, magically, become passionate bedfellows. And the offspring of their coupling will be there for us to goggle at.

I

E.P.: The Man Who
Cared Too Much

Attempting for the first time to say what Pound means to me, I find myself rehearsing my contacts with him. They were few. Several notes, one of which deserves reproduction for its typical calligraphic flourish. No doubt because of his remarks to D. D. Paige about the *Quarterly Review of Literature,* I had written to Pound at St. Elizabeth's to ask whether he would comment on the "New Critics." He replied,

Our other associations were secondhand. A few "business" letters from Mrs. Pound; a request from Pound's son; a pleasant evening with his daughter. Pound, in my correspondence with Paige, frequently passed between us. Paige saw him at St. Elizabeth's, and

on June, 14, 1947, he urged me to visit Pound (I never did); he also suggested I write to him, "something that keeps him alive," and send some poems. "He may even criticize. He has been livelier these past two weeks than before. Now feels able to sit up and type—which he didn't do before."

On June 22 Paige reported that Pound

> has an idea for you (and a couple of other folks). Says he's not interested in quarterlies. Intellectual life does not move in 3 month periods. A periodical should not be an anthology coming out every quarter. Suggests that three quarterlies unite:
>
> A to appear in Jan
> B "   "   " Feb
> C "   "   " March
> A "   "   " April
> B "   "   " May
>   etc.
>
> And to correlate or at least debate each other's editorials.* Thus giving appearance of monthly, but dividing the editorial labor and ensuring some difference of opinion.

This scheme, noteworthy in itself, reflects Pound's everlasting hunger for an intellectual community, minds striking sparks off each other, a matter especially difficult in the vast, sprawled-out USA. Wyndham Lewis could say of his old friend "he was never satisfied until everything was organized." Paige continued:

> Pound can't discern a program in your mag and thinks it too academic [because of the critical articles, often New Critical, we were still printing]. . . . EP says he doesn't mind an academic opposition; he welcomes it, especially when it's an honest one like yours.

Pound, despite his quarrel with universities, never abandoned his hopes for them as dynamic centers of culture.

Then Paige proposed that we produce an Ezra Pound number. In the ensuing months, though Paige was immersed in editing a

---

*Devoted to literature past any egotism, Pound had little patience with or capacity for the human problems involved. How many writers would support his "It is tremendously important that great poetry be written, it makes no jot of difference who writes it."?

volume of Pound's letters, the herculean task of carving some 400 pages out of more than 4000, the issue, under Paige's guest-editorship, proceeded. Meantime, Paige sent us copies of exciting epistolary exchanges, especially sections from Pound's comments on Eliot's poems. On July 22, 1947, Paige wrote: "I think that (and Pound agrees) the issue should not appear to be a yell to get him unjugged. He doesn't even want the contributors to be guided *at all* in what they write; he does not want them to write unless they *want* to." Further evidence of Pound's selflessness about literature. He wanted the issue to be effective in helping to gain his release insofar as it demonstrated his worth as a writer.

The issue appeared in 1949. In the winter of 1950 my wife and I visited Paige in Rapallo where he and his wife were living on next to nothing to be near Pound's correspondence, out of respect for him kept intact in his study with his books and other effects. Anyone interested in Pound can appreciate our pleasure at living high in that rugged, lovely hill, overlooking the sea, the mornings after chilled nights indeed Eden-dewy; at traversing Pound's haunts and recalling Yeats's visits; at browsing in Pound's jammed-up study, now a kind of shrine; at admiring the Gaudier-Brzeska bust of Pound, looking out, like Pound's own figurehead, to his Odyssean voyage. Earlier we had heard about him from Williams, whom Pound kept trying to "educate" with book lists till nearly the end* and who never wavered in his admiration for Pound's poetry. After the Pound issue Williams wrote to us to praise it, especially Pound's translation of two Cavalcanti sonnets: "They are the 'perfection' of which Wyndham Lewis speaks. There is nothing like them in English anywhere else." Pound's ear, he felt, was "unsurpassable." At the same time Williams was altogether distressed by Pound's attitudes, his violent remarks to him before and during the war.

Not much to hang an acquaintanceship on. Yet far beyond these items, for the past forty years or more Pound, rather like his relationship with Villon or Dante, has been an intimate of my mind,

---

*Thus Pound could believe "If James *had* read his classics, the better Latins especially, he would not have so excessively cobwebbed, fussed, blathered, worried about minor mundanities." On the other hand, James said to Edith Wharton of Whitman, ". . . one cannot help deploring his too extensive acquaintance with the foreign languages."

as for most serious poets. Nonetheless, in an essay on Pound, published in 1949, the year of the fiercely controverted Bollingen Award for Poetry to Pound, John Berryman could stress the remarkable fact that Pound was still regarded "with hostility or indifference." Interestingly enough Berryman rejected the other pole Blackmur set in his "Masks of Ezra Pound" (1933), an essay Berryman drew on: "idolatry" in the pair "idolatry or frightened antipathy" or "enthusiasm and hatred." Probably Berryman felt justified in rejecting idolatry because of the immense animus the Award prompted. That a fascist, an anti-Semite, an enemy of the State, should be given a major award, and in its initial granting, by that State! Quoting Pound's verses,

> In a few years no one will remember the *buffo,*
> No one will remember the trivial parts of me,
> The comic details will be absent.

Berryman could point out how mistaken Pound was: "After thirty-five years neither comic nor tragical detail is absent."

I had also thought that, as with a Villon or a Dante, Pound would be regarded mainly for his work. Yet now, nearly 30 years after Berryman's article, the situation (if one adds "idolatry" which the proliferation of books and articles would confirm) seems substantially the same. It is not alone that Pound's attitudes still rankle, that his diatribes outraged countless critics, scholars, editors, publishers, but that he was so incessantly, oppressively concerned with culture, and acted furiously as though it mattered overridingly. He was even set on changing the world's economy (here no doubt he did seem dangerous to the world's powerful people, bankers, munition makers, monopolists, government officials) to make it safe for deserving artists and writers. For he was convinced that artists, "the lead elephants,"* "the antennae of the race," were needed for preserving a society's

---

*Of course when such a leader feels he is no longer being followed, in his separation from the herd he can easily become a rogue elephant. Also, alas, many of Pound's more addled admirers, as in the parable, made things even worse for him and our understanding of him and his work. For, huge being that he was, some, grabbing the trunk, have insisted he was all trunk; others, a leg, all leg; and still others, the ——, all ——!

health; and that when that society failed its arts, it was in danger of deteriorating, even collapsing.

Irving Howe, one of our most astute critics, in his July 4, 1976 Bicentennial piece, "The American Voice—It Begins on a Note of Wonder," for the New York *Times Book Review*, seeking to characterize that voice's uniqueness, never mentions Pound, let alone his profound importance to American as to international letters. How, Pound's politics notwithstanding, ignore a writer who as much as anyone established poetry's modern voice and urged, in his passionate concern for America, the attitudes of Jefferson and Adams toward government and culture? Pound fully recognized his Americanism. His *Patria Mia* (1913) concludes:

> If a man's work require him to live in exile, let him suffer, or enjoy, his exile gladly. But it would be about as easy for an American to become a Chinaman or a Hindoo as for him to acquire an Englishness, or a Frenchness, or a European-ness that is more than half a skin deep.

And always America is the basic ache, the crucial love-hate, in his thinking. Is Pound still too hot, too nettlesome, for a popular periodical? Did Howe consider it tactless, in an article given over to celebrating a public occasion, to notice an uproarious expatriate, a verbal incendiary, branded by the US government a crackpot and a traitor? After all, did not Pound abandon, then, like a spoiled child claiming neglect, increasingly excoriate the US? (Yet one of our ablest poets and critics, Hayden Carruth, dedicated his 20th-century American poetry anthology "To E. P. from us all.") But Howe expressed his feelings on Pound some years ago (1972) after the veto of Pound for the Emerson-Thoreau Medal:

> Pound wished none of us personal harm [several times Pound did write that he could have killed this political "criminal" and that, and with glee; and though he did not believe in the murder of "the head Jews" in America, their deportation would be in happy order]; his rantings against the Jews were utterly abstract, a phantasm of ideology that is a major dimension of their terribleness. . . . But the question of whether to honor Pound involves neither the granting nor the refusal of forgiveness. It involves something else: I do not believe that we can yet close

the books of twentieth-century history, certainly not as long as any of us remain alive who can remember the days of the mass murder.

It was probably Pound's insistence on being socially responsible, his desire to serve and save America and his frustration for it that drove him to his desperate fanaticism. In 1912 he could reply to Harriet Monroe's invitation to be *Poetry's* London representative:

> Any agonizing that tends to hurry what I believe in the end to be inevitable, an American Risorgimento, is dear to me. That awakening will make the Italian Renaissance look like a tempest in a teapot. The force we have, and the impulse, but the guiding sense, the discrimination in applying that force, we must wait and strive for.

Earlier, however, his letter, emphasizing his major priorities, asked:

> Are you for American poetry or for poetry. The latter is more important, but it is important that America should boost the former, provided it don't mean a blindness to the art. The glory of any nation is to produce art that can be exported without disgrace to its origin.

Too proud for America to put up with the parochial, the second best, he shortly after wrote Monroe, "We must be taken seriously at *once*. We must be *the voice* not only for the U.S. but internationally. . . ." A little later, having mentioned how arduously, usually vainly, "I go about this London hunting for the real," he says:

> It's only when a few men who know, get together and *disagree* that any sort of criticism is born [so his scheme for *QRL*]. . . . I can give you my honest opinion from the firing line, from "the inside." I'm the kind of ass [optimism, yes, but not too blind!] that believes in the public intelligence. I believe your "big business men" would rather hear a specialist's opinion, even if it's wrong[!], than hear a rumor, a dilutation. My own belief is that the public is sick of lukewarm praise of the mediocre.

Yet who more singlehandedly than Pound did manage, by goading the old and established, by assisting the strugglingly accomplished, and by carrying on a vast epistolary kindergarten, to perform the miracle—such the powers of American optimism!—of making America poetically something of a Renaissance?

Few American writers have incarnated more brilliantly than Pound the polarities Howe set forth to account for these writers—the American dream of the new world, the Jerusalem it promised yet failed to be, or freedom from the terrible burdens of history versus the undeniable actuality. Most of his life Pound persisted in believing, with a faith tantamount to religiosity, that through economic and political changes, a more honest approach to money, and the establishment of highest artistic standards, America would indeed become a new Eden, his *paradiso terrestre*. Reality, the other pole, proved him maddeningly wrong. And finally he realized he must be satisfied with little more than glimpses of that paradise in nature, in some men and women he had known, in his mind and gifts, and in previous ages.

Among the English one can understand deep reservations for Pound and Eliot, those American upstarts who dared to take over English literature. Now that both are dead and modernism is over, the rancor, smoldering a long time, has flared out. Still, at least as remarkable as Pound's absence from Howe's article is Pound's haunting presence among writers who might well resent and dismiss him. In "Ezra Pound and the Bollingen Prize" (1949), Allen Tate, commenting,

> I cannot suppose that the anti-semitism of the *Cantos* will be taken seriously by anybody but liberal intellectuals. Anti-semites will not use it. It is too innocent. I take it seriously in the sense of disliking it, and I cannot "honor the man" for it, as the Fellows of the Library were charged with doing; but I cannot think that it will strengthen anti-semitism.

admits,

> I had, as many men of my generation might have had, personal reasons for not voting for Mr. Pound. In so far as he has noticed my writings at all, in conversation and correspondence—which the international literary grapevine always reports—he has noticed them with contempt.

Moreover, already in his "Ezra Pound" (1931) Tate has described

The Cantos as "just rambling talk." So he could say no other English poetry is "quite so simple in form . . . so simple that almost no one has guessed it. . . ." To wit, conversation, or no form at all. "Each canto has the broken flow and the somewhat elusive climax of a good monologue; because there is no single speaker, it is a many-voiced monologue." Knowing Pound's addiction to Browning, his early practice in the monologue, and his admiration for Eliot's modernizing of it in "Prufrock," "Portrait of a Lady," and particularly "Gerontion," one might be tempted to regard a monologue for many voices as *The Cantos'* form or at least a basic aspect of that form. Then, like Yvor Winters, Tate assures us *The Cantos* "are not about anything." In proof he quotes Pound who does tell us what they are about:

> And they want to know what we talked about? *"de litteris*
> *et de armis, praestantibus in geniis,*
> Both of ancient times and our own; books, arms,
> And men of unusual genius
> Both of ancient times and our own, in short the usual subjects
> Of conversation between intelligent men."

Dante, when he and Virgil meet the great Greek and Latin literary dead in Limbo, reports, "And far more honor still they showed me, for they made me one of their company. . . . Thus we went onward to the light, talking of things it is well to pass in silence, even as it was well to speak of them there." Often I have wondered, properly tantalized—for Dante has other, even bigger fish to fry and "realer" worlds to get on to—what extraordinary things they discussed. Was it mainly shop talk appropriate to Limbo? Pound, with no other journey and goal than his own life and work, whatever paradiso he assumed he was striving for, set out precisely to supply that talk "by the natural light of reason": the conversation he had carried on for many years with the selected great of the past. They, freed of the limitations of time and space in the grand vocarium of a mind, swifter than any cinema, in a sense are talking to each other through him. These voices, ancient and modern, lyrical in their moment's utterance, yet epical in their expansiveness, mason and pillar the temple of *The Cantos.* But imagine—a less sympathetic view might say—that tiny space of a brain, like a cluttered one-room

New York apartment, crammed with refugees from many countries and different times, all uttering their piece. Now and then one, momentarily outshouting the others, obliges them to listen, possibly even to reply. Is it surprising we have trouble making some order, some coherence, out of that magnificent uproar? Yet how else, like nature, manage several worlds at once? Or the multiple talk befitting that limbo, the modern world. Surely, therefore, *The Cantos* are about something? But Tate, considering these "ostensible subjects of the *Cantos* . . . only the materials round which Mr. Pound's mind plays constantly," concludes, "It is this tone, it is this quality quite simply which is the meaning of the *Cantos*. . . ." How little this conclusion would have satisfied Pound, with his great designs on his material and on us.

Then Tate decides "It is all fragmentary," "a book of marvels," "an unhistorical miscellany." Like Winters who judged Pound "merely a barbarian on the loose in a museum," "a sensibility without a mind, or with as little mind as is well possible." One ponders what kind of sensibility that could be, how it would register itself, find the language and all the rest to embody its qualities. Even Winters apparently felt obliged to make distinctions we would normally not expect of him. But his description makes Pound, beyond a lout, some carrion-fly, a mere sensorium, all feelers, gnawing at the corpses of literature, the very thing Pound chiefly abominated! However, after all this, Tate, unlike Winters, can (dare) say that Pound "is probably one of two or three Americans who will be remembered as *poets of the first order*." (my italics) Truly a judgment to give us pause. But Tate does not relent. "Yet there is no reason to infer from that that Mr. Pound, outside his craft (or outside his written conversation), knows in the least what he is doing or saying." Even so "His poetic intelligence [in contrast with general intelligence?] is of the finest; and if he doesn't know what liberty is, he understands poetry, and how to write it. This is enough for one man to know." Real specialization! How one might understand poetry and its writing without general intelligence I haven't, I must confess, the intelligence to understand. But such distinctions are there to be made. Eliot, we may recall, though he admitted Virgil inferior as a poet to Homer, maintained that since Virgil prepared for Christianity he was more for us than Homer. Like Pound I am simple enough to think that the better poet is better because more accurate about reality and therefore, whatever our special pleading, more for us.

Turning to another critic, Donald Davie, probably England's ablest on poetry, one observes a similar conflict. For decades Davie has been involved with Pound. Certainly he has been fairer than most of his countrymen to Pound; and in his *Ezra Pound: Poet as Sculptor* (1964) and his recent *Ezra Pound* he has written about him as sympathetically as anyone. Whereas Tate scoffed at Pound as "the apostle of humane culture" "crying up a rationalistic enlightenment," Davie cogently establishes the latter in *Poet as Sculptor*. Tate called Pound "a traditionalist at bottom," which Davie in his *Ezra Pound* proves by the fact that in his many admirations he "carried more nineteenth-century baggage than any comparably gifted contemporary among writers in English." To some degree this is certainly true. For with his extraordinary ambition, energy, curiosity, Pound almost alone was determined to learn from poets he could apprentice himself to. (He was also one of the last poets interested in and capable of old-fashioned grandeur and sublimity.) But, beyond the fact that one rarely escapes his beginnings, to suggest that "Pound was at bottom an Edwardian man of letters like Edmund Gosse and George Saintsbury" (how astonished those two would be to find themselves settled in such company!) is to go pretty far down for that bottom. Of course Pound respected gifts happily employed wherever he found them. From the start he went at least as much to the remote past, the Greeks, the Latin poets, the troubadours, Dante, as to his own present; but he understandably yearned for a living ambience, the stimulation of a company of fellow-workers and those already developed and strong. Good though Davie's case is and much as Pound struggled against his early archaisms, quaintnesses, aestheticism never fully subdued, that case is too partial.

Davie does not credit enough the difficulties of an uprooted, sensitive young American (Pound came to London all of 23) seeking a spiritual homeland (often the young Pound's verse speaks of his homesickness). Was not Eliot's early, important "Tradition and the Individual Talent" similarly prompted by an exile's hunger for a homeland and his finding it principally in past great literature and art? In a letter to Hardy that Davie quotes Pound accents his deracinated condition:

> I come from an American suburb [of Philadelphia]—where I
> was not born—where both parents are really foreigners, i.e. one
> from New York and one Wisconsin. The suburb has not roots,
> no centre of life. I imitate Browning.

Whatever his early rashnesses, Pound could say in his "Mang Tsze"
(1938) of Mencius, making much of his "omnipresent" "sense of
responsibility":

> His desideratum: to gather and teach the most intelligent of
> his contemporaries, unless by good fortune he find a sage from
> whom he can learn, but in any case not to start teaching
> prematurely and not to teach his own ignorance.

With America woefully inadequate to Pound—and he derived, as
Davie points out, little kinship from Emerson, Thoreau, and other
19th-century American worthies—he sought asylum in England. But
he never abandoned his flamboyant frontiersmanship; on the contrary, like a hothouse staid England sped his Americanism. After
years of effort, still hopeful of finding a true cultural capital, he
fled to France; and, finally, perhaps inevitably with his early veneration
of Dante and the troubadours and his would-be Mediterraneanism,
he landed in Rapallo. Its comparative isolation for this litterateur-at-
large, despite the many pilgrims, seems an ironic precursor of the
Pisan "gorilla cage" and St. Elizabeth's where, like the Napoleonic
campaigner he was, he eventually kept on his Elba a kind of crazy
court. Such a course does not exactly suggest Edwardianism.

But the degree to which Pound sweeps writers past their customary
bearings we see in Davie's *Ezra Pound* when, completing his absorbing
account of "Ideas in *The Cantos*," Davie says:

> As we start to read *The Cantos*, we float out upon a sea where
> we must be on the lookout for waterspouts. These, when they
> occur, are ideas, the only sort this poem is going to give us.

Davie continues:

> And meanwhile we can forget about such much-debated non-
> questions as whether this poem has a structure, and if so, what
> it is: or again, why the poem isn't finished, and whether it ever

could have been. Does a sea have a *structure*? Does a sea *finish* anywhere? The Mediterranean boils into and out of the Atlantic, past the Rock of Gibraltar.

Aside from being a tricky if not treacherous analogy, what an extraordinary conclusion, especially coming from a critic like Davie. We can see how tempting the analogy might be, particularly for an Odyssean like Pound, at tempestuous sea most of his life. But that Davie, one of our principal champions of form and of the few to hold out against modern aberrations, the riptide of amorphous, romantic poets, should not only succumb to that tide for a moment but urge it; that he should celebrate such a confusion of art and life (one gropes for the opposite of the pathetic fallacy—the organic fallacy? or, as Joseph Frank suggests, imitative form?); that he should propose a poem or what a man composes as comparable to the sea! How then deny the present swarm of frothy self-expressionists?

Davie is normally more "sensible." Whatever his awareness of the claims for it, he has little sympathy for "structureless structure," which should be for Davie, as he says it is for Robert Lowell, "a contradiction in terms."* The lure of that contradiction nevertheless remains. That Davie should even briefly be seduced by the master sculptor and craftsman Pound and compare *The Cantos* with the sea is an anomaly, as if Davie approved our time's lust for process, liquid sculpture, and ever-changing self-carving. Perhaps the Japanese painter Tao-Chi's signature for some of his works could apply to *The Cantos*: "Stone Waves."

So Pound throws his most stalwart critics into confusion. My next witness is the recent *Charles Olson & Ezra Pound, An Encounter at St. Elizabeth's*. A remarkable document, these notes of Olson's visits to Pound when the incarcerated poet was at his most distraught reveal the struggle even intelligent admirers of Pound must contend with. Olson's reaction is divided: for Pound as poet, an abiding respect; for the fanatic ideologue, contempt and hatred. Thus, commenting on Pound's "societal" sense, Olson says:

What's shallow about it is the deadness of it, the 18th century

*In a review of Robert Lowell's *Selected Poems*, New York *Times Book Review,* July 18, 1976.

lag in it, the moan for the lost republican purity, the wish to
return America to its condition of a small nation of farmers
and city-state patricians, all Boston Brahmin, and Philadelphia
brick. Nothing wrong in that either, except what happens to
political action now if it is so motivated. It turns out to be
reactionary and fascist. . . . In other words, a pitiful, sick and
dangerous defense of all that *was*, which forever and anywhere
and in all things, fears anything forward. . . . It comes down
to this: a rejection of the single most important fact between
Newton and the Atomic Bomb—the sudden multiple increase
of the earth's population, the coming into existence of the
MASSES. Pound and his kind want to ignore them. They try
to lock them out. But they swarm at the windows in such numbers
they black out the light and the air.

The last sentence's language is worth pondering. Elitism quite apart,
one might feel some sympathy for Pound's attitude. Certainly Olson's
tone hints that he is repelled by what he describes. Like Davie in
his Hardy book, he recognized things as they are (inevitably) and
accepted them: terrible, but to deny or criticize them is to risk plunging
us into chaos and fascism. Olson corroborates Tate's and Winters'
notion of Pound as a nostalgic, a conservative much exceeding Davie's
use of the word. Olson goes on:

And in their little place Pound and his kind suffocate, their
fear turns to hate. And their hate breeds death. They want
to kill. And, organized by Hitler and Mussolini, they do kill—
millions. But the breeding goes on. And with it such social and
political changes as they shall not understand.

Pound, Yeats, and Eliot never went quite this far. But it is a
fascinating and horrible picture Olson paints, on *both sides*. Olson,
I suspect, hardly objected to Pound's literary standards for perfection
and beauty. Yet how establish them, how provide the peace and
quiet needed to nurture master works, if swarming masses black
out the light and the air? Olson seems to see some of this ambiguity
when he concludes,

In Pound I am confronted by the tragic Double of our day.
He is the demonstration of our duality. In language and form
he is as forward, as much the revolutionist as Lenin. But in
social, economic, and political action he is as retrogressive as
the Czar.

Once more the divorce of form and content, precisely the lesion Pound meant to heal. One might query what the revolutionist Lenin produced that was so superior in freedom and bloodlessness to the actions of the Czar.

But the heart of Olson's notes and their relevancy to this essay occur when Olson, reporting one of Pound's most ludicrous opinions, admits,

> I record it, but here as elsewhere, it is impossible to give a true impression. For at any given point, always, there is the presence of the seriousness of the man. Even in his sickest and most evil moments.

And remarking how hate has blinded "this man of exquisite senses," Olson can say, "He remains, on the creative side of him whole, and as charming and open and warm a human being as I know." One more basic perplexity. Finally,

> It is the contradictoriness which keeps me from turning my back on him. I imagine that is why when suddenly he throws his bowels in my face I am forever surprised and react too late for anger and disgust to strike back. I am carried on by the gravity and intensity of the man, now as ever examining, examining, as puzzled as ever to the questions, as naive as your skin and mine to a new rain, an open man, the poet who does not hide his pain, joy, doubt, pride—or hate.

This "gravity and intensity" accounts for Pound's almost irresistible appeal. What artist can fail to be touched, awed, humbled by this selfless passion? I call this paper "E.P.: The Man Who Cared Too Much"; were two titles feasible, I would add "The Endless Quest for a Style." The jostle of these two matters explains much in him.

Much of this dedication I ascribe to certain American strands in Pound. No doubt, as Tocqueville reminded us, in a country as vast as America, if a writer tries to deal with all of it, an enthusiastic idealism leads to abstractness. Pound could say in 1928, "America will swallow anything in theory, all abstract statements are perfectly welcome, given a sufficiently plausible turn."* Despite his vehement

*Pound is referring to Williams' remark "All I do is try to understand something in its natural colour and shapes." Pound had said that, whatever Americans' gullibility

advocacy of accurate, luminous detail, of realism and facts, Pound was victimized by abstractness; and in his exile, even as he thought he was serving reality, the hard facts of history, theory overwhelmed him. Furthermore, his respect for knowledge that is know-how (technique) and practicality, for action and getting results, was eminently American.

Pound recognized this trait in himself. He wrote Joyce (1920), "The curse of me & my nation is that we always think things can be bettered by immediate action of some sort, *any* sort rather than no sort." And he could appreciate the wisdom of the reverse attitude. His "*Dubliners* and Mr. James Joyce" (1914) praises Joyce: "He is a realist. He does not believe 'life' would be all right if we stopped vivisection or if we instituted a new sort of economics." If only the later Pound could have remembered the good sense of the younger! Think of the Gatsby side of a young Fitzgerald, tempted to believe that 300 push-ups each day for ten years, and other such magical projects, would inevitably make him famous, a millionaire, the President of the United States. Even the subtlest Americans have a hard time altogether resisting Horatio Alger, the Calvinist formula of cause and effect, of success. Thus Pound was convinced that if people only read the right books or the list he prepared they would truly see the light. Such a faith is not far from the Hundred Best Books Syndrome.

But for all Pound's declaring, "If only I could get to those Russians I could change them" and "we have not realized to what an extent a renaissance is a thing made—a thing made by conscious propaganda," he did say, "Knowledge is NOT culture. The domain of culture begins when one HAS 'forgotten-what-books.'" (1938) Still, the books must have been read and digested to be forgotten. He saw the past and its great accomplishments, and the critic—*The Cantos* also—as meant to pick out that past's "live part." Nor are his lists merely an index, Puritan if not Catholic, by implication. "To tranquillize the low-brow reader let me say at once that I do not wish to muddle him by making him read more books, but to allow him to read

---

for theory, the "concrete example of this literary process" would seem "unrelated and inexplicable to them."

fewer with greater results." (1928). Again, after his famous, fairly Puritanical "A Few Don'ts" he can warn:

> To begin with consider the three propositions. . . .not as dogma—never consider anything as dogma—but as the result of long contemplation, which, even if it is some one else's contemplation, may be worth consideration.

Or a little earlier in the essay:

> Criticism is not a circumscription or a set of prohibitions. It provides fixed points of departure. It may startle a dull reader into alertness. The little of it which is good is mostly in stray phrases; or if it be an older artist helping a younger it is in great measure but rules of thumb, cautions gained by experience.

In 1918 Pound could say of Joyce's *Chamber Music:*

> We have here the lyric in some of its best traditions, and one pardons certain trifling inversions, much against the taste of the moment [a taste he had primarily established!], for the sake of the clean-cut ivory finish, and for the interest of the rhythms, the cross run of the beat and the word, as of a stiff wind cutting the ripple-tops of bright water.

Before such accomplished work Pound cheerfully set aside his own most precious prepossessions. Clearly he was not, in some parts of his life, as dogmatic as we tend to believe.

Another reason for Pound's appeal is that he not only believed in action but insisted that by taking thought America and the world could be saved. Fortunately for modern poetry, despite Olson's demurrer, Pound had much of the 18th-century rationalist about him (thus his enthusiasm for Jefferson and Adams who brought that thought to bear on America). He took it for granted that there is a good hard world out there, to be studied with all our senses, then dealt with. He never doubted the senses, or the reliability, properly responded to, of the reports they brought of that world. Even when he turned to China, he favored not Buddha or Lao Tse but the commonsensical Confucius. But, alas, he tried—as he cared—too much. Expecting results, as time passed and all his efforts seemed vain, as he saw what he judged an absurd catastrophe developing, he naturally became more and more frustrated, outraged, and outrageous. If a house—not to say the world—is burning and you alone see it, have the water to save it, but no one wants it, shall you smile, make clever, sardonic, or poetic remarks? Filled with his own sense of truth, yet less and less in touch with others, he could hardly help growing rabidly abstract and rabid.

Pound's self-awareness often pleasingly surprises, for one might expect the reverse from a man so engrossed in what he is doing; he was fully sensible of his impatience,* his irascibility, and its dangers. In "Dr. Williams' Position" (1928) Pound observes, "Carlos Williams has been determined to stand or sit as an American." But then, exploring Williams' diverse ethnological background, Pound concludes: ". . . he has not in his ancestral endocrines the arid curse of our nation. None of his immediate forebears burnt witches in Salem, or attended assemblies for producing prohibitions." Consequently,

> From this secure ingle William Carlos was able to look out of his circumjacence and see it as something interesting *but exterior;* and he could not by any possibility resemble any member of the Concord School. He was able to observe national phenomena without necessity for constant vigilance over himself, there was no instinctive fear that if he forgot himself he might be like some really unpleasant Ralph Waldo; neither is he, apparently, filled with any vivid desire to murder the indescribable dastards who betray the work of the national founders, who spread the fish-hooks of bureaucracy in our once, perhaps, pleasant bypaths.

Thus Williams might, ironically, be accused of

> being, blessedly, the observant foreigner, perceiving American vegetation and landscape quite directly, as something put there

---

*At the same time, for a good cause, such as his endless effort at getting Joyce published and supported, Pound demonstrated his patience. Certainly we owe a good part of Joyce's work to Pound's fantastic campaigning for him. And certainly when one publisher after another rejected both *Dubliners* and *The Portrait of the Artist as a Young Man*, books Pound recognized at once as the time's great prose, yet willingly spent their means on catering to poor mass taste, we can understand his patience's finally breaking into fury.

for him to look at; and his contemplative habit extends, also blessedly, to the fauna.

The inevitable comparison emerges, rather ruefully one might say; for Pound, even in or because of the exile his very Americanism forced on him, was, unlike Williams, unable to stand or sit; he must jump, rush, and shout because he is concerned about America. He

> cannot, on the other hand, observe the nation befouled by Volsteads and Bryans, without anger; I cannot see liberties that have lasted for a century thrown away for nothing, for worse than nothing, for slops; . . .

The ruefulness breaks out:

> And by just this susceptibility on my part Williams, as author, has the no small advantage. If he wants to 'do' anything about what he sees, this desire for action does not rise until he has meditated in full and at leisure. Where I see scoundrels and vandals, he sees a spectacle or an ineluctable process of nature. Where I want to kill at once, he ruminates, and if this rumination leads to anger it is an almost inarticulate anger, that may but lend colour to style, but which stays almost wholly in the realm of his art. I mean it is a qualificative, contemplative, does not drive him to some ultra-artistic or non-artistic activity.

Then amusingly, Pound proposes of Williams the opposite of what Williams and his admirers would claim:

> One might say that Williams has but one fixed idea, as an author; i.e., he starts where an European would start if an European were about to write of America: sic: America is a subject of interest, one must inspect it, analyse it, and treat it as a subject.

Pound, quintessentially American, had to flee to Europe to achieve some objectivity toward America. But even there the Americanism in him boiled over, scalded his calm, his meditation, even his art. Pound fails to mention the detachment of observation and analysis that Williams' medical practice must have cultivated, the immense time and energy needed to spend on it.*

Finally, praising Williams and stressing his neglect, Pound says,

> . . . when a creative act occurs in America 'no one' seems aware
> of what is occurring. In music we have chefs d'orchestre, not
> composers, we have something very like it in letters, though
> the distinction is less obvious.

Again his wistfulness asserts itself:

> . . . it is undeniable that part of my time, for example, has
> been put into orchestra directing. Very little of Dr. Williams'
> energy has been so deflected.

A touch of envy creeps in here. Pound ignores Williams' large
investment of himself in magazine editing. Pound's bitterness at having
to write "stuff as vendible as bath-tubs," at being a front man for
neglected art, overflows. Yet increasingly consumed by screeds and
manifestoes against the Volsteads and other philistines, by his need
to be a publicist and propagandist, he justifies himself:

> Orchestral directing is 'all right' mais c'est pas la même chose.
> We are still so generally obsessed by monism and monotheistical
> backwash, and ideas of orthodoxy that we (and the benighted
> Britons) can hardly observe a dissociation of ideas without
> thinking a censure is somehow therein implied.

The argument now becomes even more interesting. Pound quarrels
with the antique defense of monism ("as if the only alternative for
monism were dualism") even among his distinguished confrères:

> Mr Joyce will argue for hours as if one's attack on Christianity
> were an attack on the Roman church in favour of Luther or
> Calvin or some other half-baked ignoramus and the 'protestant'
> conventicle. Mr Eliot will reply, even in print, to Mr Babbitt
> as if some form of Christianity or monotheism were the sole

---

*Williams had written with delight of his totally self-abnegating absorption in his
countless patients. Medicine refreshed him.

alternative to irreligion; and as if monism or monotheism were anything more than an hypothesis agreeable to certain types of very lazy mind too weak to bear an uncertainty or to remain in an 'uncertainty'.

Shades of Keats' "negative capability"!

> And again, for such reasons William Williams, and may we say, his Mediterranean equipment, have an importance in relation to his temporal intellectual circumjacence.

With such thoughts small wonder Pound had to carry his Americanism to the Mediterranean, had to love his opposite. Lucky Williams already had that Mediterranean in him. But as Pound's "National Culture: A Manifesto" (1938) put it, "After the debacle of American culture [from 1861 on] individuals had to emigrate in order to conserve such fragments of American culture as had survived."

Now Pound feels obliged to deal with the charge that Williams "does not 'conclude'; his work has been 'often formless', 'incoherent', opaque, obscure, obfuscated, confused, truncated, etc." (This sounds like criticism leveled at Pound.) He accepts it; then, in a way counter to much of his own stress on form, artistry, and lucidity, he remarks:

> I am not going to say: 'form' is a non-literary component shoved on to literature by Aristotle or by some not-litteratus who told Aristotle about it. Major form is not a non-literary component. But it can do us no harm to stop an hour or so and consider the number of very important chunks of world-literature in which form, major form, is remarkable mainly for absence.

Anyone familiar with Pound will know what an exceptional statement this is for him. It seems to anticipate Davie's sea-image. Pound illustrates by referring to work he respected as much as any:

> There is a corking plot to the *Iliad,* but it is not told us in the poem or at least not in the parts of the poem known to history as *The Iliad.* It would be hard to find a worse justification of the theories of dramatic construction than the *Prometheus* of Aeschylus. It will take a brighter lad than the author of these presents to demonstrate the element of form in Montaigne or in Rabelais; Lope has it, but it is not the 'Aristotelian' beginning,

middle and end . . . of all these Lope is the only one we could sacrifice without inestimable loss and impoverishment.

This is hardly the place to argue about the *Iliad's* plot or *Prometheus'* structure, to suggest that neither Montaigne nor Rabelais was writing a poem, play, novel. Some great works, like the *Aeneid* and *The Canterbury Tales*, were indeed never "finished." But such an attitude, if it prepares us for *The Cantos*, does not quite suffice for Pound's greatest admiration, *The Divine Comedy*. When Pound concludes,

> The component of these great works and the indispensable component is texture; which Dr Williams has in the best, and in increasingly frequent, passages of his writing.

one is tempted to murmur, "So *The Cantos*."

Now I am not in this instance, as I was not with Tate or Davie, trying to catch Pound out. A genuine artist, responding to a work in its undeniable quick reality, often abandons his usual critical position. Pound can say,

> Art very possibly *ought* to be the supreme achievement, the 'accomplished'; but there is the other satisfactory effect, that of a man hurling himself at an indomitable chaos, and yanking and hauling as much of it as possible into some sort or order (or beauty), aware of it both as chaos and as potential.

The "very possibly" is amusing, as though Pound were hearing and reluctantly acknowledging his customary urgings at a great distance. Pleasing too is his capacity for several "satisfactory" effects. Is it far from the mark to suggest that *The Cantos* is a wonderful combination of both effects, abundant instances of accomplishment and of some beauty and order wrested out of indomitable chaos?

How, given a long, industrious life and the particular demands of the moment, does one keep harmonious such ideals as poetry as speech, poetry as song, music versus sculpture, matter versus form or style? *The Cantos* looms up tempest-wise before us. We know Pound's swerving between poetry as song and poetry as speech, his steadfast belief in the necessity of music in and behind every poem. Lifelong he sought a style that would not only accommodate all things but eliminate the split between words and music, words and reality; thus he opposed rhetoric, adornment, words interested chiefly in themselves. Of course there is trouble here. Speech, yes, but *whose?* Unless one is engaged in dramatic verse, in character-established monologues, what is the speech to be? An intellectual's as well read (and in several languages) as Pound? A carpenter's? A doctor's? A farmer's? A business man's? Or a mishmash of all? The varying speech of different regions? Aside from our speech's shifting before particular individuals, does it not also radically alter under differing circumstances? And where in all this the notion of poetry as something sculptured? Back to Stone Waves again?

Pound, out to educate Harriet Monroe, gave in a letter of January, 1915 his definitive answer to this problem:

> Objectivity and again objectivity, and expression: no hindside-beforeness, no straddled adjectives . . .; nothing that you couldn't in some circumstance, in the stress of some emotion, actually say. Every literaryism, every book word, fritters away a scrap of the reader's patience, a scrap of his sense of your sincerity. When one really feels and thinks, one stammers with simple speech; it is only in the flurry, the shallow frothy excitement of writing, or the inebriety of a metre, that one falls into the easy—oh, how easy!—speech of books and poems that one has read.

Words stammered out of feeling, are they bound to be fresh or frequently clichéd and little different from the frothy excitement of writing? Fortunately Pound's own practice often forgot these restrictions. Think of the reader's patience before Pound's quotations, allusions, book words, book passages! And whatever aptness his formulation may have for the short lyric, even there the idea that one is simply emitting what "one really feels and thinks" and that then "one stammers with simple speech" is highly debatable. Furthermore, with Pound exiled many years from the world of his own tongue, one might wonder what living speech he was writing, what vintage American, beyond the English he remembered from his early days. Nonetheless, as a directive to be direct and natural, his statement has its uses.

I have noted many serious critics' tendency to dismiss Pound's ideas, to reduce him to little more than a magnificent stylist, a supreme juggler of language—this in the face of his settled passion to be the opposite. Berryman quotes R. P. Blackmur's judgment of Pound as "all surface and articulation." A kind of praise almost worse than blame. Blackmur says flatly: Pound is neither a great poet nor a great thinker . . . at his best a maker of great verse. . . ." He misses in Pound "any extraordinary revelation of life . . . any bottomless fund of feeling . . . any mode of life already formulated, any collection of established feelings, composed or mastered in new form." One might ask whether the writers Pound translated—Blackmur concedes him mainly the gift of great translator—might not have so supplied him. But then the real trouble slips out: "The content of his work does not submit to analysis. . . . It cannot be talked about like the doctrines of Dante or the mental machinery of Blake. It cannot be deduced from any current of ideas. It is not to be found in any book or set of books." Pound, in short, is not for the academy. But surely the books Pound recommended so strenuously are the ones to consult? Furthermore, the vast academic analysis and talk accumulated round Pound and his work should give the lie to Blackmur. I am reminded of Eliot's similar reservation before Shakespeare: no system, no Aquinas behind him, just a flotsam of ideas. In a footnote Blackmur fails to realize how much he is contradicting and belittling his expectation above: "Most poetry is on commonplace themes [he is talking about "great poets"] and the freshness, what the poet supplies, is in the language." Then Blackmur reaches a remarkable conclusion: ". . . lacking sufficient substance of his own to maintain an intellectual discipline, Mr. Pound is always better where the discipline of craftsmanship is enough." When, unless the ideas of poetry are indeed commonplace and insignificant, can such discipline ever be enough?

In 1956, some 23 years later, in four fascinating lectures, *Anni Mirabiles 1921–1925: Reason in the Madness of Letters,* delivered at and published by the Library of Congress, Blackmur saw no reason to change his mind. Considering Pound with Whitman, a coupling that would probably have pleased as it irked Pound, Blackmur says:

> Each is a barbarian, and neither ever found a subject that compelled him to composition; each remained spontaneous all his life. In Whitman you find the sprawl of repetition, in Pound the heap of ideograms; in either case we ourselves make the thought emerge [is that so bad, not the kind of collaboration

modern poetry requires, and the felicitous "bewilderment" Davie praised?] In Whitman there is the catalogue which is not catalogued. In Pound there is the catalogue, these jewels of conversation. In both you have to know your way around and who the people are.

Yet finally, even as Blackmur calls Pound "a crackerbarrel Mencken proceeding by crotchets and idées fixes," he succumbs to the old confusion by acknowledging Pound "Il miglior fabbro"—or no Mencken at all—who "at that level knows everything, and knows besides all that his ears and eyes could tell."

To call Pound "all surface and articulation" then is to say that he is the victim of his very intention and his success in realizing it, his concentration on luminous details, on gists and piths, or an attitude approximating "no ideas but in things." Seen properly, Blackmur's judgment is a happy description of Pound's accomplishment, which derives from his passion for—these words he reiterated almost like spells—clarity, precision, hardness. Thus his first article on Joyce (1914) lauded his "clear hard prose." "He deals with subjective things, but he presents them with such clarity of outline that he might be dealing with locomotives or with builders' specifications." In his essay on Wyndham Lewis (1920) Pound approvingly comments:

> 'Tarr' really gets at something . . . when he says that art 'has no inside'. This is a condition of art, 'to have no inside, nothing you cannot see. It is not something impelled like a machine by a little egotistic inside.'

One thinks of Auerbach's illuminating discussion in *Mimesis* of Homer's radiant world, its almost sculptured visibility. Pound further quotes *Tarr:*

> 'Deadness, in the limited sense in which we use that world, is the first condition of art. The second is absence of *soul,* in the sentimental human sense. The lines and masses of a statue are its soul.'

One may balk at the extremism—the deliberate sensationalism—of this statement; it is dangerous if applied to the world beyond literature.

But it is urging, like imagism, oneness of form and content. We know that, much as he was after the great world out there and man at his most heroic, Pound was impatient with the Freudian, with the modern immersion in the personal's shadowy depths. Certainly by 1934 his impatience was complete; his later commitment to history and economics merely underscored it. Thus he wrote McAlmon:

> Lots of damn rot and "psychology," people fussing with innards which are merely the result of economic pressure. . . . I think the whole of egotistic psychological nuvveling is gone plop because the people who go on imitating Dostoiev. and the whole damn lot of 'em *won't* look at the reality.

For all his often hard arrogance, Pound at his best never pursued his own identity. Toying with motives, enthusiastic crawling about in the self's cellar, and the cant of identity crises were silly indulgences to him. And an evasion of the ideal he set himself, whatever his serious failures to abide by it, of learning to live abundantly in the larger world. He had little time for self-pity, indolence, apathy. An alien most of his life, he rarely gave way to that commonplace modern pastime—and curse—alienation, or its related cozy despairs.

Returning to Blackmur's phrase "all surface and articulation," one can propose that this was precisely Pound's success with the diverse forms he undertook. Since his life, restless as Picasso's or Stravinsky's, was a search for style, when Pound hit upon a form he admired he studied it till he mastered its unique resources. Thus his career as poet comprised a series of emergent masterworks in a variety of forms: "The Return," "The Alchemist," "The Spring," "Provincia Deserta," "Cathay," "Propertius," "Mauberley." His enthusiastic comments on Whistler surely apply to him:

> I have gathered from the loan exhibit of Whistler's paintings now at the Tate (September, 1912), more courage for living than I have gathered from the Canal Bill or from any other manifest American energy whatsoever. . . . Here in brief is the work of a man, born American, with all our forces of confusion within him, who has contrived to keep order in his work, who has attained the highest mastery, and this not by a natural facility, but by constant labour and searching . . . . work in many styles,

pastels of Greek motif, one pre-Raphaelite picture, and work after the Spanish, the northern and the Japanese models, and some earlier things under I know not what school.

The man's struggle was set before one. He had tried all means, he had spared himself nothing, he had struggled in one direction until he had either achieved or found it inadequate for his expression. After he achieved a thing, he never repeated.

(Patria Mia, 1913)

The two last poems of *Ripostes*, "The Return" and "The Alchemist," facing each other, offer a chance to watch Pound's genius quarrying out its resources. Both poems triumph in the skill with which they conjure up their particular moment; the return of the gods and the transformation of inferior—though lovely, alive—metals into gold. Both poems are miracles of equipoise. In "The Return" we must recognize the provisional, brilliant peace Pound has achieved between stone and wave. For the poem in its near Sapphic stanzas has a carved feeling indeed: cut out of a giant rock, broken off from a once mighty temple, vibrant as Valéry's notion of the dance. As with such great sculpture the poem is made wholly of movement: tentative waves, then swiftly hurtling breakers. In short, one element is composed of the other, rises out of the other: a permanent beauty out of the sea and the sea, its incessant flux, caught forever in that beauty. A frieze of a poem, it slowly thaws out and becomes frieze the more. It begins with a slow, accumulated series of waverings expressed in three-syllabled, hovering words: tentative, uncertain, wavering, half-awakened ("as half-" is echoed by the next lines "As if"), hesitant. In tune with this wavering, snow, a superb "natural" image of hesitant, late winter movement, hangs in air, murmurs, and half turns back. Then as the poem remembers what once these beings were, the mere thought of them discovers enough energy in itself to give us a moment of their powerful, ecstatic presence, not murmuring now but crying "Haie!" as they rush on "wingèd shoe" with swift hounds, sniffing not winter but blood. Then promptly, the past tense overtaking them, they dwindle again, from keen, swift "souls of blood" to leash-slow, "pallid" ghosts. Or no more than a frieze.

"The Alchemist," on the other hand, suggests a magnificent simultaneous expression of the love act, the moment of creation in the making of a poem, and actual alchemy, all done, since varyingly forbidden, at night. Beautiful mellifluous names of beautiful women, mythical as semi-goddesses and real, compose the chant, are the ritual words in a veritable catalogue of fair women. The attendant handmaids of beauty, each supplies, in her moving and her singing some basic ingredient or part (see "Το Καλόν"), almost metal already, yet alive (and perhaps already at their liveliest)—"the red *gold* of the maple," "the *light* of the birch tree *in autumn*," "the *silver rustling* of wheat," "the *molten* dyes of the water," "the *burnished* nature of fire," "the poplars *weeping* their amber," (my italics). And in the bringing, the women and their gifts not only begin the transformation but perform it until "the golden artifice of eternity" is completed as they quiet the metal. Rarely has a more sumptuous, formal, yet performing poem been composed, hard lines of verse, welded, not fused. The ingredients are properly brought at night when they are free from the office of light which imposes rigid shapes and duties on them, free in alchemy's alembic or the fragrant darkness of the imagination. One recalls one of Pound's most radiant lines, "In the gloom the gold gathers the light against it." Then the mind can enjoy the quiddity of things.

Here Valéry's contention comes to mind that genuine poetry contains no inert matter, that, on the contrary, it all metamorphoses into vibrant form. On the side of the world, not of "shadows" and "dreams," but of the "shapes of power" and "men," Pound was resolutely anti-symbolist, with imagism a direct rejoinder to it. For this insistence as for other attitudes Pound again and again has been accused of being unoriginal, lacking a matter of his own; at best merely a translator. Perhaps simply another roundabout way of saying he was too bookish, with no fund of life to draw on. Pound would have scoffed at this separation of life and literature; for life was—and is—often at its best in some great ancient text. Nobody would deny that Pound believed and lived in literature as much as in anything else, was often at his liveliest in and through it, that he made past literature one of the most impressive vehicles of reality. As for translation, in Pound's own words:

After this period [Anglo-Saxon] English literature lives on translation, it is fed by translation; every new exuberance, every

new heave is stimulated by translation, every allegedly great age
is an age of translations, beginning with Geoffrey Chaucer, Le
Grand Translateur, translator of the *Romaunt of the Rose*, para-
phraser of Virgil and Ovid, condenser of old stories he had
found in Latin, French, and Italian.

(*How to Read*, 1929)

Often too Pound has been attacked for being a bad translator,
outraging, if not his original, the "authorities" with his liberties, his
playfulness, his "howlers." One wonders what these authorities feel
about Homer, the inspired latest, we suspect, of a long line of
"translators"; about Greek drama with its few major themes and
its dependence on freshness of treatment; or, most of all, about
Shakespeare who, rarely inventing a plot, frequently, some of his
contemporaries were at pains to point out, dressed up his plays
in other men's verses. Very few of us are original; but, for our
sense of "property," we tend to absorb or conceal our sources. Pound
not only usually declared them, he advertised them. Because aside
from honesty, he was above all concerned with learning and teaching,
with exhibiting the race's great examples, his very purpose and virtue
is held against him. It was truly a matter of "surface and articulation,"
of making it new—those instances of great thought and feeling and
expression the race is always in danger of losing—in his age's unique
nuances and energies. Already in 1908 he could write Williams who
had criticized his poems, write most amiably, thanking Williams ("Your
letter is worth a dozen notes of polite appreciation."):

I have bushels of verse that could offend no one except a person
as well read as I am who know that it has all been said just
as prettily before. Why write what I can translate out of Renaissance Latin or crib from the saintly dead?

Of course a vast jumble of contradictions and torsos, especially
for one so gifted, energetic, and ambitious, is bound to be strewn
across Pound's long writing career. Some of these deserve register-
ing so as to establish, not only the tensions inherent in his work,
the complex troubles, but the riches, the dramatic delights engend-
ered by those tensions. Pound was ardently dedicated to beauty
and perfection. Lewis could say of him that, like Whistler, he certainly has been "bitten by the same inexorable bug"—perfection

—and "strained fanatically towards the same limits of human expression. . . ." Even more, "he demands perfection in action, as
well as in art. He even appears to expect perfection, or what he
understands as such, in the world of politics." At 24, in "What I
feel about Walt Whitman" (1909), from the new vantage ground
of England, Pound could say: "From this side of the Atlantic I am
for the first time able to read Whitman." "I see him America's poet."
Not, however, unmixed praise. "His crudity is an exceeding great
stench, but it is America. . . . He is an exceedingly nauseating pill,
but he accomplishes his mission." In this fashion the little essay
violently vacillates: "I honour him for he prophesied me while I
can only recognize him as a forebear of whom I *ought to be* proud."
(my italics) The trouble with Whitman is that "he is content to be
what he is. . . ." The discontent that drives one to improvements
is what Pound was after. Then he admits, "In America there is
much for the healing of nations, but woe unto him of the cultured
palate who attempts the dose." He seemed to realize his problem.
Yet he cannot deny, "As for Whitman, I read him (in many parts)
with acute pain, but when I write of certain things I find myself
using his rhythm. . . . The vital part of my message, taken from
the sap and fibre of America, is the same as his." Then a major
irony (as well as ambivalence) emerges:

> Mentally I am a Walt Whitman who has learned to wear a collar
> and a dress shirt (although at times inimical to both). Personally
> I might be very glad to conceal my relationship to my spiritual
> father and bray about my more congenial ancestry—Dante,
> Shakespeare, Theocritus, Villon, but my descent is a bit difficult
> to establish. And to be frank, Whitman is to my fatherland (*Patriam
> quam odi et amo* for no uncertain reasons) what Dante is to Italy
> and I at my best can only be a strife for a renaissance in America
> of all the lost or temporarily mislaid beauty, truth, valour, glory
> of Greece, Italy, England and all the rest of it.*

One cannot deny the appeal of Pound's confession. Or the irony
in it. Whitman, at first as collared and dress-shirted as any dandy

---

*John Burroughs in an 1871 letter described Emerson's finicky desire that Whitman's
friends urge him to be "a little more tame and orderly—more mindful of the
requirements of beauty, of art, of culture." How droll to think of Emerson and
Pound, if only for a moment, on the same side!

of his day, sloughed that role to be America's "natural" poet, a rough and tough. Pound, finding the latter condition too prevalent and longing for the culture lost or temporarily mislaid, departed for England to recover it. At first he was well pleased with what he met. Yet, defiant before English mannerliness (for some snobbery and stuffiness), he felt increasingly called on to assert bohemianism, his rampant "Americanism." In Lewis' words,

> He was a drop of oil in a glass of water. The trouble was, I believe, that he had no wish to *mix*: he just wanted to *impress*. The British in question were not of the impressionable kind— hated above all things being impressed and people who wished to impress them.—I may add they also disapproved of Americans.

After a brief honeymoon such conditions could only exacerbate both sides. Pound's "American 'strenuousness'—the Bull Moose tradition," for being despised, grew more strenuous and despised the more.

> Above all, these people were unready to be lectured to: to have their shortcomings, as to literary taste, dissected, to have their chronic amateurism exposed.

A born lecturer,* a kind of American itinerant peddler crying up his artistic wares, Pound belonged to that nettling type who expect others to be grateful—and are astonished when they are not—for telling them the truth about themselves, a telling which usually means an exposure of their inadequacies and weaknesses. But then Pound assumed that everyone is or ought to be primarily concerned with improvement and perfection, the personal be damned. The more the others recoiled, the more he attacked.

In short, Pound grew so frustrated he accused his enemies not merely of stupidity but of conspiracy, deliberate malice, downright evil. For the England which welcomed his aestheticism or at least was amused by some of his bohemianism (his poetry was at first enthusiastically received), he soon discovered, expected him to be wholly and merely an entertaining bohemian. The majority, he sadly

---

*Lewis almost makes him out *the* schoolmaster, a Holofernes, if one with genius and "*creative* sympathy": "He breathed Letters, ate Letters, dreamt Letters."

learned, deemed art chiefly an ornament, a diversion; different from Americans therefore not much more than superficially. At least as serious, the English recoil from his as he became more and more strident meant a diminution in his little income from hack-work. Thus literally as well as spiritually living in England became impossible for him and plunged him, ironically, away from aestheticism into the American practicality, the economic "hard-headedness," he had fled. Lewis quotes Pound on England:

> In a country in love with amateurs, in a country where the incompetent have such beautiful manners and personalities so fragile and charming that one cannot bear to injure their feeling by the introduction of competent criticism, it is well that one man should have a vision of perfection and that he should be sick to the death and disconsolate because he can not attain it.
>
> (*Pavannes and Division*, 1918)

Lewis agrees that

> "Professionalism" . . . was looked upon as something to shun and disown . . . . The word *Perfection* . . . has obvious professional associations. Perfection implies the highly finished product, result of competent craftsmanship, and consequently it is tabu in a society where a well-to-do class desire the fruits of craftsmanship without its toils, or in one where time is denied the workman, and what can be done can only be fragmentary, superficial, hasty, in-the-rough.

Professionalism, to the people Lewis is describing, "that, of course, was what was the matter with Americans! They take their sports too seriously."

But as Lewis rightly concludes, "Pound is—was always, is, must always remain, violently American." And he detects, after all, the "Leaves of Grass" in his "manly candour in his broad and bearded face" and the "tough guy" as well. That and the "other" Whitman also. Pound admits in his Whitman essay that "if a man has written lines like Whitman's to the *Sunset Breeze* one has to love him. I think we have not yet paid enough attention to the deliberate artistry of the man, not in details but in the large." He goes even further:

> I am immortal even as he is, *yet with a lesser vitality as I am*
> *the more in love with beauty (if I really do love it more than he*
> *did).* [my italics]

Pound concludes:

> It seems to me I should like to drive Whitman into the old
> world. I sledge, he drill—and to scourge America with all the
> old beauty, (For Beauty *is* an accusation.). . . . This desire because
> I am young and impatient, were I old and wise I should content
> myself in seeing and saying that these things will come. But
> now, *since I am by no means sure it would be true prophecy* [my
> italics], I am fain set my own hand to the labour.

But till his last years Pound was—and increasingly—"young and
impatient." Olsen speaks of his

> mere impatience, the nerves turning like a wild speed-machine
> (it is how he got his work done) and, more important, an
> intolerance of the mind's speed (fast as his goes), an intolerance
> even of himself. . . . His mind bursts from the lags he sees
> around him.

That impatience required someone important to heed it. Pound was
eagerly grateful when at last Mussolini gave him an audience and
a kind word ("*divertente*") for his work; of what other major leader
could this be said? Mussolini seemed of a mind ("right reason")
and a practicality to fulfill—such Pound's wishful, desperate thinking—Pound's ambitions for society and art. Thus he could believe
he found essential resemblances between Mussolini and Jefferson.
For the tremendous energy and will Pound thought he saw in him,
"an OPPORTUNIST who is RIGHT, that is who has certain convictions and drives them through circumstances or batters and forms
circumstances with them," Mussolini seemed a modern Malatesta.
So far the love of beauty took Pound! His Whitman essay concludes:
"It is a great thing, reading a man to know, not 'His Tricks are
not as yet my Tricks, but I can easily make them mine' but 'His
message is my message. We will see that men hear it!'" Whitman
might well have boggled at this talk of their identical message and
responded with his solitary quotation from Baudelaire: "The immod-
erate taste for beauty and art leads men into monstrous excesses."

As does the reformer's fanaticism, his single—or simple—minded-ness. Clearly Pound was meant for extremes. Not that he was oblivious to this problem. In 1918 Pound praised Joyce's comprehensiveness, his completeness, saying of *A Portrait of the Artist as a Young Man*,

> . . . there is no omission; there is nothing in life so beautiful that Joyce cannot touch it without profanation—without, above all, the profanations of sentiment and sentimentality—and there is nothing so sordid that he cannot treat it with his metallic exactitude.

And Pound can observe, in justification of the so-called "disagreeable" in Joyce, "There is no perception of beauty without a corresponding disgust." Nonetheless, Pound increasingly felt Joyce primarily satirical and analytical, both by temperament and by the nature of prose, and prone to the sordid as well, and himself as a poet given to the affirmative and to synthesizing. Plumping for balance and sanity, "Mass effect of any work depends on conviction of author's sanity," Pound maintained, "Abnormal keenness of insight O.K.. But obsessions arseore-ial, cloacal, deist, aesthetic, as opposed to arsethetic, any obsession or tic shd. be very carefully considered before being turned loose."

Yet, alas, in behalf of aestheticism and his dedication to culture, Pound was driven to what he considered fact, reality, and eventually to the fanatic's fearful partiality. For Pound discovered the artist's lot, the problem of finding means to survive while doing his work, interwoven with the welfare of all people. In 1933 his "Murder by Capital" confesses that "the unemployment problem" he had had to face for 25 years at first concerned only a handful of artists he believed in and regarded as his responsibility. But he has realized his mistake:

> If there was (and I admit that there was) a time when I thought this problem could be solved without regard to the common man, humanity in general, the man in the street, the average citizen, etc., I retract, I sing palinode, I apologise.*

*He was amply aware of the condition his passion had brought him to. In this essay he says, "What . . . can drive a man interested almost exclusively in the arts, . . . into a study of the . . . economic aspects of the present? . . . Why should

Thus Pound gave himself, with the passion he had devoted to beauty, to the study and the urging of economics, to a revision in fundamental governmental policies.

Meantime, somehow *The Cantos* accumulated. Miraculously. For embroiled as he was in endless dispatches, ukases, harangues over the plight of the world and the need for political action, and in correspondence courses with the young and the not-so-young, it is almost incredible to conceive of his writing poetry too. This is scarcely the place to examine *The Cantos* in detail. Plainly developing out of and seeking to absorb the materials, external and internal, of his life, in a most complicated way they resemble, among other things, the journal, that most popular American "form," which sanctions one's right to a world of process and action. This mode's excitements and shortcomings for the kind of art Pound desired to produce should be clear. He could introduce anything and everything* (part of his wish to reclaim for poetry domains appropriated by the novel), everything that happened to him or at least seemed important, no matter how outwardly trivial: an accidental encounter, a remark overheard, a quotation from a letter, a scrap of altogether local history involving private individuals, yet all providing evidence as Pound "read" them. This solipsism was for the material, not for Pound. Like the disparate poems of *Leaves of Grass,* *The Cantos* are kept together on the breath and by the skin of the poet.

Unfortunately now and then the form that resulted, rather than absorbing and using its materials, did appear "all surface and articulation"—the material too abruptly surfaced out of the general

---

a peace-loving writer of Quaker descent be quite ready to shoot certain persons he never laid eyes on?" He recognizes, "Head-born hate is possibly the most virulent. Leaving aside my present belief that economic order is possible and that the way to a commonly decent economic order is known. What has capital done that I should hate Andy Mellon as a symbol or as a reality?" He answers himself: "I have blood lust because of what I have seen done to, and attempted against, the arts in my time." And this he regards as ultra-important because "the effects of social evil show first in the arts."

*On March, 1917, Pound wrote Joyce: "I have begun an endless poem, of no known category, Phanopoeia (light- or image-making) or something or other, all about everything."

hurlyburly. Or it became a huge valise, jam-packed to bursting with all the valuables and not so valuables a traveler in a headlong rush might throw together. Accordingly, artistry notwithstanding, Pound's words on Williams' work may prove most relevant to *The Cantos:*

> Art very possibly *ought* to be the supreme achievement, the 'accomplished'; but there is the other satisfactory effect, that of a man hurling himself at an indomitable chaos, etc.

As I suggested earlier, *The Cantos* may be fairly judged a mixture of both satisfactory effects. A poem that will not settle down, it changes in the varying light of the reader's awareness (this, of course, is true of most good poems, but nothing like *The Cantos*). Protean like Pound himself, it will not submit to total academicizing, no matter how many literary archeologists may be diligently digging away. The crucial troubles Pound heroically weltered in, magnificently or frantically, are in the poem and in our readings of it; thus it stays obstinately, thrashingly alive.

That epithet "all surface and articulation" may prove inadequate in other ways, prove too clear, too exclusive, giving short shrift to uncertainty, doubts, flaws, Or may bring too many surfaces, and their edges, too brusquely together. Once the enamel cracked, as in *The Pisan Cantos,* much of a rather different order emerged. When Pound's hardness, the quality he always urged on writing, discovered its helplessness, he realized how imprisoned, sealed off, he had been, carrying on his dream of a great life in a foreign country. Broken open he was, at a terrible price, like Lear, to compassion, a deepened response to the world. The greatness was there to respond, whatever collapse and silence must follow. He saw that he must pull down his vanity, at last learning that "it is not man / Made courage, or made order, or made grace." He comes closest here to embracing Yeats' words that, whatever joy the artist may know in making and in mastering his materials, "with his eyes he enters upon a submissive, sorrowful contemplation of the great irremediable things." Yet even at this late date, despite his imprisonments and with Mussolini hanged, Pound could remain positive, robust, brilliantly creative:

> Yet say this to the Possum; a bang, not a whimper,

> with a bang not with a whimper,
> To build the city of Dioce whose terraces are the colour of stars.

Moreover:

> But to have done instead of not doing
>   this is not vanity
> To have, with decency, knocked
> That a Blunt should open
>   To have gathered from the air a live tradition
> or from a fine old eye the unconquered flame
> This is not vanity.
>   Here error is all in the not done,
> all in the diffidence that faltered,

He acknowledged fully what he had known intermittently:

>   nothing matters but the quality
>   of the affection—
>   in the end—that has carved the trace in the mind
>   dove sta memoria

Affection plus self-respect and the indomitable will to believe, to do, and to survive.

As the cantos came along, in operatic fashion they gathered up many leitmotifs. And with greater and greater frequency they play upon, glance off each other (or what he wished to restore: "the radiant world where one thought cuts through another with clean edge, a world of moving energies," one bird's flight cleaving in swift, sure shadow the flight of another) till, for the brevity and speed and frequency, one must read ever more slowly to supply room and time for recollection's resonance and for the turning up, in endlessly new combinations, of new gleaming facets. The cantos are often relentless in their saltancy, a seven hundred league leaping, far surpassing Yeats' or Eliot's, say, sometimes between sections of cantos, sometimes between two cantos, and sometimes even inside one canto. Some of these hurdlings it is hard not to regard as capricious, if not adventitious. The difficulties are obvious. In music we need not identify the leitmotifs (though identifying does intensify our pleasure); the music, an interwoven pattern moving along via its players and singers, plays on us. But in language, even poetic language charged with great energy, the analogy with music must break down. The vexing matter of meaning, of active understanding on the reader's part, unavoidably dogs us. How long can we hold our intellectual breath, submit to the battering waves lunged over our heads, or treat *The Cantos,* large sections of it, as an intriguing, wonderful-sounding foreign language?

Pound's was an incredible attempt to turn imagism, the epigram, and the ideogram, which by their very nature are meant for short, explosive flights, into a long epical poem. Consequently, more and more lamination ensued, images heaped on and twisted with images: a vastly intricate mosaic that does not too often compose one image or poem. At times, overseen from the distance—as from a plane—of rapid reading, details blend like tiny myriad flowers into one huge, golden-blazing field in the manner, say, of impressionist painting. At times. Elsewhere these leitmotifs become, no doubt for economy and drama, shorter and shorter phrases, sometimes a single word substituting for the whole text: a shorthand, a kind of code. Or allusions not altogether unlike those of Pound's chief *bête noire,* Milton. But Milton's allusions, in part because his audience was more homogeneous, were usually shared, not private or dependent exclusively on previous first mention, sometimes hundreds of pages earlier. Whatever pleasure Pound's method of composing may give initiates, elated with their sudden discoveries, it does seem to exact excessive labor from even the interested, intelligent, but non-professional reader. Yet, after the mine-fields of hieratic works like *Finnegans Wake,* how dare we complain?

Still we do recall Lewis' "terseness." And I cannot completely discount Pound's statement to Allen Ginsberg in 1967 that "my poems don't make sense," that they are "A lot of double talk. Bunting told me that there was too little presentation in *The Cantos* and too much reference, that I referred to things without presenting them." Or not enough surface and articulation! Pound's "Paris Letter" (June, 1922) commended the Joyce of *Ulysses:*

> . . . no author is more lucid or more explicit in presenting things in such a way that the imaginary Chinaman or denizen of the forty-first century could without works of reference gain a very good idea of the scene and habits portrayed.

Fifty years after Pound's discarded first canto, ". . . say . . . the modern world / Needs such a rag-bag to stuff all its thought in," he could tell Daniel Cory: "I picked out this and that thing that interested me, and then jumbled them into a bag. That's not the way to make . . . a *work of art*." Nonetheless, the things that interested him do constitute the poem. Like many others, until fairly recently I used to read in *The Cantos* for their lyrical moments, their sudden waterspouting into imagistic loveliness. Impatiently I leaped over much of the rest as undigested lumps, a flagging of Pound's creative powers, overridden by his other interests. But I have come to realize the importance of that rest to Pound—and to the poem. Like ideograms and other unique bits of foreign languages studding *The Cantos*, documents, passages of books, and chinoiserie become precious, sacred texts as Pound judged them the truth (therefore beauty). He must have been sorely tempted at times to reprint these texts *in toto* in *The Cantos*, claiming that the lyric moments would not have flowered without such soil. Endeavoring to remove the gap between content and form, fact and beauty, life and art, he kept insisting on their oneness. As he says in "The Jefferson-Adams Letters as a Shrine and Monument" (1937–38),

> The MAIN implication is that they stand for a life not split into bits.
>
> Neither of these two men would have thought of literature as something having nothing to do with life, the nation, the organisation of government. Of course no first-rate author ever did think of his books in this manner.

And concluding that their letters proved most cogently that "CIVILISATION was in America . . . during the decade of reconciliation after their disagreements," he has, as always, two crows to pick with the American university system: first for omitting in its teaching of history the "most significant documents" and second for doing the same in teaching literature and "assuming that the life of a nation's letters is restricted mostly to second-rate fiction." Pound would never make such a mistake. If these documents are the most significant they *must* be studied as great literature.

The problem for the reader is obvious. Let us accept for a moment the challengeable assumption that these letters are literature; but

what of the many lesser documents, drossy history books, dreary
pamphlets Pound felt called on to stuff *The Cantos* with? We have
been taught in our time, happily at its best, to see everything as
potentially poetic: either the gods live everywhere, live with and
in everything or they do not live at all. But surely the word "potentially"
means something. Unless that everything undergoes the sea-change
Eliot expected how does it indeed become poetry? Or for that matter,
if the text is already literature, who needs the poet?—What is his
use? A mere collector? Unlike the collages of a Picasso and a Braque,
say, with their browning newspaper scraps, Pound's inserts are often
long and meant to be read, pondered, digested. How many of us
bother or are expected to read the Picasso newsprint, despite his
puns and jokes in choosing it? The newspaper's "reality" quickly
becomes absorbed into the painting's ensemble, an additional, collab-
orative texture and color and—whatever pleasure of tension we may
care to find in it, even in its origins—not an obtrusive hunk of
"life." However much his inserts may now and then serve Pound
by his skill, his passion, the pressures of the context, this "method"
rarely works for others. Rather it has helped to prompt a spate
of poems, mere notations and descriptions, astonishing in their
casualness, their patent triviality. And "poetry concrete" notwithstanding, whatever love one may have for books, the letters on the
page are not normally ideogrammic, not calligraphy in themselves.
However strongly Pound may have wished for active picture-writing,
the importance of print still principally resides, not in its physical
look, but in its sound and sense.

The remarking of these difficulties and contradictions is not meant
to demean Pound and his spending himself with a prodigality possible
to very few of us. Instead it intends to underscore the richness,
often bewildering, of the mixture and of his gifts, and the intelligence
and enormous good will *The Cantos* requires to be dealt with sanely,
judiciously, honestly. But the difficulties do reflect the dilemma of
trying to arrive at a settled view of Pound and his work, a dilemma
he shared. We may dismiss his last verdict on himself and his work
as that of a disappointed, exhausted old man, readying for death,
so naturally turning on his past. Or the frustration, the sense of
failure bound to descend on most of us, if we are haunted by perfection
or ar at least by what we have yearned to accomplish. But we cannot

wholly ignore his awareness of his mistake in assuming he was a
Fortinbras, say, sent to set all right or, perhaps more accurately,
Hamlet's father, from the start directing the play from the wings,
when all the time he was—great wit, art, energy, grace, and all—much
more Hamlet, much less certain or in charge of reality, than he
knew. Also, perhaps, he saw at last the inadequacies of his tycoon-like
puritanism: his relentless, if not rigid and monomaniacal seriousness;
of his sense too not only of an ordered universe with a well-defined
hierarchy, but of his belief in his mastery of that order.

Yet caught in *The Cantos,* like iridescent insects and monarch
butterflies, shimmeringly, lovingly alive, stirred by our fascinated,
ignited, and igniting breath, glimpses of the terrestrial paradise—its
sunsets, its lightning-bright dawns—flare forth. Even to *The Cantos'*
end, for Pound—like Homer's cicada old men, the Homeric loud
in their dry rustling still, startled by the loveliness of Helen—the
beauty of the seasons, of day and night, of change prevails.

> A blown husk that is finished
>   but the light sings eternal
> a pale flare over marshes
>   where the salt hay whispers to tide's change

>   (Canto CXV)

Or admitting his errors and wrecks:

> To confess wrong without losing rightness:
> Charity I have had sometimes,
>   I cannot make it flow thru.
> A little light, like a rushlight
>   to lead back to splendour.

>   (Canto CXVI)

And finally:

> M'amour, m'amour
>   what do I love and
>   where are you?
> That I lost my center
>   fighting the world.
> The dreams clash

and are shattered—
and that I tried to make a paradiso
terrestre.

(CXVII)

Few men as valiantly, as tragically.

Wallace Stevens:
Lunching with Hoon

After a considerable correspondence relating to the *Quarterly Review of Literature*, on November 14, 1944, Wallace Stevens wrote to suggest that I visit him at his office. Since my wife and I had recently moved to New Haven with *QRL*, Hartford was close by. In the same letter Stevens, quick as always to remark possible relations, mentioned Paul Weiss, only a name to us then, later a member of Yale's philosophy department and a good friend. Weiss, questioning Stevens' concentration on James and Bergson in his essay, "The Figure of the Youth as Virile Poet," in *The Sewanee Review*, had urged, in Stevens' words, the usual "divinities of the Styx" and then, as "a relief" from them, Whitehead, Bradley, and Pierce. Stevens reflected, "I think that most modern philosophers are purely academic and certainly there is little in Whitehead contrary to that impression." He added graciously, "I have always been curious about Pierce, but have been obliged to save my eyesight for THE QUARTERLY REVIEW, etc." Stevens' curiosity was, I believe, intuitively apt. He was often occupied with matters Pierce had explored as philosopher and semiologist, and in a similar, endlessly circling fashion. For a poet like Stevens, so responsive to the weather that it became a state of mind, states of mind, especially those increasingly persistent among able, original thinkers, could quickly become a pervasive weather. Thus, apt though Stevens' intuition was, he was probably wise, for his poetry's sake, to resist his curiosity and the Coleridgean trap of an absorbing philosophy. Certainly Stevens was intrigued by the poetry of philosophy and the philosophy of poetry or at least, as he put it, "a life of ideas," "thinking about poetry," its essential nature, its place in the world, its connection and exchange with that world.

Then, on July 18, 1945—this is the invitation I remember accepting— Stevens wrote: "I shall be very glad to see you any day next week except Saturday. If you will come about 12:15, we can go to lunch together. I have been looking forward to meeting you. . . .'' My excitement at the prospect was of course complicated by uneasiness. Much as I admired his work, how dared I think to beard the mighty magician in his lair? My mind churned with notions about him: my own reflections on his poems, the bits of him I had gleaned from his letters, the stories that floated about of his very private life, his extraordinary, even difficult character, and so on. Strongly though these latter belied my sense of the demeanor of his work, pronounced themselves its diametrical opposite, I persisted in believing that, once I stepped into his ambience, by the happy ease of his powers and my enthusiasm for them, we would enjoy instant rapport. Nor was I lacking in youthful confidence.

When I arrived at the Hartford Accident and Indemnity Company, on 690 Asylum Street no less—so this, I thought, is the Palaz of Hoon!— I was amazed, naturally more than ever, no matter how much my information about him should have prepared me, by the paradox of a poet like Stevens being a vice-president of such a company, massively embodied in its edifice and its university-campus-like grounds. In Stevens' words, "The buildings were of marble and stood in marble light." Or in his letter prose: "The office here is a solemn affair of granite, with a portico resting on five of the grimmest possible columns." This description, it is true, was written to discourage a couple from calling on him "*in shorts*" [Stevens' italics]. However, he did continue,

> The idea of Mr. Ney and his wife, toddling up the front steps and asking for me made me suggest that they might like to stop at some nearby rest-house and change to something more bourgeois. This is merely one of the hilarious possibilities of being in the insurance business. After all, why should one worry?

That our most poetic poet should spend his days in such an atmosphere and at such chores! Were his life and his art as romantically chasm-split as Poe's? To think of his pen leaping the distance—chasms and mountains it would certainly seem to require—from answering surety claims to the claims of his muse demanded an alpine effort on my part tantamount to that of some of his most ambitious poems.

Yet, it must be said, Stevens believed in his position and his place's superiority. I am wryly amused to report that on July 8, 1941, in a letter to Hi Simons, Stevens could observe:

> It [his essay "The Noble Rider and the Sound of Words" which he had read at Princeton University in May] was worth doing (for me), although the visit to Princeton gave me a glimpse of a life which I

am profoundly glad that I don't share. The people I met were the
nicest people in the world, but how they keep alive is more than I
can imagine.

And with his imagination! Or precisely my reaction when I visited him
in Hartford. However it may strike an outsider, apparently each one of
us prefers his or her own nest, made indispensable, for someone like
Stevens, by its semblance of order, continuity, sanity: insurance indeed.

I entered his office, a small but high-ceilinged, airy room, its windows
looking out on the grounds, to find him at his desk, his secretary at
hers a few feet away. I was already surprised to have been invited to
his place of business; for I had always heard that he kept his daily work
and poetry strictly apart, was altogether reluctant to let his business
associates know what he was up to away from the insurance company.
By this time his attitude must have changed, and the rumor was quickly
dispelled by his warm greeting and by his introducing me to his secretary
(his manner reinforced my sense that she was not only aware of his
other life but frequently typed his literary letters and poems). Photographs had prepared me for his appearance. However, I had expected,
I must confess, some kind of supernal music to swirl round him or at
least plumes, casually and obviously stuffed away inside his daily clothes:
"A voluminous master folded in his fire. . . ." But amazement did
take me by the magic present in its very awesome absence. The big,
florid man that rose to welcome me wore a grey business suit and sandy,
cropped hair befitting any important stock broker or insurance executive.

As I tried to accommodate myself to the situation, Stevens, after
some pleasantries, promptly and proudly took me—again flouting the
notion of his secretiveness—on a triumphal tour of the "plant." While
we strolled down the aisles, I befuddled by this fairly incredible event
(would St. Peter, after all, turn out to be an insurance factor, a Vice-
President, recorder of accidents and indemnities, the angels around him,
their wings tucked out of sight, prim, neatly dressed functionaries,
banging away at their typewriters—such the music of the spheres!),
Stevens paused to introduce me to this personage and that. By the time
we came round to large, paneled doors I had no more astonishment in
me when Stevens, with an air of majestic amiability, threw them open,
ushered me in and, announcing sonorously that "This is where the
board of directors meet," pointed to painted portraits lining the walls
around the long table, with the kindly authority of a hierophant to a
lowly neophyte: "This is our present president, Paul Rutherford," that
the previous, and so on (not "photographs of the late president, Mr.
Blank").

Leaving the building, we ambled out into the park-verdant grounds. We loitered for a moment in that radiant, hot day while Stevens pointed out one office building—"That's just been sold for $200,000"—and another. Noticing my badly concealed incredulity, he smiled: "I'm afraid I'm not a raconteur like those *Partisan Review* fellers." The day before he had been to a *Partisan Review* cocktail party. Stevens, one could maintain, was occupied, in his factuality "for the courts / Of these academies," as in his poems, with "the diviner health / Disclosed in common forms," the railway stations, the court houses, the office buildings. With the statues that order the chaos and the storm, "those sovereigns of the soul / And saving banks" or the very literal Hartford Indemnity and Life Insurance Company. He might appear "a large-sculptured, platonic person free from time," but he knew how dependent we are on, how anchored to—at best happily—particular moments, buildings, places.

As we abandoned the premises, I tried to set my pace to his rolling gait, his Jovian, "large-mannered motions." For a moment in the sun he seemed "A giant on the horizon," both "rugged and luminous," at least a Roman emperor. He had been a great Wordsworthian-like walker, thinking nothing of taking 30-40 miles in a day's stride. I, feeling much diminished by his size, not to mention my troubled respect for him, recognized the portly Henry James figure he cut and, at the same time, the solid Pennsylvania Dutchman, the emperor of ice cream. A big, red man of a ponderous, almost elephantine grace, he moved rapidly yet in one piece, a little like a building, one of the buildings he lived among, regarded, evalued. At that moment, preoccupied as I was, buffeted by my own thoughts and apprehensivenesses, I hardly regarded and evalued the world we passed. Let Abraham describe his three-day trek through the desert!

Finally, we reached Stevens' Canoe Club, right for a man who loved exotic worlds yet somehow rarely managed to travel; right too for me, by now thoroughly at sea. Conversation soon became a heroic affair. Stevens, business and all, proved at once that he was not a casual conversationalist. He admitted to Hi Simons (July 9, 1941): "I am not a good talker and don't particularly enjoy exchanging ideas with people in talk. At home our house was rather a curious place, with all of us in different parts of it, reading." Holly Stevens in *Souvenirs and Prophecies* quotes her father on his:

I think he loved to be at the house with us, but he was incapable of lifting a hand to attract any of us, so that, while we loved him as it was natural to do, we also were afraid of him, at least to the extent of holding off. The result was that he lived alone. The greater part of his life was spent at his office; he wanted quiet and, in that quiet, to create a life of his own.

One thinks of Emily Dickinson's description of her father, like a loved glacier filling every cranny of the house, of her brother bending to kiss his brow in the coffin and saying, "There, father. I never dared do that while you were living." Holly Stevens comments,

> If that was true of my grandfather, and I can easily imagine it was . . . it certainly was true of my father and of our house as I grew up; we held off from each other—one might say that my father lived alone.

For, after all, Stevens as Hoon believed:

> *I was the world in which I walked, and what I saw*
> *Or heard or felt came not but from myself;*
> *And there I found myself more truly and more strange.*

His was "the complete / Society of the spirit when it is / Alone." At times he seemed to wish for a world untarnished of men, and often his poems reflect a vast, refulgent, snowman solitude. In "Sad Strains of a Gay Waltz" he acknowledges:

> *And then*
> *There's that mountain-minded Hoon,*
> *For whom desire was never that of the waltz,*
>
> *Who founded all form and order in solitude,*
> *For whom the shapes were never the figures of men.*
> *Now, for him, his forms have vanished.*

By his nature's make he embraced, was splendidly equal to embracing, the loneliness the poet knows, especially in America. His "Less and Less Human, O Savage Spirit" can say,

> *It is the human that is the alien,*
> *The human that has no cousin in the moon.*
>
> *It is the human that demands his speech*
> *From beasts or from the incommunicable mass.*
>
> *If there must be a god in the house, let him be one*
> *That will not hear us when we speak: a coolness,*
>
> *A vermilioned nothingness, any stick of the mass*
> *Of which we are too distantly a part.*

We see how positive nothingness is for him, how much to be desired.

Yet, it must be admitted, he was not always drawn to such a life. On the contrary, in his post-college years, alone in a small New York apartment, he chafed at it and in 1904 complained to his journal:

> I'm in the Black Hole again, without knowing any of my neighbors. The very animal in me cries for a lair. I want to see somebody, hear somebody speak to me, look at somebody, speak to somebody in turn. I want companions. I want more than my work, than the nods of acquaintances, than this little room.

The animal in him sought what solace it could in his long weekend peregrinations into the countryside, its trees, birds, rivers his closely observed and recorded companions, with books, concerts and plays, which he did enthusiastically frequent, and the apprentice poems he then wrote. Later more than not, habit having won and a strong inclination in his character, his work and such nods would generally seem to have satisfied him. These and the little room where he, like Emily Dickinson, quarried out the exotic riches of his imagination.

In any case, at this juncture our correspondence and our common interests served us poorly. If Stevens was a formal, taciturn, even diffident man, uncomfortable and sometimes out of step for his self-consciousness before social occasions, my confusion hardly helped. We were, in Stevens' words, "confronting fact in its total bleakness," for any poet a baffling experience. Especially if one has little capacity for being a snow man. If this was "Continual Conversation with a Silent Man" for me it came to not much more than watching "the other man, / A turquoise monster moving round." My many reasons for wanting to meet Stevens had fled from my mind as from a disaster area. Here I was—certainly a golden, privileged moment—sitting opposite one of America's major poets, some of the great poems of our time out of him, some of its great poems still to come. Yet though this be the mouth of the Nile itself, all I could do was sit as deaf, dumb, and blind as one lost in a wind storm in the middle of the Sahara. Stevens requesting a martini, I, though I never took the drink, followed suit. My misery was enhanced by his very visible delight in his martini.

Then our menus, like the most fascinating poems, engrossed us. Finally, Stevens ordered a cold consommé madrilène. I disliked iced, jellied soups, but I had no more will than to nod mutely. Let the catastrophe, some part of me seemed to insist, work itself out. A little talk, spluttering between us—could we not at least have leaned on the all-important weather?—eddied into the sands. It was then I stumbled on a perfect inspiration, a provision I must have—with the kindness of the gods—secreted just for this occasion. I had had the talent or the good sense or at least the good fortune to be, as I now mentioned, also born in Reading, Pennsylvania. With that single word an instant charm, beauty woke and leaped to her feet. The madrilène melted. The snow men thawed into glittering, voluble puddles. And the canoes, stuffed though they seemed, like the people dining around us, and dangling from the walls, exultantly rode the sparkling rapids of our conversation. Whatever his reservations for people and talk, his fundamental solitude, Stevens and I were that most instantly gratifying of things, landsmenner. Writing to José Rodriquez Feo on July 29, 1949, Stevens, referring to his lunch with three martinis at the Canoe Club a week or two earlier and to Theodore Spencer's death, said:

> While I never knew him well, I wish I had. We came from the same part of the world. We must have had much in common. And one is always desperately in need of the fellowship of one's own kind. I don't mean intellectual fellowship, but the fellowship of one's province: membership in a clique, the fellowship of the landsman and compatriot.

Obviously Stevens yearned for fellowship. But all this to a young Cuban with whom Stevens frequently, warmly corresponded, enjoying his difference and his distance! Reading a life of Conrad Weiser, Stevens could say, "This is pure Pennsylvania German and, while it might bore anybody else to shreds, it has kept me up night after night, wild with interest."

So it was reality, after all, not the imagination, which saved the day and served to let imagination out. The reality of place. Stevens most self-knowingly put it, "Life is an affair of people not of places. But for me life is an affair of places and that is the trouble." His "Anecdote of Men by the Thousand" asserts his belief in place:

> The soul, he said, is composed
> of the external world.
>
> There are men of the East, he said,
> Who are the East.
> There are men of a province
>
> Who are that province.
> There are men of a valley
> Who are that valley.

As early as 1907/08 Stevens could write his wife-to-be, "Life is a very, very thin affair except for the feelings; and the feeling of home waters the richest garden of all—the freshest and sweetest."

But stressing place simply in Stevens or overstressing it for its own sake would be mistaken. Does he not say in *Notes toward a Supreme Fiction*, "From this the poem springs: that we live in a place / That is not our own and, much more, not ourselves"? Or "We live in a description of a place and not in the place itself." However long he may have clung to Reading, his affection for it gradually faded. Even in his young manhood, whatever his feelings' fluctuation about New York during his first days in it, he could confide to his journal:

I begin to like New York & do like it hard. Reading seems childish & weak—but I like it, too—Boetia is Boetia especially when one is born in it. My liking for N.Y. & for R. are, however, quite different. I might spin any number of balanced sentences, etc, around the difference—which amounts to this, that I saw Reading first.

Going home for a few hours, he observed, "Reading looked the acme of dullness & I was glad, therefore, to get back to this electric city which I adore." So he wrote, "Reading got quite on my nerves. It is a terrible place except to the native. The country is adorable." His long walks enabled him to enjoy the latter, "the little blue hills, very pale in the light, very delicate." Or later, "If I wanted to think all of life over, I think I could do it best up the Tulpehocken, or sitting on a fence along the Bernville road. . . . Native earth! That makes us giants." Much later, on May 16, 1920, he wrote his wife:

. . . that Reading, if it ever existed except in the affections, has long since disappeared. I passed through it last Thursday on the way from Harrisburg to New York and walked up and down the train platform for five minutes in a drizzle. It was about as agreeable as a hardware store in a misty day. The houses looked dirty and shabby and the city looked like a dingy village.

Finally, he wrote:

What strange places one wakes up in! Reading was very—unsympathetic, I thought. The trouble is that I keep looking at it as I used to know it. I do not see it as it is. I must adjust myself; because I do not intend to shut myself off from the heaven of an old home.

One assumes that he means he must adjust himself to the present reality of Reading. But, knowing him, might we not be tempted to think that he means, at least as much, to the difference and, even more, to keeping his original view of Reading, the heaven of his old home? His poems do not let us overlook the enrichment his early past and its towns took on as he grew older, the glamor of his memory and imagination crystallizing them. Thus if he recalls his early days by "a Schuylkill in

mid-earth,'' it is one that has undergone, he knows, a sea-change in
his mind so that it seems capable of "Flotillas, *willed* and *wanted*"
[my italics], capable in turn of "bearing in them / Shadows [here too
he acknowledges time's passage and the imagination at work, combined
with reality] of friends, of those he knew. . . .''

Now Reading stood firm, stood us in good stead, and conversation,
as though undammed, burst forth. I, having leaped, with the magic of
one word, from limbo to paradise, gladly report that poets, living and
dead, not to say flotillas full of them, swirled up before us, were
characterized, and by a potent phrase or two of praise endowed with
exuberant life or as briefly dismissed for the ghosts they were. I mentioned Dylan Thomas, for at that time I felt some surface similarity at
least in the colorfulness, the flamboyancy, of his and Stevens' work.
Stevens, frowning, brusquely rejoined, "That's not the way to write
poetry." He did not bother to expatiate. Did he consider Thomas' work
too confectionary, too exclusively self-absorbed in its own movements
of language? Or was his attitude prompted by his Pennsylvania Dutch
austerity? On November 16, 1953, he wrote to Barbara Church about
being asked to speak at a memorial meeting for Thomas:

> . . . I don't think that I should ever have been able to get myself in
> quite the right mood for such an occasion for Thomas. He was an
> utterly improvident person. He spent what little money he made
> without regard to his responsibilities. He remarked that he had done
> what he wanted to do in this country, that is to say, that he had met
> so and so and Charlie Chaplin and had insulted a rich industrialist.
> Notwithstanding all this, he came constantly like the Sitwells and
> would have kept on coming as long as there was any money to be
> picked up. Of course his death is a tragic misfortune, but, after all,
> if you are going to pronounce a man's funeral oration, you do have
> to have some respect for him as a man.

Earlier in his office Stevens had read to me from a letter of a young,
would-be poet who had written to Stevens for help. Stevens had replied
to him, he told me—and his voice grew harsh as he recalled it—that
he had had to earn his living quite apart from his writing and the young
man would have to reconcile himself to doing the same. Furthermore,
in no way did Stevens believe a man's artistic gifts, however great,
extentuated his general conduct. He could, in response to Charles Norman's invitation to participate in a symposium on Pound, which he
declined, maintain about Pound: "While he may have many excuses,
I must say that I don't consider the fact that he is a man of genius as
an excuse. Surely, such men are subject to the common disciplines."

On the other hand, Stevens did conclude, "If when he comes over, he wants help and shows that he is entitled to it, then I, for one, should be very glad to help him and I mean that in a practical way and do anything possible for him."

Emboldened by our sudden, liberated kinship, I dared to wonder aloud at a certain falling off of color, if not sensuous excitement generally, in his more recent work, compared, say, with *Harmonium*. The lunch's success must be attested to by the fact that, rather than stiffening at my indiscretion, Stevens simply replied, "One grows older." Those accentuating the austerity of Stevens' work often seem to forget how old he was when he wrote the bulk of it. In his reply to me he had put most succinctly the predicament of poets, especially the Romantic ones. If so much of a poet's work depends on the feeling he suffuses his words with, when his senses dwindle and that feeling ebbs or fails, how shall the world and the work not also ebb—that is, unless the poet is able to discover other, deeper resources? But, of course, one may be satisfied with an accurate report of what in truth happens. Poems of frustration, of slackening powers, of sheer impotence can be among the most engrossing. Is "Tintern Abbey," exuberant memories and all, so many bosky miles from "Dejection: an Ode"? Are both poems, finally, not celebrating loss, the poets' aging, their growing estrangement and distance from nature?

I also could not resist commenting on the great frustration I assumed his daily work must cause. But he assured me that he enjoyed that work and needed it. There was little of the improvidence in him that he remarked in Thomas. Not that he had not experienced twinges of regret at his way of life. On October 28, 1922, he wrote Harriet Monroe:

> I wish that I could put everything else aside and amuse myself on a large scale for a while. One never gets anywhere in writing or thinking or observing unless one can do long stretches at a time. Often I have to let go, in the most insignificant poem, which scarcely serves to remind me of it, the most skyey of skyey sheets. And often when I have a real fury for indulgence I must stint myself.

His sense of his writing as an amusing himself and an indulgence is worth underscoring. Then the rationalization sets in:

> Of course, we must all do the same thing. . . . If farmers had summers ten years long what tomatoes they could grow and if sailors had universal seas what voyages they could take. Only, the reading of these outmoded and debilitated poems [his own] does make me wish rather desperately to keep on dabbling and to be as obscure as possible

until I have perfected an authentic and fluent speech for myself. By that time I should be like Casanova at Waldheim with nothing to do except to look out of the windows. So that I shall have to swallow the rotten pill.

As late as February 17, 1950, he could write Thomas McGreevy,

Of course, I have had a happy and well-kept life. But I have not even begun to touch the spheres within spheres that might have been possible if, instead of devoting the principal amount of my time to making a living, I had devoted it to thought and poetry. Certainly it is as true as it ever was that whatever means most to one should receive all one's time and that has not been true in my case.

As he told Mrs. Church on June 21, 1949:

One of the drawbacks of going about it [writing] in this casual and intermittent way [what he said he had always done] is that every fresh beginning is a beginning over: one is always beginning. One of the really significant reasons for devoting one's life to poetry in the same way that people devote their whole lives to music or painting is that this steady application brings about a general moving forward.

From the start this struggle went on in him. In 1901 his journal records,

I recently wrote to father suggesting that I should resign from the Tribune and spend my time in writing. This morning I heard from him &, of course, found my suggestion torn to pieces. If I only had enough money to support myself I am afraid some of his tearing would be in vain. But he seems always to have reason on his side, confound him.

A few months earlier his journal admitted:

Sometimes I wish I wore no crown—that I trod on something thicker than air—that there were no robins, or peach dumplings, or violets in my world—that I was the proprietor of a patent medicine store—or manufactured pants for the trade—and that my name was Asa Snuff. But alas! the tormenting harmonies sweep around my hat, my bosom swells with "agonies and exultations"—and I pose.

But he cannot deny that "on the whole 'money is our object.' We all get down to that sooner or later." Yet writing in 1909 to Elsie Moll, he says,

When I complain of the "bareness"—I have in mind, very often, the effect of order and regularity, the effect of moving in a groove.

We all cry for life. It is not to be found in railroading to an office and then railroading back.

His letter to McGreevy goes on,

> But, then, if I had been more determined about it, I might now be looking back not with a mere sense of regret but at some actual devastation. To be cheerful about it, I am now in the happy position of being able to say that I don't know what would have happened if I had had more time. This is very much better than to have had all the time in the world and have found oneself inadequate.

In fact, his letters, as age settled on him, fairly clearly record growing satisfaction with his daily work. On August 16, 1950, he told Barbara Church that, while most people were on holiday, "The office keeps everything together for me." Thus, despite his early passionate desire to save enough money to visit Paris (as late as 1954 he could say, "I wanted all my life to go to Paris. . . ."), after a time, with his version of it deeply rooted and defined in him, how dare confront the over-powering actuality? Ironically enough, like a good Parisian, he needed to go nowhere, beyond his own resources and Larousse-like works, to know the world, all the world such a Parisian requires or is interested in. After his experience with Reading, it is little wonder he refused to visit his imagination's home, refused to jostle his heavenly view of it with the bustling, present reality. Rather with books, letters, postcards, he preferred to fill his imaginary garden with real toads (real, if like Marianne Moore's, often plucked secondhand). On July 12, 1953, explaining the *Blue Guitar* to Renato Poggioli, Stevens analyzed one section: "Why traverse land and sea, when, if you remain fixed, stay put, land and sea will come to you. See what winter brings. See what summer brings." Similarly, in another letter to Poggioli, Stevens said of *The Comedian as the Letter C*: "The central figure is an every-day man who lives a life without the slightest adventure except that he lives it in a poetic atmosphere, as we all do." Those bent on the intrinsic poetry of living, its myriad, shimmering shades, have little time or patience for interruption. How go off on exhausting, distracting journeys or superficial adventures when so much is happening in, so much comes to, Ithaca or Hartford?

Like Walden's vast-traveling Thoreau or like Dickinson, Stevens sped in all directions in the privacy of his room and the room of his poems. His imaginings, his reading, and postcards from far-off friends and acquaintances ("In fact, I survive on postcards from Europe."), and the little boxes of their country's unique objects that he paid foreigners to send him seemed to have assuaged his hunger. Though he confessed to McGreevy on April 19, 1954, "One shrivels up living in the same spot, following the same routine," a little earlier he told Mrs. Church, ". . . I am far from poetry, and many of the other civilities of life, in all this rut of my job, which, after all, I like and on which I can so happily depend." On April 16, 1954, he wrote her: "Personally I like *not* to go on cruises. There is a specific ease that comes from the office, going to bed and getting up early which equals the relaxation of cruises." And in August, in another letter to the traveling Mrs. Church, in which he thanks her for the "collection of baroque postcards" she sent him as "super-duper," he observes, "Pennsylvania Germans have visions during their work *with the greatest regularity*," [my italics] and "Their visions gave the Pennsylvania Germans the same satisfaction that a group of New York businessmen find in bars of cruise ships." He had just said, whimsically, reflecting on these visions, "How curious it is that we don't have chapels in factories or insurance offices. What a thing it would be to find something like Venice in one of the Ford plants." (Had I not found it or at least the richest American imagining of it?) He continues,

> Our own days are the days of wind and rain, like today. Yet it is precisely on such days that we give thanks for the office. Sometimes one realizes what an exceeding help work is in anyone's life. What a profound grace it is to have a destiny no matter what it is, even the destiny of the postman going the rounds and of the bus driver driving the bus.

In *Notes toward a Supreme Fiction* he can sing the praises of at least

> *An occupation, an exercise, a work,*

> *A thing final in itself, and, therefore, good:*
> *One of the vast repetitions final in*
> *Themselves and, therefore, good, the going round*

> *And round and round, the merely going round*
> *Until merely going round is a final good, . . .*

Here his daily work and his work as a poet seem to have merged, his mode of verbal repetition much like his daily routine. Then he suggests,

> *Perhaps,*
> *The man-hero is not the exceptional monster,*
> *But he that of repetition is most master.*

This surmise certainly reminds one of Nietzsche's hero of "eternal recurrence." Till the end, Stevens worked on, as long as his dwindling strength allowed. Near his 75th birthday he wrote, "The fact that I am so blessedly busy at the office keeps me from noticing the absence of a good many precious things. . . ."

However, his devotion to his insurance work not withstanding, it was the presence of a good many precious things, the heaped-up facts of the imagination, in his poems that first drew me to him. These were among my most prized treasures, my postcards and boxes of exotic delights, especially as they were extracted from my own country. In them the self that mattered to him most could prosper, also a precious, blessed busyness. His work, like Frost's, amounted, first of all, to a great and startling discovery for me—that poetry written by grown men could happen in the United States and in my own time, could be published and even praised. In those days poetry, for most Americans, was, to say the least, remote, reserved to the tedium, never recovered from, of the classroom and to a few fuddyduds, dusty old maids of whatever sex. So I might have recognized another reason for Stevens' diffidence. He had hardly overcome this feeling of being "different," of being engaged in a "secret vice," something self-indulgently onanistic. However gratifying, it must have accentuated his sense of loneliness, of isolation, and helps to account for the impersonality, the protective coloration, as well as the jocularity, the hail-fellow tone he occasionally resorted to. After his first reading at Harvard he said, "I wonder what the boys at the office would think of this?" And a little later he concluded that "the boys would hardly be more shocked to discover him the secret head of an opium ring." At least the metaphor in its extravagance suggests the importance Stevens ascribed to poetry, even as it suggests the dream-making, intensifying powers—something so potently of this world it glorifies it as it takes one out of it—of poetry. But who could have predicted in my boyhood that being a poet, mainly because of the dogged persistence, the mighty exertions, and the consequent triumphs of poets like Stevens, Frost, Pound, Eliot, Moore, and Williams, would become a legitimate occupation, if not a pride, for hundreds of men and women and a pastime of varying passion for many thousands?

Beyond that discovery, for a good number of my contemporaries and me pleasure and encouragement derived, despite Stevens' privacy and reticence, from his poetry's confident opulence. Frost, whatever his excitements and subtleties, had made a kind of peace with his time and place. His work, at least on the surface, employed an easily accepted speech that people around him might use and concentrated on the life of those people. Even his rhymes and meters were what one might expect of well-behaved verse. But Stevens in his poems was a rather different kind of bird, nothing like the frugality of expression, the tight-pursed demeanor of his countrymen, especially the Pennsylvania Dutch or, for that matter, his later New England associates. Yet he was hardly unaware of the expense of his expression and preoccupations. His richness throve in the face of an indifferent, even hostile world, his occasional bitterness before it, and the fear it helped to prompt of impotence or inadequate inspiration, as though the very sullenness of circumstances, "the bareness," played its part in producing the poems by their defiance.

Thus Stevens' feeling of impotence, of belatedness, ironically enough, often provoked brilliant poems so gay and floribund in utterance it took a long time before I realized their underlying grimness. No doubt had I been able to appreciate their important place in his work, I should have applauded the very frustrations I questioned at lunch. But at that time I could not. Especially since his work's tantalizing, glittering surface, savorsome of itself, held one before it, almost reluctant to enter. How could one not be grateful for the sense of what poetry still could be, in its way as lavish, as glamorous—like those small kin in the grass, aglow with themselves—as Shakespeare's. Grateful also, in our modern American uprootedness, for the poems' seemingly self-sufficient nature, the wiliness with which they resisted the map-making, the prosaic "bare" order, of meaning. Not only descriptions without place but descriptions become a kind of place, a verbal paradise.

Yet, however much one might make of Stevens' writing for a long time in an indifferent, even unfriendly world, the opposite atmosphere also needs to be acknowledged: a geniality pervasive in the air of his time, an exuberance, shared by Williams, Moore, and others. Work of such ambition, originality, éclat, whatever desperations and arduous doubts these artists may have had to grapple with, must surely depend on a fundamental belief in this world and in belief, and no less in one's own senses, gifts, wits. Thus Stevens and Williams could exert themselves wholeheartedly in both worlds. In Stevens' case that belief must have been further reinforced by the good, hard common sense, the self-reliance, the ruggedness of his forebears as by the gaiety and freedom, the confident expansiveness we associate with an earlier America.

At the same time, though his self-reliance and his diligence strongly affected his poetry, another side of his nature was also clearly at work in it. Philosophical prepossessions and all, his poetry did express his delight in the world, especially its floribundity, in the luxuriance of his senses, and in language itself. As far as his vehement declaration for a poetry of earth is concerned, it is possible, as some critics have proposed, that he felt the need for his opposite, a mask, wished to be more responsive in appetite and gusto than he was. On July 29, 1949, he wrote Mrs. Church:

Often when I am writing poetry I have in mind an image of reading a page of a large book: I mean the large page of a book. [One reads as one writes: the writing is one's own, yet someone else's as well, a subtle, more accomplished accomplice, a reassuring surprise.] What I read is what I like. The things that I have just sent to Rome are not the sort of things that one would find on such a page ["A Half Dozen Small Pieces"]. At least what one ought to find is normal life, insight into the commonplace, reconciliation with every-day reality. The things that it makes me happy to do are things of this sort. However, it is not possible to get away from one's own nature.

Then he describes poems he intends to write:

At the moment what I have in mind is a group of things which mean a good deal more than they sound like meaning: for instance, airing the house in the morning; the colors of sunlight on the side of the house; people in their familiar aspects. All this is difficult for me. It is possible that pages of insight and of reconciliation, etc. are merely pages of description. The trouble is that poetry is so largely a matter of transformation. To describe a cup of tea without changing it and without concerning oneself with some extreme aspect of it is not at all the easy thing that it seems to be.

He concludes:

I have written to Tom McGreevy. Somehow my heart is not in Ireland this summer. It must be because I found out that the motor buses are much like ours and that Limerick is indistinguishable from Bridgeport. But I love his letters.

Or every-day reality, the commonplace, mediated by language, letters, if not art. Little wonder he feared visiting Paris for all his yearning after the "normal life"!

Yet why deny his delight in the earth, the amusement, the jocularity even that he did express? If a mask was necessary to allow him to say things he otherwise could not, it is also to be recognized and enjoyed for itself. Why impoverish him and his work, his sense of the whole world, by accenting one side only, the summer or the winter, the snow-man or Sunday morning: Winters charging him with being a mere hedonist, Helen Vendler insisting—and here she soberly shares with Winters a distress at Stevens' assertion of earthiness, his jocosity—on his "wintry side" as his true nature. Why diminish the drama such a tension helped to produce? Very late he could, as Ariel, say of his poems:

It was not important that they survive.
What mattered was that they should bear
Some lineament or character,

Some affluence *[my italics], if only half perceived,*
In the poverty of their words,
Of the planet of which they were part.

Whatever the Hoon of him, he also relished the Jocundus side of himself, his sense of fun and tomfoolery, his heel-kicking-up robustiousness, the early rowdiness which now and again broke into his words. Pennsylvania Dutch and Lutheran that Stevens was, even Luther, we remember, was not exactly an emaciated stripling. Because Falstaff was finally rejected and because he disturbs some scholars, are those reasons enough to think Shakespeare had no genuine capacity for him? As for the abstract, much as Stevens loved it, it had to be blooded; for it was sensuous and particular to him, a passionate pleasure of the mind, a pleasure additional to, as it was part of, nature and the world.

Thus his poetry can be regarded as a release from all that he gave himself to—and denied in himself—during his daily working hours: a happy indulgence. In 1933 he wrote William Rose Benet about his affection for ''The Emperor of Ice Cream'':

I dislike niggling, and like letting myself go. This poem is an instance of letting myself go. Poems of this sort are the pleasantest on which to look back, because they seem to remain fresher than others.

More than ten years later he told Feo, ''. . . I almost always dislike anything that I do that doesn't fly in the window.'' Similarly the postcards magically accumulating, flying in the window of his room and his office, with the intoxicating fragrances out of his boxes from strange lands: a world translated, served up in an already realized form. The image Huysmans presented in *A Rebours* of his hero Des Esseintes with his rapturous armchair travel, as he poured over maps and pamphlets, spread out like the countries themselves, and luxuriated in his many-perfumed organ, springs to mind. Des Esseintes, we recall, loved two countries that he yearned to visit, Holland and England. He does go to Holland. ''The general result of the journey was a series of bitter disappointments.'' For all his imaginings are violated: ''Holland was a country like any other. . . .'' He does not make the same mistake with England and London.

Reality or the imagination, the dichotomy between the workaday and the holiday world, had caused Hawthorne, hidden away in a room of his mother's home or in the Custom House, full anguish. He is at his most eloquent in describing his surly, worldly ancestors, Puritans that they were:

> No aim, that I have ever cherished, would they recognize as laudable; no success of mine . . . would they deem otherwise than worthless, if not positively disgraceful. "What is he?" murmurs one gray shadow of my forefathers to the other. "A writer of storybooks! What kind of business in life,—what mode of glorifying God or being serviceable to mankind in his day and generation,—may that be? Why, the degenerate fellow might as well have been a fiddler!"

One thinks too of the invisibility of an Edward Taylor as a poet and of Emily Dickinson (the world's plenty indeed hidden in a little room: we do not have to wait on a Ralph Ellison for invisible men and women in America!), of the astonishing transformation of Whitman from a dandyish journalist hack, a man of the world, to a fulltime poet—even to something like the cliché that world reduced the poet to: an unsavory, self-indulgent character, a layabout, a ne'er-do-well—with all the bravado, if not defiance, such metamorphosis required.

Perhaps Stevens better than anyone else managed this split that occupied him all his life, surely a central split in America; it involved the business man or man of the world versus the man of mind and spirit, particularly the artist. Yet Stevens, after a series of almost shattering setbacks, in making a living as in writing, enjoyed a splendid success in both worlds; as he did in those worlds presented in his poems. As late as March 20, 1951, he wrote most tellingly to Bernard Heringman:

> . . . I have no wish to arrive at a conclusion. Sometimes I believe most in the imagination for a long time and then, without reasoning about it, turn to reality and believe in that and that alone. But both of those things project themselves endlessly and I want them to do just that.

Stevens was not one to imprison himself in a single-minded attitude. Success and all, no wonder he spent his time as a poet shuttling—travel enough!—between these poles, observing with an assiduous nicety their differences, yet also their necessity to each other, their life-giving reciprocity. More times than not, I would surmise, he came down on the side of reality: "let be be finale of seem," however ambiguously one read "finale". Still, whatever his reservations, his awareness of the imagination's evasions, duplicities, inadequacies, and his mockery of it as of himself often at his noblest assertion of it, he rarely shortchanged it. He knew too well how much fiction lies at the base—if it is not the base itself—of even the most established fact and how much fact may be at the bottom of even the seemingly most outlandish fiction, supreme and otherwise.

Stevens, it is clear, hid out and recovered from his workaday world in his poetry. At the same time he found a happy camouflage, a protection, for it—possibly also an escape and rest from it—in his workaday world. Like Williams—only with a deal less complaining; in fact, as we've seen, with gratitude and self-congratulation—he, cultivating his split personality, required both energetic halves. There the drama lay. Let dissociation of sensibility go on long enough and, such are the toughness of the spirit and the will to live, to enjoy, the dissociation becomes a felicitous modus vivendi, richer in many ways than a simpler, seemingly more unified life. However, we must also respect or at least be cautious before Stevens' insistence, "I don't have a separate mind for legal work and another for writing poetry. I do each with my whole mind, . . ." So much so, one might say, that when he was busy with one the other was little present to distract it. And here we were at lunch caught between. I had certainly not come to talk about insurance. But Stevens was, on the whole, little prepared to talk about literature, let alone more private matters, especially in a place as public as a restaurant he and his business associates frequented. That is, until we discovered we had an important place in common which preceded, so wiped out, the present place and encouraged his personal side.

Of course it was a deprivation for the occasion that I could not have been in insurance or some related work as well. Who knows what precious, interconnecting secrets might have been forthcoming then. Thus even though I could hardly fathom it, Stevens had been able to bring off what, in my childhood and youth at least, would have seemed quite impossible if not preposterous: two careers normally thought of as antithetical. Naturally his poetry, by his temperament and work (and here in the abstraction of actuarial tables as of his artistic intellection one might remark a correspondence), tended to be—the licketty-split of his syllables notwithstanding, and his respect for and absorption in "things as they are"—contemplative, abstracted, often elusive; unlike that of Williams who, by temperament and profession, inclined to the pragmatic and concreteness. Ideas for Stevens were often palpable things while things themselves could become, in the transformations of his imagining, scintillating ideas. Yet he could be, in his astonishing words, close on the heels of things as he could be quick to the swift-falling flakes of naked perception, the moment of being and doing just before conceptualizing and verbalizing. He was most sensitive to the mercurial moments, their nuances, in the speeding mind, especially as they echo or reflect the fluctuations, the "fluttering things", of the world that fortunately "have so distinct a shade". For they comprise "reality" which "may be a shade that traverses / A dust, a force that traverses a shade." He may have been close—stone, buildings, statues, and all— to the modern aspect of Pound here, with an even greater love for the energies, charging and leaping through each thing and from one thing to another, than for solid, single things themselves. Little wonder his words were not free for casual talk. Not unless they could be sure of their ground, of the sympathetic nature of the one talked to.

According to Quentin Anderson's "Practical and Visionary Americans" (*The American Scholar*, Summer, 1976),

> When the practical and the visionary appear in conjunction the fact confounds us. Wallace Stevens was successful in business. We can make nothing of this. He was also a brilliant visionary and of this we can make much—even everything, as does J. Hillis Miller, who places him with "poets of reality," as if the practical were indeed the illusory.

Aside from the difficulty of trying to decide what we mean by reality, Stevens, I am convinced, would have objected to this view of him. Hardly less than a Benjamin Franklin did he respect the daily and the practical. The gusto with which he took to his martinis and his food would emphatically say so. His visionariness, like Chardin's, say, or, perhaps closer to home, the Dutch genre painters', might be called the vision of that real, the actual world. Melville's words come to mind: "Listen: less a strain ideal / Than Ariel's rendering of the real." But we know Stevens' enjoyment of the slipperiness of such terms, the enrichment they and their ambiguity allowed. Does he not say,

> *From oriole to crow, note the decline*
> *In music. Crow is realist. But, then,*
> *Oriole, also, may be realist.*

Moreover, despite Anderson's notion of Americans, one detects little feeling of guilt in Stevens about acquisitions. Here too he is close to his ancestors, feeling justified to need and happy to enjoy, having earned them, the world's "goods". Insist though he might that "It Must Be Abstract" (followed of course by "It Must Give Pleasure"), he had concluded that "The greatest poverty is not to live / In a physical world, ..." "One might have thought of sight, but who could think / Of what it sees, for all the ill it sees?"

Whether the vision of the real or the reality of vision, it was for such seeing, the seeing he had helped me and my contemporaries to, the enlargement of our worlds, that I had eagerly come to meet him. As eagerly, some time before, we had, in gratitude, begun the *Quarterly Review of Literature* out of a desire to acknowledge his work, to publish some of it and work that might share some of its qualities. Soon after announcing the magazine we corresponded with him. Now this lunch followed *QRL*'s featuring in its third issue a long Stevens poem, "Repetitions of a Young Captain," one of his fairly oblique engagements with the war and his not so oblique engagement with the "war"—and peace—between reality and the imagination. The captain, one of millions composing the army and nation against other millions like them, become a giant (an image Stevens often fondly employed) like the rest for the form and potency he takes from them, achieves "a giant sense / To the make-matter, matter-nothing mind." There the basic, fecundating contradiction thrives: the mind does make matter (or reality) and does make reality matter even as it is not—and does not—matter. Nothing in itself in the sense of the real, it is still real enough in its influence or effect on the real. And eventually this mind, "This being in a reality beyond / The finikin spectres in the memory, / This elevation" puts the captain above the ruins and the houses. Yet his "route," like Stevens', "through an image in his mind" "leaves nothing much behind." Nonetheless, the next section contends, the image in its words is more than mere sounds:

> *If these were only words that I am speaking*
> *Indifferent sounds and not the heraldic-ho*
> *Of the clear sovereign that is reality,*
>
> *Of the clearest reality that is sovereign,*
> *How should I repeat them, keep repeating them,*
> *As if they were desperate with a know-and-know,*
>
> *Central responses to a central fear,*
> *The abode of the angels?*

Such a repetition, persisted in, Stevens says elsewhere, should be enough. But then the matter-of-fact breaks in, and we leap away from this "reality," "the abode of the angels," to the railway station. The breaking in occurs for a moment only. Of the departing soldier, changing constantly,

> *The giant of sense remains*
>
> *A giant without a body. If, as giant,*
> *He shares a gigantic life, it is because*
> *The gigantic has a reality of its own.*

Even so, whatever this reality, Stevens' "few words of what is real in the world," nourishing, defend him against the bodiless "giant of sense." In those few words, but "without a word of rhetoric," "the actual, universal strength" asserts itself, "there it is." In conclusion the poem urges:

> *Secrete us in reality. It is there*
> *My orator*. Let this giantness fall down
> And come to nothing *[my italics]*. *Let the rainy arcs*
>
> *And pathetic magnificences dry in the sky.*
> *Secrete us in reality. Discover*
> *A civil nakedness in which to be,*
>
> *In which to hear with the exactest force*
> *The precisions of fate, nothing fobbed off, nor changed*
> *In a beau language without a drop of blood.*

Reality in all its exact, exacting nakedness, unaffected by an anemic—or, for that matter, ornate—rhetoric.

The issue of *QRL* containing Stevens' poem published the first installment of my two-part article on Yvor Winters' *The Anatomy of Nonsense*. This part examined Winters' view of Henry Adams and Stevens. When I wrote to Stevens about it among other matters, he refused to enter the fray. He had read, not the book, but a review of it and its charge against him of hedonism. His letter said that his recent poems were "intended to express an agreement with reality," a very different matter, he believed, from hedonism. So he could call Courbet "an ascetic", not only for all his rejections, but "by virtue of his devotion to the real." Almost a year later he wrote Feo that he still had not read any of the Winters essay since he felt that praise or blame was disturbing, especially to artists, very much more so than to politicians and businessmen. I would not have thought the latter quite so impervious to criticism, unless it be that they are much more in the public eye and less sensitive or, as Stevens seemed to suggest, less vain than writers and artists since they do not work alone and mainly on themselves. In any case, he did know businessmen far better than I do. Here at least, however, the business portion of Stevens seemed unable to protect the poet in him.

But his insurance work, in his words a "solid rock," Stevens assured me as our lunch went on, was essential for its own activity, its reassurances, and for the character it gave him. It was, he insisted, also fortunate for him as a poet: "I'm glad I'm mainly a weekend poet;

otherwise I would write too much.'' I felt obliged to agree. See how much he had already written. Furthermore, additional time to devote himself to thinking about poetry, might that not, as with a Coleridge, have led him astray from poetry itself or at least helped to make him even more abstract? But strong as his relishing was for things as they are, the goods of the world, I doubt it. He had little patience with hungry, self-consuming thought. So he wrote Feo:

> Is not a meditation after soup of more consequence than reading a chapter of a novel before dinner? We do not spend enough time in thought and again when we think we usually do it on an empty stomach. I cannot believe that the world would not be a better world if we reflected on it after a really advantageous dinner. How much misery the aphorisms of empty people have caused!

He goes on in a similarly bantering vein:

> There are no saints at all in Hartford. Very likely they exist at Veradero Beach, walking by the turquoise water and putting ideas into one's head. . . . All the time one would be finding out about life. It would come to one without trouble like a revelation and would ripen and take on color. I am speaking of Lebensweisheit, which is what one particularly picks up on beaches and in the presence of one-piece bathing suits.

Then he speaks of carrying on:

> the struggle with and against reality and against the fifth column of reality that keeps whispering with the hard superiority of the sane that reality is all we have, that it is that or nothing. Reality is the footing from which we leap after what we do not have and on which everything depends. It is nice to be able to think of José combatting the actual in Cuba, grasping great masses of it and making out of those masses a gayety of the mind.
>
> What makes life difficult here or anywhere else is not the material of which it is made but the failure to use it.

Riding home, still dazzled by the things I had seen and heard, as well as not, I decided that Stevens, despite the loneliness he, islanded almost alone at times, must know, was lucky in his life or what he had made of it: an Ariel quite comfortable, piping away to himself entertaining, complicated airs, in the commodious trunk of a Caliban. Or, as I sometimes felt about Henry James, a 200 pound humming-bird.

In a letter to Henry Church (July 26, 1945), soon after my visit, Stevens wrote with enthusiasm about Jules Renard who ''constantly says things that interest me immensely.'' But then, discouragedly, Stevens remarks:

> They are, however, on the literary level on which it seems possible to say such things for a lifetime and yet be forgotten on the way home from the funeral. The writer is never recognized as one of the masters of our lives, although he gives them daily color and form. This position is reserved for politicians. Just as someone said that a woman *is* nature, so a politician *is* life. The writer is a fribble.

Apparently his Ariel-like luck was shadowed by his Caliban sense of the world. Whatever the recent change in attitude toward writers, Stevens, we see, was saddened by the neglect of writing. But with his appetite for reality he must have shared some of the reservations of the world or at least he respected sex and politics, not normally associated with the intellect. A little earlier he had written Church about Feo's "platonism" as "a young intellectual": "He lives like the perpetual reader, without sex or politics. I speak of him because he is typical." And he concludes by commenting on Blackmur:

> As an expositor of ideas Blackmur fails, not for lack of ideas, but for not knowing what his ideas are. Nothing shows this more clearly than ten or twelve pages of his work from which one usually comes away—longing for sex and politics.

One might wonder whether this was, exceptionally, Blackmur's predicament and weakness. Did not Stevens call the writer "a fribble"? (Sex and politics, we might suggest, are not too prominent in much of Stevens' poetry. How often, given his sense of privacy, of decorum, does he speak out as directly, as unequivocally, as

> *If sex were all, then every trembling hand*
> *Could make us squeak, like dolls, the wished-for words.?*

Yet, whatever else the body exacts of us, he goes on to admit sex's fundamental power.

> *But note the unconscionable treachery of fate,*
> *That makes us weep, laugh, grunt and groan, and shout*
> *Doleful heroics, pinching gestures forth*
> *From madness or delight, without regard*
> *To that first, foremost law . . .)*

However, this attitude of doubt toward ideas and literature as well, is this not the old Pennsylvania Dutch strain in him, the American realist speaking up? We would seem to have moved not too far from Hawthorne and his dis-ease.

Then abruptly in this July 26th letter, yet probably out of his sense of the futility of the writer in the world, Stevens goes on to describe someone I am wryly amused to recognize.

A young man came up from New Haven on Monday to have lunch with me. Old people like you and me don't realize how completely young people are in the clutches of established reputations. To them these reputations are what a map is to a man at midnight in a Ford. We had a long talk during which this really accomplished youth mentioned no one of the slightest novelty. This is an instance of literary, not to say aesthetic "funding". A reputation is something in itself; it lives and dies pretty much without roots, and it produces growths out of the air that have little to do with nature.

At that time Stevens did indeed seem to think poorly of "literature" and its absorptions. He had written Feo shortly before: "Reality is the great *fond*, and it is because it is that the purely literary amounts to so little." However, reality, it would seem, is also not something we can (or should?) live in purely, entirely. So he continues: " . . . in the world of actuality, in spite of all that I have just said, one is always living a little out of it." And he quotes "a precious sentence": James' "To live *in* the world of creation—to get into it and stay in it— . . . this is the only thing!" Stevens' dual sense steadily raged away: "I have no wish to arrive at a conclusion." But, despite his reservations about literature and reputations, Stevens might have understood how a young man, caught up in the dream of literature, would be likely to be awed before the real presence of such a reputation, more importantly one whose work he altogether admired. Awed so as not to dare to venture outside what he thought would interest Stevens.

In September, 1947, we invited Stevens to contribute to our projected Pound number. He refused. No doubt a further expression of his rejection of the privileges of genius and of reputation, another "giant without a body." But his refusal, reflecting his feeling about Pound, constituted a trenchant little essay in itself, at least of Pound as a person, not a reputation:

Nothing doing about Pound. I should have to saturate myself with his work and I have not the time. Moreover, I never did care to do that sort of critical writing. In Pound's case there would be the special difficulty that he is as persnickety as all hell, if I may say so. A friend has just written to me from France speaking of

"My pink Persian

cat * * * in front of me, looking up just now with his reproachful amber eyes. He does not like to be molested even by thoughts or looks.''

That's Pound.

At some point in 1948 we apprised Stevens that we were disturbed by criticism's overwhelming of literary magazines and were thinking of devoting *QRL* exclusively to poetry and fiction. We asked him for suggestions and the names of new, likely contributors. On April 21, 1948, he replied approvingly yet practically, his sense of literature's insignificance still very strongly with him.

> Your letter about your plans is very much to the good except for the fact that this is not a creative period. Besides, anyone able to do anything worth while wants to make a business of it. The other day in New York I was talking to a man whose father is a painter in Switzerland. Ramuz, the novelist and poet, lived next door. The father has not even had a dealer for forty years. All his interest and all his strength goes incessantly into what he is doing. While, of course, we have such men over here (T. Weiss is one of them), we don't have many. One does occasionally come across a young writer of fiction who is devoted only to the job. The young poet has no choice. Is there anywhere in the country a young poet whose object in life is to think about poetry and who refuses to do anything else? Of course there is and he is precisely the sort that you are interested in. But it isn't easy to think of such people. . . .

He was plainly remembering his own dilemma as a young poet, remembering whimsically if not bitterly.

Meantime, Bard College had initiated a program of honorary degrees for distinguished artists with William Carlos Williams. In 1951 Bard offered Stevens a degree. He accepted:

> I don't suppose anyone has ever turned down an offer of an honorary degree, so that I can only say that I shall be delighted to come. Wesleyan gave me a degree a year or two ago and on that occasion two important things happened: a. it furnished the gown, and b. it did not even expect me to speak. If Bard does not have any old gowns lying around, you ought to let me know in time. You probably have one of your own that could be made over. I should as a matter of fact be very happy to see Bard and meet your friends there. But c. you speak of a literary week-end, which is rather alarming.

Alarming or not, a literary weekend was in the works. Having decided to make as much as we could of the occasion, we had asked Williams to join in a panel with Kenneth Burke and Glenway Wescott; we wanted poetry, fiction, and criticism represented. All had agreed to come. A few days before the event, however, Flossie Williams phoned to report that Bill had just had a stroke. Even as I was trying to take this news in Flossie said, "But here's Bill. He wants to talk to you." And in most broken, painstakingly detailed sentences he proceeded to explain medically what had happened to him and why he couldn't come. Naturally a pall settled on us; for a time we thought to jettison the weekend altogether. Then, despite Stevens' last words, I hit on an idea which, it turned out, was inspired. On the phone I told Stevens what had occurred and proposed that he speak in Williams' place. Stevens with little hesitation agreed to "respond" to the degree provided his response could be short. He seemed quite pleased to be asked.

The oncoming occasion did occupy him. On February 6th he wrote to Norman Holmes Pearson at Yale.

> I am sorry to bother you but you are the only person that I can think of that can tell me what I want to know. I am going to receive an honorary degree before long. The last time the college supplied the cap and gown. What is protocol on this point? Ought I to have my own or ought I to expect the college that confers the degree to have all this on hand? If I ought to have my own, is there some place in New Haven where I could pick up the right thing? The degree is to be a degree of Doctor of Letters. Since this is given by hanging an appropriate hood or some such thing over one's shoulders, I suppose there is a gown for just such an occasion, that is to say, one that does not already have a hood on it. This is all distressingly ignorant on my part.

For one awkward social experience and another Stevens was anxious to be correct. He was well aware of his capacity for contretemps. The above letter concludes with one such at a New York party.

> After three cocktails I asked them if they had ever heard the story of the man who etc., etc., etc. After making quite sure that they all wanted to hear it, I told it. It is the funniest story in the world, but, curiously, I was the only person that really laughed and I have been worried to death ever since, that is to say, until recently, when I said the hell with it.

Since I knew his sense of formality and propriety, this concern should not have surprised me. During his Bard visit he questioned me about the gown and hood several times. And after the ceremony he was especially pleased to be able to keep the hood and eager to insure its safety and his not forgetting it. On February 19 he wrote Mrs. Church that he was going to Bard:

> I know nothing about Bard except that it seems to be a scion of Columbia and that many interesting young people go there. I suppose I shall stay for a day or two but I know nothing about the arrangements except that they are going to have a lot of other people there. . . .
> The degree to be given to me is the only one to be conferred. It involves "a brief response," which I drafted yesterday, after scratching my head for two weeks—a nuisance. If one is to lead a life of ideas, it cannot be done to any advantage by fits and starts. Far more important than all this is the fact that on Feb. 16 I found the first snow-drop in the garden, under some hemlock boughs used for covering.

He continued,

> There has been a great deal more literary activity than I care for recently. The more active other people are on one's account, the more one stands still on one's own account. I like to do my work at the office and then go home to my own books—not to other people's chores. One man wants me to tell him what I think of a poem he wrote on the dedication of a new insurance building in Boston.

On March 30th Stevens and the weekend arrived. We picked him up at the train station and took him to President Case's house. There the Cases warmly greeted Stevens and, most tactfully, with a martini. Ten years later he would write William York Tindall, his escort for a Columbia honorary degree: "Personally, I shall be happy to have dinner with Mrs. Tindall and you and I know that I shall want a Martini the moment I enter the house." Stevens accepted the drink with immense, visible delight. Indeed, his slightly tremorous cupping of the glass and his pausing over it like a chalice had something of the concentration of a priestly ritual. Fortunately Case's martinis were first-rate. Case, urbane, social, Princeton-educated, and Mrs. Case, lovely, gracious, made Stevens feel at home at once.

During dinner as we sat beside each other Stevens told me that he had recently seen Marianne Moore in New York and that she had called me "a bad man." (While we were preparing our Moore issue I wrote to her for some work since we felt the issue would be incomplete without her. She replied that she had only one short poem which she sent us. Some months later, as the issue's deadline was approaching, I wrote again. And we were delighted to receive another fine poem and extracts from the La Fontaine she was translating. Apparently, I now learned, she felt that I had pestered her.) Seeing my dismay, Stevens assured me that he had assured her I was not a bad man. Then he suddenly launched a series of rather Polonius-like precepts. Among them I remember particularly such austere, high-minded counsel as that I must write my poems for no audience other than the great poets of the past, Mallarmé, Valéry, etc. An audience no doubt at that time as likely as the one I was not collecting. Actually Stevens had said in a letter that he did not write for any audience but "because for me it is one of the sanctions of life." Moreover, he continued instructing me, I must never compete for prizes, awards, fellowships. "Let them come to you." Knowing how many were groping their frantic, lost way to me through vast fog, I felt sheepish and, I must confess, irritated at what seemed fairly gratuitous advice. Its would-be fatherliness did not at the time make me happy to play Laertes. Years later, when I learned of a Wallace Stevens Award competition, I entered it and (perhaps in heaven Stevens had relented) won. I do now realize that in his somewhat gruff, brusque way Stevens was trying hard to be kind and helpful.

Shortly after he told me that he was busy tracking down his genealogy and that he had uncovered all but the last branch. He knew where it was but the people of the house thought he was crazy and would not let him in. Even so he was set on getting that branch. The fervor with which he expressed his determination convinced me that, if necessary, he'd blow the house down. On October 11, 1943, he had written Hi Simons about this interest: "This was a subject that I scorned when I was a boy. However, there has become a part of it something that was beyond me then and that is the desire to realize the past as it was. . . . the whole thing has been an extraordinary experience: finding out about my family, etc." We know what time and money he spent on this interest.

That evening in Bard's gymnasium, the only building large enough to contain such an event, the degree was presented. A storm had suddenly blown up. As with "Repetitions of a Young Captain," "A tempest cracked on the theatre" and "The people sat in the theatre . . . / As if nothing had happened." But this was no ruin-making, rather the reverse. By the time Stevens rose to reply, lightning and thunder and a driving rain were appropriately at work. As he read his paper, the sound effects, the rain clattering on the tin roof, drowned out the early spring voices and his words for anyone beyond the first row. He made no effort to be heard. But in this setting the event and Stevens' presence were so impressive no one seemed to mind. It was as though we were privileged to be watching this big red man reading—or creating—to and for himself. A kind of intense privacy, a trance-like hearing, settled on us all. Perhaps in that spring-early time we were, like the season, the "ghosts that returned to earth to hear his phrases," and as we stepped "barefoot into reality" listening to him, to "the literal characters, the vatic lines," no more and no less than "the poem of life," "the pans above the stove, the pots on the table, the tulips among them," in our ears these "Took on color, took on shape and the size of things as they are / And spoke the feeling of them, which was what they [we] had lacked." A Chardin visionariness indeed, the daily things made feelingly realer through art. As Wescott told us, he had traveled to Bard on the same train with Stevens; but though he sat near him and watched him all the way, he never dared approach him. When Stevens finished, the thunderous applause mixing with the metallic rain, he said to me, "Well, we didn't need the old man after all, did we?" This was obvious if mild amusement and pleasure in his being older and healthier than his friend Bill.

After the ceremony a group of us retired to the Case House. There, to the consternation of those of us who thought we knew Stevens, one of the more innocent members of the group piped up, "Will you read to us, Mr. Stevens?" To my amazement he, smiling broadly, said he would be delighted to. He must have felt unusually relaxed. As he wrote Mrs. Church a few months later, classmates and people he was visiting in Brookline at his 50th reunion and his reception of a Harvard honorary degree ("For me personally, this degree is the highest prize that I can ever win.") tried to get him "to recite poetry, which I don't do and did not do." Perhaps his reply to Karl Shapiro, then editor of *Poetry*, rejecting Shapiro's invitation to read in Chicago, helps to explain: "It is one thing to go to New Haven or Cambridge and to read to a small group of people and it is quite different to do what seems to be almost a professional job." We were such an informal, small group and, like the weekend, entirely given over to him. Then my consternation, allayed, turned to pure embarrassment when Case had to admit that he had no copy of Stevens in the house. Stevens promptly put all embarrassment to rest: "It just happens that I have a copy of my poems with me." And, going upstairs, he brought down *The Auroras of Autumn* with many dogears sticking out of it. Obviously, he hoped to be asked to read. Reading a number of poems slowly with genuine relish, he also helpfully commented on them.

I remember particularly his remarks on "Angel Surrounded by Paysans." The poem was prompted by a Tal Coat still-life Stevens had received from his dealer Paule Vidal. He bought paintings, sight unseen, through her mainly by his specifications of size, color, etc. and her response to these, a little like the boxes he had acquaintances send him from remote countries. The Tal Coat greatly pleased him. On receipt of it he wrote her,

> I was happy . . . to find that it is so much cooler and richer and fresher than I had expected. It is young and new and full of vitality. The forms and the arrangement of the objects are, both, full of contrariness and sophistication. . . . For all its in-door light or in-door objects, the picture refreshes one with an out-door sense of things.

These observations and others following stimulated him to his poem.

> The strong blue lines and the high point of the black line in the central foreground collect the group. The wine in the glass at the right edge warms, without complicating, the many cool blues and greens. This is going to give me a great deal of pleasure and I am most grateful to you.

A few days later he wrote, "Now that I have had the picture at home for a few days, it seems almost domesticated." Then he explained his poem:

> I have given it a title of my own: *Angel Surrounded by Peasants* [later Paysans]. The angel is the Venetian glass bowl on the left with the little spray of leaves in it. The peasants are the terrines, bottles and the glasses that surround it. The title alone tames it as a lump of sugar might tame a lion.

Some weeks later he wrote Mrs. Church, "My Tal Coat occupies me as much as anything." And his title and poem had not, after all, completely "tamed" it.

> It does not come to rest, but it fits in. R. R. Cogniat speaks of his [Tal Coat's] violence: that of a Breton peasant from the end of the earth (Finisterre). . . . Note the absence of mandolines, oranges, apples, copies of Le Journal and similar fashionable commodities. All of the objects have solidity, burliness, aggressiveness. This is not a still life in the sense in which the chapters of de Maistre are bits of genre. It is not dixhuiteme. It contradicts all of one's experience of a still life and does very well for me in the evenings when its vivid greenish background lights the lights, to make the most of it.

On the same day he had written McGreevy of the picture: "The man puts up a great deal of resistance to the effort to penetrate him."

A month after the picture's arrival Stevens felt called on to tell Paule Vidal about it again:

Since my last letter to you about the Tal Coat I have reached what I think is my final feeling about it, although one never knows what prompts an artist to do what he does. It is obvious that this picture is the contrary of everything that one would expect in a still life. Thus it is commonly said that a still life is a problem in the painting of solids. Tal Coat has not interested himself in that problem. Here all the objects are painted with a slap-dash intensity, the purpose of which is to convey the vigor of the artist. Here nothing is mediocre or merely correct. Tal Coat scorns the fastidious. Moreover, this is not a manifestation of crude strength of a peasant, to use a word merely to convey a meaning. It is a display of imaginative force: an effort to attain a certain reality purely by way of the artist's own vitality.

One can understand how Stevens, burly man that he was and, at the same time, most fastidious connoisseur, might admire this quality, especially as it, like the lion asleep in the stone or the lute, lodged at the heart of him and expressed itself at times in his poetry. Being with him, one could sense the vigor reposed in him, the imaginative force. It was "a magnificent fury" he believed in. He deplored to Feo literature which is "a form of self-indulgence" and complained that "The savage assailant of life who uses literature as a weapon just does not exist, any more than the savage lover of life. Literature nowadays is largely about nothing by nobodies." For it is "a good barbarian, a true Cuban, or a true Pennsylvania Dutchman" he is after. So, though he admits Arp's exquisiteness, he finds that "His imagination lacks strength. His feelings are incapable of violence," and "he is too much a man of taste to be a leader, like Picasso." Let us have postcards from the volcano. But love of life or not, nature, the barbaric, savagery generally had to be mediated by Stevens' meticulous, magnificently complex mind. Yet it is the combination in his work that at its best saves it from being lopsided or too simple, establishes the happy coupling of earth and heaven, almost, one could say, that wonderful fruit: an austere abundance and its reverse.
A month later in a letter about the poem that Victor Hammer considered printing—but never did—with an illustration by Fritz Kredel (all this very much a Stevensesque "translation": from a painting to a poem to a drawing!) Stevens could admit:

The question of how to represent the angel of reality is not an easy question. . . . I was definitely trying to think of an earthly figure, not a heavenly figure. The point of the poem is that there must be in the world about us things that solace us quite as fully as any heavenly visitation could.

As the angel in the poem rejects an "ashen wing" and a "tepid aureole" and maintains that it is one of us and in so being "Is being and knowing what I am and know," so it insists,

> *Yet I am the necessary angel of earth,*
> *Since in my sight you see the earth again,*
> *Cleared of its stiff and stubborn, man-locked set. . . .*

So, as ever, it is the earth Stevens desires but as it is, uncontaminated by man's limited awareness. At the same time, in proper paradox, the angel suggests that it is "only half of a figure of a sort, / A figure half seen, or seen for a moment, a man / Of the mind, . . ." Finally, on May 29, 1952, Stevens wrote to Sister N. Bernetta Quinn:

> . . . say that . . . the angel is the angel of reality. This is clear only if the reader is of the idea that we live in a world of the imagination, in which reality and contact with it are the great blessings. For nine readers out of ten, the necessary angel will appear to be the angel of the imagination and for nine days out of ten that is true, although it is the tenth day that counts.

Locked away as we are in the world of imagination, our own exclusive, even hermetic view of things, we must hunger for reality, its occasional breaking in on us so that we are shaken and refreshed.

The next day of the conference, before Wescott's talk, in a pause of conversation among a group of us around Stevens and Burke, the latter looked up at Stevens fairly tentatively, then with a touch of defiance in his voice said, "I think I've cracked 'The Worms at Heaven's Gate.' " Stevens regarding him sceptically, he plunged on: "It's all in that name you chose, Badroulbadour. As I repeated it over and over it came clear to me. Bad, bad, bad on to bawd, bawd, bawd, then behind it body, body, body, all the way to a stress on the final ur or manure, the whole course of life." Stevens, snorting, walked away. With his belief in the "tougher" aspects of reality he might have been more sympathetic. Just before this conference he had written Peter H. Lee on some of his poems:

> They do not penetrate very far into the tough material of this world. . . . Isn't it the function of every poet, instead of repeating what has been said before, however skillfully he may be able to do that, to take his station in the midst of the circumstances in which people actually live and to endeavor to give them, as well as himself, the poetry they need in these very circumstances?

But then perhaps Burke had failed to attend to the reverse enough, the worms *at heaven's* gate or, in Stevens' words, "The poet makes silk dresses out of worms." His letter to Lee makes it clear that he is "trying to persuade you to forego the familiar for the unfamiliar"—that is, for the local "circumstances in which people actually live," the "tough material" of actuality. Out of that the poetry, the silk dresses, must be made. Burke was being perhaps too familiar or at least was losing sight—and sound—of that beautiful mouthful "Badroulbadour."

When I came to pick him up at the Cases, as he said goodbye to them and thanked them for their hospitality, he felt obliged to say to President Case, "Now I suppose you expect me to send you a big check for the college. Well, I won't." Obviously, since Case had had nothing to do with our initial plan to invite Stevens, he had had no such expectation. Instead Stevens sent Mrs. Case a little carton of apricot jellies and on April 5, 1951, a letter to us:

> I enjoyed my visit to Bard more than I can tell you. One grows accustomed to the larger colleges and takes them for granted. But a visit to one of the smaller ones refreshes one's sense of what underlies the larger ones. I find, too, that this new honor made quite as much of a splash, here in the office, which is my only milieu, as any other. After so much publicity recently I expect to retire to the first desert I come across and then try to recover myself.

The interruption of his privacy did trouble him. A little earlier he had written Sister Quinn, "There has been entirely too much activity for me recently and I am beginning to feel that publicity is definitely a thing that degrades one." Then on April 23rd he felt called on to write to Williams.

> I heard the other day that you will not have too much damage to show for yr recent collision with Nature and I hope that this is true. . . . The affair at Bard College was extremely pleasant—sort of early American with rain on the roof and the voices of the first frogs competing with the voices of the speakers. I enjoyed the experience, which was new to me, although I had to leave without hearing Kenneth Burke whom I should have been much interested to hear. . . . Your illness saddened and disturbed everyone. I do hope that the news I have heard of you is true and that you will send me word, if you are able to do so. You have worked hard all your life and now that you are at the top and need only time and the care of old age and leisure, I hope that what has happened will lead to some resolve (or to the necess'ty) to be more saving of what you have left. Let me withdraw the words old-age. As the older of the two of us, I

resent those words more than you do. If a man is as young as he feels you are, no doubt, actually twenty-five and I am say twenty-eight. And I know lots of people of our age who are no older than they were half as many years ago. I still come to the office regularly because I like to do so and have use for the money, and I never had any other reasons for doing so.

We did not print Stevens' response until 1955. By its ardent confirmation of his belief in the imagination, its indispensable place in our lives, and yet its reliance on reality, the little essay deserves excerpting, especially:

The poet finds that as between these two sources: the imagination and reality, the imagination is false, whatever else may be said of it, and reality is true; and being concerned that poetry should be a thing of vital and virile importance, he commits himself to reality, which then becomes his inescapable and ever-present difficulty and inamorata. In any event, he has lost nothing; for the imagination, while it might have led him to purities beyond definition, never yet progressed except by particulars. Having gained the world, the imagination remains available to him in respect to all the particulars of the world. Instead of having lost anything, he has gained a sense of direction and certainty of understanding. He has strengthened himself to resist the bogus. He has become like a man who can see what he wants to see and touch what he wants to touch. In all his poems with all their enchantments for the poet himself, there is *the final enchantment that they are true* [my italics]. The significance of the poetic act then is that it is evidence. It is instance and illustration. It is an illumination of a surface, the movement of a self in the rock. Above all it is a new engagement with life. It is the miracle to which the true faith of the poet attaches itself.

Stevens must not be—as he said he would not be—pinned down. A little earlier than the degree-awarding he had written Bernard Heringman:

A week or two ago when I was down for the National Book Award one of the newspaper men asked me why it was that I did not write on the level of intelligence in the literal sense. I told him that when one wrote on a literal level one was not writing poetry.

Nonetheless, he continues: "The fact remains that in facing reality one of the most intense necessities is the need of facing it literally and writing about it literally." On June 19, Stevens wrote Charles Tomlinson about *Credences of Summer*: "At the time when that poem was written my feeling for the necessity of a final accord [stronger even than "agreement"] with reality was at its strongest."

QRL's last literary contact with Stevens involved the article he contributed to our Marianne Moore issue. His affection for her apparently dispelled his reluctance before such assignments. Nominally "About One of Marianne Moore's Poems," Stevens first juxtaposed her "He 'Digesteth Harde Yron,' " with an essay, "On Poetic Truth," by H. D. Lewis. The yoking reflected Stevens' long absorption in philosophical matters, especially as they related to poetry. Nevertheless, here too it is the real, the creature, ostrich or poetry, that can digest hard iron, which concerns Stevens. His reasons for being drawn to Lewis' paper are clear in the first few lines of Stevens' essay:

> Mr. Lewis begins by saying that poetry has to do with reality in its most individual aspect. An isolated fact, cut loose from the universe, has no significance for the poet. It derives its significance from the reality to which it belongs.

After comparing a stanza of Moore's poems with an extract from the *Encyclopaedia Britannica* on the ostrich, Stevens remarks:

> The difference signalizes a transition from one reality to another. It is the reality of Miss Moore that is the individual reality. That of the *Encyclopaedia* is the reality of isolated fact. Miss Moore's reality is significant. An aesthetic integration is a reality.

Then Stevens says that poetry's

> function, the need which it meets and which has to be met in some way in every age that is not to become decadent or barbarous, is precisely this contact with reality as it impinges upon us from outside, the sense that we can touch and feel a solid reality which does not wholly dissolve itself into the conceptions of our own minds. It is the individual and particular that does this.

"The angel of reality" it is that makes this contact possible, provides us through the senses with a sense of things as they are that resists the mind. And having made a case for the unique accomplishment of poetry, Stevens concludes: "Considering the great purposes that poetry must serve, the interest of the poem is not in its meaning but in this that it illustrates the achieving of an individual reality." We turn to the poem for "its potency as a work of art," its making us "so aware of the reality with which it is concerned, because of the poignancy and penetration of the poet, that it forces something upon our consciousness." Stevens ends this section by paraphrasing Lewis:

It is here . . . that the affinity of art and religion is most evident today. . . . both have to mediate for us a reality not ourselves and . . . this is what the poet does and . . . the supreme virtue here is humility, for the humble are they that move about the world with the lure of the real in their hearts.

Are we here not approaching Keats' "negative capability" but with a sense now of some "higher" reality?

The second section of Stevens' essay, which seems to abandon Moore and her poem for a personal recollection, poetically reflects that lure. But Stevens was being especially faithful to her; for he knew how deeply the lure had bred humility in Moore, a respect and capacity for the reality not ourselves. Stevens recalls his visit to the old Zeller house in the Tulpehocken, in Pennsylvania, part of his appetite for the past, especially his own remote past. He stresses the Zeller family's faith and happy worship: "Their reality consisted of both the visible and the invisible." At another time, Stevens reports, he visited Christ Church near Stouchberg with two of its elderly members. It was the church's old graveyard which detained them with its limestone wall "about four feet high, weather-beaten, bald" and its eight or ten sheep, "the color of the wall and of many of the gravestones and even of some of the tufts of grass, bleached and silvery in the hard sunlight." These are particulars, but of a most exiguous kind. It was "the sense of aban-donment and destitution, the sense that, after all, the vast mausoleum of human memory is emptier than one had supposed." And the two elderly men "could not be any effective diversion from the reality that time and experience had created here: the desolation that penetrated one like something final." It sounds like the snowman talking. What, as Hamlet could say in his graveyard, poor Yorick in hand, is all the wit and poetry in the world against this? We have come here to the blank, the final slate, the nothing that is not and the nothing that is at the heart of nature.

Yet having faced the blank page with all the capacity of a Mallarmé, Stevens can go on to another "supreme fiction" or at least an inter-mediate, superior one. For he believed that the same mind and imag-ination that had conceived that supreme fiction God could, now that God had grown anachronistic, go on to creating other, more viable fictions. It is his awareness of the fictional aspect of these creations and yet his sense of assent to them that is extraordinary. Most of us are naive enough to need to believe in what we believe. However, his wish to believe rarely reached the pitch and power of will, the brio of a true new god-maker; it may well be that his very scepticism, his awareness of the fictive aspect of all gods, had to dilute his mythopoeic faculty. Returning to New York after the graveyard visit, Stevens went to an exhibition of books in the Morgan Library. There he found an answer, art's answer, to the earlier desolation.

> The brilliant pages from Poland, France, Finland and so on, books of tales, of poetry, of folk-lore, were as if the barren reality that I had just experienced had suddenly taken color, become alive and from a single thing become many things and people, vivid, active, intently trying out a thousand characters and illuminations.

The base, the barren reality, miraculously blossoms, by way of the imagination, into life's plenitude. And mainly the flowerings of particular exotic places, but pressed between pages and sent forth like his loved postcards or his spice-fragrant boxes. Such glimpses of the world in poem and picture, often more effectively than whole or actual experiences, freed and fed and fortified his gallant imagination: as much in love, it is true, with the final slate as with the floribund. But though Stevens may at times have proposed that "the wise man avenges" every leaf that falls "by building his city in snow," here as elsewhere he shows himself decorating the cemetery with jubilant blossomings.

At the same time reality must be treated in a special way. Having read my first book of poems, on April 7, 1951, Stevens wrote:

> I have been paying special attention to THE CATCH and have therefore been in no hurry to write to you about it. The first impression that I have is of the book's polish or finish. This is a precious quality which the first book of a man often lacks. Perhaps its accomplished quality is a better way of describing it. On the other hand, the last poem, the long one, I did not like and as this is the most important poem in the book I ought to have liked it most of all. I did not like the subject. It is easy to pick up words and phrases that touch one. But the reality of the subject is a reality that presents nothing but difficulty to a poet.

It would seem that reality, however much Stevens believed in it, must not be dealt with too directly, at least not this kind and not on so large a scale, lest in its squat, unbudgeable way it prove undigestible and overwhelm the poet and his imagination. We know, despite his words on sex and politics, Stevens' feelings about "the literal level." So he deplored what he called the "gross realism" of a Faulkner. He had little patience with, let alone practice in, narrative or the dramatic. Place, yes, but not people in their time and place. History itself—the poem, "Shades of Caesar," is much occupied with Mussolini, fascism and that time—too unwieldy, oppressive, even general, ought not to detain the poet. "I shall not play the flat historic scale." Furthermore, "Given an actuality extraordinary enough, it has a vitality all its own which makes it independent of any conjunction with the imagination." (Actuality here probably ought not to be confused with what Stevens normally called reality.) Such matters of actuality, in short, remain altogether recalcitrant before poetry, refuse to be dealt with in anything other than their own opaque, bristling, iron terms: with a bird as black, as actual, as powerful as Mussolini how treat—or contain—it in thirteen ways? It is the personal and the individual that Stevens advocated, the life locally lived. And at the same time dealt with at a distance, the aesthetic distance that provides an amiable space for the real and the imagination to interplay in. For a poet what can society, the bustle of nations, especially gigantic war mean but interruption and frustration. Writing to Feo on December 5, 1949, about letters of Romain Rolland, Stevens says:

> Last night one of his letters was full of complaints about a noisy neighbor. Somehow it interested me immensely to know that one has noisy neighbors in Paris. Rolland, apparently, lived in an apartment where his wife, Clothilde, was no more hostile to a little dust than we are at home but the neighbors seem to have moved the chairs every Thursday and cleaned the windows every Friday, polished the kitchen floor every Saturday, did the laundry on Sunday, dusted on Monday, etc. Rolland thought that was the last word in being Bourgeois. How much more closely that sort of thing brings one to Paris than remarks about the growth of interest in Socialism, the artificiality of Sarah Bernhardt, . . .

This is what Stevens desired, news of the world, daily news, but not out of newspapers, not of large historical events, rather of individual lives living themselves, realistic postcards from the daily world, especially as here the world he loved as much as any, Paris. But even this news, and especially this, must be heightened and "transformed" by poetry. One of his Adagias says, "To give a sense of the freshness or vividness of life is a valid purpose for poetry. . . . It is not that one purpose is as justifiable as another but that some purposes are pure, others impure. See, those purposes that are purely the purpose of the pure poet." So in a letter to Hi Simons in 1940 Stevens wrote:

> The purpose of writing poetry is to attain pure poetry. The validity of the poet as a figure of prestige to which he is entitled, is wholly a matter of this, that he adds to life that without which life cannot

be lived, or is not worth living, or is without savor, or, in any case, would be altogether different from what it is today.

But then he comments:

> Poetry is a passion, not a habit. This passion nourishes itself on reality. Imagination has no source except in reality, and ceases to have any value when it departs from reality. Here is a fundamental principle about the imagination: it does not exist except as it transforms. There is nothing that exists exclusively by reason of the imagination, or that does not exist in some form in reality.

A poem dealing directly with history in its totally human preoccupation and its entanglement with "facts" must prove impure, must successfully resist the imagination. Stevens' letter to me continued:

> However, I don't believe that that sort of thing is going to be your sort of subject. The extraordinary activity of your mind makes your choice of subject sound casual. You have yet to find, that is to say, identify what your imagination will choose to struggle with.

On November 26, 1935, Stevens had written Ronald Lane Latimer, "One of the most difficult things in writing poetry is to know what one's subject is." And then again, reality and the daily world notwithstanding, "One's subject is always poetry, or should be." Perhaps this poetry nothing but poetry is a language like and onto the language of the world, reality itself, one unsullied by man's moods and failures, even feelings, as though the very air, the very Ariel, should speak. The world so seen, without humanizing or interiorizing, might return us to that plainness, that directness, of a Homer whose "surfaces" were sufficient and therefore at once profound or the all that there is. Yet think of the actuality in Homer's work!

The last personal note from Stevens came on May 5, 1953. I must have asked for some poems and mentioned that I had been awarded a Ford Fellowship which would enable my wife and me to take off for a year of Europe. He addressed me for the first time "Dear Ted Weiss."

> I am sorry; no poems. I wrote hardly a line during the winter. Now that the time for sitting on the nest has come around, the damn thing is full of water. As someone in the office said the other day, it rains every hour on the hour and has been doing so for several months.
>
> The news about the Ford Fellowship almost makes me feel young again. At last the right people are getting a chance to see a bit of the

places that are supposed to be the right places. Good luck to both of you.

His great vicarious powers, call them the powers of the imagination, responded to the occasion as ever. We had shared Reading, the real place of our births; now I could go on with his blessing to the Europe he had loved and passionately lived in in his mind.

RETROSPECTING THE RETROSPECTIVES

This issue of selected criticism and reviews completes the celebration of *QRL's* thirtieth anniversary. Originally we had expected to produce only one anthology, a miscellany composed out of all the material at our disposal. But we soon discovered that the work's abundance would not let us limit it to a single volume. In fact, even a much larger scope did not entirely subdue the feeling of occasional arbitrariness in our choices. The first anthology was devoted to poetry; the second, to fiction; the third, to our special issues, each occupied with one major writer, original work plus articles on it; and the present, to general criticism.

Now there may be some point in submitting the whole enterprise to a last overview: what does it come to, editing a little magazine, a paper boat launched among breakers, battleships, oil-laden freighters. Engrossing though the role may be to editors, at times, whatever their convictions, their passion of commitment, they must feel like unlicensed peddlers, pilots of a paper boat indeed, in a swirling street, furtively urging a cargo of precision glasses on the blind mob rushing by. In a little mag's tiny world editors can anticipate, a few scattered readers apart, relationships with this writer and that, good will for the hospitality provided; the irritation of others, even when one has accepted their work; and the indifference of the great majority. These, if they read little mags at all, consider editors, perhaps rightly, a necessary parasitic nuisance, little better than publishers and booksellers.

On the other hand, one of the chief gratifying surprises of editing has been the enthusiastic response of others, even some whose work we have rejected but with comment. We have considered it one of our important functions to acknowledge any flickering promise, let alone actual flashes of talent. We soon realized the patience our reading would require: full-fledged, established writers often need many pages to warm up, to find their true voice and subject; younger writers, groping in the dark of their not yet explored resources, are

bound, most of them, to be intermittent. Lonely and uncertain as writing is, people are usually grateful for a serious
response. Several have even been gracious enough to say that
QRL's rejection in its care proved more meaningful to them
than some of their anonymous acceptances. Finally, there is
the satisfaction of knowing we encouraged neophytes who
eventually became writers of substance.

On the negative side again, readers occasionally blame – if
not praise – editors for what they print, as though they had
written it all themselves, or deliberately chosen only poorer
work. Editors cannot publish material they do not receive.
Of course by their attitude they do attract or discourage
writers. And they may set a good pace of standards and
expectations. In addition, most people are unlikely to
recognize – for a magazine is in itself a slight, ephemeral
object – editing's underside, the hidden work: reading and
choosing manuscripts (in one unguarded, self-lacerating
moment I calculated that we receive about 20,000 manuscripts a year); arranging an issue; proofreading and the
rest; coping with printers and distributors; sometimes packing
and mailing; attending to subscriptions, inquiries, complaints;
and trying to maintain some regularity. Like houseplants and
pets, a magazine requires fairly continuous attention. And if
for financial reasons the magazine is printed abroad (ours has
been, first in Belgium, then in England), one must anticipate
additional large expenditures of time and the risk of a magazine's going astray. Somehow, miraculously, we have never
lost an issue.

Attempting to awaken interest is a further trial. One fact
we have never been able to reconcile ourselves to: the indifference of most Americans, with so-called literate college
graduates no exceptions, to literature. Of the millions able to
read and also the overwhelming thousands that scribble, no
matter how one may appeal to them to support writing, only
the tiniest percentage respond. (The writers, aside from what
one might consider a necessary curiosity and a desire to learn
from others, fail to realize how much their individual fates as

writers depend on the larger fate of writing itself. Even the heroic example of Pound in this regard has not taught them.) In short, nervous people, ones upset by frequent difficulties and given to great expectations, had better not take on editing.

Yet, hardships and all, the recent past has had its share of editors who, considerable writers themselves, thought editing an important activity: Pound, world-wide honey-making bee that he was, flitting from magazine to magazine as from movement to movement; Eliot with the *Criterion*; Marianne Moore and her schoolmarmish scissors, snipping away for the *Dial*; William Carlos Williams in several magazines, midwifing the interests that he believed in and felt were neglected or threatened by the successes of figures like Eliot. Other writers, Ransom, Tate, Robert Penn Warren, made editing, at least for a time, an intrinsic part of their lives. Of course in these writers' editing days, with the New Criticism regnant, a poet was expected to prove himself by his powers as a critic and his command of earlier literature. How else could readers be sure they were dealing with a poet they could trust? And editing a magazine, for its concern with taste and quality, the propagating thereof, was approved as a worthy critical occupation. But the times changed and, quite predictably, veered in a kind of vertigo to the reverse. The less a poet knows about earlier poetry and the past the likelier, many now think, he is to be fresh, original, uncontaminated by oppressive, antiquated influences.

Pound, in his total dedication to poetry, could say that great poetry must be written; it does not matter by whom. No doubt editors should strive for such attitude, such Poundian self-denying. Yet sooner or later, they arrive at what is for them the crucial question: What does editing a little mag mean to the editors themselves: how does it affect their lives, their thinking, their own work. Usually an unpaid position, little-mag editing has to be carried on in catch-as-catch-can fashion, with other jobs, as well as one's private life, at one. A certain amount of Spartan conduct is inevitably required. One might wonder how, in such helterskelter, anything gets done. Yet actually one irritation, even as it prompts another, often helps it. Editing plunges one into the middle of writing itself and supplies a curious — chiefly paper — companionship. The correspondence with many a writer at every stage of his development is exhilarating when it is not exasperating. Letter friendships, especially those based almost exclusively, at least to begin with, on literary work, can enjoy an intensity, a purity, surpassing that of more personal ones.

In fact, one of our early naivetes was the assumption that a letter intimacy amounted to an actual friendship. Several times we were shaken by the evidence of our mistake. Edith Sitwell, for instance, after an exchange which resulted in our printing a group of her poems, urged us to visit her at her ancestral Renishaw Hall. And when she came to the United States in 1948 we were invited to the reception for her at the Gotham Book Mart. When we met, she, her hand momentarily in ours the weight of tissue paper, hardly acknowledged us. In fairness it should be said that the party, crammed into that small, book-crowded shop, was a huge, crushing one. By the time our section of the seemingly endless line reached her she was, like a seeress hypnotized by the giant, snake-eyed gem flashing on her own brow, clearly befuddled in her vermillion, serpentine turban. At one point, shortly before confronting her, we experienced the same theme in another key. There, suddenly sprung into sight directly ahead of us, in tricornered hat, protoplasmically white, looking like a child's version of George Washington, stood Miss Marianne Moore. Having recently published an all-Moore issue, we had corresponded with her a good deal. But even as we introduced ourselves, with a startled look she seemed to dematerialize. Only later would our puzzlement be settled by Wallace Stevens, who, when he came to Bard College to receive an honorary degree, explained that she had been annoyed with us for keeping after her for work of her own to strengthen the issue.

However, some of the correspondence did blossom into friendships and memorable occasions. The value of this correspondence to us we have not begun to estimate. After all, in one sense, all writing constitutes a letter to the world. What a pleasure when one's letters receive replies that encourage replies in turn. Who would not like to have corresponded with Homer and Shakespeare or Wordsworth and Whitman or, for that matter, Stevens and Williams, especially while they were producing some of their most exciting work, you possibly abetting it? And now and then the man or the woman behind the work emerged to confirm it in his or her own person.

At the University of North Carolina, where I had just begun to teach, we met Warren Carrier who, out of common interests, quickly became a good friend. And when in 1943 he proposed starting a literary magazine I strongly encouraged him. Though my chief absorption was my own poetry, what harm could a nearby, amiable magazine do to that? Warren urged me to join him. I had no particular interest in being an editor, but I agreed to help and to review books of poetry. So, with two other North Carolinians, I became an 'Assistant'. For the first issue we sent out announcements, a half-sheet advertisement, to the world. In our happy, youthful innocence we assumed that much of that world would rush to our side in awed gratitude and delight. Nothing quite so ecstatic happened. Yet response did collect. Almost at once our first subscription arrived with a very enthusiastic letter. However, when the first issue appeared, that subscriber, demanding his money back, excoriated us for our deception; how dared we appropriate such hallowed title, then print under it the nonsense we did, poems and stories, often impenetrable at that. Marianne Moore promptly replied to our modest circular: she wished us well, admired our courage and economies, and returned the announcement; she thought we might, as part of the war effort, wish to reuse it! Some writers, like the little-mag-supporting E. E. Cummings, sent work at once; thereafter, contributing regularly to *QRL*, he helped to keep us alive through editorial doldrums. His work we supplemented with that of writers we knew, some friends, and ourselves.

By the second issue, I became an editor; and D.D. Paige, also teaching in the English Department and eventually to edit Pound's letters, became an assistant. Aside from local lights the magazine began to sport names like Henry Miller, Mark Van Doren, Harry Levin, Thomas Merton, Ramon J. Sender. The third issue proudly presented work by Wallace Stevens. From then on we maintained a relationship with him, at times intermittent but most reassuring to us, till nearly his death. This relationship involved several meetings, many letters, and poems and essays in QRL. He, like Cummings and Williams, rarely turned away the appeal of a literary magazine, no matter how little or obscure. Of course at that time little mags and magazines interested in modernist poetry were not too abundant. We had written to Stevens for work shortly after the magazine's beginning. His long poem, 'Repetitions of a Young Captain,' one of his fairly oblique engagements with the war, soon followed.

We also ran articles by critics like Edouard Roditi and Edwin Berry Burgum, a considerable range to say the least — from the esthetic to the Marxist. But though in its first years QRL was a fairly normal literary magazine; like other college-based periodicals sharing out its space among poetry, fiction, articles, and reviews, from its inception it reserved pride of place for poetry and fiction. In the words of QRL's 30th Anniversary Poetry Retrospective's introduction: 'Despite its university location it was very much a private enterprise. And unlike its fellow periodicals it was set on stimulation and innovation rather than on consolidation, evaluation, and scholarly taste-making.'

The second issue included Part I of a two-part article that I wrote on Yvor Winters and his volume, *The Anatomy of Nonsense*. The second part appeared in the next issue. What began as a normal review turned into a forty-page, youthfully exuberant counter-attack. Irritated by Winter's highhandedness with Henry Adams, Stevens, Eliot, Pound and others, I felt called on to pay Winters back in kind, to expose his weakness and aberrations as a critic. The article prompted a response perhaps as vigorous as that for anything I have published since, and not alone from the writers Winters had mauled. A response from many, but not from one of the chief figures involved. Having occasion to write to Stevens, I commented on the exchange. Stevens replied:

> As soon as I saw what your letter of March 24th was about I stopped reading it. This was at the end of the first paragraph. I have not yet read Mr. Winters' essay. But I have read a review of his book and gather he considers my poems to be expressions of Paterian hedonism. Poems written over a long period of time express a good many things. *Certainly the things that I have written recently are intended to express an agreement with reality* [my italics]. I need not say that what is back of hedonism is one thing and what is back of a desire for agreement with reality is a different thing. There is also the possibility of an acceptable fictive alternative. I am, of course, not willing to be drawn into any debate between you and Mr. Winters. Probably all three of us are equally concerned about the same thing.

Of course we invited Winters to reply. He wrote to accept, saying,

> You are behaving like a gentleman in connection with your invitation, and I regret what I am going to do to you. You must be very young, because you are very ignorant and very inexpert. You ought to remember that print, like a pistol, is a deadly weapon, and if you start a fight with it, you must take the consequences. The academic profession and the literary profession are full of people who believe whatever they read. One member of my department actually took your remarks seriously. I am going

to defend myself, and if you suffer, why that is your funeral.

Best wishes for the future,

Yvor Winters.

He did indeed reply in a typical scorcher. I had clearly not pleased him.

Rexroth, with whom we had begun to correspond at this time, when he learned that I was about to undertake Winters, wrote:

You havent any business belaboring Winters. First — who can denie [sic] that he is as good as they come these years as a poet. . . . Second. It isnt polite to refer to folk's infirmities. Everybody knows he is quite a little touched in the role of M. Arnold Redivuus. . . . Where I come from people are polite and I would no more dream of referring to Winters' critical ideas than I would to Orrick Johns' one leg, or Max Bodenheim's no balls, or. . . . Poor unfortunates they are and deserving of pity.

Really — Winters is unquestionably the best of the constipated school of poetry —. . . . I havent any quarrel whatsoever c̄ him qua poet — except that I think that he thinks 'the art of versification' is hard come by — as it obviously is for him — and that most people would write like Barnaby Googe if only they could.

Like Williams, Rexroth told us that Winters had once written him that he had very genuine but indifferently employed talent and urged he let Winters teach him versification which would make him a major poet. Since I was not challenging Winters as a poet but as a critic, and of writers I admired, I saw nothing impolite in doing battle with him along the lines he had himself long ago established.

Having read my review, Rexroth wrote:

Whee.

Still, I think it is kinda shooting fish in a barrel. What did Winters do — tell you he had once been boxing champion of the University of Chicago and you could put on the gloves c̄ him? That's his usual response. [Fortunately by the time of my essay Winters had given up boxing for the more pervasive pugilism of rigorous criticism and teaching and for the raising of prize airedales.] . . . so much hinges on his parvenu notions of metrics. This goes to unheard lengths. I once asked him what he thought of Dostoieffsky — to which he responded that he didnt read Russian. I then asked him what he thought of St. Augustine. And got quite a speech. I then reminded him that St. Austin was unaware of the existence of the very language in which the gospels were written — i.e. Aramaic. He was quite put out. Odd little facts like that Japanese poetry is based on Chinese poetry which is read from Chinese characters directly into Japanese with no knowledge of the original language leave him utterly buffaloed.

But then Rexroth continues:

Winters is something like Henry Miller — [a comparison, I'm sure, Winters would have been everlastingly grateful for — not to mention Miller] integrity is so rare a thing that one is willing to put up with much.

Finally:

I think you missed an opportunity to concentrate on the absurd notion of salvation by seminars which is the denouement of Winters book. We are now entering that period of decadence when rhetoricians are teaching Virgil and Horace from the cannibals of the Blue Nile to the painted Picts. . . . This is the age of college professors. . . Dr. Winters can have it.

After an interval Rexroth wrote,

Where are you at? What happened? Or do I owe you letters? And what happened to your magazine? Winters, who gave a paper at the Am. Soc. of Aesthetics in Berkeley at the same time I did said you had suspended publication to

avoid printing his crushing rebuttal. I told you he is para-
noid. His paper was all about how Hopkins was a moral
leper because he didn't scan by Winters system. The
parvenu English professors who cant understand a word of
Hopkins, and hate him from the bottom of their rabbit
hearts ate it up. It reminded me of nothing so much as Ben
Gitlow before the Dies Committee. Beat me teacher, once
I was a modernist. Fortunately, they didnt understand a
word Rexroth said.

Later Rexroth commented, 'Poor Winters. I almost cried
when I read his answer — it's a pity you had to print it.'

Eventually, I must admit, I began to feel that my essay had
been excessive, the pawky work of a young man who enjoyed
his spurs, the exhibition of them, too much. When Winters
concentrated on writing that did not personally involve him,
poetry other than that of his own students and contemporaries, he was often a most acute critic. However, more than
ten years after my essay (1956), Winters published a long
summarizing article, 'Problems for the Modern Critic of
Literature,' in which he gave literature from beginning to end
specific grades. Often his judgments were, I thought, whop-
pingly and exactly wrong. Thus he could conclude that much
of Homer's material 'is only imperfectly fitted to verse' and
'only imperfectly fitted to interest the civilized mind.'
I felt somewhat relieved for my essay, if not fully vindicated,
when Winters further observed that it was a shame that minds
as good as Homer's, Virgil's, Dante's, and Milton's should
have been wasted on a creaky form ('. . . we have lost the
literary innocence which made it possible for men of such
extraordinary gifts to be satisfied with such unsatisfactory
methods.') and that the one thing Homer couldn't handle was
action, and when he maintained that literature from its beginning has been straining to become one form, the short poem
and one short poem in particular ('. . . in my opinion it is the
greatest poem which I have ever read, regardless of kind.'),
Valéry's 'Ébauche d'un Serpent.'

Shortly after this exchange, Carrier left to join the English Ambulance Corps (World War II had begun). Thus the first issue of Volume II came out under my name as editor and Renée, my wife, as managing editor, with Ernest Morwitz, once an important member of the Stefan George circle, as our 'Foreign Advisor.' As though to signalize this change, we moved, lock, stock and mag, to New Haven where I became an instructor in the Yale English Department. However, before his departure Warren and I had planned an all-European issue. And Volume II, no. 1, contained translations of Juan de la Cruz, Alberti, Hölderlin, George, Corbière, Rimbaud, and Yvan Goll, as well as articles and reviews on Rilke, Corbière, Malraux, Perse, Mann, and Lautréamont. The issue amply reflected our determination to do what we could to break down parochialism and to make good literature-at-large available.

But here we were, my wife and I, suddenly the step-parents of a little mag. Neither of us, certainly not my wife, could, less than a year earlier, have anticipated this egregious turn of events. Still, it did prove advantageous in several ways, most basically in Renée's effectiveness, her managing the magazine's meager finances, so that by the second volume they no longer needed supplementing. She also acted as the magazine's designer and joint editor, primarily occupied with fiction but also with choosing the poetry. Usually I read the poems first, separating the clearly (reassuringly!) bad from the possibly and certainly good. The latter I would read aloud to Renée whose musician's ear often quickly remarked false or weak notes.

With Volume II's second issue we formed a relationship that was most important to us. William Carlos Williams became a frequent contributor and correspondent, writing to us sometimes two/three times a week. In that issue we featured 'The Words Lying Idle,' the fifteen poems that constituted Williams' poetic output for the past year. On September 23, 1944, he wrote, 'Since you intend to feature me I'll give you everything I've got, to put it that way. Let's make a splash — if you have the room for it.' The issue also printed his brief essay, 'The Fatal Blunder.' In a July 29, 1944, letter he had said: 'Having just finished enjoying your shots at Winters — how richly deserved! — I've gone and dug out the enclosed note on Eliot which I dashed off in a fit of anger some months ago. If you won't use the bit who will?' In addition, we ran Williams' enthusiastic review of Rexroth's book of poems, *The Phoenix and the Tortoise*. Thereafter, Williams became a kind of vibrant, overseeing presence for *QRL*. He could write on September 28,

> I feel very grateful to you for your support, you'd be surprised how isolated one feels at times and how many small irritations one must face to keep writing. I was sixty one a few days ago, let's hope that in the next twenty years I shall find more ease.

'Surprised' indeed! What sentiments could be more heartening to young, unknown writers like ourselves?

Rexroth also appeared in the issue (we enjoyed and sought out such crisscrossing and interconnecting reinforcement) with two of his more memorable, sensuous poems, one amusingly enough about Winters' book of poems *The Giant Weapon*. Rexroth wrote when he sent his second poem, 'Maybe it goes well & will give the impression of a little group of serious thinkers. *Wms* on Rexroth, Winters on Winters, Rexroth on Winters.' Beyond that I had reviewed, among others, Williams' *The Wedge*. The review stressed his (and Marianne Moore's and Stevens') remaining in this country to fight it out for poetry on home ground. More than not, however, they were inward expatriates; working in obscurity, they hardly needed to flee to Europe. For us, as soon for many others, Williams was a shining example. In his life and his work, so passionately carried on, he proved that America even in its most impoverished and seemingly dehumanized aspects, looked at honestly, lovingly, still could sustain and comprise poetry. Looked at also with legitimate anger.

On October 2, when his poems had appeared, he wrote:

I feel happy that I'm able to please you for I like the tone of your article in the last Quarterly — as I have told you. Yes, I'd appreciate it if you'd send the issue containing my stuff round here and there for I think this small collection is about as good as anything I have ever done. It's good to be alive again.

Then on October 14 he sent the following:

After a day batting around the city, yesterday, I came home to my evening off and an hour or two of reading. I wanted to finish your Winters critique. . . Then I got to reading the Three in One review [my review, in Vol. 1, no. 4, of books by Stevens, Cummings, and Robert Fitz-gerald]. I didn't bother to look to see who had written it — I never look till after. When I got to p 330 my admira-tion got beyond bounds. It struck me that here at last I had come upon an intelligence that found it possible to get beyond intellect — the rarest thing in the world. Beside, your language, your use of the language, delights me. This together makes great reading. I congratulate you as I envy you your use of words.

However prepared we were by now to expect generosity from him, the reader can appreciate the feelings this letter caused. On December 28 he congratulated us on moving to New Haven:

Yale should enhance the prestige of your magazine. As the Norweigians [sic] say, When it rains on the parson it drips on the sexton — so that I too may look for a benefit from your advance. . . . There's no need to feel embarrassed over the plethora of my sendings, do what you can to print what you will have of mine and I'll ask no more. I am greedy, naturally, for as much space as I can get but I have also an experienced appetite that has passed through many famins. [sic]

He did not realize that the magazine had little to do with our moving and that I was probably lucky that my editing and my own poetry writing were not held against me. On January 26 Williams wrote with a touching zeal few men can equal:

> Cheerio and let's see these next three issues of your all important magazine. After that I'll practically be your slave, order what you please and I'll bust a gut to satisfy you, just name the shot — call the shot I am to attempt.

At this time, and for months after, he referred to the finishing of *Paterson I* and complained of delays, printing failures, etc. On August 22 he wrote about the *Quarterly's* new issue with his usual enthusiasm, but as for his own part in it:

> Curiously or not I for myself want to go bury my head in a manure heap. It may be the times or it may be something else but I come away from a look at myself as a writer profoundly depressed. One or two of the poems, yes, but the prose, no, absolutely no. My mind is to [sic] accurately reflected in all its unquiet, its uninstructed toment [sic] that is not, positively not attractive. If I write again it will have to reflect quiet and instruction. I am depressed.

Apparently he did not altogether share his followers' assumption, some of them, that the mind, whatever its turmoiled or confused state, must be accurately recorded. After commenting on some of the issue's items, particularly the Taupin essay, which he much enjoyed, and the Winters' reply ('Winters is horrible to me, he is the very antithisis [sic] of a mind that might produce a poem'), Williams went on

> Oh well, I'm low and I know I'm low. I waken, like all old men or old shits at around 2 a.m. and lie there and ponder the world and my fly speck of a place in it and there I lie and look up into the dark and its like the inside of a sewer drain. I see nothing good but only my own weaknesses and unpreparednesses. The first light of dawn does cheer me, I get up and go to work, only they [then] do I feel light-hearted but the work is too hard and I cannot always do it

to my own satisfaction. Congratulations on your issue — it is human, it is faulty but it's enthusiastic and in spite of that emanation of the pit Winters it is honest, beautifully honest, unpretentious and non-sectional; local.

His depression continued. On September 8 he wrote:

> Thanks for this, that and the other — encouraging words, kindly expressed etc etc I appreciate it all. I hate to say this — but I dread the appearance of my Paterson (1st part, of 4) this fall after seeing the galleys. It is just dirty sand when I thought I was building at least a rock shelter. I'm ashamed and yet can't quite bring myself to suppress it. I am not kidding, I am sick over the matter. And yet, bad as it all is, there is something there I want to say. If I quash the whole now I'll never do it again. So I am risking a fiasco for that poor lost thing. And for the sake of common honesty DON't say what isn't true of the thing if and when it gets into your hands. Don't try to be a friend — for if I detect it we're through.

Fortunately *Paterson I*'s reception was splendid; and with the help of enthusiastic reviews by Lowell, Jarrell, and others, Williams began to receive the general attention and praise till then stinted him.

With Volume II, no. 3, we inaugurated a project we had long contemplated: the giving over of an entire issue to one writer, usually a foreign one, we believed neglected or inadequately understood. We agreed with Pound that one of the primary functions of a literary magazine was the crossing of national boundaries, the presenting of first-rate work lost to most of us for the alien country of a foreign language or a distant age. We knew how enriching such transplanting could be. Had we and our generation not benefited tremendously from translations of Rilke, Lorca, the French Symbolists? Thus through our friendship with Angel Flores we conceived an all-Kafka issue, one that would print not only examples of his work never before (or newly) translated, ranging through his whole life as a writer, but also articles on his work and, wherever possible, on his particular pieces in the issue. Such weaving back and forth gave, we felt, an integrity to the issue and in the interplay made it many times richer.

While the issue developed, my correspondence with Rexroth flared like a straw fire. My earlier quotations from his letters should indicate what lusty, formidably learned, entirely enjoyable flailings out his letters often were, a happy combination of abuse and warmth; setting us and the record straight, he was full of ardency, a mentor and tormentor in the Pound vein. He found some merit in the magazine and us, but excoriated our having anything to do with the, as he saw it, altogether decayed world of the academic. We must in no way resemble *The Kenyon Review* or *The Partisan Review*. He was especially upset at our announcement of the Kafka issue. And when it appeared he saw little reason to change his mind.

> I didn't like your Kafka number. Prewar but definitely. Leave that sort of nonsense to Partisan Review and Kenyon — the OWI generation. All the little kafkaites have had their day and are now utterly spurlos versunk. It does rather amaze me tho- how misrepresentative your number was — not a single adverse criticism — are you and your set totally unaware that there are large numbers about who think Kafka stinks — that it is what he stands for that is wrong with the world? And who have very clear, definite reasons to give? . . .Do you ever read NOW? Retort? Illiterati? That is where the health is — and those are the people who are going to dominate postwar letters. . . . For God's sake get out of that Kafka-Kierkegaard-Henry James-Rilke-Proust cul de sac full of castrated Phi Beta Kappas — it is not for you.

But in a letter later he admitted:

> I prefer Kierkegaard to Kafka, however. As for James — I

am very fond of him — the only trouble is, the boys from CCNY dont know that he is a comic writer, writing about very filthy people — they think he is so rafinee and what a pity mama and papa didnt use it such distinguitched languich. No matter — after 35 only idlers read fiction anyway, and women, of course.

A little later:

Dont you be mean to Kenny. He is Agin Art, and that is very important. Anybody can be E. . .B. . . , all you need is a good sharp pair of shears and a hemostat. It is like the dodos who think Ezra's epigrams and DHL's Pansies and Nettles aint art. *Only* artists write things like that. Imagine Parker Tyler *writing* a Pansy? . . . Valery me no valeries. Everything he says — the opposite is true. I hear he died. Too bad, once & a while his poetry is very pretty in spite of his silly affected notions. What poets think they are up to is of no importance. Look at his master Mallarme — pure art, my ass — all that wonderful froufrou and patchouli — fans and handkerchiefs and rose bud slippers and the gels kicking holes in silk hats full of champange [sic] and piss — listen — Mallarme is just the highbrow's Merry Widow, and very good at it too. As Charley MacIntyre . . . says 'Yu know whut dat June Park is about?' 'De etoinal feminine.' But not enough of the patchouli rubbed off on Valery.

But what seemed to irritate Rexroth most was our failure, so he thought, to appreciate as fully as he did certain writers: 'You and your Kafka-Valery-Pound-Moore numbers! . . . Why not a full dress study of Patchen or Miller.' So too:

Honey — you is getting some sense at last! But what good my advice will do is another question. You dont like the Post War II generation. I find your opinions of Patchen, Miller, Lawrence etc infuriating. You have never printed Everson, Lamantia, Duncan, Greer, etc etc. . . . The future in poetry belongs to us — just as painting for the

next 20 years will stem from Tokey, Graves, etc. No more
R P Blackmur, nor more Dr. Mizener.

Actually we had printed Miller, valued Patchen's first two
books of poems (if not his prose and later work), especially
prized Lawrence (most of all in his stories) and, admiring
Duncan's remarkable lyricism, published him several times.
Finally, Rexroth wrote on this matter:

> I think Patchen is pretty much a touchstone. Those who
> cant see what his antiliterary behavior means are lost — he
> is the best of his generation and already a classic c̄ the
> young — Dont forget — as Stalin long ago forgot — the
> future is always poor, unknown and young. And *not* too
> skillful!

Our objection to the later Patchen, no longer a boy, was not
that he was antiliterary but, on the contrary, too typically
'revolutionary' and too slapdash, too self-indulgent. We saw
in him already the orthodox 'experimenter'.

Our third volume opened with a selection from the un-
published poetry of David Schubert whose work was much
too inadequately known. He had died in April, 1946, the
year of the issue. He and I had met in 1938 when we both
began graduate work in English at Columbia University.
Though he was only a few years older than I, he was in life as
in letters many years ahead of me. And our friendship sped
my interest and development in poetry, the understanding
and the writing of it. As the poet David Ignatow wrote
shortly after we printed Schubert's work,

> I was very much pleased by your presentation of some of
> the last of David Schubert's poems. Your foreword was
> filled with understanding and appreciation of the basis of
> his work, the city. I too was born and brought up in the
> city, but unlike many poets of my background have not
> attempted to obscure my source. I feel myself to be one of
> the group, of which Schubert was an outstanding member,
> that finds itself impelled more and more to write out of its

origins for the freedom and power of its art.

Many years later, Macmillan having published Schubert's volume, *Initial A*, Ignatow, commenting searchingly on Schubert's work, said: 'I was born in 1914, a year younger than he, but at thirty three when he died he was so far ahead of me in technique and understanding that I can only guess in wonder what he would have attained to today.' From the start Schubert's life was as troubled and tormented in its way as Crane's, a paradigm of what a good number of first-rate poets would later become. So too his work magnificently anticipated the absorption of later poets in city living and dying and in the personal, its anguish, turned into splendid poetry. We featured twelve of his last poems. Williams, with his habitual, spontaneous warmth and no doubt recognizing a younger brother-in-arms, responded at once:

Many thanks for the Schubert poems, they are first rate — more than that, far more. They are among the few poems I read that belong in the new anthology — where neither Eliot nor, I am afraid, Pound belong. I wish I could get up that anthology where the rails are polished silver they are so clear in the sunlight I should provide. There is, you know, a physically new poetry which almost no one as yet has sensed. Schubert is a nova in that sky. I hope I am not using hyperbole to excess. You know how it is when someone opens a window on a stuffy room.

Meantime, in that same issue, I reviewed Randall Jarrell's second volume of poems, *Little Friend, Little Friend*, with Ernest Morwitz and Olga Marx's *Poems of Alcman, Sappho, Ibycus*. Jarrell's individual poems, when I read them for the first time in magazines, puzzled and disturbed me; but together in one book they impressed me with a wholeness, a reciprocal strength, I was hardly prepared for. My review reported that feeling with great enthusiasm. And some time after Jarrell wrote from Greensboro, North Carolina, where he was teaching:

Would you care to use these poems in your magazine? I've meant to express, in some way, my pleasure at your review of *Little Friend, Little Friend*, and I can't think of any other way except to send some poems.

I hope you get to review my new book this winter — I thought your *Little Friend* review extremely accurate about what the poems say, and I was particularly pleased with the remarks mixed in the Sappho part; I don't have the regular modernist-poet attitude toward ordinary people, and am extremely glad to have that said.

More letters and poems followed, and several meetings, fiercely argumentative as well as most memorably pleasant. Eventually Bard College awarded him, as it had Williams and Stevens, an honorary degree in literature.

In *QRL*'s fifth year, increasingly disturbed by the New Criticism's hold on criticism and poetry alike, we decided to concentrate exclusively on poetry, fiction, and drama, especially large amounts of each: poems in ample selection whenever possible or long poems, whole plays, the novella. We found the New Criticism with its inevitable stress on English poetry much too provincial. Moreover, it seemed to us to be strait-jacketing writers. A kind of formula had emerged for the making of a poem: it must be well-behaved; self-conscious; mindful of its ironies and paradoxes and learning; metrically proper. So we proceeded to our changed format. Stevens greeted the change though he recognized the difficulties it entailed, but several writers demurred. Marianne Moore, for instance, admitted that she often preferred articles to poems, found the former more interesting and useful. But we understood that she was a writer, rather than a reader, of poetry and that her method of composition would naturally incline her to articles over creative work.

The change generated additional excitements in our involvement with the work of new, most promising young writers like James Merrill, John Gardner, James Dickey, Jean Garrigue, Robert Coover, Donald Finkel, Denise Levertov,

David Galler, Hayden Carruth, Arthur Gregor, Gil Orlovitz, Linda Pastan, George P. Elliott, W. S. Merwin, Roger Hecht, James Wright, Harvey Shapiro, Leonard Nathan, and a host of others. The exchange of letters with many of these and the witnessing of their development were as stimulating as they were pleasurable. If we had been bolstered by older, more experienced, established writers to begin with, now we were grateful for and encouraged by the support of writers just coming on. We felt, happily enough, the labors notwithstanding, like pilots of a paper boat miraculously able to accommodate a full roster of fascinating passengers at their entertaining best and improving as the cruise continued.

We are amused to observe, if somewhat wryly, that soon after, with the bursting forth on the scene of the Beats and outrageous happenings in the world at large, New Criticism was unseated, in poetry and criticism alike. Eventually, as though in revenge on New Criticism but on this new, often would-be intuitive, if not mindless poetry as well, the criticism that emerged abroad and in this country began to express its impatience with literature altogether and proposed that it was at least as valuable, if not as literary, as poetry and fiction. *QRL*'s position seemed more important and precarious than ever. Now the sociologizing, psychologizing, philosophizing, politicizing of literature and culture, certainly the cerebrating, was on full blast, with woeful, frantic attempts to find an equally opaque, ponderous 'professional' jargon. One might look back wistfully, not to say nostalgically, at the gentler, innocent-seeming time of New Criticism when a poem, however much it might be entered into, even overrun, did not, like Patroclus's body, disappear altogether in the tug-of-war among furiously rival contenders for Achilles' armor. Reasonable midwives are most urgently needed: essays, reviews, magazines like *Parnassus* (and *QRL*!) that will attend to the poetry and fiction itself, not to the superstructures of criticism, jerrybuilt as they may be, intent on replacing creative work.

The Blight of Modernism
and Philip Larkin's Antidote[1]

One can say at once that, on the whole, Anglo-American relations in poetry seem to be at low ebb. Recent English poets have made little visible mark on American poetry's turbulent course. Beyond importations from South American and iron-curtain poets and a preoccupation with tribal utterance, surrealism, and the East, American poetry appears engrossed in its own churnings. Some English work, however, does trickle over, and Ted Hughes for his ferocities has probably had the largest impact. A few poets like Gunn, Tomlinson, Davie, Hamburger and Kinsella, by teaching and reading widely in the United States, and like Dannie Abse, for winsomely human qualities, have attracted an audience. It is regrettable that the witty, compassionate work of a D. J. Enright, say, or the original, powerful, if often fairly hermetic poems of Geoffrey Hill[2] have not reached farther.

The English, for the most part, have also—if they have been aware of it at all—dismissed most recent American work. Robert Lowell has been among them but more, it would seem, as an admiration and a problem than an influence. Similarly John Berryman and Sylvia Plath. With the collapse of the empire and England's growing crisis, it is

---

[1] Delivered in December, 1975, at the MLA in San Francisco, California.

[2] Since this paper was delivered, with the recent publication in this country of his work Hill has received considerable—even at times one might be tempted to say extravagant—attention and praise. Harold Bloom, who wrote an introduction to the Hill volume, using his strongest word of praise, one he metes out begrudgingly, calls Hill a very "strong" poet. Donald Hall, who links Hill with Hardy and Lawrence as one of the three best modern English poets, goes on, fascinatingly—here he reflects the uneasiness between the two countries—to say that did Hill write in the United States he would be terrible (Hill has admitted the influence of Ransom and Tate), but since he writes in England he is magnificent. Lucky accident!

understandable that its poets might fall into retrenchment and resort again to the conservatism, the traditionalism, deep-rooted in many. The Ginsbergs, the Blys, and scions of the Olson group, however doubtful their effect, do seem to have a considerable English audience, at least among the young and the would-be far out. Their difference, their oddity, has also made them appealing to some more sedate Englishmen. The English tend to ignore those American poets who equal—if not better—what they do. The wilder sort, however, the English can enjoy because they are what one might properly expect of Americans. Enjoy and at the same time depreciate for their extravagance, self-indulgence, sensationalism (even as the Americans scoff at the English for their tepidity, their blandness).

Until recently, intimidated, whatever their fundamental chafing, by the awesome practice and presence of Eliot and Pound, English poets did little more than mutter. But the mutterings have gathered for a long time. Years ago John Wain could defiantly assert of himself and his contemporaries, members of The Movement, that avant garde writing is whatever is going on now; they were going on now; therefore they were the avant garde. A. Alvarez's Penguin Anthology, *The New Poetry* (1962), with its manifesto which denounced most contemporary English poetry for its gentility, its failures to grapple with the mad modern age, and sought to shame it by stressing Lowell and Berryman and later Plath and Sexton, may have helped to repress some of the resentment's articulation.

But with Eliot and Pound adequately dead, more and more English poets and critics have felt emboldened to speak out. And Donald Davie took basic, often cogent issue with Alvarez at once. Then in his *Thomas Hardy and British Poetry* (1972) Davie's lifelong demurs, his ample praises notwithstanding, for those foreigners, Yeats, Eliot, and Pound finally came to the vehement fore. Hardy, indigenous, a poet in the old style, and liberal, is the model to follow: and the best English poets, Davie maintained, have done so. His position, however, for some of the poets he proposed in proof, is rather hard to take seriously. Even his two likeliest candidates prompt reservations. Tomlinson, whom Davie especially admires, is a rather ambiguous case and an exception among his English contemporaries; for he himself has made much of his debt to Americans like Williams, Marianne Moore, and Oppen. Larkin, Davie's prime example, is, by Davie's own admission, a shrunken poet, one who has faithfully followed Hardy's diminishings to their much greater point today. But Davie, recognizing those diminishings, approves them; in a shrunken, threatened world they are all that is possible. Anything else is a lie, irresponsible and utterly dangerous. Badly off as England and democracy are, one must not shake the leaky boat with extreme criticisms or extravagant imaginings. But this attitude derives, I suspect, mainly from Davie's English pragmatism and scepticism, his frequently valuable conservatism.

Larkin himself in a recent essay, "It Could Only Happen in England," an introduction to the American edition of John Betjeman's *Collected Poems*,[3] ostensibly intended to help the American reader with Betjeman's very English, very local qualities, has also taken up the cudgels, rather more savagely than Davie. Another English poet and critic, John Press, in the "General Introduction" to his *A Map of Modern English Verse*,[4] having discussed modernism, says:

> We may, of course, believe with Robert Graves that 'foul tidal basin of modernism' is merely an ignoble deviation from the mainstream of English verse. It is conceivable that the course of true poetry in our century descends from Thomas Hardy through Edward Thomas, W. H. Davies, Norman Cameron, and Alun Lewis, to finish with Graves himself; . . .

A rather extraordinary "conceiving," I would have to say and, aside from my opinion of the worth of the names he mentions, beyond being, after Hardy and before Graves, mainly pleasant minor poets, a conceiving dismal even in Press's terms: a "descending" and a "finishing." Is this the conduct of a mainstream? Press continues:

> and that modernism, as Philip Larkin has observed [this already in a review in November, 1958], "is fun no more. Deserted by the tide of taste, the modern movement awaits combing like some cryptic sea-wrack."

Here, we see, modernism is not even a deflection of the mainstream, a sink of stinking waters, but a shore-dumped seaweed. "Fun" is apparently what Larkin is after, and fun is what he finds in Betjeman. But it would seem that by the 70's Larkin had grown tired of waiting for someone to do a thorough job of combing and for the seawrack to be disposed of. Accordingly, in the Betjeman introduction he decided he must do it himself. Press, in his balanced view, I should point out, concludes:

> While sharing this admiration for Hardy I am convinced that the major poetic achievement of the century is the work of the modernist

[3] Houghton Mifflin, 1973.
[4] Oxford University Press, 1969, pp. 4-5.

poets, of which the three major representatives are Yeats, Pound, and Eliot.

Larkin in his Betjeman introduction, however, is hardly so temperate. Coming from so gifted a writer, one so important to the English, thought by many their best poet, if not the best writing in English today, Larkin's statement deserves careful consideration. To be fair and to illustrate his powers as critic and stylist, within my space's limits, I shall let him speak for himself.

First of all, the essay is astonishing—at least to this American reader— for its claims for Betjeman. Whatever Larkin's qualifyings, at the outset he calls the *Collected Poems* "the most extraordinary poetic output of our time." And from what follows we can be sure that Larkin does not mean by extraordinary odd or egregious. In fact, one would not, I believe, far miss the mark to suggest that Betjeman is the poet Larkin would most like to be. And precisely for his quirky, low-hedge-rooted qualities. One might also understand a Larkin, withdrawn if not diffident, hyper-responsive to all kinds of depression and horrors, those our age has excelled in, and dubious of any answer to them, envying or at least admiring the robustious Mr. Betjeman, the immediacy, the local gusto, the ability—as we shall see—with roaring laughter and a "Gosh" to run roughshod over modern actualities. The essay first tells us what Betjeman is not, not one of the landed gentry, not a member of some university "that provides him with a comfortable stipend." Rather, his public image is of one "who crops up in cultural TV panel games," etc. However, the story is more complicated and serious than that. For Betjeman is "a Commander of the British Empire, a Companion of Literature, a Royal Fine Arts Commissioner, a governor of Pusey House, a holder of honorary doctorates from six universities." At the same time he is

> one of modern England's few upper-class licensed jesters: usually photographed roaring with laughter, he will ride a bicycle through crowded London, dress up in Henry James's morning clothes (which he seems to own) and explain how much he still loves his old teddy-bear Archibald.

Or Monty Python here I come. The line, it is true, is sometimes hard to find in English Literature (and England) between eccentricity and substance. Larkin, like Betjeman, well knows this fact, even to the point of applauding the deliberate cultivation of eccentricity or seeing one's tastes and inclinations through, giving them—against society's increasing pressures—their triumphant, impressive head.

From the start, Larkin assures us, Betjeman was pretty much himself, with themes "resolutely opposed to the spirit of the century in two major ways: they were insular and they were regressive." For Betjeman is in no way cosmopolitan. With architecture, not poetry, what most occupies him, he himself has said, "I only enjoy to the full the architecture of these islands." One can respect this view since he feels ignorant and therefore frustrated abroad; for it is the whole town, not individual masterworks, he relishes. In his words, "I like to see the railway station, the town hall, the suburbs, the shops, the signs of local crafts being carried on in backyards." Or "our whole overpopulated island." At this point Larkin remarks,

> If the spirit of our century is onwards, outwards and upwards, the spirit of Betjeman's work is backwards, inwards and downwards. If the architecture of our day is high-riser flats, its heroes the working class, its environment motorways lit with sodium, Betjeman exalts Comper interiors, clergymen's widows, and gaslight. If the age is agnostic and believes everyone is a socialist nowadays, Betjeman embraces the Christianity of the Church of England and proclaims a benevolent class system the best of all possible worlds. In a time of global concepts, Betjeman insists on the little, the forgotten, the unprofitable, the obscure . . . .

Before such nostalgia, however ardently espoused, one wonders what real broad enthusiasm can prevail. And Betjeman's poetry is no less insular and regressive. Having bypassed symbolism, the objective correlative, and all such mental complications, he considers poetry "an emotional business." (Eliot, I had thought, also put feeling first in poetry.) Thus Larkin assures us, Betjeman's poems,

> however trivial or light-hearted their subjects, always carry a primitive vivacity that sets them apart from the verses of his contemporaries and captures the reader's attention in advance of his intellectual consent.

Certainly recent American poets, longing for the primitive, should take little exception to the above. But it is possible that they and Larkin (and I) mean rather different things by "primitive vivacity." For "forthright, comprehensible," and "personal" though Betjeman's poems are, they are "couched in the marked buttonholing rhythms of Praed or Tennyson."

Here I must confess my abashment, my deep sense of inadequacy as a reader of English verse, before the profundities Larkin finds in the quatrain he quotes as evidence. Never has Shaw's quip that the thing that separates Englishmen and Americans is the English language seemed more appropriate.

> *Miss J. Hunter Dunn, Miss J. Hunter Dunn,*
> *Furnish'd and burnish'd by Aldershot sun,*
> *What strenuous singles we play after tea,*
> *We in the tournament—you against me!*

These verses open a love poem; yet Larkin says,

> What could be simultaneously more personal and ironic than the first line? The passionate [sic!] reiteration of the beloved's name in a form in which it would appear, say, on her visiting card conveys that she is clearly seen by the poet in the context of the middle classes, and that this increases her attraction for him.

We poor Americans, before such subtleties, such excitements, must hang our visiting-cardless, unclassed heads in loutish shame. But the significant truth is out: "Betjeman is a true heir of Thomas Hardy, who found clouds, mists and mountains 'unimportant beside the wear of a threshold or the print of a hand'. . . ." I can appreciate such humanism; yet why, in any genuine, large poetry, need clouds, mists and mountains be deprecated, for themselves as for their part in the human condition? Or has poetry changed that much? Even England has some mountains (still), and surely it would be an act of excessive, excessively exerted myopia, whatever England's industrializing and over-population, to ignore its clouds and mists. And is it not a little odd to visit a modern view on an earlier time, on a writer whose novels at least are soaked in, if not dependent on, the natural scene? Yet Larkin assures us that Betjeman's "gusto embraces it all," as well as "the mouldy remnants of the nineteenth century," the twentieth also. And Larkin confesses,

> I have sometimes thought that this collection of Betjeman's poems would be something I should want to take with me if I were a soldier leaving England: I can't think of any other poet who has preserved so much of what I should want to remember, nor one who, to use his own words, would so easily suggest 'It is those we are fighting for, foremost of all.'

Most important of all, Betjeman has brought poetry back to the general reader. His *Collected Poems* in its first edition sold more than a hundred thousand copies. Larkin does, it is true, acknowledge difficulties in Betjeman's verse, all the unknown place names, etc. In fact, Larkin admits that "Some of Betjeman's poems are completely incomprehensible to me . . . while remaining emotionally potent." Aside from the plausibility of observations like Eliot's that the music of Dante's poetry can move us even if we know no Italian, one might wonder at Larkin's easy acceptance, hard-headed as he means to be, of such a split and wonder further about the clarity and immediacy he praised. But he sees, despite his scorn for modern poetry's obscurities, that a work may be entitled to, may need, such difficulties. Furthermore, Betjeman has enough "universal situations" and "fun" in his rhymes and meters.

And now, as Larkin underlines Betjeman's uniqueness, the chief point of this piece emerges: Betjeman's remarkable popularity in England is partly due to his having little in common with modern poetry. In fact, as Larkin emphasized earlier, "The first thing to realize about Betjeman . . . is that he is a poet for whom the modern poetic revolution has simply not taken place." However, Larkin insists, ". . . it is as obvious as it is strenuously denied that in this century English poetry went off on a loop-line that took it away from the general reader." Of course the United States via Eliot and Pound with "their culture-mongering activities" was responsible for the loop-line. But I might ask who those looped English poets are. For as far as I can see, the majority, as though nothing especially striking or unusual had happened, went on writing generally well-behaved verse, this with very little of the lyrical power, the daring, the range of Eliot and Pound. Yet Larkin maintains, ". . . the aberration of modernism . . . blighted all the arts." Davie has also accused modern poetry of alienating the general reader. Why then has English genteel poetry on the whole failed to hold him? But one might question how many general readers read older, ambitious poetry or, for that matter, exacting literature of any kind. One recalls Valéry's grave prediction that soon, for the expanding modern media, no one would read, or be able to, writers like Pascal. I also wonder whether, at present, the attempt, however laudable, to recover the general reader may not entail far too many sacrifices of poetry itself.

Larkin continues his attack against English literature's becoming an academic subject. Obviously when students had English literature securely in and behind them, literature as an academic subject would have been superfluous. He deplores "the consequent demand for a kind of poetry that needed elucidation." For a time poetry almost did become university property. Alas, in an increasingly unliterate, if not illiterate, age where else can poetry be preserved? And are even Chaucer, Shakespeare, Pope, Browning so readily available to, so popular among, modern readers? Also, if criticism prospered in sponsoring complicated poetry, at least it did help to enrich its readers. (How does Larkin feel, one might ask, about that latest criticism so called which is impatient with, if not contemptuous of, literature altogether?) In one sense Larkin should be happy now; in the United States, with the Beats and their followers, poetry has become direct and—at times painfully so—simple; at last it is once more out in the streets. Yet I suspect that this is not what Larkin is after; I doubt that he fully relishes the likes of the Liverpool poets. (Perhaps these are even some of the looped poets he objects to? They do have an audience; but surely they require little elucidation, are not culture-mongering, and can in no sense be considered the offspring of Pound and Eliot? Nonetheless, it may be that I underestimate their disturbingness to an Englishman like Larkin. But an ocean away poets of such kidney seem Liverpiddling indeed, and I cannot resist the suspicion that it is the success itself, the enthronement, of Eliot and Pound that Larkin chiefly resents.) In any case, Larkin concludes, ''the strong connection between poetry and the reading public that had been forged by Kipling, Housman, Brooke and *Omar Khayyam* was destroyed as a result.'' Does Larkin really want us to take this list seriously? But singlehandedly Betjeman has

> restored direct intelligible communication to poetry, not as a pompous pseudo-military operation of literary warfare but simply by exclaiming 'Gosh, how lovely' (or 'Gosh, how awful') and roaring with laughter.

Is *this* the answer to the efforts and accomplishments, or even for that matter the aberrations, of modern poetry? Maybe it is the Liverpuddlers Larkin longs for after all! Or is ''Gosh'' Larkin's notion of direct appeal to all those benighted Americans, the silent and not-so-silent majority?

Eliot, it seems, caused the trouble, especially with his ''Poets in our civilization, as it exists at present, must be difficult.'' Nonetheless, Eliot and Betjeman, Larkin assures us, are closer than one might think. Eliot also urged poets to express ''the whole way of life.'' Should that way, one might ask, exclude mists, clouds, mountains and even mountainous, sometimes complicated ideas? What is poetry, especially of the major variety, if it fails to encompass the all that there is or not only the whole way but the whole of life? Larkin approvingly quotes Eliot's list of the whole-way-of-life's properties:

> Derby Day, Henley Regatta, Cowes, the twelfth of August, a cup final, the dog races, the pin table, the dart board, Wensleydale cheese, boiled cabbage cut in sections, beetroot in vinegar, nineteenth century gothic churches, and the music of Elgar.

This list appeared as late as 1948 in Eliot's *Notes Towards the Definition of Culture*. Amusing in its coming from an American, if by then a thoroughly transplanted one, it reflects the side of Eliot that dominated after the energy of his originality as a poet was over.

I am further amused to put beside this list a similar one from perhaps the single most telling fillip to the creation of an American literature: Emerson's "The American Scholar," his address at Harvard University in 1837, when, dismissing "the great, the remote, the romantic; what is doing in Italy or Arabia; what is Greek art, or Provençal minstrelsy" [Pound beware!], Emerson declared: "I embrace the common, I explore and sit at the feet of the familiar, the low. Give me insight into today, and you may have the antique and future worlds." For, like Eliot, Betjeman, and Larkin, he goes on:

> What would we really know the meaning of? The meal in the firkin; the milk in the pan; the ballad in the street; the news of the boat; the glance of the eye; the form and the gait of the body.

But he does not stop at such a list alone, for he requires

> show me the ultimate reason of these matters; show me the sublime presence of the highest spiritual cause lurking, as always it does lurk, in these suburbs and extremities of nature; let me see every trifle bristling with the polarity that ranges it instantly on an eternal law, and the shop, the plough, and the ledger referred to the like cause by which light undulates and poets sing. . . .

In short, it is already the democratic and the colloquial Emerson is after but because he believes in their potency and in the gods in them and not as a retreating, last-ditch measure. Little wonder the greatest "scholar" of them all, Walt Whitman, the one who went most diligently to school to Emerson, took fire from such sentiments, exploited the potency of the democratically divine to its utmost. It is this potency which Eliot, Pound, and Williams also, at least occasionally, discovered in their work and which Larkin and Betjeman for their good, hard, common sense (so Amis, Davie, Wain, etc.) tend to suspect, belittle, and recoil from. And in this recoiling they are eminently modern. Thus Larkin, however he may set himself apart from modernism, in his latest collection's title poem "High Windows" demonstrates again how much he participates in one of modernism's more painful, impoverished aspects: at what seems about to be his loftiest he comes—such his vision, his spurning of deception—to nothing more than "nothing."

But having made his case for Betjeman, Larkin concludes, "Can it be that, as Eliot dominated the first half of the twentieth century, the second half will derive from Betjeman?" Anticipating the incredulity of at least some of us, Larkin defiantly continues: "I do not think this as completely unlikely a suggestion as it might first appear." It is one thing to put one's money on a dark horse; quite another, on a horse (let alone a bicycle) not even in the race. However, as we have seen, Larkin would have it that the race left the track a long time ago.

Now I also have reservations before modernism's worst antics and aberrations. Furthermore, I can sympathize with a poet's need to take, for his and his work's sake, what might appear to be a violent stand. We remember the troubles Keats had, for instance, in trying to get round—the "anxiety of influence"?—that overwhelming Alp in his way, Wordsworth. Such a poet's need to recover and to champion an earlier tradition, say, especially as in Larkin's case one he considers more indigenous to his world, is surely acceptable—at least for him— when it supports work of his quality.

But Larkin, it seems to me, cuts poetry's roots off much too short and, at the same time, fails to recognize the life-giving importance, the enrichment, of all kinds of importations. Has not English poetry been at its best in its times of outgoing? Obviously English poets have a right to their own expression, and they ought not to be swamped by any other nation. In fact, English and American poets should be different, as different as their worlds. Moreover, they should be grateful for poetry's magnificent variety, and not indulge a commissar-like, party-line notion of one sort of poetry only; so too they should appreciate what benefits derive from their acting as each other's stimulating counterpart. In my Lord's house of poetry, that mighty Ark, let not all inhabitants be crows or pigeons, bears or hares, but respecters of each other's distinctive characteristics and of poetry's hospitable ecology. Would it not be sad indeed if, after the heroic accomplishments of Yeats and Eliot, and others, England, in its time of distress, cut itself off from other worlds (even the modern) of thought and feeling? To deny that modern world, however bewildering or intolerable it may be, is to deny the reality we live in. Furthermore, to ignore the internationalism more and more common is also to ignore reality, as it is to lose sight of most men's uprootedness and mobility today. To ignore or to despise it is no way of dealing with it.

Many American poets, some of them among our best, in revulsion from our world, our own present debacle, are also nostalgic, plumping for regionalism, American Indianism, etc. All over America poets have staked claims on particular localities. In England's bad time it may be similarly natural for its poets to draw back, to want to protect themselves, to seek to make the most of what is left. Yet how gainsay the great world out there willy-nilly operating on English (and American) life? The Georgian tradition (or its curiously translated American version), even if not at present asserting itself overtly in pastoralism, in clouds, mists, mountains, may be a legitimately persistent one. But should it, any more than in American art the Grant Woods, the Wyeths, the Currys, overwhelm or displace more ambitious work?

The Many-sidedness
of Modernism

A number of English poets and critics, some of the best among them, have understandably long resented Pound, Eliot, and Yeats as well. Foreigners, they dared to absorb, if not divert, the main stream of English poetry or make it turbulent at least with their thrashing presences. And how many years they occupied its centre! Shipping out with Odysseus, Pound's poem demonstrates, was altogether hazardous. And who beyond Odysseus survived to tell the amazing tale? Philip Larkin has several times inveighed against Pound and Eliot, the agents provocateurs of that aberration, modernism. Donald Davie, after a long and impressively fruitful relationship with the three poets, in his *Thomas Hardy and British Poetry* came to the conclusion (at least for the time being: poet that Davie is, his judgment naturally alters with his poetic needs) that they must be set aside for the poet who most valuably maintained the great tradition, Hardy. In fact, Davie claims, the setting aside has happened: "In British poetry of the last fifty years (as not in America) the most far-reaching influence, for good or ill, has been not Yeats, still less Eliot or Pound, not Lawrence, but Hardy." This conclusion may seem extreme. Yet a close look at modern English poetry would probably reveal that the bulk of it does hark back to an earlier tradition.

Most recently Frank Kermode, in *Critical Inquiry*, after admitting his reluctant ("puzzling") attraction over twenty years ago to the "irrational wisdom" of the image, a wisdom "which I have never had much time for . . . and particularly fear . . . when it is systemized or when it is dispensed in the tone of priestly rant occasionally adopted by Yeats", can say, "In the end my distaste proved stronger than my interest, and I simply gave up Yeats." "Simply" is rather breathtaking:

such casual dismissal of a major poet! The telltale words, I suspect, are "fear" and "distaste", reflections of the not unusual English disposition to rationality. Davie's book makes much of Hardy's modesty, civility, liberal reasonableness, his desiring little more than to appear in Palgrave's *Golden Treasury*. Sharing Kermode's scepticism, Davie applauds Hardy's refusal to traffic with the transcendental. But aside from the hunger for common sense, does this attitude not smack, in some large measure, of nostalgia, a yearning for the quieter days, a return to something like the Georgian poets? Fortunately Hardy was a good deal better than that.

A similar reaction has occurred in the United States. A number of poets and critics have deprecated Yeats and Eliot (if not so much Pound). Even Irving Howe, in a recent issue of the *New York Times Book Review*, noting that "Serious readers and critics in recent years have found in his [Hardy's] poetry values that make it attractive at a time when the great figures of modernism may have come to seem a bit questionable", proposes:

> To turn back to Eliot takes on the character of a cultural event. Between his work and a reasonably sophisticated reader there intervenes a thick partition of ideas about modernism, myth, the modern historical crisis, etc. With Hardy it is, or seems, otherwise. Reading his lyrics we experience a direct relation with language, immediate renderings of crucial moments, and a modest voice of contemplation.

No one would deny the greater consciousness and self-consciousness enveloping the work of Eliot and Yeats. But the crucial word in Howe's observations is the twice-repeated "seems". He is too acute a critic not to qualify his own attitude: ". . . no literary experience can be unmediated. There is always . . . the resonance of tradition and the pressure of cultural assumption—as much in Hardy as in Eliot". No American primitivist, Howe knows we cannot throw off our age or the past to become naked, pure, wholly original.

One of the major impulses of modern times has been to see how close to life (or nature) art can come. In fact, with the aleatory and the improvisational, with happenings and action painting, both in America and England a huge bid has been made to break out of culture altogether or to identify nature and culture. Recently, in a perceptive review of John Bayley's *An Essay on Hardy* for the *TLS* (July 28, 1978), Robert Langbaum reports that Bayley shows how Hardy is modern yet different from the modernists in that his ideas do not control his work. One thinks of Eliot's "James was not violated by ideas" or, for that matter, Williams's "no ideas but in things". But Bayley, amplifying this notion, says that Hardy's ideas are "quite separate from his observations of persons and things". In short, whatever Hardy's culture, nature in his work happily prevailed. (We are, I think, not far from Howe's position.) Langbaum further reports, "The disunity accounts for Hardy's lack of that 'fluency' which signified the Victorians' power over the material and interfered with the feel of life". Too great fluency can indeed drown the very things it assumes it is presenting.

But more than that danger is at stake. Bayley has it that Hardy was so "helpless" he willingly "let his text fall flat when life does." Do we then prefer writers so powerless before their material that it comes out raw? Beyond that, our disappointment in reading Hardy may be attributable to "a formalization of disappointment as a bulky ingredient in life".

Though Langbaum finds this formulation applicable to Hardy, he recognizes it for the imitative fallacy it is. In fact, Bayley goes so far as to say that "Hardy is most present in a work when he is being most inconsistent, when the elements of the work are most separate. The conscious rendition, which may seem inept, is a feint that releases unconscious perceptions . . . ." It is hard to know how much Bayley means us to stress "may *seem* inept" and "a feint" or "formalization", but here we seem to have the artist as victim, prostrate before life and, apparently, at his best in that state since most accurate about things as they are. Is such a view not in danger of surrendering the artist as artist, of abandoning the ancient, deep conviction that he is a maker, at least somewhat in charge of his material, using it, discovering its wholeness in likely patterns? But how complain when an Ashbery is praised for being "true to the mind's confusions"? Accurate reportage, rather than making and comprehending, would now seem to be the poet's business.

The final truth appears in Bayley's "The fact was what mattered to Hardy's romanticism, not what he made of it". Does such an interpretation not encourage a basic confusion, not only of art and life but of our notions of life and life itself? Are not "facts" (here we see the pervasive influence of science) a tacit agreement on how to see nature or, in fact, an expression of culture? Surely it is a remarkable moment that can applaud "separation", "inconsistency", "unconscious perceptions", remarkable when the "made" no longer strikes us as "natural". But perhaps life has become so difficult, so overwhelming, that many of us can trust a writer only when he threatens to fall to pieces. However, one might be tempted to ask, why go to so much intellectual trouble when one can simply say that we have had Yeats, Pound, and Eliot and have had it? After all that high accomplishment, give us the drab, the ragged, the mistaken, the indifferent.

Or in Ammons's words "give me / the dumb, debilitated, nasty, and massive", which he seems to find the chief if not only alternative to "good poems, all those little rondures splendidly brought off" and which he is "sick of". Of course one longs for a medium able to accommodate everything: boredom, folly, stupidity, etc, this without lying about the nature of any of them, yet somehow, perhaps by the intensity of the concentration on them, the loving human care, redeemed; else why have art in the first place and not simply living itself?

Yet Howe similarly compromises the issue. For though he acknowledges the intellectual forces at work in Hardy, he maintains they

> do not hover so loomingly, so fiercely, so brilliantly as do those that surround Eliot (and again, even Yeats). In Hardy the pressures of culture have been more thoroughly subdued, or occasionally evaded, than in the great figures of modernism.

We might boggle at this conclusion, especially as we recall those Hardy poems which do grapple with religious problems of his age or recall his pervasive melancholy, surely a consequence to some degree of that age. And we might ask whether Hardy is not more simple-seeming because his times are not so present, their problems, unlike those of Yeats and Eliot, not our problems. But praising Hardy's naiveté, which "now comes to seem a source of strength", Howe maintains that Hardy moved beyond the shaping thought of his time to "his own unique way of looking at things, the bias of a temperament drawing from country life but rubbed raw by modern ideas". According to Howe, culturally-conditioned ideas do not "clog" Hardy's poetry, and "they do not require elaborate glosses. Whatever is abiding in our life—and something must be!—survives in Hardy."

Being "rubbed raw by modern ideas" does not sound like too much of an escape from culture to me, or too different from Yeats, Eliot, Pound. Also, I would have thought that in their best poems these poets likewise move beyond their age's ideas (in fact they were often dead set against them) to their own unique way of looking at things; nor do history, myth, etc, clog these poems.

But elaborate glosses or not, I wonder how immediately one reads most major poets in their more ambitious work. The short lyric is one thing; the long, meditative lyric or the sequence, quite another. In undertaking to encompass a world the latter is likely to make far greater demands on the reader. Yet the simple truth is out. According to Howe we turn back to Hardy for relief from our age's tyrannical spirit. However, much as we may "want to rest with the security of Hardy's old age, his balancing of finalities", Howe knows we cannot long escape our own time. A desire to do so is, he admits, "merely foolish". But rather than finding security in Hardy's lyrics, I have always found in them a poignancy that is an outcrop of their gloomy doubts and foreboding. Still Howe's honesty in words like "escape" and "rest" helps to make clear what it is that now, after the battered 1970s, attracts us to Hardy. And we can accept Howe's view since it recognizes the escape as temporary. The return to Hardy, it would seem, cannot be much more, except as a great poet of any time and place proves a delight and an inspiration.

Nonetheless, a growing number of American poets and critics agree with Larkin, Davie, and Kermode in giving Eliot and even Yeats short shrift, though, ironically enough, they do so for reasons usually the opposite of those of the English, i.e., they object to Yeats's and Eliot's formality, cerebration, internationalism, historicism and, finally (at least with Eliot), devotion to the establishment. I have been puzzled that Yeats's absorption in the mystical and the occult has not made him more popular with recent poets. The answer must be that he was too accomplished and elegant, too formal (at least externally) in his verses for them. The use he made of forces beyond the mind resulted, despite his passion and rages, in poems too controlled, too realized.

I find this cudgelling of Yeats and Eliot with either the tough old gnarled hickory of Hardy or, more commonly in America, the crab-apple bough of William Carlos Williams, most regrettable. Despite Williams' modernism, he and Hardy have had a similar appeal. However different they may have been, both, though rubbed raw by modern ideas, were essentially pastoral poets, rooted to their respective places.

And they and their work have encouraged the present ardor for the local and, being misunderstood, for an often unfortunate simpleness. Much as I admire both poets and for their earthiness I do not mean to cudgel them in turn. But surely one may complain about critical positions and poetic practices that, whatever their reasons, tend to shrink the world of poetry, to limit its possibilities.

Many recent American poets have wanted to leap over Yeats and Eliot and, via Pound and especially Williams, to find their way back to that shaggy bison (at least as they misread him), that wild original and aboriginal of the American past, Whitman. One of America's better poets, Galway Kinnell, in would-be all-out romanticism has said, with truth but also with what seems enthusiasm: "There is often a deep anti-intellectualism, a lack of balance and reasonableness, even a certain stupidity, in American writers." Even more impressively, as he gets on to his ideal: "Had Whitman been more clever, conceivably he could have turned out to be as good a poet as Whittier or Longfellow. He was too awkward, too unschooled, too mad.'' Clearly Whitman has proved too clever for Kinnell. (Fortunately in another context Kinnell declares ''. . . the best poets are the sanest''). Then he assures us, ''Of course, the universities suppressed his discovery for a hundred years, always preferring lesser poets, including, in our time, Ezra Pound and T. S. Eliot, whose work is so much better suited to the classroom''. Kinnell does not bother to mention the long and painful time it took before Eliot and Pound were accepted. And did not even fairly academic centres swear Whitman in as a substantial part of the curriculum quite a few years ago?

But both in theory and in practice these newer poets plump for immediacy, a kind of magical realism that hopes to make excitement of the moment beyond the urgencies and outrages of our age. This magic, a reading of the best of them reveals, can be thoroughly impressive. They have staked out regions of the luring islands our three Odyssean poets paused in and sped on from.

One can applaud these younger poets' desire to recover poetry's basic feeling, its primitive power of mystery. But may concentration on it not amount to a retreat to poetry's final fastness, a retreat already evidenced in the romantic poets before the always more triumphant prose of the world: journalism, the novel, science, commerce? The potential risks and costs of such magic grow ever clearer. Like Howe's fairly wistful yearning, such work in its instinctuality, its elemental, shamanistic tone as though from under rocks and roots, expresses an understandable desire to escape our age's oppressiveness. But the jettisoning of syntax, out of distrust for its consciousness, its complications, and the stripping of poetry in general to a kind of spooky, husky muttering, do they not result in a minimal language, mainly dependent on a powerful ellipticality? Result also in a failure to grapple, except indirectly by all that the work stoutly denies or ignores, with the world around it?

One might suggest that magic abundantly obtains in Yeats and Pound, and in Eliot as well, in his unmistakable resonance out of mysterious sources. Eliot could say, ''The artist, I believe, is more primitive, as well as more civilized, than his contemporaries, his experience is deeper than civilization, and he only uses the phenomena of civilization in expressing it.'' But, in addition, these three poets exploited their whole beings, their minds no less than their instincts, memory and learning no less than the local and the immediate; for them the remote past could be as present as the here and now. When Howe speaks with approval of Hardy's ''modest voice of contemplation'' is he not echoing the present's suspicion of the large, the noble, not to say the sublime? Wearied by our age's holocausts, many of us have submitted to the contrary of the grand. The uprootedness, the fragmentariness, in much of the brief magic of some of our better recent poets is one thing; the triviality that pervades vast reams of modern poetry, the downright drabness (except as it is tarted up by easy neo-surrealism), is quite another. Many poets seem content with a mere rehearsing of their routine, daily movements.

Democratization, one could say, has advanced so far in poetry that even the dull, the ordinary—even prose—have found their lobbyists. Williams, despite his lyrical mercuriality and his patent, deep sympathies, has been misread, run down into the pedestrian: things as they are but drably, journalistically, are, presented without imagination or vision, as though these were deceptions, as though prose-drabness by its oppressive presence confirms the poem's authenticity.

Yet though ambition, range, complexity have been turned away from, might we not do well to remember that most of the modern poets we have regarded as major attempted work of considerable scope, usually sequences, whether it be *Song of Myself, The Cantos, The Waste Land* and the *Four Quartets, The Bridge, Notes toward a Supreme Fiction* or, for that matter, *Paterson* (and Hardy's *The Dynasts*)? The authors of these poems, whatever their preoccupation with the self, acknowledged and sought to realize the world out there, one that always needs to be dealt with. Can we really hope to return to the woods or think to lose ourselves in the primordial self? How, beyond some enormous catastrophe no one with any sanity would begin to dream of, can we expect our huge populations to return to "natural" conditions? Hardy and Williams may have come closer to some aspects of reality than Yeats and Eliot, and these aspects deserve to be attended to. But stress the former poets to the diminution or neglect of the latter and our whole reality, as much as not a product of the human imagination, is bound to be beggared. Rather, as with the basic differences between English and American poetry, naturally prompted by their very different worlds, we are better off being grateful for the riches of those differences.

But the detractors of Yeats, Pound, and Eliot, especially the more vehement among them, may be doing these poets a service. They are voicing the inevitable human reaction to success: our tiring of the triumphant, in itself and in our applause of it. This would-be dethronement— the reasonable desire of new poets to throw off the past and to find their own voices notwithstanding—may help to preserve and eventually restore our three poets.

After a time readers and writers, young ones particularly, needing to react to their present's fix, may seek out Yeats and Eliot again. To prosper, literature requires hindrances, oppositions.

It is all this that makes M. L. Rosenthal's *Sailing into the Unknown: Yeats, Pound and Eliot* sharply pertinent. During the years that he has had the work in mind, books about these poets have appeared in swarms. Consequently, one might think his volume belated. However the time and its havocs have ripened Rosenthal's powers and afforded him an important perspective. So has the most recent poetry. In the interim he has written volumes of his own very considerable poems and several books of criticism on modern poetry that have established him as one of our most valuable critics. He has also been prominent as an editor and a teacher, activities that have kept him at the centre of our poetry. Moreover, it is precisely at this moment, when we are in danger of discarding these three poets, that we need a reassertion of their relevance. Rosenthal's book reminds us of what we are always inclined to forget: how much a poem can come to. He urges us not to settle for too little, not to be too easily satisfied. Out of his respect for poetry's basic significance to our lives and his refusal to allow critical theorizing to eclipse poems themselves, he is ideally prepared to demonstrate the pertinancy of Yeats, Pound and Eliot in the only way that matters— through their work. We must esteem the intensity of his involvement and his direct but highly discriminating love of that work.

His book offers an accurately bifocal view: Yeats, Pound and Eliot in their poems and in their appositeness to us. He emphasizes their innovativeness, their great Odyssean daring, their ability to exploit and make prominent "the implicitly presentative and improvisatory character of poetry", or structure and process, the structure frequently made of and by the process.

However, he does not blink his poets' weaknesses, their programmatic impulses that sometimes weighed upon their imaginative powers. He prizes them for their part in establishing a new genre, perhaps the most significant in modern times, the poetic sequence, which enables the poet to exercise his whole being. Rosenthal's experience in writing sequences himself, most recently his moving *She*, enables him to respond to them with special rapport. It is something like Elizabethan completeness he is after, a recovery of the total human condition.

Undertaking his journey through the work of his three poets, he proposes that we try to read them "with mind entire", in the way they read their lives and the work of their great predecessors, in the way they wrote their poems. By this proposal Rosenthal means the reverse of a removal from society or life itself. Plunging into Canto 47 as it "directly acts out that communion of past and present which, felt at the pitch of experience is nothing less than our human meaning in process", he enlightens us on the brilliant experimental use Pound made of traditional or archaic materials, on the mystery and the energy he released in bringing Odysseus up to date.

As he proceeds to a larger exhibiting of Pound's dimensionality, Rosenthal rightly says, "Assimilation of life's plentitude into his created world is Pound's artistic purpose". But it is this inclusiveness, when it becomes excessively complicated and defiant of assimilation, that causes trouble. Late in life Pound could confess, "I don't have a one-track mind". *The Cantos'* free-moving tracks, crowded with speeding, loaded trains that cross and threaten to collide, leave many of us stranded. Pound continued, "When I talk it is like an explosion in an art museum, you have to hunt around for the pieces". Rosenthal considers *The Cantos* "a sequence of sequences". Because of the half century in which the work accumulated and because of its improvisatory nature he thinks it absurd—and I agree—to expect the poem to have a single integrity. Rosenthal would, I believe, assent that *The Cantos* are a texture and a contexture rather than a text.

The Cantos constitute a texture, the weaving and reweaving, like Penelope's endless industry, of a most extraordinary poetic mind. Or rather, like Odysseus himself, one twisting in and out and back and forth on its long journey. And Rosenthal is most helpful in following the intricate movements of Pound's imagination. In his examination of the first *A Draft of XVI Cantos* he establishes the pacing of the process and, at the same time, the emergent moments of ecstatic yet completely lucid loveliness; these, like imagism itself, stabilize the poem and focus, even while they underwrite, its riotous energies.

Rosenthal recognizes the "tendentious" material that invades the later *Cantos* and the mechanical that now and then overtakes the organic. However, sympathetic to what he calls their "found poetry", he applauds Pound's "genius in deploying documentary quotations and other data". Pound, it is true, almost persuades us to share his enthusiasm for his sources, as important to him in their original utterance as the unique moments in the languages he admired. Despite his aversion for abstractions, the fact of his documents, their very literalness, saved them from being mere ideas to Pound. Rosenthal reads *The Pisan Cantos* with great, delicate sympathy. So much so that one might feel some uneasiness before statements like "change the names [here Mussolini and company] and a few specific details, and the same passage could be used to memorialize a political martyrdom or defeat in a cause cherished by more of us. . . ." No doubt, but surely the names and the specific details, especially to anyone as sensitive to them as Rosenthal, make a fundamental difference?

With Yeats's "Civil War Sequences" Rosenthal pauses briefly to discuss the poetic sequence itself. He finds it a natural outgrowth of the modern sensibility. Whatever diverse elements it may include, he concludes that "its ordering is finally lyrical, a succession of effects . . . openly improvisational and tentative in structure. . . ." Indeed the lyrical is the core of modern poetry, out of the person of the poet.

But is he, like many recent poets, satisfied with the lyrical alone, or does he make more of it? Narrative of an extended sort is no longer available to most poets; similarly overt statement and conventional forms are recoiled from. Thus the poet has had to develop another resource—an astonishing one—the lyric "writ large", expanded to accommodate a great variety of materials, yet charging them with its emotional energy. The lyrical passages are the islands Odysseus, pausing on, gathers refreshment and supplies from for the next step of his voyage. In short, what we have is a process something like the reverse of that of ambitious older poetry. Rosenthal explores the rich struggle in Yeats's sequences between change (or process) and structure, between the political and the artistic, one pitted against and reinforced by the other, arriving at best at a precarious equipoise or "the transforming conversion of defeat into a kind of power". And for him out of this struggle "Yeats remains our greatest modern architect of structures made up of lightning flashes".

In his chapter "Uncomfortable Choices" Rosenthal suggests that Eliot, falling somewhere between Yeats and Pound, was less rooted than Yeats but, his greater "orbit of association" notwithstanding, "always more deliberate" than Pound. The uncomfortable choice, as Rosenthal sees it, was Eliot's deciding increasingly that his didactic Christian message must be openly expressed; for Rosenthal this tendentiousness mars the work: Eliot ". . . took the risk of bringing the whole baggage of his mind along, cluttering the aesthetic field of action as he went". Certainly the religious and philosophical matters in the poems can constitute a problem. But Eliot's tendency to elaborate his ideas, one might observe, did find great precedence in Dante, who never hesitated to bring the whole baggage of his mind along, especially in the purgatorial cantos. And, of course, Pound stuffed his *Cantos* with all kinds of recalcitrant materials. In his wariness before ideas as ideas, his suspicion of abstractions, Rosenthal seems closer to Pound, despite his actual practice, than to Eliot or Yeats—closer, that is, to the more recent prevailing attitude.

In spite of such reservations Rosenthal, impressed with Eliot's precocity, says that, from the start of his writing, "Everything Eliot does is experimental in some genuine sense''. At the same time he examines Eliot's gradual (sometimes years-long) building of a poem, occasionally out of seemingly discrete, separately published sections. And he admires the depth and extent of feeling such building elicits (and requires) to make a whole poem.

Referring to Eliot's "supreme buffoonery", the consequence of "more feeling than it [Eliot's sensibility] can express directly", Rosenthal, to my surprise, designates Eliot's early "Hamlet and His Problems" his best critical essay. Indeed, with Eliot's own later reservation about it as a comment on *Hamlet* and Shakespeare, and with the many strenuous objections to it from other critics, one might wonder. But Rosenthal's additional references to the essay indicate that by best he means in its reflection on Eliot's own poetry and method. Though Eliot in this essay dismisses—rather contemptuously, it would seem—as immature the impulse that Rosenthal concentrates on, an impulse belonging to ado- lescence. Rosenthal finds it most apt for explaining Eliot's ability to explore a multiplicity of feelings. "Eliot's primary center of reference, as a poet, remains 'the intense feeling, ecstatic or terrible, without an object or exceeding its object' that is the real subject of his *Hamlet* essay and the heart of his poems''. This observation may well contain a penetrating truth about the nature of Eliot's poetry, a respect for the mystery at the heart of our existence. Yet is not Rosenthal ignoring the problem at the base of this awareness of Eliot—one of the chief modern problems, the abyss between our feelings and the world? Deeply re- gretting it, Eliot sought to heal the breach and to recover the oneness of fact and feeling, to reunite our outer and our inner life, by discovering adequate objective correlatives. Here Rosenthal might appear to be applauding the very subjectivity he usually questions.

But it would seem that Eliot did not trust his intense feelings enough. In one of the most interesting portions of his book Rosenthal ponders what *The Waste Land* would have come to had Eliot held onto those feelings and to the poem's original sections deleted at Pound's urging. A very different poem, Rosenthal believes, would have emerged, one closer, in being "much more confessional and vulnerable", to what "a Lowell and a Ginsberg later dared to do. Neither his [Eliot's] nor Pound's taste was ready to be confident about doing so in 1922. . . .'' A different poem *The Waste Land* would certainly have been, but whether better because of its indulging the relaxations recent poets have allowed themselves is, to say the least, debatable. Aside from the question of the deleted sections' quality, might their inclusion not have resulted in a slacker, baggier poem? At the time he submitted the first draft to Pound, Eliot thought *The Waste Land* a collection of poems rather than a whole work. He later said that Pound's editing turned *The Waste Land* "from a jumble of good and bad passages into a poem". Nonetheless, Rosenthal considers *The Waste Land* which we now have a structure with undeveloped potentialities. But he does admit that "Every poem is after all open in the sense that it could be developed further, it could be improved, if only the poet's energies and state of readiness were a trifle beyond their actual state." Improved, yes, but also possibly weakened? One might wonder whether, in his view that Lowell's and Ginsberg's self-exploitation amounted to an improvement, some kind of belief in progress, at least in techniques, is not lurking behind Rosenthal's thinking here.

Be that as it may, for Rosenthal "Eliot never again matched the combined richness, volatility, and dance of voices . . ." of *The Waste Land*. Eliot's plays passed over, Rosenthal adjudges the *Four Quartets* inferior, at best intermittently effective, weakened by their "mechanical parallelism". Also, he thinks them not of "a single prolonged impulse or predicament". With their various settings and occasions one might wonder why they should be or, arguing the opposite, whether an overarching predicament does not in fact subsume them all. He finds them no less deficient in unity than *The Cantos*.

But perhaps asking them to be "a fully integral sequence" is asking too much or rather something other than Eliot intended. They are, after all, four discrete quartets, not one. Obviously the pattern Eliot developed for them was meant to ensure them a shape and containment *The Cantos* lacks. Again, despite his tolerance for the documentary in *The Cantos*, Rosenthal declares the *Four Quartets* cluttered with the making of doctrinal points (Is it that he feels more accord with Pound's "doctrines"?), consequently possessing a boringly slack verse line as well as "prose-dreariness". Whether one accepts this judgment or not, I do agree that ideas, to serve in poetry, must come vibrantly alive, must be felt and must make us feel. And in poets like Lucretius, Dante, Donne, ideas often do live by being ideas. Theirs was the healing of the breach that Eliot desired: a thinking at the fingertips and a feeling with the mind. The opposite of the discontinuity, the radical disunity, which Bayley discovers in Hardy.

In his last chapter, "Continuities: Lessons of the Masters", Rosenthal stresses the three poets' continuing presence. Deftly and briefly, commenting on other poets, mostly more recent ones, from Lowell and Creely to Ashbery and Snyder, he remarks their debt to Yeats, Pound, and Eliot, but their lesser stature for exercising only a small part of the earlier poets' mastery. In one sentence he can summarize: "A good deal of the later Wallace Stevens suffers from overexpanded musing with virtually no intensity, and a fair amount of John Ashbery's writing is an endless proliferation of tones without focus.'' Before the praise recent critics have meted out to the later Stevens, usually at the expense of the earlier, and before the fairly indiscriminate enthusiasm for Ashbery, such reservations are well worth weighing. So are the remarks that follow.

> Openness is hardly an end in itself, even when the sensibility at work is as entranced with itself as in these two poets. Nevertheless, the experiments of Yeats, Pound, and Eliot probably made this problem inevitable with highly gifted poets who have infinite patience and can burn quietly along forever in their low-flickering way.

The reverse, he is confident, is what Yeats, Pound and Eliot were after. However, Rosenthal does not pause to remark the number of critics who prefer complexity, obscurity, prestidigitation to intensity. Nor does he remark the large, if not pervasive, suspicion which many poets, English as well as American, have toward such intensity. They will not be taken in by their own feelings any more than by their age. Even Yeats declared passionate intensity to be the possession, at present, of ''the worst''. Not only the centre, alas, but the circumference cannot hold.

Returning, finally to his initial image of the Odyssean model that Pound employed, Rosenthal accents the past, its use, as a vital presence and reassurance, a source of strength rather than of anxiety. ''The normal poetic position—from a poet's point of view—is that communion with the sensibilities of the past is necessary both to self-location and to learning what it is to explore the hitherto unknown.'' But the normal poetic position does not seem to be so normal today. It is ironical that for almost diametrical reasons many poets and critics concur in distrusting the past. The poets shy away from it out of their gainsaying its worth, its relevancy, and out of their desire to be themselves, wholly here and now.

Rosenthal cites a number of more recent sequences with their like reliance on the poem's speaking personality as its unifying centre (something he seemed to feel Eliot might have relied on more in *The Waste Land*). He finds this inadequate, and also the assumption that ''sheer drifting along, and the variations of theme and feeling time provides, will create structure enough''.

Much as Eliot figures in their work, Rosenthal thinks it surprising that the Black Mountain poets and others should have rejected him. But was it not because of his religion and his politics and the ideas (Rosenthal himself, we have seen, objected to some of them) more and more prominent in Eliot's work? Rosenthal is to be commended for pointing out that Williams, an immense influence on recent poets, was, especially in *Paterson*, much closer to Eliot, Pound and Yeats than he or his followers have recognized. Convincingly, Rosenthal compares elements of *Paterson* Book I with the much-earlier *The Waste Land*. Then he suggests the vast reach of the three poets' influence, and in England the impact of Yeats (not Hardy) on Auden, Empson, Larkin, and Hughes—though not one of these, Rosenthal contends, possesses their model's many-sidedness. But, Rosenthal judiciously concludes, what poets after Yeats and Eliot have done and are doing helps, like more news of Odysseus, to reveal additional facets of the latter's great, still richly living art, helps us also to realize more than ever the breadth of their poems. New poems help us, and so do books of criticism as astute as this one.

II

The Nonsense
of Winters' *Anatomy*

T HERE IS SOMETHING to be said for Winters' critical position; but Winters, as his latest book* copiously illustrates, is not the one to say it. Let me suggest at the outset that Winters, with many other schoolmen, (starting as long ago as *The Treason of the Intellectuals*), has, I believe, overestimated the significance of the intellectual. This exaggeration is, no doubt, not only a perverse flattery, but unwittingly a bit of personal backslapping—belief in one's own position as the most paramount is almost inevitable. Not that the intellectual ought not or could not be a leader; but with our education's depths what they are today, I fear he cannot. Thought, even the loftiest, does percolate down to the masses. But look what happens to it by the time it reaches them. Look what happens to it by the time it reaches litterateurs like Winters.

This book attempts through Henry Adams, Wallace Stevens, T. S. Eliot, and John Crowe Ransom—key presumably to four major attitudes in our times (though actually they lump into one position: Winters' opposition)—to arrive at Winters' own credo. Winters is not so much anatomising as using their dead bodies for posts on which to hang his barbed-wire line. Of distinguished choler, he is strainingly like Samuel Johnson (a critic he regards as the "greatest" in English) in everything except style, wit, and observation. Out of insatiable querulousness and doughty provinciality Winters would make a world order. His tactics nicely recall propagandists who tailor the facts to fit their desires. He most fiercely resents the "determinists," those who believe that a writer cannot escape his time. Winters would substitute his determination, his thundersome insistence on "morality" and the eternal verities. Into the procrustean bed of his beliefs, then, the world must go.

Oddly enough, Winters has browbeaten not a few otherwise acute critics into humble acceptance of him and his. For this reason, among others, I believe that his wellnigh peerless inconsistencies should be exposed. Even in review of this latest book, Cleanth Brooks, in the spring issue of *The Kenyon Review*, can say, "He is perhaps our most logically rigorous critic; he is certainly one of the most intelligent." And a little later: "I suppose one should be grateful for the presence in modern criticism of a powerful corrective force like Winters who is always on

---

* Yvor Winters: *The Anatomy of Nonsense*. New Directions. $3.00.

the alert to pick up the critic who is inconsistent—alive to every *non sequitur*, censorious of every fuzzy term"—except his own! Brooks' commendation harmonises with that of Ransom whom Winters in this book proceeds to pulverise. In his *New Criticism* Ransom also dubbed Winters "The Logical Critic" and declared him "the critic who is best at pouncing upon the structure of a poem." I will try to prove that Winters too often pounces only to destroy.

Not that these critics fail to qualify their applause: Brooks admits that Winters is "cantankerous," "not amiable, not charming, obviously very earnest, and willing to split a hair to any distinguishable degree of fineness." So too he comments on Winters' resolute myopia concerning Eliot and Ransom; still Brooks' respect for this "certainly one of the most intelligent" critics remains steadfast. In fact, Brooks' observations seem to imply an admiration for Winters' very blindspots. "He exhibits all the rancor of a man who has pondered a matter long and carefully, and knows that he is right." Or gathering a little anthology of Winters' critical gambados, Brooks can savor them as instances of Winters' "sheer guts" and "blindsides." "Our most logically rigorous critic [*sic!*]."

Sections I and II of this essay, reviewing general critical principles and Winters' treatment of Henry Adams, have been eliminated.

III. WALLACE STEVENS

Our examination of Winters on Adams has stressed, I believe, not only Winters' inability to read, but also, and more flagrantly, his inability to write. As we turn to Stevens, however, we shall realise with deepening conviction Winters' inability to understand poetry. In prose analyses his derangements appear those of commission and falsification; in poetry, omission and sheerest ignorance. The best or at least most glaring example—here I violate the development of his book to reach at once the climax of Winters' inanity—of his ineptitudes is his brilliant blundering through the second stanza of Stevens' "Le Monocle de Mon Oncle." I quote the stanza for reference:

> A red bird flies across the golden floor.
> It is a red bird that seeks out his choir
> Among the choirs of wind and wet and wing.
> A torrent will fall from him when he finds.
> Shall I uncrumple this much-crumpled thing?
> I am a man of fortune greeting heirs;
> For it has come that thus I greet the spring.
> These choirs of welcome choir for me farewell.
> No spring can follow past meridian.
> Yet you persist with anecdotal bliss
> To make believe a starry connaissance.

Winters summarises:

> The first four lines are incomprehensible, except as description, and the claim of the fifth line is unjustified; the remainder of the stanza, however, displays a combination of bitterness, irony, and imperturbable elegance not unworthy of Ben Jonson.

Interesting, is it not, his yoking of bitterness with imperturbable elegance, not to mention the irony I nowhere see.

Clearly Winters cannot relate the obvious. He does not recognise that the red bird flying across "the golden floor (like Blake's "starry floor") and through the different seasons (choirs to themselves but rigorous challenges to it), that this bird immediately corresponds with the "I." Just as this bird seeks its own choir (its ripeness or spring) and finding it, next meets only, inevitably its deathsong (a torrent), thereby dropping to death beyond our reach; so the "I" also seeks his choir (or heirs). And as with the bird, his spring in welcome bids farewell; for welcome is farewell. Love's consummation is likewise its consuming.

Winters says that the poem "endeavors to treat the subject of love in hedonistic terms and confesses ironically to encountering more than one difficulty." It confesses difficulties but hardly "ironically." Winters confuses polish, balance, earnest ease with irony. Unless you are carefully crude (though he resents "roughing up" a verse, as we shall see), you are guilty of irony. And the poem achieves much more than such mere confession. It concludes that though love is variously trying, now as age increases, through love's very shrivelings, the "I" appreciates love's substantiality amid all its flutterings (one shade among the many).

Certainly stanza six gives the open lie to Winters' claim:

> If men at forty will be painting lakes
> The ephemeral blues must merge for them in one,
> The basic slate, the universal hue.
> There is a substance in us that prevails.

Here, I believe, Stevens is voicing his belief in the permanence of the universe, and so of us, part of it. As young-men we can chase all the maneuvers, important and trivial, of love; then hedonism can be a fulltime allout occupation. But such athletic business must be reserved to young-men. Let those at forty pursue the universal hue.

Thus in another poem that Winters neatly hops over, the well-known "The Emperor of Ice-Cream," Stevens concludes with the extremely tantalising "Let be be finale of seem"—again, I think, a thoroughgoing denial of the hedonism Winters charges. Whether we take this abundant ambiguity to mean (1) let what is be the end of seeming (its death) or (2) let what is be the grand finale of seeming (imagination's final, finest product must be the world as it is)—whether we accept either, clearly Stevens is in no way evading reality and hiding behind the shutters of trickery. For all his elegance Stevens is no "fop of fancy." He knows that reality and imagination are not only inextricably intertwined, but in the greatest minds one. But Winters is not basically concerned with Stevens' grip on the world as it is. It is Stevens' manner that mortally offends him—Stevens' ease and grace, his failure to show the wrinkles of worry and wear.

Here we encounter a major problem—the value of "nonsense." "Metaphors of a Magnifico" is scarcely "wilful nonsense," though assuredly Stevens willed the poem's effect. The nonsense, as Winters means it, is, I believe, purely and wilfully Winters. Stevens' nonsense, in his skilled use of it, is consequential indeed.

Thus in "The Revolutionists Stop for Orangeade" Winters is unable in his sobriety to appreciate the potency of the clown, the tear of laughter (as the poem implies)

> Hang a feather by your eye
> Nod and look a little sly,
> This must be the vent of pity,
> Deeper than a truer ditty
> Of the real that wrenches,
> Of the quick that's wry.

and the vastness one can approach and "get away with" under the guise of buffoonery. Stevens' elegance is a similarly successful mask. Like a Sidney, Stevens knows that courtly grace can cloak earnestness. As Stevens says in his latest book, "Life's nonsense pierces us with strange relations." How can Winters, submerged in seriousness, distorted by his fanaticism, realise that in nonsense often the greatest depths reside and even stand revealed? Thus Shakespeare's "fools," professional and otherwise, are frequently the profoundest witnesses of life. As Theseus remarks,

> The lunatic, the lover, and the poet
> Are of imagination all compact.

a realisation that Stevens with his sauntering profundity has not been slow to use. And what of Shakespeare's spoofing about poetry? Does this also offend Mr. Winters? He does not see that the tragic and otherwise intolerable can, not occasionally, be handled only by the superficially flip or casual. Thus it is in poetry that we can accept and enjoy situations and utterances in themselves too terrible: "a tale told by an idiot." In fact, even as poetry makes terror's expression possible, it can augment the terror. In his resentment of wit, humor, and nonsense, Winters seems to be making a plea for Romanticism and, even more painfully plain, Victorian earnestness.

Similarly Winters misconstrues "A High-Toned Old Christian Woman" which opens: "Poetry is the supreme fiction, madame" ("supreme fiction" becoming part of Stevens' latest title *Notes toward a Supreme Fiction*). Winters forensically denies Stevens' statements by paraphrasing the poem: " . . . we learn that the 'moral law' is not necessary as a frame-work for art, but that 'the opposing law' will do as well." Winters, a non-Christian, is again assuming that the moral law of Christianity is the only one.

We might find point in quoting Aristotle's distinction between a poet and a historian here: "The difference between a poet and a historian is this: the historian relates what has happened, the poet what could happen." Poetry is a human laboratory in which the poet can witness all the possibilities of life. Not a few of Shake-speare's main characters are not men as they are or men as they ought to be, but men as they would be if they were what they deeply wish to be. I will discuss this freedom further, however, when I reach Ransom. Stevens may simply be suggest-ing that in poetry as "in the planetary scene" many ways of living are "proper" and "holy"—one not necessarily better or worse than another. Anent this poem Winters compares Stevens "final doctrine" with that of Winters' favorite irritant Poe whom he quotes:

> It may be, indeed, that here this sublime end is, now and then, at-tained in fact. We are often made to feel with a shivering delight, that from an earthly harp are stricken notes which *cannot* have been un-familiar to the angels.

"Poe's statement," Winters observes, "is made, of course, in the tone of saccharine sentimentality which is Poe's nearest approach to sincerity." No doubt it is the "of course" that proves Poe's constant insincerity. Obviously Winters is mistaking a fairly common 19th century rhetorical tone for sentimentality. But he dare not brook the idea for a moment that earth may be our Eden and the only heaven (tormented as it is) we as men can know. Even our notion of heaven and angels derives directly from the earth and our experience of it.

> Stevens' statement [Winters continues] is made ironically, but one should not be misled by this fact. For though Stevens is ridiculing himself and his artists, he is ridiculing his old Christian woman, the representative of the moralistic point of view, even more severely.

The "ridicule," I maintain, much like the "irony," is little more than Winters' imagining; he has a fertile eye for bogeys and insults. Stevens, he goes on, "is offering his opinion as more nearly tenable than hers, notwithstanding the fact that he cannot offer his opinion with real seriousness." Not possessing Winters' divina-tory powers, I am unable to see why Stevens cannot be offering his opinion "with real seriousness." From these judgments Winters leaps to his pet conclusion: Stevens' attitude "eliminates the possibility of the rational understanding of ex-perience." Again I must remark Winters' refusal to admit the limitations of the mind *per se*. He does not see how superior we as whole men are in our living than in our single thinking (if we could sever mind from the rest of us). Nor does he appreciate how little ideas often amount to, their transiency and foolishness from one time to another. Could we expect him to realise that a writer might use them simply to portray people who do believe in them?

Thus, for all his bullishness, Winters breaks the jar in "Anecdote of the Jar," transparently to buttress his case. The jar is, as he says, "vulgar and sterile" and therefore does domesticate the wilderness, but not because it is "symbolic of the human intellect." On the contrary, the jar (and the word should tell with its "gray" and "bare") represents for Stevens, I believe, modern standardisation, un-beauty, hardly intellect at its best. Rather than converting the wilderness into powerful human beauty, like signboards the ugly jar conceals and vitiates the wilder-ness. Such control is destructive.

Winters' insistence on Stevens' hedonism, or his belief in the primacy of the feelings and confusion, leads Winters to amusing parallels. Stevens in his roué's desire for always stronger sensations like Poe, also always chasing after bigger and better thrills, found adumbration in Poe's fatuous inference: "The desire of the new is an element of the soul. The most exquisite pleasures grow dull in repetition." The source of this statement, I suspect, is what frets Winters. Similar sentiments in the mouth of Winters' admiration Sam Johnson, I equally suspect, would not distress Winters a fraction as much. According to Johnson, "The great source of pleasure is variety. Uniformity must tire at last, though it be uniformity of excellence." Once again I ask, shall we describe the world as it is (as much as we can) or as we wish it to be?

But I challenge not only Winters' saddling of Stevens with "romantic irony" to the exclusion of humor or the ability not to take oneself too seriously, but also his assuming that Stevens is his characters, particularly Crispin. Stevens may have thought of Crispin as one of his masks or personæ (so Eliot with Sweeney); Stevens may have flirted with the prospect of a life exclusively of action (a mask that constantly fascinated Yeats), but these are hardly reasons to decide that Stevens' poetry is bankrupt. Do we disparage Browning for the characters in his monologues? Was he the Bishop Ordering, Andrea del Sarto, and Caliban? And suppose Crispin was a reflection of Stevens' feelings at the time of the poem's composition. Do we denounce Shakespeare for his dark comedies, or Hopkins for his terrible sonnets?

Thus Stevens' longest work, "The Comedian as the Letter C,"* Winters interprets as an example of Stevens' impasse: having driven feeling as far as he can, Stevens must now decide between silence or incomprehensibility. "The Comedian as the Letter C" Winters considers the major battleground of this conflict. A major battleground it is, but not of the conflict Winters names. Rather it grapples with the growing realisation that the world and its simple things are poems enough, "The veritable *ding an sich*"; their interpretation is what a poet should busy himself with. It is the age-old conflict between fancy and imagination, the turning toward "Let be be the finale of seem." Stevens is making a bid here for the very matter Winters thinks he himself has been yammering for! "all the arrant stinks / That helped him round his rude esthetic out."

> It made him see how much
> Of what he saw he never saw at all.
> He gripped more closely the essential prose
> As being, in a world so falsified,
> The one integrity for him, the one
> Discovery still possible to make,
> To which all poems were incident, unless
> That prose should wear a poem's guise at last.

---

*Winters says, "the significance of the title, I regret to say, escapes both my learning and my ingenuity." Obviously "C" equals Crispin.

For Crispin could no longer

> be content with counterfeit,
> With masquerade of thought, with hapless words
> That must belie the racking masquerade.

Turning out dreams, he is "tiptoe cozener" no more, "preferring text to gloss," "veracious page on page, exact." Crispin even reaches the conclusion that life without poems may be joy and imagination enough; then life becomes the poem.

> He first, as realist, admitted that
> Whoever hunts a matinal continent
> May, after all, stop short before a plum
> And be content and still be realist.
> The words of things entangle and confuse.
> The plum survives its poems.

Winters the inkblood, who seems to think that life exists for literature's sake (as I will attempt to show: literature is his religion), cannot help being horrified by such conjecture. How dare he even think: "For realists, what is is what should be."

Now Winters flouts "the fallacy that the poet achieves salvation by being, in some way, intensely of and expressive of his country." Winters must not forget his eternal verities. The poet does not achieve salvation; but by looking home (so Chaucer and Joyce and Yeats), the poet can become universal, even to the intensity of his superficial provincialisms. Such doing is the very practice Winters earlier seemed to insist on: the truth of our own experience and the value of using it. He reviled Adams for failing to recognise the validity and reasonableness of at least his own experience.

In that it finds divinity enough in the quotidian "The Comedian as the Letter C" plainly answers "The Man Whose Pharynx Was Bad." Again, in the man with the pharnyx Winters assumes that the poem is the whole truth about Stevens. Winters calls the poem "a statement" of Stevens' growing "boredom ["the boredom which eventually overtakes the man who seeks for excitement instead of understanding"] which is both extreme and explicit." On another page Winters says that Stevens uses the landscape in the poem "to symbolize his own frustration." Winters will not permit a poet variousness or the airing of doubts, even when as in the bad-pharynxed man, the poet can make melody out of the malady of the daily. I wonder if Winters' every moment of every day is gay and poem? His poems would hardly say so.

> The poet [Winters interprets] has progressed in this poem to the point at which the intensity of emotion possible in actual human life has become insipid . . . the figurative opposites of summer and winter here offered suggest the opposites of the moral and the anti-moral which appear in "A High-Toned Old Christian Woman."

The interpretation, I submit, is unconditional highclass poppycock. In the first place, as the title suggests, one might break through if strong enough. In the second place, the "intensity" has not become insipid; the weather is and the man's ability to pierce it to the everlasting freshness. The man admits that he is caught in surfaces, locked in "an icy haze." But he has not lost awareness in winter of its "final slate" persisting through all winter's purples. This final slate reminds us, of course, of

> The basic slate, the universal hue.
> There is a substance in us that prevails.

emphasised in "Le Monocle de Mon Oncle." As for "the figurative opposites of summer and winter here offered," I think it should be by now incontrovertibly clear that Stevens recognises the seasons as centrally one.

Winters, I suggest, will not permit Stevens variousness since it might weaken Winters' campaign. But at the end of this chapter on Stevens, Winters concludes: "His ideas have remained essentially unchanged for more than a quarter of a century." No doubt Winters is correct if we agree to strip away or blink all the differences. Thus all great poets are the same if we pluck them of all differences. But what naked unrecognisable birds our bards become at that point! On such a flimsy premise Winters dismisses the four books following the first. He does not (dare not?) even mention the next in order, *Ideas of Order*. For the very title (after all Winters' bluster about order), might prove a little disconcerting. Here Stevens (actually preoccupied as he is with the "blessed rage for order") directly handles Winters' todo: our experience for the wisdom it can teach us. Winters' statement on *The Man with the Blue Guitar*, "merely a jingling restatement of the old theme of the severance between the rational understanding and the poetic imagination" (with Winters "things as they are" and the "rational understanding" —sanity?—are synonymous) is exactly half of the book's contents. The more significant half, the first group giving the book its title, "deals" as Stevens says, "with the incessant conjunction between things as they are and things imagined."

> I am a native in the world
> And think in it as a native thinks,
>
> Gesu, not native of a mind
> Thinking the thoughts I call my own,
>
> Native, a native in the world
> And like a native think in it.
> * * * * * *
> And things are as I think they are
> And say they are on the blue guitar.

[Let be be the finale of seem.]

In addition, Stevens' latest *Parts of a World* and *Notes toward a Supreme Fiction* prove not only that his world has not "remained essentially unchanged for more than a quarter of century," but that, on the contrary, it has come more and more to grips with the world as it is.

Finally, coming to the center of the Stevens' essay, "Sunday Morning," by way of "Stars at Tallapoosa," I maintain that Winters botches the latter unequivocally. It is *not* trying to pull the intellect and the emotions apart; only a thickthumbs like

Winters would think or try to do so. Nothing, I believe, could be remoter from the truth than his by now creaky claim

> As far as I can penetrate this poem, I judge that it postulates the absolute severance of the intellectual and the emotional: the lines between the stars are the lines of pure intellect; the earth-lines and the sea-lines represent the non-intellectual experience (loosely speaking) of daily human life. Both modes of experience have beauty and should be pursued, but they are disparate and unrelated to each other; and it follows, although this is not stated in the poem, that the intellectual experience, since it bears no relationship to the rest of our life and hence is in no way useful, is valuable simply for the independent emotional excitement which one may derive from it.

At least Winters owns to "looseness" in his interpretation and Stevens' recognition of the beauty of "both modes of experience." Not only does Stevens recognise their beauty, but, Winters to the extreme contrary, he demonstrates in this poem the oneness of the mind and the emotions at best: sense coupled with sensuousness, one meaningless and lost without the other. For Stevens the star-lines are the very ones (verses) that Stevens wants and believes we are central to, mind and body (*univ*erse).

> Making recoveries of young nakedness
> And the lost vehemence the midnights hold

is what Winters particularly fears. Beware of life, especially fresh vibrant life.

On "Sunday Morning," "probably the greatest American poem of the twentieth century," Winters wages his mightiest campaign. Winters, I would expect, must immediately like this poem for its religious occupation.

> The second stanza asks the question which provides the subject of the poem; it asks what divinity this woman may be thought to possess as a recompense for her ultimate surrender to death."

The second stanza says,

> Why should she give her bounty to the dead?
> What is divinity if it can come
> Only in silent shadows and in dreams?
> Shall she not find in comforts of the sun,
>
>   *   *   *   *   *   *
>
> Things to be cherished like the thought of heaven?
> Divinity must live within herself.

Surely the stanza has little to do with the woman's "ultimate surrender to death." Rather she wonders why she should recognise and revere the dead, "silent Palestine / Dominion of the blood and sepulchre," and established ancient shadowy religion (the god of these dead), especially if divinity appear "only in silent shadows and in dreams." For the living life must serve. Thus the woman seeks comfort in the multifarious beauty of the earth and in herself: divinity lives within herself and the world around her, the immortal now, not in the dead past or theology. In the third stanza Stevens suggests that *we* blooded and bodied Jove (god).

Shall our blood fail? Or shall it come to be
The blood of paradise? And shall the earth
Seem all of paradise that we shall know?
The sky will be much friendlier then than now,
A part of labor and a part of pain,
And next in glory to enduring love,
Not this dividing and indifferent blue.

In the fourth stanza [Winters criticises] . . . the protagonist objects
to the concept which has been offered her; she states that the beauties
of this life are transient and that she longs to believe in a Paradise beyond them. The remainder of the stanza, and the greater part of it, is the
poet's reply: in a passage of great rhetorical power, he denies the possibility of Paradise, at the same time that he communicates through the
feeling of his language a deep nostalgic longing to accept the ideas which
he is rejecting.

Winters is one with the many nostalgics for God, common in our day, scholarly men
who, confessing that they are no Christians, look longingly after the spiritual comforts of the past. Principally because Stevens describes the religious ideas brilliantly,
Winters discovers his own nostalgia in the brilliance. But let us look at the fourth
stanza:

She says, "I am content when wakened birds,
Before they fly, test the reality
Of misty fields, by their sweet questionings;
But when the birds are gone, and their warm fields
Return no more, where, then, is paradise?"
There is not any haunt of prophecy,
Nor any old chimera of the grave,
Neither the golden underground, nor isle
Melodious, where spirits gat them home,
Nor visionary south, nor cloudy palm
Remote on heaven's hill.

[here Stevens points out how of all the religions man has made there is none]

                          that has endured
As April's green endures; or will endure
Like her remembrance of awakened birds,
Or her desire for June and evening, tipped
By the consummation of the swallow's wings.

The earth is Paradise, permanent even in its moment of loveliness; for beauty is
forever in the flesh. So "Peter Quince" says,

Beauty is momentary in the mind—
The fitful tracing of a portal;
But in the flesh it is immortal.

At this point the woman yearns for "imperishable bliss"; and Stevens explains
the value and necessity of death.

In the sixth stanza the poet considers an hypothetical paradise, and since he can imagine it only in terms of a projection of the good life as the hedonist understands the good life, he deduces that paradise would become tedious and insipid: we have in this stanza the first sharp vision of the ennui which is to obsess the later work of the poet and which is ultimately to wreck his talent.

Indeed, as we are now constructed, paradise would grow "tedious and insipid." See Milton's. Man and woman probably had to get out by any hook or crookedness. The monotony overpowered them and perhaps God too who sent Satan to relieve them! Even as our winters are a biting beauty of their own, they strengthen and salt away our summers. As for the "ennui," Stevens is simply expressing our need for change, even for death. I repeat Samuel Johnson's observation: "The great source of pleasure is variety. Uniformity must tire at last, though it be uniformity of excellence." Winters cannot see that we, hardly "ripe" for a screwed-tight paradise, would be even more unhappy in its confines than we may be where we are now. In his *Parts of a World* in "The Poems of Our Climate," considering an utterly pure world, a paradise, Stevens remarks:

> There would still remain the never-resting mind,
> So that one would want to escape, come back
> To what had been so long composed.
> The imperfect is our paradise.

The imperfect, except as it means the past, can do nothing but infuriate Winters with his stalwart distemper. To a considerable extent at least we have witnessed how rigorously unreasonable Winters is in the pursuit of his reasonable ends. For his wooden insistence on morality above all, he cannot see the trees of poetry. Nor does he know that reason, restrictively as he would use it, can also become a blind tyrant. But I wonder what it is he abides by other than himself? Though everyone agrees (including Winters) that Winters is a thoroughgoing moralist, no one pauses to question or define the basis of his morality. It is not, he avers, Christianity. At most it is the "practical" end of Aquinas: what man's senses and intelligence, meeting experience, have "always" told him. In brief, it is a belief in this earth and its permanence. In very brief, how except for its medieval hauteur and crabbedness does this morality differ from Stevens' socalled "hedonism"? But Winters identifies his crabbedness with the traditional which, present in Stevens' early work, "enables Stevens' talent to function at its highest power; but it is not only unjustified and unsupported by Stevens' explicit philosophy, it is at odds with that philosophy." We must be traditional not only in form but in attitude and content. Such belief smacks a little too much of ancestor-worship. What did the poor writers (innovators!) do who established the tradition? What did they ape? God-forsaken Stevens, alas,

> is not like those occasional poets of the Renaissance who appear in some measure to be influenced by a pagan philosophy, but who in reality take it up as a literary diversion at the same time that they are beneath the surface immovably Christian. Stevens is released from all the restraints of Christianity, and is encouraged by all the modern orthodoxy of Romanticism.

We end where we started. Winters preempts all "restraints" for Christianity—either you are a Christian or you are immoral. What did all the wretched Greeks and Romans do? What does wretched Winters do? For he has disavowed Christianity. Or as in his use of Aquinas, for him do the restraints exist apart from the religion—ethics without belief?

IV. T. S. ELIOT

IF WINTERS' grotesqueries of interpretation, as presented in Part I, have seemed surprising, his fumbling of other men's criticism is even more incredible. His treatment of Eliot is perhaps the most precise illustration. Winters has somewhat anticipated and crystallised the growing tendenz away from Eliot. Now that the epigone have entered their physical maturity, chafing at their former submissiveness, they must trample their champion under. I am not suggesting that Eliot is superior to criticism. Elsewhere I have sought to discover his nuclear confusion. But most of the arraignments, as exampled in Winters' practice, endeavor to injure, I maintain, Eliot's more substantial work. Again we will pursue Winters' sleights-of-head, not only to expose his egregiousness, but also to attempt to restore some of Eliot's more trenchant insights and, simultaneously, to mirror the tendenz I mentioned.

Winters begins his inquisition with a quotation from Eliot's "The Function of Criticism" which I repeat for reference:

> No exponent of criticism . . . has, I presume, ever made the preposterous assumption that criticism is an autotelic activity. I do not deny that art may be affirmed to serve ends beyond itself; but art is not required to be aware of these ends, and indeed performs its functions, whatever they may be, according to various theories of value, much better by indifference to them. Criticism, on the other hand, must always profess an end in view, which, roughly speaking, appears to be the elucidation of works of art and the correction of taste.

Immediately Winters detects a basic fissure or "problem."

> How . . . can an artist perform a function better for not knowing what it is? Is Eliot assuming an automatic, or unconscious art, an art which is an extreme form of romantic mysticism?

Eliot did *not* say "unknowing"; he said "indifferent." His meaning—a commonplace one, eminently acceptable—is clear: art need not pursue didactic or political ends. Though it may serve them, purposeful attempts to do so frequently hamper the art, so thwart the service to additional ends. Nor did Eliot say that art is unconscious about itself; he said indifferent to ends other than itself. If the art is "good," it will satisfy the moral with grace. We teach best by avoiding the chalky atmosphere of pedagogy. Eliot warns in the same essay: "There is a tendency . . . to decry this critical toil of the artist; to propound the thesis that the great artist is an unconscious artist, unconsciously inscribing on his banner the words Muddle Through."

Unperturbed, Winters continues his questions.

Are we to assume that there is no art in expository prose let us say in Johnson's Introduction to his dictionary? Or merely that there is no art in that branch of expository prose which we call literary criticism?

Of course there may be art in expository prose, but expository prose cannot be a work of art. If it is creation, patently criticism is no longer criticism. Winters fortunately forgets that later in the same paper Eliot suggests:

> If so large a part of creation is really criticism, is not a large part of what is called "critical writing" really creative? If so, is there not creative criticism in the ordinary sense? The answer seems to be that there is no equation. I have assumed as axiomatic that a creation, a work of art, is autotelic; and that criticism is about something other than itself [Winters quotes this last sentence, but neglects its ambience]. Hence you cannot fuse creation with criticism as you can fuse criticism with creation. The critical activity finds its highest, its true fulfilment in a kind of union with creation in the labour of the artist.

Exactly as others misunderstanding—most recently Eliseo Vivas in the Winter, 1944, *American Bookman*—Winters insists that Eliot's "objective correlative" reflects his tendency "to assume the emotion as initial." The reverse is true; for Eliot the emotion is consequence, the effect of the cause the writer must carefully pose. Winters would have Eliot say precisely what he already has—namely, that things produce emotion. But an artist must work somewhat in reverse. Knowing what effects he wishes to engender—or does Winters demand inspiration, "romantic mysticism?"—the artist must set up objects to engender these emotions in his audience.

Winters, however, declares the objective correlative "a reversal of the normal processes of understanding human experience, and a dangerous reversal." On the contrary, the ability to employ this necessary device requires intense human insight and detachment antipodal to the romantic manner Winters thinks he is deploring. He refuses to regard art as a deliberate craft, a strategy. Though things determine our thoughts and feelings, an artist working in reverse—that of mirrors—cannot afford romantic seizures. Winters is confusing art with life, creating with the "normal processes."

But Eliot, for some unexpressed reason, "is unable to adhere to his position"—an additional witness to Winters' remarkable talent for combining creation with criticism. How does Eliot betray his defection?

In the same essay—indeed on the same page—he writes:

> "Hamlet is up against the difficulty that his disgust is occasioned by his mother, but that his mother is not an adequate equivalent for it; his disgust envelops and exceeds her. It is thus a feeling which he cannot understand. . . ."

Winters properly elides the rest of the quotation: ". . . he cannot objectify it, and it therefore remains to poison life and obstruct action. None of the possible actions can satisfy it." How this utterance violates Eliot's position I cannot remotely say. Eliot maintains that because Hamlet has no objective correlative, no cause or reason for his emotion, the play is unrooted in tangibles and fails. Hamlet has no background of object or image to move and mirror his emotion, so define it. And Shakespeare failed him in presenting the emotion without the motive. "Now finding an 'objective correlative' for an emotion," Winters goes on, "is not the same thing as understanding it: to understand it we must know and correctly judge its motive." Hamlet did *not* know his motive. Had he been able to discover the correlative, Hamlet could have known and correctly judged the motive. In a sense, the correlative is the motive. But once more Winters is artfully confusing audience and artist and, a further complication, the character in the work. More, he is blunting the divergence of attitude in the lyric and in the drama.

Then he adduces a section of the Lancelot Andrewes essay as a "more explicit" instance of Eliot's inconsistency: I repeat the section:

> Andrewes' emotion is purely contemplative; it is not personal, it is wholly evoked by the object of contemplation, to which it is adequate; his emotion is wholly contained in and explained by its object. . . . Donne is a 'personality' in a sense in which Andrewes is not: his sermons, one feels, a 'means of self-expression.' He is constantly finding an object which shall be adequate to his feelings: Andrewes is wholly absorbed in the object and therefore responds with the adequate emotion.

Winters comments:

> . . . Andrewes is praised because he adheres to my principles, whereas Donne is blamed because he adheres to those of Eliot. Eliot does not explain his self-contradiction, nor does he give any evidence that he is aware of it.

Winters, I believe, is obscuring Eliot's intentions. First of all, if we are to be honest to Eliot, he is discussing sermons or morality (the "normal processes"), not art. Second, the piece is Eliot on impersonality again. Winters has shifted focus: Eliot is attacking Donne because of the opacity of his personality. The greatest writers are clean windows through which the world clearly shines; the romantics are generally stainedglass windows *for* which the world shines. Eliot is complimenting Andrews for suppressing his personality in the face of his object. Donne, on the other hand, permits and encourages his personality to appear, obstructing the religious experience. He who loses himself shall find himself. Andrewes is concerned with his object; Donne with his reaction to the object. Thus he shifts from object to object in a futile effort to appease his personality. Such hotspurrish personality is not to be denied, and would be restless even in heaven. By its very strength it denies the world and itself. So a Milton and his Satan; so a Donne, and an Eliot. By their prides humility is their hunger.

"The theory of the 'objective correlative' rests," Winters penetrates, "on the assumption that the poet is trying to express an emotion, not on the theory that he is trying to understand it." Eliot scarcely says so, any more than he asserts the "primacy of the emotion." His words are: "The only way of expressing emotion in the form of art is by finding an 'objective correlative.' . . ." "The only way of expressing emotion," if such expression is desired, is hardly the same thing as saying emotion is the only thing to be expressed!

Exhaustless, Winters takes Eliot up for the rank heresy of observing in his "Shakespeare and the Stoicism of Seneca" that the poet "is not necessarily interested in the thought itself." Winters wonders:

> And if the emotion is to be considered as motivated by the thought, what are we to think of the poet who can express such emotion when he is not 'interested in the thought itself?' Furthermore, how can such emotion be expressed except in terms of the motivating thought unless we are to falsify it utterly? And how can it be precise unless the motivating thought is precise?

Winters persists in confusing the artist with his art, which, apparently, must always be intense personal expression. Winters is incapable of seeing that a writer often uses ideas he may have little or no personal sympathy with, as a Shakespeare or a Chaucer, desiring to reproduce sundry people who do believe in and live by (or at least express themselves through) such ideas. For, artistically, ideas in themselves are minor, important only as they embody people. Winters, believing in permanent values, can hardly brook such an idea. But as Eliot says in the same essay, on the same page, a Shakespeare is not interested in the thought for itself. Shakespeare

> . . . was occupied with turning human actions into poetry. I would suggest that none of the plays of Shakespeare has a 'meaning,' although it would be equally false to say that a play of Shakespeare is meaningless.

For as far as attitudes of philosophies were concerned, Shakespeare "used all of these things, for dramatic ends." When Winters asks, how can emotion "be precise unless the motivating thought is precise," he disregards once more the fierce disinterest the artist enjoys. One can be precise about a thought without owning or believing in it. If not, study of civilizations, philosophies, and religions other than our own, would be ridiculous.

Eliot, considering Shakespeare and Dante, indulges the rashness that an artist's thoughts are incidental to his time. "Anti-intellectual and deterministic," Winters storms. "We may observe from this that the quality of a writer's thought is at once enforced upon him and is irrelevant to the quality of his work." It is the treatment of the thought that matters, how dramatically he incarnates it. Thus we can delight in arts whose thoughts themselves no longer vitally concern us; by artistic treatment humanity is still in them.

But Eliot in this very essay anticipated writers of Winters' stripe—partial reason, no doubt, for Winters' pique:

> The people who think that Shakespeare thought, are always people who are not engaged in writing poetry, but who are engaged in thinking, and we all like to think that great men were like ourselves.

As Eliot has it, "In truth, neither Shakespeare nor Dante did any real thinking—that was not their job." Both borrowed freely. Tolstoy was right in denying Shakespeare originality; it is not his "philosophy," but his understanding and realisation of human beings that endears him to us. And he used commonplaces, *their* commonplaces, to contain them. "I doubt whether belief proper enters into the activity of a great poet, *qua* poet"—that is, in the performance of his art. He may have whatever private thoughts he cares to, but as an artist he rises above them to the self-forgetting, the objectivity of creation.

The absurdities accumulate. Mightily Winters scoffs at Eliot's "distinguishing between Dante *qua* Dante and Dante *qua* poet. Anyone who can take this sort of thing seriously is welcome to do so." We should thank Winters for his rare tolerance. But clearly poets as men and poets as poets *are* different individuals. At their best in their writing they can attain a peace, a clarity, a power they may seldom know in their lives. But such ideas, Winters assures us, evaporate before Eliot's "mystical determinism." How shall we expect Winters to understand that we are inevitably the children of our age. Winters in his pulling away from it is shaped by it; Joyce in his upheaval from Jesuitism became what he did. But our art depends on us; and to an extent our age too; the molding is mutual. As for our art, regardless of what material we use, if we can fuse it emotionally, it becomes important.

> It is possible . . . to admire a poem deeply [Winters admits] without wholly understanding it; but such admiration must rest on an understanding at least imperfect, and the idea that this admiration is adequate as compared with that which comes with full understanding is mere nonsense. . . . If the meaning is important in the creation of the poem, at any rate, it is foolish to suppose that one can dispense with it in reading the poem or that the poet did not take his meaning seriously.

More nonsense. Where does Eliot say that the admiration for a poem is "adequate"? On the contrary, in the very essay Winters is analysing, Eliot concludes:

> My point is that you cannot afford to *ignore* Dante's philosophical and theological beliefs, or to skip the passages which express them most clearly; but that on the other hand you are not called upon to believe them yourself. . . . You are not called upon to believe what Dante believed . . . but you are called upon more and more to understand it.

After declaring for belief to appreciate Dante's "final vision of beatitude," Winters shortly turns on himself. Looking at Stevens' "Sunday Morning" again, Winters pontificates: "It is no more necessary that one be a hedonist in order to enjoy this particular poem than that one be a murderer in order to enjoy Macbeth." The parallelism is hardly accidental on Winters' part! Attacking Emerson's "The Problem"— hedonism presumably since pantheistic—Winters cannot understand Emerson's identification of man with nature. Nor can he realise that poets (so men) at their best are free, momentarily immortal, Eden-dwelling, conversing intimately with the beasts and the birds and the saintly trees—free of the drudgeries that stand between us and understanding. So en rapport do they become with the thing they view, they hardly know they are.

> If we could force ourselves [Winters believes] to see what Emerson meant, and refuse to be misled by the traditional associations of the language when it is considered fragmentarily, then the poem, it seems to me, would be damaged past remedy. Of course we can never quite do this; the traditional associations are there, and they keep the poem alive in a

marginal and unsatisfactory way, but nevertheless alive, and this is true of much similar poetry.

In other words, the poem is alive because we do not understand it!

Similarly Winters jumps on Blake whose "philosophy resembles that of Emerson, except that it is not pantheistic[!]" Blake's "Introduction to the Songs of Experience," Winters insists, "rests on a precise inversion not only of Christian mythology, which perhaps does not matter, but of Christian morality as well." Here we have reached the hob of Winters' concern and belief. As he splits Aquinas from his faith, so Winters accepts Christian morality without its root in Christian mythology. Amazingly, he suggests that we may reverse the poem's meaning: ". . . we may reasonably take the poem in that condition of generality and not trouble ourselves about the difficulties of Blake's philosophy until we actually trip on them." Now, Winters believes that we need not know the poet's meanings, let alone agree with it! Abruptly, then, Winters tries to regain himself: ". . . the thought is of the greatest importance as a part of the poem itself."

Eliot, when he knows what he is doing, Winters admits, reprehends determinism. He quotes from Eliot's "The Function of Criticism":

> The critic, one would suppose, if he is to justify his existence, should endeavor to discipline his personal prejudices and cranks—tares to which we are all subject—and compose his differences with as many of his fellows as possible, in the common pursuit of true judgment.

Winters, sensibly enough, neglects to quote the next sentence:

> When we find that quite the contrary prevails, we begin to suspect that the critic owes his livelihood to the violence and extremity of his opposition to other critics, or else to some trifling oddities of his own with which he contrives to season the opinions which men already hold, and which out of vanity or sloth they prefer to maintain.

Instead Winters stretches the quotation to include a defence of an "absolute norm." So also, strategically, he skirts a later declaration in this essay:

> . . . to those who obey the inner voice . . . nothing that I can say about criticism will have the slightest value. For they will not be interested in the attempt to find any common principles for the pursuit of criticism. Why have principles, when one has the inner voice?

Winters would inflate his inner voice into such eternal principles and vice versa, just as Eliot's recent religious supernaturalism suggests conversion to the inner voice. Actually Winters and Eliot enjoy a tight sodality of idea. Whether it be reason or religion, both are not far from Babbitt's ridiculed Inner Check brought out, "revealed." Winters' chief resentment of Eliot is that he is not Winters or, better, that Eliot beat him to the draw of ideas Winters would claim as his own. He is a schism not for differences, but for temperament. To paraphrase Eliot, "In Eliot's beginning is Winters' end."

What Winters, in sermonic anger and fear, is accusing Eliot of is corruption of the young and the feeble-minded; Eliot is a modern Socrates. So Winters quotes Eliot's own words against him.

> No sensible author, in the midst of something he is trying to write, can stop to consider whether it is going to be romantic or the opposite. At the moment when one writes, one is what one is, and the damage of a lifetime, and of having been born into an unsettled society, cannot be repaired at the moment of composition.

Caustically Winters comments:

> At the moment when one writes, one is what one is: one has, in other words, no power over that moment; one must surrender to one's feelings and one's habits at that moment if one is to achieve sincerity.

Eliot means nothing like Winters' interpretation. But at this juncture we touch one of their few fundamental disparities. According to Eliot: "in one's prose reflections one may be legitimately occupied with ideals, whereas in the writing of verse one can only deal with actuality." Thus he ascribes the mediocrity of most religious verse to its "pious insincerity." Winters, on the other hand, advocates poetry as a vehicle of ideals and idealism. Eliot is thinking of lyrical or personally reflective verse, and is objecting to the pious insincerity of pretending to think, feel, be what one is not. Of course, here for a moment Eliot himself is taken in by what he has warned against, confusing art with religion and morality. He sounds here very much like the Winters good saltpillar of society Cummings capsulely captured, the pillar who "respects artists if/they are sincere." We can understand such belief in a Winters, a provincial of art, with moralism mistaking itself for art. Normally Eliot is guiltless of such befuddlement, but his velliety to believe is, no doubt, responsible. Eliot does not say that the poet should not improve his habits, but he says that such improvement cannot be affected "at the moment of composition"; it can be won only with difficulty. However, he fails his own earlier realisation, that Dante the poet need not be Dante the man and that poetry can be the ideal (the man at his best) and criticism the real (the world as it is).

Concluding his harpooning of Eliot with an examination of his "poetic practice," Winters devotes at least half of it to the lupus-in-fabula and, as far as he is concerned, the villain in modern poetry—Ezra Pound. Eliot, in this medieval drama, is merely Beëlzebub, yes-man to his master, Satan Pound. "The Chinese poets," Winters tells us, "like Pound, were primitive in their outlook, and dealt with the more obvious and uncomplicated aspects of experience." Ultimates of sophistication would be more like it. Earlier Winters attacked Eliot for insisting on the complex and the subtle. Having convicted Pound, to his huge satisfaction, of being "a sensibility without a mind, or with as little mind as is well possible" (again rejecting the intelligence implicit in articulated sensibility), Winters easily dismisses Eliot as poet; for "it is this Pound who provides the foundation for the more ambitious work of Eliot."

V. John Crowe Ransom

Despite the extreme gentility Ransom accords Winters in *The New Criticism*, Winters spares him no jot of his contempt. Before he proceeds to the pulverising, however, he pauses to reiterate his "concept of the morality of poetry" "which Ransom misapprehends." This reiteration leads us through the weary morass of connotation versus denotation or perception versus concept. Winters makes the futile distinction between perception and concept common to many critics, not recognising that perception involves the mind, and a "refined sensibility" (as he says of Pound) a refined mind: ". . . the feeling, evocation, or connotation is directly the result of the concept and dependent upon the concept for its existence." No doubt, but it is in the connotation and the writer's control of it that the affect on the reader appears. ". . . when we come to use the language," Winters insists, "it is the concept which evokes the feeling." Hardly, it is the use to which the concept is put, the focus and aim. We need simply refer to the vast shifts of meaning a single word experiences in different contexts.

I think, however, that I have already expressed my agreement with Winters that a poem need not be overtly didactic to be moral. But when Winters tries to make Ransom out something of a critical simpleton, when he tries to make a case against "Ransom's difficulty . . . that he can understand the idea of morality . . . only with reference to an act of simple classification"; I think we can readily detect Winters' manipulating of Ransom's recognition of "the innocence of nature, which the poet [here Keats] aspires to but cannot sufficiently realize because he is a moral and human being."

Distinguishing between science and poetry, Winters informs us that "the scientist is interested in ideas, not in the feelings they motivate; his interest is purely conceptual and amoral." Is it in feelings then that men become moral? If so, Winters is denying himself; morality lies in concepts not at all! Feelings for him are apparently perceptions; he does not know the reciprocity of mind and emotions. But if we can allow the scientist detachment, why not the artist? No, Winters would reply: "The subject matter of poetry . . . is human experience, it can therefore be understood only in moral terms." But aren't "ideas" human experience? Isn't the scientist's work human experience? What magical release does a scientist have? Or are feelings, since the scientist is concerned only with ideas, alone the world of human experience? If so, the poet violates this experience when he thinks on it (as Winters would have him do); for then he approaches the scientist. We see what muddle develops when men who know little or nothing about science olympically generalise about it. How can we expect Winters to appreciate that science in its austerity, in its total devotion to a discipline, in its pursuit of "realistic" truth is also a morality and splendid idealism?

Again Winters comments on Ransom's comment on him.

> I do not know how a poem can evaluate an experience or do anything else with it except by 'just imagining' it; for the poem exists on paper. One cannot commit a murder and write about it at the same time; the two acts are distinct. I can imagine further that both 'Une Martyre' and *Macbeth* might indispose us to murder, but I can see neither harm nor decadence in that; I can imagine no good reason why most love poems

should indispose us to fall in love or why most descriptive poems should indispose us to take walks in the country.

When Ransom characterises poetry's indisposing us to experience, as a "kind of moral decadence," he does not mean decadence morally; rather the breakdown of morality as an active or practical force. For poetry of this kind eliminates it by making action unnecessary. Morality then shrivels (decays) out of existence. But Ransom seems here, according to Winters, "a defender of overt action," though he has acclaimed art "valuable as a check to action." Exactly, a check to action as futile as murder, and therefore not "decadence" as harm. But Ransom was not defending action; he was admitting that morality is a matter of action, not of art. Winters himself quotes him: "Morality is for the practical rather than the æsthetical stage; coördinate with greed, or envy, or lust, or whatever appetites and affections it sets itself up in opposition to."

"The work of art, for Ransom," Winters tells us, ". . . is an act of sensibility, or, as he sometimes puts it, of cognition." Winters permits Ransom's own words to explain:

> In order to be human we have to have something to stop action, and this something cannot possibly be reason in the narrow sense. I would call it sensibility.

Reason is not enough; so Aristotle prescribed drama which cleansed by an appeal to the emotions draining them, certainly as much as by an appeal to reason. As Winters avows, everything human beings do is a judgment. But most writers are not large or deep enough for direct, all-inclusive judgments. Their work is to present the world they know by the bent of their vision as precisely as they can. And lo, even as it is accurate, it will be judgment, but judgment realistic and trustworthy. So a Twain, a Fitzgerald, a Hemingway are obviously best when they avoid comment, philosophising or moralising, and attempt "merely" to reproduce what they see.

Amazingly enough, at this juncture Winters confesses: "The other objection by Ransom . . . is better founded, for it rests on a careless statement of my own." Winters had analysed:

> These relationships [between words in a poem] . . . extend the poet's vocabulary incalculably. They partake of the fluidity and unpredictability of experience and so provide a means of treating experience with precision and freedom.

The amazement grows that Winters should recognise "unpredictability." Ransom takes exception:

> The freedom does very well; the freedom is unpredictability, and the unpredictable or free detail cannot be precise in the sense that it was intended, that it unfolds logically according to a plan. To have an unpredictable experience seems quite different from treating experience with precision.

I here, with some amusement, am inclined to differ with both of them. Why cannot these relationships be free, the fluidity of experience, and yet precise to that experience, even to its unpredictability precise? They do partake of the experience's condition. In that it grows directly out of it, language is very much like its parent life; the artist tries to recapture the relationship and even the identity.

"What I meant to indicate," Winters rationalises, ". . . is that the poetic medium has a more finely detailed vocabulary than has the medium of prose." Does Winters mean, as his first quotation on words partaking of the fluidity and unpredictability of experience certainly declared, that the poetic medium is closer to infinitely nuanced life—more accurate than prose? If so, poetry is superficially less accurate. Thus Joyce's poetic prose in its precision appears chaos. So an Eliot and a Pound, perhaps too precise for a Winters to see. Winters, however, tries to exclude the possibility of such a conclusion by waving the red flag "irrelevancies."

> . . . the writing of a poem involves a good many unpredictable ex-periences. But if the poet allows himself irrelevancies in any true sense of the word, his poem will be damaged, and if he allows many it will be spoiled. A good many unpredictable experiences will have to be pruned away, and those which are kept should be kept for their accuracy.

First, who is to decide the "true sense of the word?" Second, if as Winters long ago premised, the world as-it-is is our desire, what are these unpredictable experiences that must be pruned away? Finally, these unpredictable experiences which are kept, shall they be kept "for their accuracy" to a preconception, an abstract idea or judgment, or for their ability to be precise to the unpredictability of life? As always, Winters must have the poet use a pointer to indicate to the reader what is and what is not right. Science with its minute computations is an art too, but it is too accurate to itself and not the flashing, shifting life. Thus to date the scientist has always had to change his theories and measurements, and we have dumped earlier expositions; whereas a Shakespeare, copying the mer-curial, the precise lineaments, is as accurate and final as he can be. Not theory his, but practice. Though practices change, we cannot gainsay the truth of his practice to his time and experience.

Once more Winters revives the business of realism versus nominalism. "Ransom is a nominalist . . although the entire business gives him a good deal of embarrass-ment." I wonder if Ransom knows he is embarrassed? So we are back to Platonism again. With reluctance, Winters assures us, Ransom would admit

> that he and I both are men and that the concept *man* is of the first importance if we are to be understood; this in spite of the fact that he and I are able to conduct an argument on what we take to be the same subject, and, when all things are considered, to understand each other fairly well.

What Winters says is very true for philosophical discussion and speculative ex-pediency. But actually, for poetry, no such thing as man exists: it is an abstrac-tion formed from examination of many individuals for convenience, but hardly for accuracy. The poet tries to arrive at men first. After endeavoring to trace the rich confusion that exists between Winters and Ransom, we are perhaps entitled to question the correctness of Winters' "he and I are able . . . to understand each other fairly well. . . ." Yet these are men born in the same time, of somewhat similar backgrounds and interests. Think then what confusions must creep in between men centuries apart.

Winters concludes his discussion of this problem:

> . . . any feelings one may try to express about the object will be expressed through the connotations of those words, that is will be motivated by abstractions—not by the object but by our understanding of the object.

In short, we do not, cannot know the universals or even the thing, but ourselves, our reactions! What happens to realism? Or is Winters turning realism inside out and saying that the universals are the abstractions our minds contain?

Then the cat is out of the bag; Ransom, heaven help him, is a hedonist.

> . . . it is natural [Winters assures us] that he should endeavor to justify a hedonistic philosophy; and it is natural that he should fail in this attempt at justification . . . it is in nature to offer a rational defense of one's way of life, real or imagined, even if that way of life is anti-rational . . . it is impossible to devise a philosophy which will show us how we can enjoy a universe from which all distinctions have been eliminated.

Yes, it is human nature; but what is Winters' nature which offers an unrational defense of the rational way of life? How Winters can accuse Ransom's universe of being one "from which all distinctions have been eliminated" is beyond me. I quote Winters' early quotation of Ransom:

> The myth of an object is its proper name, private unique, untranslatable, overflowing, of a demonic energy that cannot be reduced to the poverty of the class concept.

Then, to add injury to insult, Winters interprets: ". . . as a matter of fact, Ransom is not able invariably to get along without some sort of idealism." To confirm this conviction, Winters adduces Ransom's essay on "Lycidas" which "deals primarily with the function of the poet as a kind of ideal and highly generalized spokesman." Finally, as the "*coup de grâce*," he poses Ransom's essay on Millay in which Ransom "objects to female poets . . . because he finds them insufficiently intellectual and too inclusively and sentimentally devoted to objects of sense." Let us see what these accusations amount to. In the first place, all workers, whether artists or scientists, in that they are striving after certain goals, usually beyond them, are "idealists." So the poet may be "a kind of ideal and highly generalized spokesman," but his words need not be. As for the female poets, what contradiction is there in Ransom's charge of insufficient intellectuality? Must one be an idealist before one can use one's intellect? Where has Ransom scoffed at the value of thought? Apparently for Winters only non-idealists are sentimentalists! To the extent that a man who has ideas of what art should be, who respects certain ideals of conduct and wisdom, Ransom is an idealist; but in Winters' sense hardly. Winters quoted him less than a page before to my purposes here:

Persons who are idealists by conviction, or on general principles, are simply monsters. (I mean the Platonic ones) the kind of idealists who worship universals, laws, Platonic ideas, reason, the 'immaterial.'

Winters is such a cave-dweller, but one who, in reverse, worships the material as though it were immaterial.

To shame Ransom in permitting his hedonism to influence his theory of poetry, Winters cites Ransom's admirable definition of the æsthetic attitude.

> The æsthetic attitude is the most objective and the most innocent attitude in which we can look upon the world, and it is possible only when we neither desire the world nor pretend to control it. Our pleasure in this attitude probably lies in a feeling of communion or *rapport* with environment which is fundamental in our human requirements. . . .
> I should say the æsthetic attitude is definable with fair accuracy in the simple and almost sentimental terms: the love of nature.

"Nature" for Winters must eliminate man. For he writes: "This statement, if taken in the narrowest possible sense [the only sense Winters would take it in], would appear to limit poetry to the description of landscape!" Winters goes on in a sweep of glory:

> But how applicable is it [this "formula"] to the treatment of *Macbeth* or of *Othello?* Were these plays written because of the love which Shakespeare felt, either for their actions as wholes or for any major part of their actions? Did Shakespeare love the spectacle of ambition culminating in murder, or of jealousy culminating in murder? Did he write of Iago because he loved him so sentimentally that he wished to render him in all his aspects? To ask the questions is to render the theory ridiculous,

or perhaps the asker of the questions. Plainly Shakespeare *did* write these plays for love, love of the opulent, wellnigh overwhelming spectacle of life. The fascination and love for whatever is is transparent in a Shakespeare and a Chaucer. Even when they attack they attack *con amore*. Winters means sanction or approval by "love"; Ransom means gusto and profound pleasure, such as Chaucer's enthusiasm for a villain's sweat or for that magnificent scum the Pardoner. But Winters has found a much deeper reason for the genesis of the plays:

> Shakespeare wrote the play in order to evaluate the actions truly; and our admiration is for the truth of the evaluations, not for the beauty of the original objects as we see them imitated. And how, one may wonder, can Shakespeare evaluate these actions truly except from the position of a moralist?

To repeat these words is to render their theory ridiculous. Where does Shakespeare evaluate? For all Othello's mighty blindness we admire him in the end; and even Iago, perfect in his villainy, to the end. So capable is he, such a splendid artist in action, we even look for motives for him!

Ransom's identifying a "poem with its subject and our feeling for the poem with our feeling for its subject" provides Winters with another opportunity for sneer. Though he deplored, out of misunderstanding, Eliot's and Ransom's considering art an end in itself, certainly Winters seems to be appealing for such an attitude here: a poem independent of its subject-matter. Criticising further, Winters writes: "we see identified explicitly our liking for the poem and our liking for its subject. . . ." By "like" Ransom does not mean "approve"; he means "liking is interest," as we are interested in lust, greed, murder, and whatever passions absorb people consumingly. But Winters denounces:

> To identify liking with interest is preposterous. We may be interested in communism, cancer, the European war, or Ransom's theories of poetry without liking any of them.

Winters must morally sanction something before he can like it. We wish he would at least try to understand the object he evaluates before he evaluates it.

One of the high watermarks of Winters' extreme earnestness plunging him into the ludicrous occurs when he tries to denote how expensive Ransom's sensibility can be:

> Ransom's devout cultivation of sensibility leads him at times to curiously insensitive remarks. In comparing the subject of a poem by Stevens with that of a poem by Tate, he writes:
>
> > The deaths of little boys are more exciting than the sea-surfaces—
>
> a remark which seems worthy of a perfumed and elderly cannibal.

What rejoinder is there meet for such irrelevancy? Ransom merely means that a human death, especially a young one, is much more humanly concerning than sea-surfaces. See Shakespeare, who did recognise the cannibalism of us all and gorged his audience with as much raw red meat as his stage could hold. Winters reserves his cannibalism for critics; no wonders he suffers of indigestion.

Winters thinks he catches Ransom in a central weakness in "Art as Imitation of the Unique Experience and Art as Unique Experience." If art is an imitation of a unique object and unique in itself, how can it be a replica? Ransom did not say it was. In fact, on the next page Winters quotes him: "it [a painting here] is the imitation of something rather than the original." "Art," Ransom writes, "celebrates the concrete, the richly sensible. . . ." Winters demurs:

> Such a position, however, leaves him with some need to justify the existence of art in a world which without its help is already teeming with natural uniqueness; especially as the work of art appears in this passage to be merely an abridgment of the original object.

What Ransom called the work of art was "an abridgment of the *infinity* [italics are mine] of the original." The justification is easily arrived at: art exists for its humanising, a presentation of the world for men by (and through) men. The bee makes honey; man makes guns, tractors, poems. So in the next quotation Ransom accounts for art's attractiveness and necessity in its freeing: "An imitation is better than its original in one thing only: not being actual, it cannot be used, it can only be known." This is the detachment of art. But Winters garbles it into "a check to action." In no sense here does Ransom suggest this check—simply that in itself the painting cannot be used; it is not a tool but an end. From such garbling it is but a step to "here as throughout Ransom, we see the constant straining to define an art, which shall subsist as nearly as possible without rational content." Use and reason for Winters are clearly one. Thus Ransom is correct in his identifying morality with the practical. But Winters' blatant insistence that Ransom would push rational content out of art is something I cannot understand, particularly since it comes hard on the heels of Ransom's own statement that "Art exists for knowledge."

Winters follows Ransom's theory of imitation as it reappears in *The New Criticism*.

> He [Ransom] states that our emotion for the artistic object cannot be the same as our emotion for the original object. 'The original emotion blinded us to the texture of the object, but now there is leisure for the texture.' In other words, our imitation in retrospect is more complete than was the object imitated, at least as we saw the object, and is no longer an abridgment.

There is leisure now for the texture because in art we do not experience the urgency of use. But I see no reason to think that Ransom has wandered from the idea that art is an abridgment of the infinity of the object. In itself, however, art is a new infinity.

> Ransom [Winters writes] says that the work of art is objective: it deals with the object itself, not with the artist's feelings or emotions, except, I suppose, the one emotion of love for the object, yet Ransom repeatedly speaks of the emotions communicated by the poem. . . .

Like many others, Winters persists in confusing a poem's contents with its author and his feelings. To use Winters' own analogy, am I to think that Shakespeare was preoccupied with the idea of killing his wife because Othello is preoccupied? Of course there is always the story of the second-best bed!

We are ready now for one of Ransom's most significant ideas: "For each poem even, ideally, there is distinguishable a logical object or universal, but at the same time a tissue of irrelevance from which it does not emerge." Gleefully Winters pounces on this nonsense:

> We may observe here again the characteristic elements of Ransom's critical theory: the concept, inescapable and necessary, but regrettable, and having no definable function, hopelessly entangled in detail which is admirable largely in proportion to its being irrelevant to the concept.

Ransom, I believe, means that the concept or object is a commonplace in most poems and so fairly anonymous. It is how the poet treats it in details that distinguishes it and him, how he enlivens it to and in the air of reality. But let Ransom speak for himself. I quote what Winters has pared away.

> The poet perpetuates in his poem an order of existence which in actual life is constantly crumbling beneath his touch. His poem celebrates the object which is real, individual, and qualitatively infinite. . . . The poet wishes to defend his object's existence against its enemies. . . . The critic should find in the poem a total poetic or individual object which tends to be universalized, but is not permitted to suffer this fate. His identi-

fication of the poetic object is in terms of the universal or commonplace object to which it tends, and of the tissue, or totality of connotation, which holds it secure. How does he make out the universal object? It is the prose object, which any forthright prosy reader can discover to him by an immediate paraphrase; it is a kind of story, character, thing, scene, or moral principle. And where is the tissue that keeps it from coming out of the poetic object? That is, *for the laws of prose logic* [my italics], its superfluity; and I think I would even say, its irrelevance.

Winters, roundly slating Ransom for "the anti-intellectual tendency of this doctrine," concludes:

> . . . Ransom wants as little rational content as possible, and . . . sees texture or what I should call feeling or emotion, as existing independently of structure and yet in some obscure manner not wholly escaping from its presence.

To begin with, I would deny that Ransom is necessarily militating against rational content; but he would not have it the be-all and end-all of poetry. So also I would question Winters' analysis of "texture" as "feeling or emotion." But he must analyse so, if he is to set up the repugnant and for him obsessive struggle between mind and emotion. By texture Ransom means the details of a poem, the circumstances that provide and are immediacy and particularity. These by their attractiveness, even as they environ "the commonplace object," sometimes almost seduce us to themselves. Shakespeare, again, is the likeliest example of this frequent tug-of-war between subject and surroundings, a pleasing internecine affair. Sometimes even characters in the plays by the fascination of some object, a mirror or a pen, momentarily forget the major movement and destiny of their roles. It is a case of delightful split allegiances. No doubt Winters will consider my language woefully illicit. Going beyond Ransom, I would propose that detailedness, by its very density, not rarely brings us variously, so more clearly, to the central idea.

> One is inclined to wonder [Winters says] at this point what has become of the unique object, of love for the unique object, and imitation of the unique object. The only object left to us now is the universe, and the universe is so chaotic that it can scarce be called unique with any real sense of security. . . ."

It is more than passing strange that this eternal-veritist should describe the universe as "chaotic." Because of his garden variety of Platonism, he cannot see it one. We love the unique object for its uniqueness, but also because its uniqueness sharpens and shapes the rest of the world and at the same time heightens the object's identicality with the rest. The object then is not only itself, but by being itself a focus for the lover, a lever to lift the world into delight.

On the way to exposing one of Ransom's "two major concepts of the nature of irrelevancy," Winters does not realise what damaging admission he makes. Talking of Ransom, he says:

> He sees the texture of irrelevancies as that which is left over when one has made a formal outline of the theme of the poem. That is, if one

should take a narrative poem with a descriptive background . . . a summary of the plot would exclude most of the descriptive detail, along with other material [Before Winters called texture "emotions"?] ; and it would no doubt be possible to rewrite the poem from the summary, even with the use of the same general setting, in such a way as fill in with other details.

If new details can be set to the summary without upsetting the summary, what inevitable relevancy do the original details have? Winters cannot defend a tenable point he seems to be attempting to make—the fact that the concept and its details are mutually influential. The change of one must change the other. But clearly then there are no root-relevant details. The artist's genius determines what seems inevitable; he might have put it another way equally inevitably. Thus several poets approaching a similar situation from different attitudes are "inevitable." Each poet looking at the world has a sight different but "equally valid." As Winters himself puts it, writing of "two poets of talents equally sound and essentially similar in scope": ". . . it is very unlikely that we can imagine them writing the same poem."

Ransom's second mistaken "major concept of the nature of irrelevancy" has to do with "metaphor and simile: the importation of irrelevance."

Ransom regards metaphor and simile as a direct means of introducing irrelevance into the poem: that is, if the poet compares Time to the driver of a winged chariot, then a winged chariot, which is essentially irrelevant to the subject under discussion but pleasant to contemplate for itself, is introduced to dissipate the interest.

More accurately, metaphor enriches the interest. Certainly the chariot is irrelevant to Time itself. Metaphor introduces new objects; it is a door to the world. First, however, it more deeply defines the original object; then it suggests its relationship to other objects and even to all. By its abundant enriching, metaphor may at first seem to distract.

Despite his denigration of the 18th century and what he called its "intellectual deficiency," Winters is fighting for its beliefs in generalised man and life and is using very similar logic. For all his protests, he wants the attitude present in science; he resents poetry's putting on flesh and blood, immediacy. Though he seems to recognise the point of metaphor, he dismisses Marvell's "winged chariot":

. . . the physical embodiment of the enemy is perhaps arbitrary, the chariot being chosen as much for its picturesque qualities as a chariot as for anything else. It seems to me very doubtful, however, that the chariot has any great vigor in itself and distinct from the idea of Time. . . .

Why think of it here "distinct from the idea of Time"? Surely more than for its "picturesque qualities," the chariot was chosen for its vigorous connotations of speed or racing, war, and triumph. To see where Winters' logic may lead him, we need simply consider his evaluation that Marvell's

. . . poem has been overestimated, I believe, largely as a result of Eliot's admiration; Herrick's "Gather ye rosebuds," on the same subject and with no irrelevancies worth naming, is clearly superior.

Herrick's poem is general and casual enough to satisfy even Winters.

But the most shameful indignity finally appears: Ransom does not respect poetry enough. Unfortunately his comprehension that "the disinterested love of the artist for the object . . . is preferable to the object, does not at all times convince him." Foolishly, with Stevens, Ransom prefers the plum to its poem. Determinism is at the bottom of such preference: Ransom is as much victimised by determinism as Eliot. Winters must conclude by having Ransom and Eliot collide. "The systems are not strictly consistent with each other, but, as Eliot would no doubt remind us, consistency is not one of the virtues of our age." Winters need not be so modest; why subpoena Eliot when he himself will more than do?

VI. Post Scripta

In his "Post Scripta," Winters sums up the ambition of *The Anatomy of Nonsense*. Running through the figures he has fulminated against, Winters laments the extent to which critics like Eliot and Ransom, "men of some native ability," have slipt from the straight and narrow and so led others astray. Winters admits:

> On the other hand . . . I have yet to discover a professor of English, except for a few relatively young men who are also poets, who could judge a new poem accurately—

one of the best things Winters has said. But later he will recover himself. Some pages on Winters' conclusion comes clear. Commenting on the humanists, he fronts one of the objections made to them—an objection, incidentally, drawn from Eliot's "The Humanism of Irving Babbitt"—namely, that humanism is not a substitute, but a feeble, temporary alternative for religion, chiefly because humanism lacks a central strength, such as the Church. Winters confesses:

> I do not consider myself one of the Humanists. . . . But the student of literature who takes his profession seriously, who wishes to quicken it and make it important, has an institution nevertheless. That institution, in spite of what I have been saying, is the university.

Is he suggesting that humanism does have an institution and that the student of literature is inevitably a humanist? A theologian without religion, a preacher without a church and a heaven other than his pen and his self-belief, Winters would make the university his pulpit; he would no doubt keep the religious air. His poet-scholars, as the hope of poetry and of civilization too, I suppose, compare favorably with the medieval monks. Since Winters wishes literature to inflate itself to include or be religion, what better priests than monkish scholars?

Winters anticipates protest:

> This statement, I dare say, will amuse the reviewers for the weekly journals. But notwithstanding all the sins of the literary scholars, the popular view of the academic world, as something cloistered and remote

from reality, peopled by souls who have failed in the practical struggle, is a product largely of the Romantic Movement and of the colored funny papers.

One may be forgiven, I hope, if, after having spent some time actively in the academic world and having read this book, he slightly demurs. It is not so much the scholar's failure in the "practical struggle" as in the educational one that troubles me. The methods of industry have invaded education; the standards of mediocrity, perhaps naturally, are most zealously adhered to.

Then, not satisfied with the big game he has, he thinks, accounted for, in this last bit of rifle-practice Winters briefly knocks off Parrington for his history's "exceptional badness" and his refusal to make "any attempt to understand the art as art." Parrington is exclusively devoted to the ideas in art.

> The essay on Melville, for example, is merely a pseudo-poetic summary of the sensational and uncritical book by Mr. Raymond Weaver. . . . The value of the essay, if it has any, lies wholly in the soundness of Parrington's unguided personal impressions (not to mention Weaver's), and in the beauty of his prose; the virtues are purely belletristic.

How can a man whose essay is dismissed as "merely a pseudo-poetic summary" be praised for the "beauty of his prose" in this essay? Or is Mr. Winters agreeing with Parrington, after all, that treatment does not matter, does not influence the contents and vice versa?

But though Winters' sympathy and touching affection for professordom continues, of course, the scholar must extend himself. Thus Winters pauses to acquaint us with flagitious oversights in scholarship. Ernest Fenollosa is an instance. Even an averagely opaque scholar should be able to appreciate his importance. For

> . . . his contribution to Japanese culture was regarded by the Japanese themselves as so great that the emperor had his ashes removed from London to Japan, and, according to the story, in a Japanese battleship. . . . These facts have nothing to do with American literature, but they are the sort of thing that might help the scholar to notice Fenollosa, who is in other respects important.

Even a scholar ought to be able to recognise a battleship, especially a Japanese battleship. Furthermore, Fenollosa, Winters assures us, *is* "in other respects important." His work on Chinese poetry and Japanese profoundly influenced the arch-fiend of American literature—Ezra Pound. Other grave omissions exist. Almost no scholar has examined Indian poetry which, Winters much earlier told us, Pound's *Lustra* "greatly resembles." Then Fenollosa's widow entrusted her husband's literal translations of the Chinese and Japanese to Pound—happily, it seems, for "the Chinese poets, like Pound, were primitive in their outlook. . . ." But the most criminal neglect of all is the failure of two scholars in their fairly recent histories of American literature to mention

> . . . Adelaide Crapsey, who died in 1914, who antedates many of the writers discussed, who is certainly an immortal poet, and who has long been one of the most famous poets of our century.

It is true that Louis Untermeyer's anthology of *Modern American Poetry* does include her. But beyond that I wonder with whom she has "long been one of the most famous poets of our century"? In an earlier book Winters listed her as one of the most distinguished experimentalists. For how has Pound surpassed her? Did she not exploit the Japanese "hokku"?

Finally, Winters reaches his climax:

> One of the most curious facts about the poets of my own generation and of the generation following—that is, about the poets now, roughly, under fifty years of age—is this: that many of the best of them are teaching in the universities. There has been no comparable unity of profession among able poets since the 17th century, when most of the best poets were members of the clergy.

Yes, many of the best are teaching in universities—including thee and me. From clergymen to school teachers is for Winters a minor happy step. Yet, as I quoted him before: "I have yet to discover a professor of English, except for a few relatively young men who are also poets, who could judge a new poem accurately."

These young poets, apparently, are to become the academic, literary, and intellectual leaders of our day. As Winters' last sentence goes: "A handful of brilliant poets, even if congenitally minor, scattered judiciously throughout our best universities, might easily begin to turn us a little in the direction of civilization." He mentions at most twenty poets, several dead, several not affiliated with universities, as the mighty leaven—mighty indeed if this handful can stir as many convention-ridden universities as we are. Not a few of the poems Winters lists from these poets are, surprisingly, of a religious complexion. Several of these poets sound as though they are salvaged out of obscurity itself, anonymity's best children. Almost half of his favorites fall into this category. But "a few . . . seem to me among the major talents of our time." Here he names Louise Bogan, Tate, and Baker. After Winters' denunciation of Tate this designation is more than passing strange. Damon and Stafford might be major talents; "the main difficulty with Stafford and Damon being the scarcity of mature poems on which to form a judgment." In other words, if they wrote mature work, they would have written mature work. At length Winters admits that as far as academics is concerned, eight of the poets mentioned operate on academic faculties. Two of these, Van Doren and Ransom, he has himself estimated as "certainly very minor." Ransom and Tate he has "exposed" as intellectual neerdo-wells. Briefly, five young poets remain—two of these, Damon and Stafford, unsure—the burning hope of our educational system. I hope they are "judiciously scattered"!

Winters does not bother to mention how little creativeness is respected generally in universities; how not seldom it is almost a detriment to academic recognition; and how often a poet advances for drudgery done, in spite of his poetry. One might easily essay this book a self-justification, a lengthy apologia with the wouldbe blistering and back-breaking of many to do it. Even if the intellectual were in a position to exercise leadership, if Winters is representative, imagine how improved our world would be. Aquinas parted religion and reason; Winters makes reason his religion. Fanaticism ineluctably follows. We have seen the violence he must resort to, the violation he must commit upon experience, to assuage his rabid logic.

Between Two Worlds
or On The Move

Anyone acquainted with Donald Davie's work will not be surprised
at my calling it one of the more considerable ventures in literature
in our time. He has from the start, with *Purity of Diction in English
Verse* (1952), attempted to counteract what he regards as the most
pernicious tendencies in modern poetry. And though with twenty
years elapsed, symbolism, the brand of Romanticism he objected
to, hardly dominates today, many qualities he reprehended still prevail
in American poetry—the intuitive, the improvisatory, the fragmentary
as against reason, syntax, order. Challenging modern poetry's failure
to exploit traditional verse's resources, Davie has stressed the grievous
losses of expression and content poetry sustains when it abandons
the poetic past. On the other hand, one of Davie's striking traits
is his openness of mind, his sympathy, despite his basic reservations,
for poets like Charles Olson and Edward Dorn. "To *move*, to *keep
moving*" (Davie's italics), an "imaginative response," has been his
comportment, if not his strategy, in his work as in his life. Yet whatever
detours he may undertake, the conservative standpoint persists
throughout his work. Because of that standpoint and what he
understands by it, his work generally reflects the quality he most
appreciates and wishes restored: a generous civility. Whatever demurs
I may have for Davie's position, I admire his struggle toward honesty,
his intelligence, his defense of the quieter, less impressive, since
less assertive, virtues. The struggle he is involved in is nothing other
than that of poetry and life itself, not only in a wounded, diminished
England, but in the world at large. At the same time, though this
paper primarily treats his criticism, readers should recognize its

relevance to his poetry. Here too he moves between two worlds with graceful agility.

Several decades ago, being an excellent critic would have provided Davie with the certification poets were expected to have: knowing about poetry proved the poet's trustworthiness as a poet. Today, except in the universities, and often not in them, the reverse obtains. With the fierce insistence on instinct, the magical, "the dark and mysterious," if a man is that learned, especially in past English poetry, how can he be free to create new work? Of course learning, and of the most obtrusive kind, hardly impeded Pound and Olson. But theirs, existing chiefly programmatically, always came at one with enormous certainty and powerful exclamation. In short, as the reaction set in against New Criticism and its devotion to English poetry, the Pound and Olson variety of learning appealed precisely for its cantankerousness, its often shrill authoritarian tone. Davie, however, though as unorthodox in his championings as Pound and Olson, has usually been modest, making points for poetry as seemingly remote and irrelevant as that of the late 18th century in England.

But if Davie's defense of the unpopular "center" has, like much modern English poetry, seemed too mild, especially for an age as tempestuous as ours (one further reason for his urging modesty), we might do well to heed the English view that American poets are frequently forced, melodramatic, sensational. Davie is definitely not a world-shaker. He knows the world is being shaken more than enough. He does not want to change his reader or life itself. Rather, he wishes to preserve the precarious, precious stuff and the equally precarious democratic society that he feels alone makes life of any decent sort possible. So if he has written enthusiastically on Pound, Olson, Dorn, he has also recognized the hazards and costs of such work. I am reminded of a statement by Picasso that Françoise Gilot quotes in her *Life with Picasso*.

> . . . as soon as art had lost all link with tradition, and the kind of liberation that came in with Impressionism permitted every painter to do what he wanted to do, painting was finished. When they decided it was the painter's sensations and emotions that mattered, and every man could recreate painting as he understood it from any basis whatever, then there was no more painting; there were only individuals.

Davie would, I think, agree with this observation; and coming as it does from one of the greatest experimenters painting has known, it might give us pause. But I would go farther. Modern poetry, dismissing established conventions and the tradition behind them, has established a new orthodoxy; out of the eccentricities and the powerful, idiosyncratic style of a Pound, a Williams, an Olson, younger poets have tried to make a style of their own. Or a very limited style indeed.

As Davie points out in his first book, the Romantics already rarely recognized more than one kind of poetry. But Davie does appreciate the "web of responsibilites" enmeshing the poet mindful of the importance of poetic diction. For such a poet—and here's the rub for us—even as he is sure of his audience, must share its basic assumptions. "Strength of statement" is primary to him; his poetry must possess the virtues of good prose (shades of Pound and Eliot). Pure diction in its "economy in metaphor," achieving "judgment and taste . . . preserves the tone of the center, a sort of urbanity." Unfortunately a poet seeking these qualities may win his reader's respect but never his love. For it is not the appeal of a powerful individual at work. Borrowing Eliot's definition of Dante's diction as "the perfection of a common language," Davie says we find this perfection not in the great English poets, who apparently ignore or exceed it, but in the good ones. So he cites Gower and Greville and Denham, Parnell and Goldsmith, Johnson and Cowper. One wonders how many present American poets would be persuaded by such examples or by the good sense that a poet look not for greatness but goodness.

Like Pound, Davie cares greatly about accuracy in writing. But a fundamental difference occurs in that Pound, Davie maintains, minimized and even dismissed syntax. However, a moment later, in one of the many reversals Davie is given to, he admits that, for what the dislocation of syntax can produce, we may not be able to return to pre-symbolist syntax. But a reversal again:

> Finally, of course, one cannot avoid the fact that the poet's churches are empty, and the strong suspicion that dislocation of syntax has much to do with it. After all, there is no denying that modern poetry is obscure and it would be less so if the poets adhered to the syntax of prose.

One might wonder whether it is really the poets' fault that the churches are empty. Do most people read any poetry today, go to church even to the best, syntactically clear poetry? On the other hand, how much is Davie taken with recent outdoor churches, jammed as they often are with the young, most enthusiastic for a poetry, a religion, almost oblivious to syntax altogether?

Belatedly Davie acknowledges historical changes as well as the effect of changes in men's philosophy and conduct on language. He also rightly insists on the reverse. This is the tantalizing question: which affects which first. Nevertheless, abandoning syntax in poetry, as Davie sees it, amounts to throwing away "a tradition central to human thought and conduct. . . ." "Throw away" sounds immensely deliberate, if not cavalier. But so he says of Pound. And he abruptly links Pound's abandoning of syntax with his fascism.

> By hunting his own sort of 'definiteness' (truth only in the particular), he is led to put his trust not in human institutions but in individuals. Similarly he pins his faith on individual words, grunts, broken phrases, half-uttered exclamations. . . . Hence his own esteem of the definite lands him at last in yawning vagueness, the 'intuitive' welcome to Mussolini. . . .

Or "one could almost say, on this showing, that to dislocate syntax into poetry is to threaten the role of law in the civilized community." This statement is tantamount to the old charge of the "treason of the clerks." And indeed soon after Davie instances Valéry's admission that he attends more to the composition of a work than to the work itself as a "*trahison des clercs* on the grand scale." Despite his respect for history Davie has paid little attention to modern historical circumstances or to the prevailing poetry that Pound and his associates violently and justifiably reacted against. Davie does not apparently believe that language in poetry, as it ages, hardens, and seals itself off more and more from contemporary experience and a changing world, becomes useless if not dangerous. Rather, principally concerned with coherence, he inclines to the language and its laws as an innate, lasting thing. A page later he seems to relent: Eliot may have "done all that was practicable and renovated only so much as is appropriate to the present day." But persisting in his desire for a pure diction, Davie maintains that such diction was damaged by the appearance of the "improvisor," "a heroic figure of the Romantic movement throughout Europe." Through him poetry went from the notion of the maker and the poem as a made object to the poet as "legislator, seer, scapegoat and reporter." Men moved from poetry as "artificial" to an enshrining of the "natural." And the equating of the natural with the spontaneous, the amorphous, the artless, and the personal "is still a potent force in the writing and reading of poetry." Still indeed. This statement is more apt today than ever.

But troubles do accumulate for even a sympathetic reader, especially an American. Praising Coleridge's "Dejection" as a great poem and attributing its greatness to its reliance on tradition, to its being impersonal in expression though prompted by personal anguish, Davie ascribes the poem's purity to "good breeding." In earlier good times, the Elizabethan, the Caroline, and the Augustan, the poet enjoyed a stable proper society with "ceremonious" manners. "The courteous usages were mostly hypocritical, but at least they were consistent." Manners even superficially observed are no doubt preferable to no manners or destructive boorishness. But what intrinsic value have hypocritical courteous usages? For such nostalgia, little in tune with the democracy Davie would preserve, is it really only the ideal, a Platonic notion of poetry, we are after? Yet again, since Davie acknowledges that the Industrial Revolution destroyed "the established codes of social behavior," how can he expect "exquisitely assured" poetry to be written now? Nonetheless, a little later he praises a poem by Shelley for reflecting "the habit of gentlemen" and civilizing the reader simply by its manner. But then Shelley was the only English Romantic poet "with the birth and breeding of a gentleman, and that cannot be irrelevant." One might wonder, class-structured England notwithstanding, where and when Davie is living.

One of the most revealing passages in the book is Davie's treatment of Hopkins.

> Such self-regarding ingenuity may be called decadent. Hopkins wrote in a decadent age, and if he is its greatest poet, he may be so because he cultivates his hysteria and pushes his sickness to the limit. Certainly he displays, along with the frantic ingenuity,

another decadent symptom more easily recognized, the refine-
ment and manipulation of sensual appetite.

Our age is surely more decadent than Hopkins'; therefore, to follow
Davie's reasoning, if a poet is to be its greatest, he must cultivate
his hysteria even more than Hopkins did. Actually Hopkins' sweet
reasonableness, his profound good sense, is everywhere evident in
his letters and journals. But Davie insists that, lacking respect for
language, Hopkins' is "a muscle-bound monstrosity." For his is "the
Keatsian luxury carried one stage further, luxuriating in the kinetic
and muscular as well as the sensuous." It is hard to see how one
can "luxuriate" in the muscular, especially if one is swooning in
the sensuous. But Hopkins, according to Davie, wanted verbally to
get "a more exquisite tang" than there is in life. We see what can
happen when one, embracing the mean, follows it to the extreme.
In this mean's conviction of authority, it assumes that what is life
for it must be life for all; anyone who feels, sees, says more—usually
thought an enhancement of our awareness of life—is indulging or
overdoing. Davie admits that Shakespeare's language is similarly
daring. But in Shakespeare's time language was still free and fluid.
By the 18th century it was permanently fixed. Therefore Hopkins
should not have taken such liberties. As though in a world of
tremendous upheaval, language can—or should—stand still. At such
moments Davie sounds not like a modern Englishman but an 18th
century French academician. Always, however, his thinking is haunted
by the fact, contrary to his wishes, of fundamental change. So he
must admit that Landor, whatever his efforts, had nothing but his
own voice; "for there was . . . no Regency or Victorian culture to
speak through his mouth as Caroline culture spoke through Carew."

In his next book *Articulate Energy* (1955) Davie set out to defend
syntax in poetry against modern practice. Here he especially opposes
modern poetry's preference for musicality (or post-symbolism in 1955)
to syntax and formal, logical order. He is right, I think, to object
to the modern poet's preoccupation with the lyric as the ultimate
poetic expression (a notion the New Critics endorsed). However,
I doubt that many poets today would consider a poem lyrical simply
because it was sprinkled with vocatives and "exclamation marks, dashes
and rows of dots." Such poems do exist. But to find this practice

not only in late Victorian conservatives, but in an "agressive modernist" like William Carlos Williams, constitutes an extraordinary coupling or guilt by association. Williams' ability to discover legitimate poetic excitement in the daily and the commonplace, without blinking their ordinariness, might well have appealed to Davie. But Williams' abandonment of poetry's conventions offended him. Thus, though the *Cantos'* dislocated syntax may look like that of Williams, the *Cantos* are "articulated most closely," if by a musical and not a linguistic syntax. Surely musical organization occurs in Williams?

Here the basic dilemma emerges. "Verse may be 'strong' or it may 'aspire to the condition of music'; it cannot do both." Poetry to be strong must be syntactical. But since both strong verse and musical verse have produced great poems, and since we are lucky to have both, and since they cannot be both at once, what are we to do? Write sometimes one, sometimes the other? Spurn the facts of our age's basic attitudes and live with the past? Or do the best with what we have and try to absorb into it as much as we can of the past's accomplishments? Again Davie cites Landor, who paid too much for his syntax. Why? because he is strong, not like Denham, Pope, or Crabbe, but like Milton, with English treated like Latin, In short, we must go back, but not too far, only to that time which set language, the late 18th century. Does Davie really expect us, beyond parody, little as we share Pope's premises, to emulate his syntax? However much he may appreciate them, can Davie gainsay the diminishing returns in Pope's imitators?

Yet poetic syntax is so valuable because it achieves "objective" effects: ". . . it follows a form of action, a movement not through any mind, but in the world at large." This assumption ignores what, beyond "divided sensibility," philosophers like Kant and his successors did to unhook our minds from the world. Davie persists: before Mallarmé, all syntaxes were mimetic; so they justified themselves by something outside themselves. Mallarmé's syntax, however, is concerned only with itself. Now Mallarmé's ambition was absolute poetry. But insofar as words continue to be words, not mathematical signs, with roots and earthly meanings, such ambition must always be frustrated. Davie, believing that man's established constructions and nature's relate, scoffs at the modern notion that the poet in being "natural" breaks through artificial constructions to the world as it is. What distresses Davie is that such poets flout their "established contract" with their readers. Without such a contract the poet loses his hold on his reader by way of the "accustomed." But for a poetry based on the assumption of making it new, as well as on an impatience with, if not aversion for, the well established, the accustomed is the last thing wanted. Furthermore, Davie did see (as we today too clearly do) that a new way persisted in can also become customary, so tediously much that it likewise needs breaking. But we are at a basic opposition: the individual, whether person or poem (as unique), versus the community (or established contract).

In this book Yeats, for his rejecting both free syntax and free verse, its inevitable concomitant, emerges as the modern English hero of poetry. Pound and Eliot unfortunately went too far. So since his rhythm abandoned customary "metrical landmarks," Pound requires "blind faith." But at least Pound and Eliot do not deceive by using mere empty forms. It may be such either/or preference which leads Davie to pay little attention to the many good American poets—not only "traditional" ones like Robinson and Frost or the more "modern" Stevens and Moore—somewhere between his position and its polar opposite, and to concentrate on "far-out" poets like Olson and Dorn. But does abandoning syntax inevitably reflect "a failure of the poet's nerve, a loss of confidence in the intelligible structure of the conscious mind and the validity of its activity"? Or does it at its best acknowledge that there is more to the mind than consciousness alone and more to language than a contract with society?

Davie maintains that "things," emphasized by modern poets and critics, are not concrete but rather, since plucked from experience, abstractions, whereas "the experience" is the only "ultimate concretion." Accordingly, he is confident that thoughtful men can no longer deceive themselves into believing that by way of things they are breaking through grammar and logic to basic Edenic nature. I have considerable sympathy with Davie here against such naiveté, such would-be primitivism. But the fact remains that many poets, no longer trusting old ways of thinking and feeling, clutch things, not so much like drowning men (though that too), but for the tangible realities they are. Nor can we forget how much Pound and his coevals despised the vagueness and looseness in most of their predecessors' poetry, the straw these latter had accumulated that must be flushed out even if it threatened to drown the horses (Pegasus?) and to destroy the stables themselves. But David rightly recognizes the deep modern desire to shake off all bonds or, as the phrase goes, to blow the burdensome mind.

In the book's conclusion Davie urges, surprisingly, "the reek of the human." He praises a Wordsworth poem for being, unlike a self-sufficient symbolist poem, open to the outside world, that of common experience, and for having "the smell of soil and soiled flesh, . . ." If such reek is what Davie wants, surely he can find it in Yeats' Crazy Jane poems, in Eliot's *Waste Land* and Sweeney poems, and in the *Cantos,* and not merely the hell *Cantos.* Furthermore, much recent American poetry should please him since it is passionately occupied with the reek of humanity. In fact, its reek may be a good deal stronger than any Davie ever bargained for (such reek is not exactly copious in his poetry). Those poets who hunger to recover a Golden Age are at least as busy with this world that obstructs or destroys the possibility of that recovery. Recent poetry, unlike the symbolist variety, prides itself on being "open," open in itself as to the world the poet occupies. It is traditional verse this poetry considers closed and remote from our world. In Williams' words, "The world without smell is the world without me."

Amost ten years elapsed before Davie's next book of criticism, *Ezra Pound as Sculptor* (1964) appeared, certainly one of the best studies of Pound that we have. And indeed much had happened in that time not only to the world and poetry but to Davie's thinking. Thus, after his many fundamental reservations, here he comes closest to Pound. In fact, examining Pound scrupulously, Davie finds that Pound was rather other and more than he had suspected or rather more like him and his 18th-century attitudes. Nonetheless, throughout, as he meets them, he does quietly remark failures, aberrations, pretences in Pound's work. What is it then that provides the grounds for Davie's change? For all Pound's abuse of syntax, it is basically not symbolism with its appetite for the indefinite that appeals to Pound but "hard distinctness" or his own imagism, which Davie now is at pains to distinguish from symbolism. For Pound there is indeed a world out there; and however much music may attract him, it is stone and sculpture—as with Davie after him—that becomes the master metaphor of emulation. For Pound is, unlike Eliot and Yeats (who now, despite his well-behaved syntax and metrics, seen as an egotist sublime, preoccupied with his own responses and his "vision" rather than with the world itself, shrinks into a lesser figure), a realist, attached to the French 18th century, the Age of Enlightenment. The analogy with science, in Pound's precise observation of the external world, is stressed. So Davie can praise Pound's "lineation" and even sanction his seeking "an effect of improvisation, ·of haste and rough edges. For only in this way can he be true to his sense of the inexhaustibility of the human and non-human nature he is working with, a sense which makes him feel not noble but humble."

Davie grapples with Pound's fascism. And now he appreciates Pound's yearning for a culture that would encourage simplicity as compared with the solitary artist's struggle. Davie delights in Pound's "painful self-assessment" in *Guide to Kulchur,* which derives from Pound's enthusiasm for Hardy, and in Pound's about-face disavowal of "modernist intricacy and technical sophistication in favor of a limpidity he considered 'totalitarian.' " Davie does admit a struggle in Pound between his natural enthusiasm for the 18th century (and realism) and his conscious thought, which inclines to technique, particulars, post-symbolism. But we learn in a moving passage that

> Pound's whole philosophy of history is in the strictest sense "Augustan" . . . like Pope and Swift . . . he sees the course of human history in terms of prolonged "dark ages" interrupted by tragically brief islands of achieved civilization. . . . Like Pope at the end of the *Dunciad,* Pound has written and acted as if the precarious islands of achieved civility were maintained only by unremitting vigilance on the part of a tiny minority, typically a group of friends, who must continually (and in the end always vainly) stop up the holes in the dikes against which the sea of human stupidity, anarchy, and barbarism washes incessantly.

No wonder Davie, in the precarious island England has become, now feels large sympathy for Pound.

Consequently, whatever his previous admission of inadequacy, not to say wrong-headedness, in Pound, after Davie's impressive patience before Pound's more dubious aspects, it is fairly startling as late as the book's last pages to see Davie stridently attack Pound. Davie blames him and him alone for poetry's present loss of status. In his vast but inadequate reading of history "Pound has made it impossible for any one any longer to exalt the poet into a seer. . . . Pound's arrogance . . . has overreached itself not only for him but for all poets." Why should the errors of one poet, even a major one, spoil it for all the rest? Surely like anyone else, the poet, when he succeeds in being a seer, succeeds; when not, not. Perhaps the moral is that our times are so extreme in their exacerbating that they drive even so moderate a man as Davie to rancor. But in the end he underscores Pound's "responsibility" in earning his poetic "freedom." He concludes by prizing Pound the translator, as he does his use of rhyme in the *Classic Anthology,* since the poems "celebrate the decorous in private and public life." For "without a master to translate," Pound, as in "the lawless world of the *Cantos,* cannot be decorous.

After eight years, simultaneously with his *Collected Poems,* Davie published his latest book of criticism, *Thomas Hardy and British Poetry* (1972). Here, in defense of civility and moderation, he is often at his most opinionated and quite irascible. But perhaps, desperate as the book in many ways is, almost a last-ditch engagement, he is understandably so. For Davie does see England as a kind of Augustan Rome, an island in its latter days threatened by engulfment, not only by the roaring sea of America and the rest of the world, but from within. And this book is an attempt to raise some sea wall against both encroachments. Therefore Davie recommends—what he thinks he already finds operating among the best contemporary British poets—England's own culture as a model, particularly as embodied in Hardy. It is amusing to remember that Emerson, Whitman, and Williams similarly urged the U.S.: give over English manners and matter and look homeward. Why should the English not also resist foreign influence and cleave to their own best voice?

We might consider it sad, however, that, even while the English world is shrinking, its poetry should also shrink, that it should defiantly set out to be provincial. (Davie's practice, happily, hardly conforms to this notion.) Surely English poetry, like any other, can benefit from foreign infusions—that is, if English poets are able to naturalize them. But from the start Davie has been concerned to show how the great foreigners, Yeats, Pound, and Eliot, whatever their triumphs, have failed or flouted the central English tradition. Thus this book is his most immediate call to arms and at the same time an elegy for England's poetry, at least the glory it has been. Also, in Davie's devotion to things English and his understandable sense of the present moment's frailty, the book might be read as a capitulation to England's industrialization so complete that it seems to view any criticism of England as "irresponsible" and likely to encourage chaos and/or fascism. It is, apparently, even too late for a minority like Pound's. Not that Davie blinks the dinginess and the painful cost of all this; on the contrary.

But why Hardy? For his concentration on specific times and places, his sense of history. It is the hard-headed, pragmatic, even anti-poetic English nature Davie is approving, Hardy's suspicion of the transcendental, a Yeats' striving for the visionary. One must, it seems, choose one master or the other. (So happily, after an initial absorption in Yeats, Larkin "converted" to Hardy.) Accordingly, Davie means this book to do what has not been done: prove Hardy the equal of—and, for English poets, superior to—Yeats, Pound, and Eliot. Given the Hardy limitations that Davie admits, this might seem hard to do. But Davie will embrace those very limitations as admirable and necessary (and not for this troubled time alone). It is Hardy's "scientific humanism" he commends against Yeats', Pound's, and Eliot's "anti-democratic opinions," a humanism reinforced by "the ethic of the laboratory." Thus Davie endorses Hardy's exhorting "loving-kindness, operating through scientific knowledge." Such sentiments, appealing though they may be, must strike one now as naive, at best wistful thinking. Already in 1922 Hardy called what he desired

> a forlorn hope, a mere dream, that of an alliance between religion, which must be retained unless the world is to perish, and complete rationality, which must come, unless also the world is to perish, by means of the interfusing effect of poetry.

And Hardy had not lived through Nazism, not seen the complete divorce between technology and rationality or at least humanism, what hideous uses—and in behalf of a mad religiosity—technology would be put to. Davie fully appreciates "the human cost" of Hardy's basing what hopes he had on science and its industrial technology. And Davie admits post-Hardy British poetry's "apparent meanness of spirit, a painful modesty of intentions, extremely limited objectives.

. . ." But those qualities are acceptable if one realizes that this poetry is trying to solve the problems Hardy's poetry raised for the 20th century. For Hardy and his followers, "in severely curtailing for themselves the liberties that other poets continue to take," avoid the latter's childish irresponsibility.

At this juncture Davie examines "Hardy as Technician." Hardy's attitude to technology emerges, not from the little his poems say about it, but from its basic informing of his art. His attitude, it turns out, since too much a matter of will, often proves negative, if not destructive. Sometimes his poetry's "form mirrors a cruel self-driving, a shape *imposed* on the material, as it were, with gritted teeth." This wilfulness derives from Hardy's reliance on Victorian "self-help," from his being "the poet of technology" out of his training in Victorian architecture. Aside from being pretty hard to prove, such speculation makes one wonder whether the reverse might not be at least as seriously proposed—to wit, the Hardy poem Davie presents as evidence, "Lines to a Movement in Mozart's E-Flat Symphony," is ponderously bad for its too obvious notions of, its too heavy leaning on, the "poetic": clotted alliteration, forced, rigid pattern, etc. So too the proof Davie discovers in another Hardy poem, "The Wind's Prophecy," of its formal reflections of technology seems to me altogether challengeable. The line "And gulls glint out like silver flecks" Davie calls technological because the gulls glint with a metallic glitter. Metal, I should think, has been with the race, and glinting too, for some long time. So the sea sounds in the poem, a slamming and a hammering, are for Davie "industrial associations." But actually the sounds are "like the slam of doors," hardly modern industrialism. As for the "hammerings on hollow floors," one need not resort even to such primitive "industrialism" as ancient blacksmiths to account for them. But now Davie admits that his reading of the poem has amounted to "special pleading." The poem's references to technology are "not so unambiguous, not so insistent, as I have made out." Then why make them out so?

He tries again with another not-too-successful Hardy poem. Not too successful because the work of " 'a superb technician' who dismays us precisely by his *superbia*." Yet precisely this, Davie says, could be the grounds for calling Hardy a very great poet. Why? Because no contemporary of Hardy could—in his art, not just in his content—grasp so well "the essential nature and life style of late Victorian England, an England which rested on mechanical technology, on heavy engineering." A most ingenious argument! What is the heavy engineering in the poem? Because its swallows are "like little cross-bows," they have according to Davie, become machines. I would have thought crossbows medieval rather than late Victorian or modern technology. But Davie's analysis is most perplexing when he says that we get in this poem "some sense of what it was like to be married to a Victorian engineer (whether in steel or in language) or to any man vowed to the Victorian ethos of self-help." What kind of example for later poets, also accepting technology, is this version of Hardy, a Hardy bad as he is when he reflects that technology? Well, at times ". . . the drilling and the riveting stop . . . when the civil engineer who was once a mason finds that he has to chip with his own chisel." But is such response not nostalgia for an earlier time rather than belief in technology? A mason is fairly remote from a civil engineer and, for that matter, from the urbanity Davie has wanted. Here Davie singles out an endearing quality from Hardy's work, interesting in itself and as a reflection on Davie's poetry: though Hardy imposes himself "imperiously" on his medium, he imposes himself on his readers hardly at all. But is this civility "scientific humanism" or rather old-time gentleman-liness?

Now we reach a remarkable passage.

> A technician such as Hardy was . . . needs to believe that decisions are being wisely taken elsewhere about what the ventures are to which his technical expertise shall be applied. . . . Major issues of national policy were among the matters that Hardy was too modest to concern himself with.

Or a real specializing and a hard-and-fast separation of functions. Is such modesty commendable or an abdication of responsibility? The laboratory technician preparing a poison gas is, so an Eichmann would have it, simply carrying out his job? And this he must do unquestioningly in the assumption of wisdom in those who have ordered the gas? But Hardy's modesty prevailed. Unlike "the literary man or the philosopher, who has the presumption to question the

whole cultural design, and offer to set the whole world to rights,"
and like the modest, honest scientist or engineer, Hardy was a
"cop-out, a modest (though proudly expert) workman in a corporate
enterprise which from time to time publishes a balance-sheet called
The Golden Treasury or *The Oxford Book of English Verse."* Apparently
modern times are so different, so much more precarious, that the
ancient assumption that the poet should be radical, "go to the roots,"
no longer applies. Hardy and his heirs have wisely spurned that
assumption. This seems to recommend establishment verse or at
least the poet's being, not a seer or sayer, but a keeper to his last—in
the making of poems. Yet even with Hardy it was not merely accepting
things as they are, but advocating an alliance of religion and rationality.
Poets may not be called on to question the whole cultural design
as Pound did; but is it wrong or irresponsible for poets and thinkers
to remark the outrages of a modern technological society? Is it better
to let such a society go down of its own grinding, ponderous weight
than to try to warn it with earnest criticism?

In the chapter "Hardy Excelling," Davie focuses on Hardy at his
best: the poet in him who surpasses his technology (technique?).
But first Davie denounces myth and mythology and the suprarational.
Or the hungering in our day for something beyond our crushing
materialism. One can well appreciate fears of drugs, facile mysticisms,
magic, especially in a rationalist-based society, even as one can also
understand the turning to them for that society's oppressiveness.
Davie confesses that when someone speaks of "meeting Artemis"
or "turning into a tree," he can in no way understand it. He finds
such thinking "dangerously self-deluded" and closely related to
matters like Pound's anti-semitism. It is "in fact the central and
unavoidable question about Pound's poetry, as about Charles Olson's
and Robert Duncan's." Still Davie does admit how much the English
are barred entrance in poetry, even from imagism itself. He commends
the latter in Pound and in Pasternak (a very considerable presence
in Davie's thought and poetry). Pasternak is an imagist, it seems,
as much as Pound or a poet concerned with the world out there.
But since readers always prefer the subjective, and since the subjective
uses the objective for its own purposes, for most Hardy's poetry
will always seem "insufficiently exciting." Apparently Pound, Pasternak, and Williams, whatever their imagism, have something else

(subjectivity or simply the numinous?) that does make them sufficiently exciting.

Finally, and after all, we must recognize how different Hardy
is from Pound and Pasternak:

> All these poets claim, by implication or else explicitly, to give
> us entry through their poems into a world that is truer and
> more real than the world we know from statistics or scientific
> induction or common sense. Their criticism of life is radical
> in that they refuse to accept life on the terms in which it offers
> itself [that is, if you identify life with statistics or our society's
> official version of life], and has to be coped with, through most
> of the hours of every day. In their poems that quotidian reality
> is transformed, displaced, supplanted; the alternative reality
> which their poems create is offered to us as a superior reality,
> by which the reality of every day is to be judged and governed.

Davie is clearly caught between the daily, practical world and the
world of contemplation and vision. But since the English tend to
have ample dailiness, the silent majority in the U.S. as well, do they
need more of it from their poets or rather refreshments, enhance-
ments from elsewhere? One remembers Lenin's resentment at the
beauty of Mozart's and Beethoven's music (how dare they?) in a
world riddled with suffering. Is not the failure to recognize the
sacramental, the something else, in our lives well on the way to
denying poetry altogether? The grimness of Davie's tone would
suggest to me that he is fully, sadly aware of this possibility.

Yet Larkin is England's chief poet now because the England in
his poems is the England that is. Apparently it is enough—if not
best—for the poet to be an accurate recorder of what is. It is revealing
to put little congested England beside the vast, open spaces of the
U.S. That difference alone accounts for the very different kinds
of poetry arising from the two countries, precisely as their poets
are filled with a sense of place. One culture is also saturated with
history, further "congested" and heaped up with lives, the failures,
of the past; the other is still quite new and (even now!) hopeful.
In Larkin we see the English poet so habituated to industrialization
he does not complain about it but takes it for granted, or is, like
most men and women, "numb" to it. Feeling for them, Larkin ignores
"dignity" or "sanctity" since that would interfere with "his level-toned

acceptance of that England as the only one we have, violated and subtopianized and poisoned as it is." Thus men and women are regarded as "victims" of polluting history, never its "makers." What about their conduct now and in a democratic society? Is their will of no account? To object to this world is to be arrogant. Davie can say, ". . . either we accept that we deserve no better then the gracelessness of scene which surrounds us, or else we shut ourselves off from our neighbors who seem to ask nothing better and are doing their best to make it worse." Is this not *the* loss of nerve, the collapse of spirit, Davie has several times attacked?

But late as it is, Larkin even more than Hardy has had to lower his sights and surrender. Both have settled for "parliamentary democracy as a shabby, unavoidable second-best." They have "sold poetry short" to go on being human, "a citizen of some commonwealth." And Davie doubts that anyone can escape. Dismal though the sell-out may be, it must continue. For since 1953 it has been the "loss of nerve" that has saved us. So no war over Budapest in 1956 or in 1968 over Prague. It was an "alarming recovery of nerve" that took America into Vietnam. But one might ask who beyond the poets and the thoughtful opposed that war. However, the British intelligentsia (whom by analogy Davie identifies with Yeats, Pound, and Eliot), since they have been "a perpetual opposition," can only be irresponsible. And since British society is not repressive, the intelligentsia have no right—have not earned it—to be irresponsible. But where does the reverse take one? Davie himself concedes, ". . . if all these poets [Hardy, Auden, Prynne] are scientific humanists . . . what we have is scientific humanism at the end of its tether." Plainly a most desperate situation. Nonetheless, for England it must be Hardy or closed forms (to provide a bit of privacy, no doubt, little clearings) and vertical as against Whitman and the Open Road, the sprawling expansiveness, the horizontal of the U.S.

In a last, brief section, "Afterword for the American Reader," Davie observes that Americans cannot hear British poets and British readers only pretend to hear American poetry since Williams. However, a basic change has set in: Americans' contemptuous tolerance" of British poetry versus Englishmen's "resentful fascination" with American poetry. And like American politics, American poetry, though it opposes that politics, is, Davie accuses, "chauvinistic."

American poets appropriate foreign poets with the "imperious rapacity" of their own country. But Davie qualifies: ". . . doubtless it is only sour grapes" for an Englishman to think this way. In any case, a fundamental difference remains: English poets think historically and complexly; Americans, simply and utopianly. So Americans respond to British poetry with "a post-colonialist backlash." And the British, alone regarding poetry as "a modest art," in their feeling inferior have only themselves to blame. For the last time Davie underscores good manners. Why should they be held against a poet? Thus Davie defends as "civic sense" what has been derided in the last half-century's British poetry as "gentility."Whatever good sense may inhere in Davie's argument, I doubt that it will seriously affect American poets. However, with the death of Eliot and Pound, the two panjandrums of "modern" poetry, English poets and critics have begun to dare to fight back. And Davie's book, whatever its low-keyed hope, may help to reinforce that fight—that is, if poets can find comfort and energy in a stance that seems to espouse the downward aspect of modern democracy, the anti-poetic commonness in us all.

II

After this examination of Davie's criticism readers should be prepared to learn from their scrutiny of his poems that they have been, as the flyleaf says, "written in the faith that there are still distinctively English—rather than Anglo-American or 'international'—ways of responding imaginatively to the terms of life in the twentieth century." (One might demur, at least a little, for the many poems under the influence of foreign places and poets, especially Pasternak.) And readers should be prepared to hear in the first poem—appropriately, "Homage to William Cowper"—that Davie, even as he is aware with Cowper that "Honor starts, like Charity, at home," regards himself "A pasticheur of the late-Augustan styles." Fortunately he is also rather more than that. The first three formal, witty poems, set apart almost like epigraphs, establish basic themes; all three recognize the troubles and failures, if not horrors, of domesticity, geography, society, and reason—Davie's essential concerns. The second poem, "At Knaresborough" involves a meeting with a countryman who warms to Davie at his familiar accent. But Davie "feels little":

> Believe me, sir, I only ply my trade,
> Which is to know when I am played upon.
> You might have moved, you never shall persuade.
> You grow too warm. I must be moving on.

Properly the volume's first collection is titled *Brides of Reason (1955)*. And the first poem, "Among Artisans' Houses," conveys Davie's sense of present British civilization via such houses: their "Clothes-lines run to a handy cleat,/ And plots are furiously neat." Unfortunately, "There are not many notice this/ Resourcefulness of citizens,/ And few esteem it." But he does; for it is what he clings to. So he queries:

> And if civility is gone
> As we assume it is, the moulds
> Of commonwealth all broken down,
> Then how explain that this still holds,
> The strong though cramped and cramping tone
> Of mutual respect, that cries
> Out of these small civilities?

That tone can occur only here "where continuity is clear" and life is "sanctioned by the use of time." But then—for he will not lie, not impose "a moral" where there is none—he admits the scene a "Curious relic from the past." But meager though this remnant of civilization may be, Davie is grateful for it, if no more exuberant before it than it is; for soon, he glumly predicts, it too will be gone. Already his doubts, aware as he is of the cost, the losses, on both sides, are fighting it out. In "Creon's Mouse" he poetizes what he has said in prose:

> If too much daring brought (he thought) the war,
> When that was over nothing else would serve
> But no one must be daring any more,
> A self-induced and stubborn loss of nerve.

For neither Antigone nor Creon can win; this—Davie urged in his prose—only yielding Ismene understands.

In 'Puskin. A Didactic Poem" (many of Davie's poems are moral meditations), Davie finds Pushkin impressive because

> The poet exhibits here
> How to be conscious in every direction
> But that of the self, where deception starts.
> That is nobility; not lost
> Wholly perhaps, if lost in art.

For beyond Pushkin self-consciousness took over.

> Self-consciousness is not at fault
> In itself. It can be kept
> Other than morbid, under laws
> Of disciplined sensibility, such
> As the seventeenth century Wit.
> But all such disciplines depend
> On disciplines of social use,
> Now widely lost.

Poetry should be as good as prose. This writing is prose-clear, but rather too essayistic. Recovering some of his late-18th-century poise, Davie resorts to the quatrain and, in its formality, to some hope:

> Remains the voice that moves on silence
> In moral commonplace, where yet
> Some thwart and stern communal sense
> Whispers before we all forget.

Davie is at his best in "Remembering the 'Thirties"; here, by the subject matter they operate on, his urbanity, his wit, his precision prosper. About the before and after and what happens to them in styles of poetry: how easily a manner, even one guarding against appearing foolish, turns what were agonies into mere stories for the reader. Those of the 'Thirties, playing "the fool, not to appear as fools," were caught by their act:

> And curiously, nothing now betrays
> Their type to time's derision like this coy
> Insistence on the quizzical, their craze
> For showing Hector was a mother's boy.

Still, much as Davie in his criticism seems to respect his own day's strategy: "A neutral tone is nowadays preferred," he has—and this is what lifts his work above society (or light) verse—his reservations:

> And yet it may be better, if we must,
> To praise a stance impressive and absurd
> Than not to see the hero for the dust.

Davie, fortunately, does not have it too easy. At the same time, "An English Revenant" acknowledges in a series of apposite "nots" the mean, the moderation, Davie has arrived at:

> My home is in the west,
> But not in the far west;
> And though I was born in the north,
> It was not in the far north;
> I am lately returned from the east,
> But from the middle east;
> My songs aspire to the south,
> But not to the deep south.

But he does confess in the section's last couplet: "Now only my singing mouth/ Thirsts for the springs of the south."

In the ambitious "Hawkshead and Dachau in a Christmas Glass," Davie juxtaposes Wordsworth and Coleridge and Nazism. As with "An English Revenant" he says,

> As I shall not aspire
> To wear the coat of fire
> Which (we have proved) incinerates the heart;
> Because the human mind
> Cannot be far refined,
> But must admit its grossness from the start; . . .

His discretion, he maintains, arises from his fears and the world's failures; fire is bound to result in Dachau. As he says later, "At Dachau man's maturity began. . . . At Dachau Yeats and Rilke died." Here he sounds rather like an Alvarez. But for the latter this must mean the end of gentility (civility?) in poets; for Davie it means the opposite: we must, to preserve the little left, do what we can not to start the fire again. "Eight Years After" convincingly insists, "Enormities should not be scrutinized."

> For fearsome issues, being squarely faced,
> Grow fearsomely familiar. To name

> Is to acknowledge. To acquire the taste
> Comes on the heels of honouring the claim.

Thus in "Method. For Ronald Gaskell," in defense of his style and in answer to the charge,

> For such a theme (atrocities) you find
> My style, you say, too neat and self-possessed.
> I ought to show a more disordered mind.

Davie avers, "And stains spread furthest where the floor's not cracked." Now he has it both ways: enormities in not being named, a naming whereby they grow commonplace, are more enormous, not simply ignored. Such verse, however, can sound rather comfortable, too sure to begin with of—so almost superior to!—failure.

In the next volume, *A Winter Talent and Other Poems (1957),* an Augustan formality normally prevails. In the attractive "Obiter Dicta" Davie again acknowledges his liking, shared with his father, for "moral commonplaces," denounced though they be by modern romantics. But he wonders whether he does more with his father's "pearls of wisdom" than "snap the elastic band/ Of rhyme about them." And in the skillful "The Wind at Penistone," meeting a "reserved" wind, "A plain-ness rather meagre than severe" in the streets, and a "dour" young housewife, he has to admit that ". . . even I,/ Liking to think I feel these sympathies,/ Can hardly praise this clenched and muffled style." But his, alas, is indeed a winter talent: ". . . coming home,/ The poet falls to special pleading, chilled/ To find in Art no fellow but the wind." As though Italy, the south, were truly an inspiration, the poems under the heading "Italy" strike me as much more incisive and, at the same time, graceful and interesting than the previous poems under "England" and "Ireland." Here too one should be grateful for the neatness of Davie's wit. "The Pacer in the Fresco. John the Baptist" is a fine, richly realized poem. And "Hearing Russian Spoken" is at least candid:

> If broken means unmusical I speak
> Even in English brokenly, a man
> Wretched enough, yet one who cannot borrow
> Their [Dostoievsky's "debauchees"] hunger for indignity, nor, weak,

> Abet my weakness, drink to drown a sorrow
> Or write in metres that I cannot scan.

For one born to the manner metrical, breaking out is as difficult as it is for latecomers to poetry-making (Americans) to write well in formal verse. Still Davie sees that "Abandonment," whatever the tongue, "trades on broken English with success/ And, disenchanted, I'm enamoured yet." "Rejoinder to a Critic" repeats Davie's doubts about—and his preoccupation with—feeling, its dangers and its costs.

> You may be right: "How can I dare to feel?"
> May be the only question I can pose,
> "And haply by abstruse research to steal
> From my own nature all the natural man"
> My sole resource.

He is large enough to recognize, "And I do not suppose/ That others may not have a better plan." But then he rejoins, "Donne could be daring," but only because "he never knew,/ When he inquired, 'Who's injured by my love?'/ Love's radio-active fall-out on a large/ Expanse around the point it bursts above." And if the critic says this is "Not love, but hate," "Well, both are versions of/ The 'feeling' that you dare me to." So better "Be dumb!/ Appear concerned only to make it scan!/ How dare we now be anything but numb?" After such holocausts, perhaps not too egregious a question. Yet surely mankind must struggle on to try to distinguish between love and hate, must not lose one for fear of the other.

From *New and Selected Poems (1961)* contains several important, effective poems. "To A Brother in the Mystery," dealing with stone and its shaping, contrasts Davie with a poet he admires, Tomlinson (despite—or because of—modern American poetry's influence on him, his absorption in nature, and his fierce refusal of "the Hardyesque surrender"?); and accents their influence on each other. In fact, Davie cautions Tomlinson against his warmer, softer, more "human" nature. "With the Grain," a key poem, grapples directly with the problem of ideas versus experience. Davie admits the poem is "obscure," then with his customary honesty reprints the "vulnerable" note, written three days before the poem. From this note:

It is true that I am not a poet by nature, only by inclination; for my mind moves most readily and happily among abstractions. . . . I have little appetite, only profound admiration, for sensuous fullness and immediacy; I have not the poet's need of concreteness. I have resisted this admission for so long, chiefly because I mistook my English empiricism for the poet's concreteness, and so thought my mind was unphilosophical whereas it is philosophical but in a peculiarly English way.

This comment obviously sheds much light on his work. (One cannot resist the double sense of "natural" in his "a natural poet," one by nature a poet and the other a poet occupied with nature. Davie has made much of nature's "disappearance" in industrialized England and so in its poetry as well. For an American, delighted by England's nature, this view is hard to accept, even harder after Raymond Williams' illuminating *The Country and the City.*) Might Davie not, however, have made more of the immediacy, the sensuousness, the reality of ideas themselves, as with a Lucretius, a Dante, a Donne? Or is Davie too late-18th-century for such intensity, not to say passion?

We can readily understand why such a poet would be suspicious of, unavailable to, the immediacy of being a tree, a river, a goddess, would be sceptical of the mythical. It is the human, reflected in ideas and laws, defined by the resolutely other world (though if nature disappears what is that other world but other people and man-made society?), that he is after, and not the identification with that world (usually the "natural") of a Keats or a Rilke. Davie's lyricism is often personal but (as he said of Hardy) in an impersonal, if not "reposeful," way, concerned more than not with lack of feeling and related problems of style. The writing, usually hard and definite, but rather metallic than of carved stone, is rarely possessed of the evocativeness Pound, say, often magically managed. At his best, perhaps by the very divisiveness in him that Davie has well described, Pound achieved both precise denotative expression and a richly reverberating suggestiveness.

A *Sequence for Francis Parkman (1961),* out of Davie's first visit to North America, is, as befits the new world, more relaxed and "open." But Davie is still his wry, dry, witty self. And now and again close rhyming does take over, as does history with its remoteness. *Events and Wisdom (1964),* though it may contain too many weather reports and travelogs for some tastes, is one of Davie's most appealing volumes. Marked by short, easygoing lines, it is simpler, more direct. The danger in all this buoyancy is that some of the poems may fly off for very lightness. *Essex Poems (1969)* seems grimmer and even more stripped, as in "July, 1964," "Thanks to Industrial Essex," and parts of "Sylvae." In the first he experiences three deaths. But by the third stanza he says:

> The practice of an art
> is to convert all terms
> into the terms of art.
> By the end of the third stanza
> death is a smell no longer;
> it is a problem of style.

Where then is the reek of humanity he strongly urged?

More Essex Poems (1964–68) sports an interesting pair in "Revulsion" and "Oak Openings," appropriately side by side. The former is unusually confessional, touchingly so: "Angry and ashamed . . .

> My strongest feeling all
> My life has been,
> I recognize, revulsion
> From the obscene; . . .

Not an altogether promising passion, he realizes, for life or art. "Oak Openings," answering "Revulsion," also answers the relentless modern lust for the new, its failure to recognize that every advance of novelty means some loss. "To Certain English Poets" clearly anticipates the polemics of Davie's book on Hardy.

> Like you I look with astonished fear and revulsion
>   at the gross and bearded, articulate and good-humoured
>   Franco-American torso, pinned across
>   the plane of human action, twitching and roaring.
> Yet a restlessness less than divine comes over us, doesn't it, sometimes,
>   to string our whole frames, ours also, in scintillant items,
>   with an unabashed crackle of intercom and static?
> Or will you, contained, still burn with that surly pluck?

Again, in "Epistle. To Enrique Caracciolo Trejo," Davie remarks
"A shrunken world/ Stares from my pages." One might wonder
why he makes so much of his sense of diminishing. What of his
objections to the overly self-conscious (not to say the confessional)?
So he tells us, "I cannot abide the new/ Absurdities day by day,/
The new adulterations." This sentiment does not exactly square with
the acceptance, the resignation, his Hardy book recommends. Thus
in the next *Los Angeles Poems (1968–69)* we meet "England," a scratchy,
poor man's Poundian diatribe. Prosy enough in its short-lined free
verse, as it spreads over many pages, it resists this reader's interest.
His *Recent Poems*—mainly "Six Epistles to Eva Hesse (1970)"—in
bouncing, humorous rhyming couplets, are a catch-all, a *tour de force*;
they use Davie's knowledge of the past to twit the present with its
fix and fixes. Thus his note reports that the poems, all written
"light-heartedly," are "to show that . . . as much variety of time,
space and action can be encompassed" in a traditional English form
as in the "much vaunted" *Cantoesque* free form. He affectionately
mocks Eva Hesse and other Pound enthusiasts, as well as Olson.
To wit, "No, Madame, Pound's a splendid poet/ But a sucker, and
we know it." A great deal of historical matter, much of it obscure
(at times as dull as Pound's) if not very minor, has been crammed
into the poems. But savory bits of the personal are sprinkled here
and there, and pointed moral observations, as well as artistic ones.
A vigorous instance follows:

> But rhyme in less licentious mode
> Ensures a wavering switchback road
> Which, I aver, I trust much more
> Than five-lane free-verse highways for
> Egotists to roar along
> In self-enclosed unmeasured song.
> Theirs are the closed forms, theirs the flat
> Fiat of synopsis that
> Makes every goddess the Great Mother
> And women types of one another,
> And Hathor, Circe, Aphrodite
> One pair of breasts inside one nightie.
> That closed-in Kosmos served by myth
> Is just what Rhyme must quarrel with.

They are an amiable set of poems to end (almost) this ample *Collected Poems.*

III

But even as we think we know pretty well what Davie is at, happily (and waywardly) he upsets our assumptions by being on the move again. The Fall 1972 *Mosaic* published his essay "Eliot in One Poet's Life." Here, taking stock, Davie finds his discovery "much less depressing than surprising." And so, I think, might we. For after all his concentration on Hardy, Davie announces "the surprise was that I discovered, as soon as I thought about it, that the late Mr. Eliot has been a presence in my life more insistently influential than any other writer whatever." Would it be unkind to suggest that, for all the criticism he has expended on such matters, we might have expected him "to think about it" rather earlier? But perhaps we can consider this civility and English fair play, as well as the mind's natural tendency to change and to have different needs at different times. As we have traced it, first Yeats had been most important; then Pound edged him out; now, after the intense interlude of Hardy, Eliot comes out on top after all.

Eliot's criticism initially influenced Davie. Mistakenly he thought he must imitate Donne and Herbert. But then his writing was released by his sudden realization that the Romantic movement was not a superficial fashion. Contrary to his previous criticism, he now observes that it is impossible to return to the 17th or 18th century "except by . . . arriving permanently travel-stained." Fortunately Eliot's poetry had another effect on Davie; the *Four Quartets*, freeing him of the notion that only metaphor could impart meaning in poetry, impressed him with the usefulness of abstract words and "sustained and elaborately correct syntax." But why has Eliot, beyond the above and his "believing in the right to personal privacy," meant more to Davie than any other poet, even Hardy? Davie was born twenty years too late for Hardy. And though Davie felt much more affection for Hardy, Eliot elicited "infinitely" more "professional respect." (Such conclusion after a very recent book making most arduously a case for Hardy and as a professional poet?)

This might seem like a pretty jagged note to end on. But, no, Davie will, fortunately, not rest. In the Autumn-Winter 1972/73

Agenda what do we find but a longish poem, "Reticulations," in manner and matter very much like Pound (here called "my master") and Olson; more like them than any earlier Davie poem I've seen. Apparently and gratifyingly wonders, as far as Davie was concerned, will never cease. Nor the need (via "*Guide Michelin*"—Davie is teaching in France that year—the subtitle of the poem) to be moving on, even if it be mainly a flying back and forth from past to present, history to geography, England to U.S. and back again. In Picasso's words:

> . . . even if you are against a movement, you're still part of it. The pro and the con are, after all, two aspects of the same movement. . . . You can't escape your own period. Whether you take sides for or against, you're always inside it.

Thus in the latest Davie piece I've read, a review of George Oppen's *Seascape: Needle's Eye* in the Spring 1973 *Shenandoah*, poems Davie admires ("Not for him . . . the naive pastoralism, the harking back to a pre-industrial economy, which is the stock-in-trade of the American poets currently most popular. . . ."), Davie concentrates on Oppen's foreigner's sense of precariousness on the San Francisco coast, his sense that not the past, not poetic art, will help us. In this, his "disarmingly modest" claims for his art, Oppen is, Davie maintains, unlike the Williams he resembles—for Williams was "after all a mythopoeic poet (*Paterson*) . . . in his last years a master or a prophet"—but like Hardy. Nonetheless, Davie disagrees that the time for traditional splendors and clarities is past. For whatever traditional technical devices Oppen's art rejects, it has its own splendors and clarities. If we truly abandoned the past in poetry, we would be left with "grunts and yelps." And rightly Davie declares that Oppen has relinquished old rhetoric for new (for "rhetoric is inseparable from language"). Davie admits however that this new rhetoric allows Oppen, as sometimes it did Williams, "an extraordinary directness and gentleness of intimacy," a tone of voice beyond the older rhetoric's reach. From the ashes of the old, the phoenix of "the elegant as well as the touching" springs again. "Whether you take sides for or against [a movement], you're always inside it."

T. S. ELIOT AND THE COURTYARD
REVOLUTION

I

THE revolution began innocently enough, with laudations of Eliot even, as the largest tributes were being heaped upon him. John Crowe Ransom, easily and graciously in *The New Criticism* among the foremost critics who have written on the subject, presents Eliot as a pioneer of this "new criticism." Ransom says: "It is likely that we have had no better critic than Eliot." Yet he reaches this conclusion by curious circumlocutions. Wishing to clarify the direction of the new criticism, he concentrates on what he regards the faulty links in Eliot's critical armor. Unwittingly, Ransom has paved the way for the interpretations of Yvor Winters and Eliseo Vivas. Even as he intended praise of **Eliot**, Ransom supplied these later critics with cues that they have inflated in a fashion Ransom, I believe, would little approve. As Ransom is moderate in his appraisal, they deliberately seek out only the negative.

Thus Ransom's designation of Eliot as "The Historical Critic," a description certainly inadequate to the accommodating of Eliot's abilities, has no doubt helped to implement Winters's detraction of Eliot as a "determinist." And as we collect and estimate Ransom's objections to Eliot as a new critic, we discover that they do generally incline to the views held by the men who accuse Eliot of anti-intellectualism and romanticism. It is not to be wondered that the suspicious have suspected Ransom of praising Eliot in order to bury him. Of course Ransom says nothing so explicit. Yet extracted and concentrated on, his demurs—three basically, all stemming from one root—must awaken suspicion as to the fundamental soundness of Eliot's criticism. First, he remonstrates with Eliot for being insufficiently theoretical or philosophical; second, he chides him for suggesting "automatic writing in art"; and finally, he laments Eliot's anti-intellectualism or indifference to the "affirmations" or meanings of poetry.

Briefly sketching Eliot's literary career, Ransom comments on the excitement provoked by Eliot's "complex personality." The Jekyll of Eliot's criticism, Ransom tells us, clashed with the Hyde of his poetry. But though the word was sought in the Jekyll to justify the Hyde, "the word was not there." For "the drift of the criticism was heavily against the drift of the poetry." Eliot himself recognized and indicated this disparity. He even offered it as an essential of the two occupations: ". . . in one's prose reflexions one may be legitimately occupied with ideals, whereas in the writing of verse one can only deal with actuality." In his criticism Eliot expresses by implication what he would like to do and be; in his poetry he expresses what he is and at the particular moment of composition must be, without assuming pious poses. Thus he has, naturally enough, defined the purposes of poetry and of criticism according to his practice.

Yet it seems a little peculiar to declare "the drift of the criticism . . . heavily against the drift of the poetry," or to maintain: "In no formal sense did the poetry become more traditionary." Even as Eliot's later poems clearly ramify from his earlier work, so a unity does play between the criticism and the poetry. In addition, Eliot's poetical style surely reflects his critical cynosures; are not the metaphysical, the Dantean, and the Elizabethan abundantly busy in his art, absorbed into his own personality and time? Eliot has historical sense enough to know that that poet most successfully imitates the best who expresses his age in itself. Tradition, to live, must breathe contemporary air. Finally, the dramatic irony active in Eliot's poetry, the criticism operating on what Eliot treats, is consonant with his prose concerns. If we examine sympathetically, the word is there.

Following Eliot's development, Ransom now commends him for not permitting his creative talents, his critical judgments, and his religious convictions to compromise one another. "One of the best things in his influence has been his habit of considering aesthetic effect as independent of religious effect, or moral, or political and social; as an end that is beyond and as not coördinate with these." But though Ransom believes Eliot's critical attitude "still unchanged," he thinks the religionist in Eliot is overtaking the critic and the poet; religious opinion has nearly supplanted the criticism. As we shall see, this later flowering should please Ransom.

Eliot as a historical critic next occupies us. And what does the title amount to? Eliot resembles "certain academic literary scholars . . . having the historical scholarship." Ransom justifies the identification by assuring us that Eliot "is learned in the precise learning of the scholars, a Pharisee of the Pharisees." A remarkable compliment, particularly for its overtones. It seems to me that Ransom is confusing Eliot's precision and a certain primness with the precise dullness of many scholars. Why does Ransom elect him a Pharisee? Because the universities have not seriously impeached his learning! Elsewhere, in his "Criticism, Inc.," Ransom admitted the studious indifference of universities to criticism. Is it daring to venture the speculation then that scholars have not impeached Eliot's learning simply because they have shied clear of it? They fear him; for he is not afraid, very unscholarly-like, to hazard critical opinions. Ransom himself conjectures that if the scholars fail to recognize him as belonging to them, "it is because he turns his scholarship to pointed critical uses." Something of a distinction, I would say. And now Ransom turns upon himself. Establishing Eliot in the critical line of Dryden and Doctor Johnson, Ransom acknowledges that "that is a kind of scholar which our wonderfully organized Departments of Literature . . . have simply not turned out, nor dreamed of turning out." For "it is likely that we have had no better critic than Eliot." Yet he is a Pharisee of Pharisees.

But here the first significant fracture appears. To the "absolute aesthetician, the philosophical critic," the historical approach is insufficient. Yet as Ransom repeats, though historical in base, Eliot does not fail to apply his learning; and so he is "critical in the end." For "Eliot has nothing like a formula ready in advance." What more could we, or Ransom, ask? Much, it seems. Investigating Eliot's essay on Swinburne, Ransom infers, "Little is 'formulated' in this essay in the technical terms of some critical theory, even of some theory of his own." In short, Eliot should pause to write pure aesthetics—one of Ransom's abiding beliefs. But a theory accumulates behind Eliot's critical comparisons, a technique that has served Ransom himself admirably. Must Eliot state theory nakedly, passively? Rather he demonstrates it in action. Accordingly, later critics have built whole theories and furbished reputations on Eliot's *obiter scripta*. Ransom earlier cautioned us against philosophical critics whose "theory is very general" and who have "not proved that they can write close criticism by writing it." Even those casually acquainted with Ransom's writings must know his profound affection for the particular and his reprehension of generalizing and categorizing criticism. Yet these absent in Eliot distress him. As for critical principles, look at the critical to-do Eliot's dropt-in-passing "objective correlative" has stirred up. But no, Eliot fails to make "ultimate generalizations"—a strange complaint for one who has consistently abhorred the fiercely Platonic in our world. Eliot suffers of "a theoretical innocence." Eliot himself has accused Pater, Arnold, Ruskin, and Carlyle of being anti-intellectual or worse, unable to follow a thought. Now with poetic justice, if no other, the accusation is brought against him. As Eliot has denied his teachers, so our time has begun to deny him.

Out of his theoretical innocence must grow Eliot's tendency to fall back upon "some inaccessible entity which he calls 'the tradition' "—something Ransom regards as semi-mystical. Yet Eliot never says that this tradition relieves the individual writer of his responsibility or alleviates his effort. On the contrary, it jealously requires utmost vigilance. For "probably, indeed, the larger part of the labour of an author in composing his work is critical labour." According to Eliot tradition is the unbroken continuity of culture, the interplay and interdependence of the great works of art that constitute its members. But even as Ransom seems to be attacking, he withdraws. Eliot is a traditionalist, but only "up to the point where it would obscure and dull his critical judgment of a given poem. Then he reverts simply to the good critic. . . . No mischief is done."

At this juncture, however, Ransom discovers "great difficulties" for Eliot. These occur when Eliot "theorizes about the function of the ever-living tradition at the moment when actual new poetry is being written." Ransom here regrets what he earlier desired of Eliot—theorizing. Poor Eliot collides with the "insuperable fact" that "each new poem must after all compose a new poem which cannot be exactly what any previous poem has been." How has Eliot impugned this newness? In Ransom's mind, Eliot tries to handle this fact by maintaining that tradition supervises and composes the poem while the poet is a mere writing hand. On the contrary, Eliot considers tradition a living thing, "a mind which changes." As the past influences us, so we affect it. Ransom tackles a "strange" passage from Eliot's "Tradition and the Individual Talent" in which Eliot presents "as a principle of aesthetic, not merely historical, criticism" the communality of art. "The existing monuments form an ideal order . . . modified by the introduction of the new . . . work of art among them." The order adjusts itself as a family, whole before, makes room for a new child. When a new masterpiece appears, though it initially may upset privacies and relationships, we soon tuck it in and consider it inevitable. So the past is altered for us in that we have changed our attitude toward it to include new work. Ransom recoils at the idea that the "new poem will automatically make an alteration in the tradition." By new Eliot meant "great"; if the work is great, the change in the past will be automatic. Ransom confesses ignorance before this passage. He will not see that in a sense we know Shakespeare better than he knew himself. In that poetry grows out of the past, it "explains" or elucidates the past. So a Joyce's *Ulysses* heightens the *Odyssey* even as the *Odyssey* reinforces *Ulysses*. The "body of poetry has increased itself in the past" in understanding: a great art-work more than any scholarship illuminates the past. Ransom wants to know if the increase will happen "automatically." How can it if, to quote Ransom and Eliot too, the additions are "deliberate"?

Immediately Ransom encounters Eliot's theory of depersonalization, his insistence that the poet be not seduced by personality, as the romantics often were, yielding to his idiosyncracies and weaknesses. Ransom boggles at the chemical metaphor, as others after him have done. He protests that Eliot "does not identify the chemicals in this reaction, other than the catalyst . . . the poet's mind." Are not the chemicals, the oxygen and sulphur dioxide, our feelings and emotions that Ransom later quarrels with? This process he judges "very nearly a doctrine of poetic automatism." Either he forgets or does not understand the emphasis Eliot puts upon the critical faculties focused upon the raw product of the imagination. To begin with, a passionate detachment is at work, an objectivity of concentration surpassing science. The artist is a negative plate that focuses both scene and sun. But Ransom thinks this theory "not very realistic belief" in "insisting that even the apparent innovations of poets were really fulfilments of history." These innovations are fulfilments of the poets' personal histories, in turn—if the poets are substantial ones—a fulfilment of the history of the world around them. Ransom, however, seems to forget Eliot's avowal that such work helps shape history—a reciprocity.

Again Ransom executes an abrupt about-face. Eliot "is not without a theory of poetry, and he does not write specific criticism without conscientious references to his theory." This time Ransom turns Eliot aside with the judgment that the theory is "one of the most unmanageable theories that a critic could profess." For Ransom considers "the feelings and the emotions" unmanageable. Let us talk about the "cognitive objects, or the cognitive situations, which identify them" instead. And so normally Eliot does. Ransom seems to be unaware that his belief in the cognitive object resembles Eliot's objective correlative and its indispensability. But Eliot is at this point not talking about the work of art but what happens in the artist's mind. He equally insists that the artist must furnish us with cognitive objects and that these objects concern us in studying a work of art. The matter of feelings and emotions comes to a head in Eliot's famous "Poetry is not a turning loose of emotion, but an escape from emotion." In itself it is true the statement is elusive and, as Ransom says, may strike the "humble reader" as "something esoteric." It does so until we remember Eliot's insistence on detachment. Ransom has said with equal esotericism, "Poetry is beyond passion." So in his essay "Henry James," printed in 1918, the year after "Tradition and the Individual Talent," Eliot continues this idea by complimenting James for his critical genius which

> comes out most tellingly in his mastery over, his baffling escape from, Ideas; a mastery and an escape which are perhaps the last test of a superior intelligence. He had a mind so fine that no idea could violate it.

In brief, Eliot is extolling control: he resents one's being hit-and-run over by ideas or emotions. Mastery means submitting or assimilating ideas and emotions to an artistic purpose rather than allowing them to dominate and submerge one. From the essay "Tradition and the Individual Talent" to the "Henry

James" to the "Metaphysical Poets" is a clear line of developed theory. Reading various Eliot essays, we can piece together his critical ideals by nõticing what he respects similarly in different men and different times. After exploring Eliot's analysis of Jonson, Ransom concludes: "It is Eliot's theory . . . which is at fault if anything is. His perception, within human limitations, is nearly perfect, and a critic can go a long way with that." Earlier Ransom denied Eliot any theory; then he hesitated; now he finds fault with it. But Eliot's perception is nearly perfect. Need I remind Ransom of his maintaining elsewhere the inevitable mutuality of concept and percept? "No percept without a concept, sharp percepts mean sharp concepts, rich percepts mean a multiplicity of concepts; and lacking the latter he [Ransom is criticising the original Adam] could not have had the former. . . ." If Eliot is the peer of all our critics, are we bold in believing that his perceptions involve actively penetrating concepts?

But Ransom seems to be playing several critical rôles. Thus tackling Eliot's "The Metaphysical Poets," he comes upon thought-versus-feeling. Knowing their dependency, as I have shown above, he here argues that for us they are split awry. Strange again for one who, demanding the "whole man," later rebukes Eliot for separating art and religion. Ransom has continuously lamented the specialist tendency in our world; nonetheless, he avers that feeling and thought "ordinarily repel one another: the abstracted exercise of reason . . . and the inclusive experience. . . ." But how shall we enjoy this inclusive experience without thinking? Eliot is not singling out the *abstracted* exercise, but that involved in the fully functioning whole man. Thoughts and feeling are basically one—the one impossible for us without the other. Here Ransom acknowledges scientific practice and the weight of history: "There can be no undifferentiated unity again: no return." We will see shortly however how, when he wishes to, Ransom can resent and battle history. Actually Ransom seems to mean by thought systematic or schematic reasoning. Eliot, I take it, means thought as the word is commonly defined.

Finally, we come to the third charge: as far as poetry is concerned, Eliot "waives the necessity of belief." In other places Ransom has described the basic ideas in poems as their prose commonplaces and has accented the treatment of the details or the "irrelevancies." He has also again and again rejected the philosophers and moralists in poetry who go to it for ideal or moral reinforcement or employ the poem as a sugar-coated illustration. Here Ransom becomes the Puritan. Yet, at the beginning of this essay, he commended Eliot for "his habit of considering aesthetic effect as independent of religious effect, or moral, or political and social. . . ." Here we reach one of the major conflicts in Ransom; he espouses the autonomy of poetry in his belief in close criticism but renounces this autonomy practically in his predilection for poetics. On the one hand, he would safeguard poetry's purity and freedom in a world of specialization. If our day is divisive, let poetry be spared division. On the other hand, he respects the unity of life he discovers in the past. What Ransom does not see consistently is that art at its best includes all interests—political, social and religious—but so fused that it is none of them. Having, apparently, finally submitted to moralism, he now does what he found "particularly depressing" in Blackmur: he approaches a poem as a moral tract; it is a fillip to theory. But as he says of Blackmur, Ransom "of course, is not really a moralistic critic at all when he is going properly, but only nominally, and perhaps only in desperation. . . ." For Ransom the problem of belief now becomes almost identical in poetry and religion.

He discovers another considerable shift in his thinking for us, one closely resembling the submission I have just mentioned. He feels an increasing sympathy for the naturalists, positivists, scientists. "The forces that have captured the world are trying to found a new civilization; it may turn out oddly like the old one." Briefly, he sympathises with them but hardly agrees with or thinks like them. But "there might be something in having one's own civilization anyhow." A rather startling statement for Ransom to make, much as he has protested the always increasing scientism, Platonism, Puritanism, as he has variously called it, and poetry's desperate fight against it. Has he capitulated to the time? If so, what relationship does be observe between the specializations now? One recalls his former excoriation of "Platonic Poetry" and his arraignment of those who study nature only to use it.

The core of the problem is, he says, the "supernatural fact" which "appears constitutionally in every religious discipline, but it appears luridly and with the greatest frequency in poetry." What has happened to his dismissal of Santayana's Platonic essences and his conviction that poets are "prodigious materialists"? This supernatural fact must be dissected philosophically, and scientifically too, presumably. Then in support of the present erroneous notion that Eliot considers poetry purely emotional, Ransom tells us that for Eliot poetry is free of "real factuality" "since it only wants to offer emotional experiences, and these can feed on fictions and fancies as well as on facts." I wish Ransom were a little more substantial in this opinion. Is he not ignoring the objective correlative and Eliot's desire for a poetry written by the whole man?

But Eliot, Ransom says, does draw a firm line between fact and fiction in religion. Ransom approves this line, and wishes it for poetry too. For, differing with Eliot, he asserts that Religion is Morals, that Religion is Art. "Orthodox religious dogma is closely comparable with some body of Platonic or poetic myth; it is poetry, or at least it once was poetry. . . ." Should we worship poetry then? Though he has come dangerously close to it in the past, Ransom has never admitted the Platonic background of religion. How could he, condemning the Platonic as he did? Now religion is not only Platonic but poetry is too.

But he has come close to the truth, when he says: ". . . at least it once was poetry." To begin with, animistically, worship was poetry; God was everywhere and everything. Such belief soon shrank; and religions employed poetry or ritual for illustrative purposes, to reach and seduce the people to moral teachings. But it is dubious that art and religion were one; the artist of the Middle Ages utilized religion as a language, the only cultivated idiom present. Today other languages are perhaps available.

Finally, Ransom regrets that Eliot has served his literature with less than half the zeal he pays religion. For as Ransom showed, Eliot is sound on literary facts and suspect on religious ideas. But Ransom should not be uneasy; for as he says, the religious in Eliot has begun to invade the literary, in poetry and criticism alike. *After Strange Gods* ought to please Ransom. Has he forgotten that there Eliot finally succumbs, claiming that literature's problem is a religious one and that literature needs religion? "I can see no necessity," Ransom says, "for waiving the intellectual standards on behalf of poets." Eliot has never done so. "If Shelley's argument is foolish, it makes his poetry foolish." Exactly what Eliot has said. In *The Use of Poetry* Eliot reminds us that Shelley was the victim of his ideas; devouring him, they emerge triumphant everywhere in his work. A Dante absorbs his ideas into his living expression. Shelley's ideas stand in the way like Sin at the gate, not to be denied. As Eliot explains it:

> When the doctrine, theory, belief, or "view of life" presented in a poem is one which the mind of the reader can accept as coherent, mature, and founded on the facts of experience, it interposes no obstacle to the reader's enjoyment, whether it be one that he accept or deny, approve or deprecate. When it is one which the reader rejects as childish or feeble, it may, for a reader of well-developed mind, set up an almost complete check.

Ideas grow out of their time and climate. If the poet converts them into living flesh, into experience rather than naked belief, though we may be of another time and thought, we can delight in them.   But if the poet cannot see his world for his struggle with insubordinate beliefs, his work and his readers are throttled by them.   It is the price one pays, and should, for the luxury of excessive theory—whether in criticism or poetry or religion.

II

Eliseo Vivas in his article "The Objective Correlative of T. S. Eliot," in the Winter, 1944, issue of THE AMERICAN BOOK-MAN, amply illustrates the growing animus harshly aimed. Vivas's indebtedness to Ransom is fairly transparent.   It is interesting merely to juxtapose the conclusion of Vivas's article with a critical remark from Ransom's *New Criticism*, first expressed in the pre-face and later centering on Eliot.   Ransom says:

> I think it is impossible to talk clearly about these matters until we drop the vocabulary of emotions and talk about the respective cognitive objects, or the cognitive situations which identify them.

Vivas evidently agrees with this view; for according to him,

> The vocabulary of the emotions is thus confusing, if not indeed irrelevant, to literary criticism; and if it were drop-ped, and the critic confined himself only to the objects and situations and values communicated by the poem, there would ensue an enormous clarification in the practice of criticism.

Need I point out how much these quotations owe to Eliot? More's the amusement when we realize that Vivas opposes it to Eliot even as Eliot is deprecating Shakespeare's omission of a significant object in *Hamlet* and stressing art's constant need for such object.

Vivas's essay is an excellent example of what happens when

such critics, assuming Ransom's negative inferences on Eliot and shunning the homage, derange the inferences for their own purposes. Furthermore, the article illustrates the prevalent critical practice of calculated misquotation. In that Eliot proposes the objective correlative, "he accepts with the vast majority of his contemporaries the modern dogma that the artist is primarily concerned with emotion." Such a conclusion does not wrench the facts; it breaks their backs! Eliot never said, as Vivas has it, "The poet expresses his emotion . . ."; nor did Eliot stress the primacy of emotion. To quote Eliot accurately: "The only way of expressing emotion in the form of art is by finding an 'objective correlative'." As he says in his "The Metaphysical Poets": "Those who object to the 'artificiality' of Milton or Dryden sometimes tell us to 'look into our hearts and write.' But that is not looking deep enough. Racine or Donne looked into a good deal more than the heart. One must look into the cerebral cortex, the nervous system, and the digestive tracts."

Furthermore, Vivas blinks the fact that at this point Eliot is examining a particular play, *Hamlet,* and accounting for its failure in the unmoorage, physically, of its emotion: Hamlet's (and so Shakespeare's) inability to discover an object or situation which would satisfy and thereby, at its proper stage, induce the acting emotion (like the Ghost) to appear. This very realization Yvor Winters, another anti-Eliot critic, has attempted to palm off as his own: the "pseudo-reference"—that is, romantics finding their feelings first and then trying to pin them on inappropriate objects, a rupture between cause and effect. Winters, however, fails to allow for that state of well-being, that moment of ipseity which seizes on anything that comes to its hand as delight, praise, and gratulation. Such divine inflatus like sunlight plays no favorites.

All that Eliot is essentially saying is that we cannot have an emotion without an object or symbol to body it (almost bait to capture it); the better, the more intelligent the poet the more likely the symbol he chooses. So, in little, Hamlet's playing on the flute or Richard II's wielding of the mirror is a perfect reflection of feeling. In a sense, these objects "explain" the emotion— that is, show us its *raison d'être* and so produce the emotion in us. Shakespeare was here incidentally offering the artist's craft. The artist must work in reverse. First he determines his purpose; then he provides the causes, the scenery, the background so that the emotion can "naturally" arise in us. To present the end-product ("I fall upon the thorns of life! I bleed!") as a Shelley does and to expect the reader to feel any more than a faint regret for the poor (obviously weak) young fellow, is poppycock. We must be permitted to participate. In *Hamlet*, Shakespeare has posited the emotion without proving it or showing its reasons to us. We cannot discover what shaped the passion. Perhaps this incompleteness, however, is Hamlet's central problem and basic attractiveness? So Falstaff is most himself when he is least himself.

Eliot is seeking artistic "inevitability." Put fire to a hand and the hand burns; bring certain objects and situations to bear and the character, as a piece of paper under a steady lens, must also burn. We, the readers, identifying ourselves with the character, as we see through the artist's lens, are likely to burn too. As Vivas insists, ". . . no artist, however skillful, can possibly control the subjective affective responses of his readers. . . ." True, but that need not prevent the writer from trying. Thus intelligence must do its deepest critical work in creation (in preparation of the trap for the reader as well as for the emotion). Furthermore, we expect on the part of a fairly literate, practised reader a certain willingness to adjust himself to different times, places and situations. If what Vivas says above were wholly true, then communication would be impracticable and art futile. Recognizing the barriers, we strive against them or, better, use them.

It is amazing how these critics impugn Eliot for the very thing he attacked, romantic emotionalism, and impugn him with and in behalf of romantic emotionalism. They accuse him, it would seem, of being romantic because he has not been romantic enough for them. Furthermore, they forget the intellect, the critical faculties which Eliot predicates. This romanticism appears later in Vivas when he speaks of the artist's "problem of sincerity or of integrity" as though art were not in itself an integrity and, by it, sincerity enough. He tells us that as "there is a vast difference between justice and legality" (justice being some abstract permanent value quite apart from living): ". . . so the artist in regard to his original emotion: how outrageously do the demands of form violate it, how deeply do they transmute it! For no form really suits it, no public means through which it can be communicated brings it utterly out of the shadow of its own ineffability." And Vivas accuses Eliot of being "primarily concerned with emotion"! This idealism, a desire for naked emotion, the impossibility of which Eliot has indicated: this regret that we are unable to express our emotions directly, rawly, without the ordering that means understanding: this resentment of forms is, I believe, opposite the truth. Form alone permits the poet mastery of the emotion by way of comprehension.

Apparently, a page later, Vivas changes direction; for talking of Lorca and his "Llanto por Ignacio Sánchez Mejías," Vivas suggests that "the whole episode, name and all, may have been imagined. . . . It is not necessary to assume that the actual emotion that is worked up by the poet into the poem is the actual occasion of the creative act"—meaning, so far as I can tell, that the emotion in the poem need not be the engenderer of the poem. Reluctantly he admits that art is "artificial," a doing, a making, by no means necessarily identifiable with the poet's spiritual state at time of making.

"Eliot," Vivas maintains, "grafts a somewhat revamped doctrine of catharsis on to the popular theory of expression, and uses the product to justify poetry therapeutically." Mr. Vivas is to be congratulated on his clairvoyance. Eliot, to my searching, is not remotely concerned with a "popular theory of expression"; nor is he attempting to justify poetry, therapeutically or otherwise. Eliot is sane enough to know it needs no such justification. Again, he simply says that emotion, ignorant of its causes, blurred, and larger than its possessor's (or possessed's) understanding, by the confusion makes action of a directed intelligence naturally impossible: so Hamlet. Eliot is not discussing poetry: he is discussing the emotion in *Hamlet*.

Quoting from Eliot's "Tradition and the Individual Talent," Vivas analyzes: ". . . according to Eliot's opening sentence, the stuff which makes up the poem consists of emotions and feelings." Repetition of this opening sentence in itself denies such interpretation: "The experience, you will notice, the elements which enter the presence of the transforming catalyst, are of two kinds: emotions and feelings." Naturally, our feelings—sensations or responses to our world—(Eliot, knowing how difficult it is to discover the border between feelings and emotions, ignores it) and our emotions are the raw materials of a poem (for they are all we have); but they are the *raw* materials: it is what happens to them in the mind or imagination of the poet, the transforming catalyst, that matters, that determines the shape of the poem. Neatly Vivas ignores this obvious distinction. Then he spots "the source of a serious confusion": ". . . it would seem as if the feelings which inhere for the poet in the phrase or image which he chooses also inheres in it for the reader." First of all, the "feelings, inhering for the writer in particular words . . . or images, [which] may be added to compose the final result" is an afterthought Eliot tacked on; he says nothing about the feeling inhering for the reader; what he does say is: "The effect of a work of art upon the person who enjoys it is an experience different in kind from any experience not of art. It may be formed out of one emotion, or may be a combination of several: and various feelings, inhering for the writer in particular words or phrases or images, may be added to compose the final result."

Countering again, Vivas recognizes: ". . . it also happens that a poem or any other object of art seems to possess among its objective characters emotion or feeling values, which 'inhere' in it irrespective of our reactions to it." *Seems* is the word. A poem—words, as the semanticists have taught us—has no value beyond what we can discover. More, it is memory of the object and not the poem itself that arouses emotion. But Vivas says in a different connection: A poem "expresses" emotion "whether it arouses it or not"—innately it seems. Need we remind him how often the emotion and the meaning of a poem grow as later generations add their thoughts and feelings to it?

A little later Vivas scores Eliot for "the very assumption that a feeling can exist by itself in the mind and wait without symbolic expression of any kind whatever." I challenge Vivas to produce such a statement on Eliot's part. All Eliot said was that "the poet's mind is . . . a receptacle for seizing and storing up numberless feelings, phrases. . . ." He did not comment on the clothed or naked condition of these feelings. But I think we can assume that Eliot is well enough educated (certainly his objective correlative would say so) to realize that feelings cannot exist without symbols or words to contain them.

Vivas poses a Sphinxish question: ". . . exactly how can feelings, something subjective, attach to images, something quite objective?" The fatal dualism once more: feelings enjoy a seity quite detached, it seems, from the external world. Yet a moment ago Vivas regretted what he considered Eliot's tendency to believe that "a feeling can exist by itself in the mind." A moment ago also Vivas had taken the attachment for granted: now he sees in Eliot a failure to explain the happening. For Eliot, to begin with, "The *only* way [my italics] of expressing emotion" is by evoking or arousing it. Next, let me say that feelings, subjective, attach to images, objective, in the mind: what are feelings but our responses to these images reflected within us? Perhaps the *how* of this relationship cannot be "explained." Eliot never tried to do so; he merely offered a fairly obvious mechanism or "formula" for recalling emotion. As I have mentioned earlier, at the end of his article, oddly enough, Vivas himself concludes: "The vocabulary of the emotions is confusing, if not indeed irrelevant, to literary criticism; and if it were dropped, and the critic confined himself only to the objects and situations and values communicated by the poem, there would ensue an enormous clarification in the practice of criticism." Why then censure Eliot for not doing what no one else has ever done and what you do not, apparently, wish done?

"But even if poetry always did arouse emotion, we would still have to ask whether poetry *should* seek to arouse emotion. . . ." The "always" is curious. Again, I must insist that Eliot did not romantically demand that poetry must "seek to arouse emotion." He said, *if* emotion is to be expressed, it can be only by. . . .

Finally, Vivas asseverates the "importance for criticism to realize that the emotion expressed through the objective correlative is not that which the poet felt before the poem was written"—as though to say that Eliot insists on their identity. Nowhere in his essay does Eliot attempt to confuse the poet's personal feeling with the feeling in the play. Actually, using Vivas's own much earlier quotation, I find that Eliot believes that a great poem (by implication) is "a new compound," hardly a single, simple emotion. Even should some powerful emotion be the initial motive power, as in Lorca's poem, say, his poem, if it is worth while, even as it expresses his sorrow (so arouses it), controls and orders the sorrow by the very properties that produced it; and by ordering it, the poem makes the sorrow a new magnificence. "The assumption," Vivas goes on, "that we can criticize the play *Hamlet* by comparing the emotion expressed in the play with Shakespeare's emotion, or that through the play we can discover the emotions that went into it is a confusing illusion." No doubt, if that had been Eliot's intention. As I have suggested, he does not compare the play's emotion with Shakespeare's to criticize *Hamlet*: rather by the confusion of the emotion in the play, Eliot infers that Shakespeare did not know exactly what he wished to say, that he had not found efficient fact enough to warrant the emotion's presence. Eliot is not interested here in the emotions that went into the play. What he notices is that we cannot discover the sources of the emotion and therefore cannot feel either the emotion or Hamlet clearly.

HOW TO END THE RENAISSANCE

ONCE more in old tones of new triumph we are being told by various artists and critics that at last something utterly new, new for the first time in some "40,000 years of aesthetic activity," is being achieved by the most audacious sector of the avant-garde, that embracing the position of "radical empiricism": we are at last on the way to being, through their enthronement of chance and the random (but the rigorously objective as well), free, particularly of our whole long burdensome past. According to the French painter Georges Mathieu, quoted by Professor Leonard B. Meyer in his article, "The End of the Renaissance?", in the Summer, 1963, *Hudson Review*:

> Our whole culture has allowed itself to be permeated, since the end of the Middle Ages, by Hellenistic thought patterns which aimed at bringing the cosmos down to human proportions and limited the means of access to an understanding of the Universe to those provided by reason and the senses [no reference to feeling, intuition, inspiration, imagination?] . . . . For the past ten years, painting . . . has been freeing itself from the yoke of this burdensome inheritance. After twenty-five centuries of a culture we had made our own, we are witnessing in certain aspects of lyrical non-configuration a new phenomenon in painting—and, one might add, in the arts in general—which calls into question the very foundations of 40,000 years of aesthetic activity.

Aside from Mathieu's highhandedness with chronology, the ease with which he leaps from the end of the Middle Ages over twenty-five centuries and, magnificently expanding his conquest in a phrase, past 40,000 years, exhilarating as all this may be, one might question his confident belief in the uniqueness of the past ten years of painting and of the arts in general.

At the risk of being contemptuously dismissed as academic by such new men, I would also like to rehearse some history, but that more modestly recent. Over fifty years ago Ezra Pound, with what became known as Imagism, proposed to the young poets around him that they cleanse poetry of the late Victorian litter into which it had fallen. Their effort constituted one of the periodically necessary purifyings of the language of the tribe. Much later William Carlos Williams, perhaps the most persistent of the lot, could say: "No thoughts but in things." Beyond their suspicion of generalizations no longer relevant to experience, in the pragmatic spirit of the age these poets longed for precision, that which the practice of their senses could thoroughly, empirically account for.

At the same time we note a complex impulse at work here, one rather at odds with itself: on the one hand, the ancient desire to bring the word as close as possible to the deed and, on the other, delight in the resources of words themselves, the rich private lives they possess. So similarly artists have been preoccupied with their materials, the fundamental nature of their medium. A Mallarmé made poetic capital of the virgin-white page; it became the theater of his delicate surgical operations on language. And his follower, Valéry, concerned to redeem words from their plebeian prose entanglements, declared: "I did not want to say but wanted to make." Behind this contrary desire, however, lies a further embarrassing wealth, the world within the artist. We confront the dilemma at once by juxtaposing "no thoughts but in things" with "abstract expressionism." Joyce's work, in his Laocoön-like struggle to reconcile these several worlds, indeed to discover the oneness that should operate behind them, is perhaps the most impressive witness of this dilemma.

So it has gone in all the arts: the media as mirrors to be cleansed to reflect the world more accurately versus the media as worlds in themselves. Composers like Schoenberg and Webern, eager to break out of the late romantic fix, established a new one, an almost hermetic vocabulary for music. One of their followers, Pierre Boulez, has announced that "the composer should play the game with the most rational dice and according to the strictest rules he can imagine." Many of us no longer believe in innate laws or at least our access to them or, for that matter, in the conventions that grow out of established practice and the artistic community. "The composer," as Robert Craft sees it, "is therefore obliged to invent rules just to have rules and because he must work according to something. In practice this is apt to lead to a new system for each work." In painting also Kandinsky and others, under the impact of an always more abstract scientific description of the nature of things, threw off the tenure of the external world, at least the world as men till then had usually seen it, so paving the way for abstract expressionism and additional recent developments.

Here we encounter an interesting shift, one of the myriad secularizings that have been going on for centuries. Medieval and Renaissance artists, employed by the religious view that saw heaven and the spiritual world as the reality, dutifully painted angels, saints, and devils, but at their best these were brought splendidly to earth. Now with science's supplanting for many of the religious view, artists again are dutifully trying to portray the new reality. However, since this view has little interest in man as a unique, subjective creature, still committed in most of his daily life to the experience of his senses (rather it is this present view's very remoteness and would-be objectivity which makes it convincing to most of its exponents), it is hard indeed to relate its reality to man, to involve it in the realm he normally occupies. And though habituation may eventually change this, for the time being some serious blur inevitably sets in.

Another strain in modern art, however, even as it is devout before the objective, concentrates almost entirely on the daily, especially as it stresses "the ugly and sordid, the decayed or rotting figure." A recent article, "Why Not Pop Art?", by Nicolas Calas, in the Spring, 1965, issue of *Art and Literature*, presents this aspect of new art with a good deal of sympathy. In his words: "Pop art is sharpening our sensitivity by emphasizing the objective aspect of being at the expense of the subjective one. . . ." But a little later he admits, without any seeming uneasiness at what his admission betrays, "In fighting for their place in the galleries of Madison Avenue [inevitable locale!], the brightest of the younger New York artists were impelled to reverse the position of their elders"—that is, the abstract expressionists. But perhaps his most revealing statement is the following:

> Pop art focuses on the popular ready-made image. This is undoubtedly a healthy reaction to the cult of the dream image of the interbellum period with its political and sexual wishful thinking by the fellow-travelers of Marx and Freud. [Pop art then is realistic and brave: it sees and celebrates things-as-they-are.] Pop art is tailored to the needs of 'the lonely crowd' which congregates in subways and fills highways, gazing at ads and billboards with the fascination medieval masses gathered in churches gazed at holy images —ikons. Pop art is the art of making pop-ikons in an era when magic has withdrawn from mosaics and stained glass to reappear on the television screen. "I am so mesmerized by television that I want to buy all that it advertises!" a City College student was heard to exclaim.

As I have suggested, this is part of the new "religious" art, but one apparently altogether compatible with and worshipful of its world. But does Mr. Calas really so casually equate "holy images—ikons" and what they stood for with "pop-ikons" out of ads and billboards? And the lust for buying that he seems to applaud as a proof of the mesmeric power or magic of television, does he really regard it as similar to or an apt substitute for what holy images might have meant (or, as he might say, for what they made their worshipers "want to buy")? He goes on, again with what seems to be consent if not approval:

> Pop art rests on the assumption that man is no longer a child of nature but of the machine [one might ask who made the machine, where it came from]. Warhol may be the purest of art-popists when he says: "The things I want to show are mechanical. Machines have less problems. I'd like to be a machine, wouldn't you?"

If he has not already made it—and such statements as well as his work would seem to say so, with some luck and continued effort Warhol ought to make it soon.

On the other hand, for a world always more oppressive to them, many artists, yearning to be free as well as immaculate, conceived a new sense of the powers and rights (rites) of art itself. As I proposed earlier, their mirror, not satisfying them as a mere docile reflector, became an immense, luxuriant, crystal jungle. Art alone and the artist's absorption in his creative life, whatever formidable hazards it produced, constituted the sacred and real, the last refuge against a pernicious world. And following in the wake of World War I, such an attitude proved extremely valuable. Whatever their eager response to and participation in chaos, even the surrealists, dadaists, and all the rest, in their more extravagant experiments seeking out the limits of their media and therefore of man also, were useful (especially as genuine artists absorbed the lessons of such sacrifices into larger, more relevant undertakings). The conventions of our civilization, officially supposed to be moored in the rational and the orderly, had failed to hold. Rather than serving to maintain sanity, reason—at least its more mechanical offspring, logic and technology—had been commandeered by the worst passions of our time; in fact, the horror of the age has been this hideous cohabiting of those offspring with barbarism and madness, this and the minotaurs begotten. Little wonder that the artist in furious disappointment and contempt has felt obliged to flout his world's conventions.

At their best, however, these floutings were ways of cleansing the stable, not of sweeping all its occupants and the stable itself away as well. Tried as man has been, on the whole his most fruitful response has resulted from his tenacious belief in man and man's unique contribution to his world. Much as the image of himself and his art as a pure mirror or an aeolian harp has attracted him, the work that has continued to matter has reflected his refusal to relinquish altogether his human role in the exercise of that art or, flagrant as its failures have been, reason and the other faculties of the mind. Failures of themselves do not necessarily accredit the basic weakness of a faculty; they may have resulted from its excessively simple or excessively confident employment.

But now, according to this new sector of the avant-garde, its members have taken the final major step, and by the "breakthrough" of their experiments they are freeing themselves and us from ancient slavery. One can scarcely challenge the right of such artists to carry on their experiments or the possibility that what seemingly suicidal enterprise they are involved in may continue to prove fruitful. Furthermore, who would want to deny the arts their amusements? These, especially if carried off with gusto, are, in what always threatens to become solemn—never more so than in a time as grim as ours—devoutly to be wished. But the prevailing spirit of these artists seems to be one depressingly pretentious and inquisitional. It is the outrageous restrictions of their aesthetic and the arrogant, not to say absurd, claims made for it as *the* interpretation of life that vexes. These are resolute martyrs, exhorting us all to share their happy martyrdom, gloating over their capacity to slough centuries of human accomplishment, and so the race itself, as it is something more than a momentary mechanical response.

In his article, "The Premises of Action Painting," in the May,

1963, *Encounter*, Harold Rosenberg, one of the most stalwart champions of the new, puts extremely well the postulates that underlie recent painting. I quote him at length:

> Another vanguard assumption was taken up by Action Painting with full intensity—that which demanded the demolition of existing values in art. The revolutionary phrase "doing away with" was heard with the frequency and authority of a slogan. The elimination of subject matter was carried out in a series of moves—then came doing away with drawing, composition, colour, texture; later with the flat surface, art materials. (Somewhere along the line Action Painting itself was eliminated.) In a fervour of subtraction art was taken apart element by element and the parts thrown away. As with diamond cutters, knowing where to make the split was the primary insight.
>
> Each step in the dismantling widened the area in which the artist could set in motion his critical-creative processes [the word "critical" is worth emphasizing], the irreducible human residue in a situation where all superstructures are shaky. It had become appropriate to speak of the canvas as an arena (at length the canvas was put aside to produce "happenings").
>
> On the "white expanse" a succession of champions performed feats of negation for the liberation of all . . . behind Pollock came a veritable flotilla of icebreakers. As art dwindled the freedom of the artist increased, and with it the insignificance of gestures of merely formal revolt. Content became everything.

This last, after the early rejection of "subject matter," is somewhat mystifying. But I suppose we are to understand by it that after the clean sweep had been made and we had been thoroughly doused in the icy waters of truth the whole world in its own unmediated immediacy could begin again for these artists.

In any case, a moment later Mr. Rosenberg derides the academic for whom, whatever the situation or state of the artist, the only thing that "counts" is the painting and the painting itself counts only as line, colour, form. . . . But the net effect of deleting from art the artist's situation, his conclusions about it and his enactment of it in his work is to substitute for the crisis-dynamics of contemporary painting and sculpture an arid professionalism that is a caricature of the aestheticism of half a century ago.

A similar attitude has been operating in a considerable sector of poetry with its addiction to the highly personal, the intimately autobiographical. I am afraid I must say to the above what I would say to this poetry: devil take the "artist's situation." Who is he, any more than the rest of us, that we should be concerned with it except as he is able to change it into something rich and strange, something in its power and its revelation apposite to us all? Let him keep this work to himself or, after he has found out what he wants to and has to about himself, let him turn it into something past the merely personal or destroy it. Shakespeare's "crisis" would no doubt be fascinating to learn about, but chiefly because he wrote his great plays out of it, *not* vice versa. Archeology physical or psychological, as it amounts to little more than exhuming and venerating things simply because they happen to have been buried, leaves me fairly cold. In a desperate time, however, when all seems fundamentally shaken, the clutching of self, the exploiting of one's own predicaments, may seem legitimate and, by its desperateness, authentic. Moreover, as the individual becomes scarcer and scarcer, the capacity for deep relationships more and more difficult, the hunger for gossip about others, whether true or fictive, is bound to grow.

Perhaps at this point, since it is one of the few popular, yet would-be serious attempts at a thoroughgoing apology for this far-out sector in all the arts, not painting alone, Professor Meyer's article affords as good an opportunity as any for examining what he calls the new aesthetic behind them. Prompted by a commendable desire to be receptive and fair, he sets out to describe this aesthetic in a positive, generous way. We have all learned the risk of being reactionary in the arts. In his *The Tradition of the New* Mr. Rosenberg points out, "In the arts an appetite for a new look is now a professional requirement as in Russia to be accredited as a revolutionist is to qualify for privileges." (Of course he is contemning the look, not the new, the tendency of our day to accommodate itself to "imaginative discontent" by emasculating it into mere technique and art history. I too regret the enthusiastic, cheerful public embrace of whatever is produced, particularly as it has an unusual cast, an embrace which usually comes to nothing more than a crushing bear hug.) Professor Meyer means to show that "Whatever one may think of the art of radical empiricism, the philosophical position of which it is the expression is . . . a consistent and tenable one." Yet as he counts off one loss after another, much like the strippings Mr. Rosenberg summarized, one cannot help wondering whether his essay is not a poker-faced attack. But knowing how uncertain standards are today, can we afford such luxury (if indeed satire is his intention)? Too readily now hoaxes are turned into seriousness.

Whatever his intention, let us look at the arguments he presents for respecting this new aesthetic. We start with music since in painting, even the most advanced, the purely "accidental" is harder to establish. But for music of this order "chance procedures" are not in their application random; on the contrary, they are as rigorous, as "systematic" as the objectivity required by the "new novel." Professor Meyer quotes John Cage who, explaining that "Those involved with the composition of experimental music find ways and means to remove themselves from the activities of the sounds they make," suggests, ". . . the interpretation of imperfections in the paper upon which one is writing may provide a music free from one's memory and imagination." Till now we have believed that art is largely of man's making, perhaps the realm most characteristically his own, the moment in which he and his world most happily meet in a medium like himself derived from that world, yet out of him and developed by his unique gifts. Thus we may ask why we should want such removal, such freeing from memory (the muse of the arts since the Greeks) and imagination (the source of art for much of our past).

Considering the focuses available to a critic discussing works of art, Professor Meyer informs us that "completely random or indeterminate music," since it is "purposefully without any organization," cannot be discussed or analyzed in itself. Furthermore, the random procedures themselves are not his concern since "they are more interesting as symptoms of a new aesthetic than as techniques for creating works of art." But is this the point of this new revolution? The works it is producing matter mainly as they enable us to ponder the new aesthetic underlying them? No wonder analysis has been—at last!—disarmed: it has engulfed the art itself. We need no longer, in this age of criticism and analysis, worry about troublesome works. For "random procedures are a means to an end and their real significance begins to appear when one asks why—for what purpose—they are employed."

Reminding us of the common pattern of all previous music in that "tones are related to and imply one another," in that it has a grammar, a syntax, "a purposeful direction and goal," and thus predictions are possible (so too with painting and literature), Professor Meyer proposes that this new art seeks to break out of this age-old conformity. It establishes no goals. "It arouses no expectations, except presumably that it will stop. . . . It is simply *there.*" Music and art have hitherto presented themselves in patterns as a great deal of literature has proceeded with plots. And till now the ability to articulate sounds into such patterns or materials drawn from or resembling life into plots has been regarded as the chief mark of the artist's worth. When Aristotle stressed plot's primacy in tragedy he assumed his reader would understand that plot is not merely a miscellaneous collection of events, but an ordering, a discovering of order in and through the establishing of it, a managing of material so that it could be most intelligently responded to. So too Aristotle underscored metaphor, the artist's capacity for witnessing a living, cogent unity in the world for us; the deeper, the richer the metaphors or the unifying, the greater the work, the fuller and more exciting our appreciation of our world. But at this juncture, it seems, for this new aesthetic we must abandon all the above or a major part of human significance as mere routine and, much worse, a fundamental deceit. Against the backdrop of the huge losses, the wastes and hideous prodigalities that spell out much of our past and present, one might question whether we can afford to be so cavalier with our hard-won accomplishments.

Again John Cage crops up for his urging the composer "to give up the desire to control sound . . . and set about discovering means to let sounds be themselves rather than vehicles for man-made theories or expressions of human sentiments." Beyond the fact that genuine music or art is never merely a matter of controlling sound or of conveying man-made theories (certainly not in the way that work of this new aesthetic seems to be; it is at least as much a matter of discovering and freeing sound), one is obliged to say that man, short of suicide or total mystical transcendence, can never "escape" himself, never except as he learns to know himself and his media, himself through his media. If a *man* is hearing the sounds they inevitably become human in the hearing. Not totalitarianism, not even madness, frees him; nor drunkenness and drugs: by them he becomes a creature of mechanical response. In addition, only as man masters his media can their elements achieve real freedom and selfhood; only as they are related do they discover their distinction. As the whole is larger than the parts, in this one true instance of aristocratic democracy, can the parts be larger than themselves alone. Break the containment of form and each sound not only becomes independent of every other sound, but becomes (what other word will do?) meaningless. "Sounds as sounds—as individual, discrete, objective sensations." Among other obvious questions one might ask, Why several sounds? Why not just one, since in each expression different, listened to indefinitely?

But I feel it time to try to clear past art from the imputation of guilt by association with the regnant philosophy of the modern Western world. Certainly art grows out of its world, uses it as material, is for—if not concerned with a defense of—it. But words like "purposes" and "goals," applied to past art with the implications of materialism still attached to them, are surely misleading. Form, with its assumption of a beginning, middle, and end and of the inter-relationship of its parts, can be spoken of as having a goal. But the principal fact ignored here is that formal art is its own goal, has no goal beyond its self-realization and a repetition or extension of that realization in its audience; in a basic sense, by its livingness it is never finished. So music can be seen as time used against itself or, better, time attended to for its own sake, shaped and so enlarged to be itself. Not business and materialism but a feeling for the organic is what has inspired the best work, a sense of wholeness, the unity of things, whether it be a horse, a tree, an event. If these and the other phenomena of nature have no form then it is true that art should not have it either.

Yet apparently Professor Meyer agrees with these new artists that involvement in relationship blinds one to "things in themselves—as pure sensation." He offers as evidence a radio or TV gone "haywire so that the sound was completely distorted . . . you became very aware of sound *qua* sound—you became conscious of the bleeps, bloops and squeaks." (Whatever reservations we may have about the purity and pleasure of a diet of bleeps and bloops, welcome momentary relief though they may be from TV programs, if such sounds are, as it seems, destined to be more and more with us, it may be the better part of wisdom, not to say necessity, to make the best of them!) Again I detect a basic confusion. No doubt if TV and the ordinary comprise the range of our experience, they do "prevent us from seeing and hearing what is really *there* to be perceived." What, however, have TV programs and the like to do with our past great art? Who can really say that the assumptions lying behind these programs are congruous with the attitudes inherent in that art? A Greek temple, a Lear, a Cézanne, if we are not already ground down by our day's clichés, precisely break through them and jar us at depths we did not know we have. But how long can we concentrate on "pure sensation" without being utterly frustrated, nerve-racked, maddened? It is the tedium, the dullness, the shallowness of much of the art based on such aesthetic that most convincingly turns one against it.

Two things only seem real to many today: the extreme of sensation or sensationalism, whether it be dope or rape or other violence, and its apparent opposite which is actually the same thing (one the inevitable consequence of the other): boredom, emptiness. In itself the ability to face the worst is of course a most admirable strength, as is the ability to wring delight out of what to most would seem trivial or repellent.

> All the world is full of inscape and chance left free to act falls into an order as well as purpose: looking out of my window I caught it in the random clods and broken heaps of snow made by the cast of a broom. The same of the path trenched by footsteps in ankle deep snow across the fields.

It is amusing to realize that these sentiments, with words like "chance," "left free to act" and "random," belong to one of English literature's most painstaking formalists, Gerard Manley Hopkins. But he is talking about nature here, *not* art. The last thing he would have advocated was man's abdication of his unique qualities. His yearning for openness to experience, experience as splendor and loveliness in its totality, is further evidenced by his:

> It is not that inscape does not govern the behaviour of things in slack and decay as one can see even in the pining of the skin in the old and even in a skeleton but that horror pre-possesses the mind.

This yearning, aside from his being a religious and possessed of the artist's devotion to the sacramental, was natural to one gifted with almost preternaturally passionate senses.

It has usually been one considerable part of the artist's province to extend the range of human capacity as well as to absorb the new in its seeming hostility, to warm and humanize the strange and forbidding. Who does not want his response to experience, his delight in it, improved? But may he not boggle at a theory that would exclude most of his previous capacity, turn almost all of him out for an engrossment in "slack and decay"? The desire to see and to present the world freshly must be as old as art itself. But as art has gone out eagerly, heroically to other things and beings, as with Odyssean curiosity it has sought to identify itself with them in their own terms, it has known that it has done so mainly to return, renewed and deepened, to its own identity and the human condition. Else like the lotus-eaters it could be lost forever.

On the other hand, since life is boring and empty for a great number let art in its adherence to things as they are be even more intensely boring and empty. In a time as bombarded as ours, such extremes of sensationalism and boredom, if they make little sense, especially as the major concern of the artist, are at least understandable; for battered senses only such outrage, always more outrageous, can seem convincing. Also, ironically enough, our affluent society, much like a monstrous supermarket, curses us with a welter of ideas. Laid out, brightly packaged in loudly advertised terms, equally available and jostling, for the myriad choices possible they are likely to produce bewilderment and nausea. What else is left, the cry goes up, but the random choice by chance or machine?

Then it is out that this art, "perhaps at least in part a reaction to the mess that goals, purposes, and strivings have got us into," would be like "nature" itself which "simply is." First I would like to ask what tools these artists have to calculate the natural and the unnatural. Why is a full employment of all our powers, including the mind with its memory and imagination, necessarily "unnatural"? Where has man found and developed his faculties if not in and from his nature in nature itself? But man, aside from the inevitable fact of society, of memory, his own and his race's, is not *simply* nature. No other creature would—or could—go to such fantastic extremes to prove it is natural or to attain the natural.

Thus I would like to inquire whether, in this aesthetic's own terms, TV, radio, computers, electronic devices can be regarded as natural. Are they not products of man's ingenuity, his logic, his theories? So the modern city itself, splendid monument as it is to the random, the broken, the shapeless, is *not* natural. On the contrary, it is the work of many exploiting nature, often as not—if one can still believe in its laws—against its essential grain. Much of what is happening now in technology, politics and art, may it not be man's desperate will against nature, a using of it against itself and himself? Yet if we wish to be as impressively inclusive in our definition of nature as this aesthetic would seem to profess to be, then since whatever happens exists and by existing in real and/or natural, the stench, the luridness, the outrages of the city, all this and much more—murder: torture: war—must be regarded as natural, so acceptable. Certainly the orgiastic, the Dionysian, in man and nature cannot be denied; nor in its fecundating and renewing powers should it be. But when it alone prevails, if disaster is to be thwarted, the Apollonian in collaboration with it must be renewed. I too admire

Blake's "Whatever lives is holy." But however strong our yearning for total comprehension, short of religion we begin to be in trouble when we try to say, Whatever *is* is holy. In any case, I have tried to show that for these new artists only what they approve—really fiercely exclusive—is holy. The negative capability, appealing as it is, does not mean capability for the negative alone.

But what does it matter in a world always more triumphantly stripped? Earlier Professor Meyer had admitted: "It is easy, of course, to ridicule art created by accident—by . . . asserting that 'my little child could have done that.' And perhaps the child could." Why perhaps? Is a child not less burdened with memory and training and complicated thinking than the rest of us? Here, it seems to me, we have the real failure. A good number of these new artists, unable to compete with the accomplishments of the past, understandably, touchingly, have tried to do something else. But what, alas, has this something else often come to? A mere negation of that past and a sad assertion that whatever one happens to do is not only worth doing, but "realer" in its bareness than anything done before. So our incompetences (obsolete word!), our ignorances, our absurdities are sworn in as preciously significant. Obviously "the value of the work of art cannot be judged—any more than one can judge nature or natural objects in themselves." In the words of Mathieu: ". . . if we reduce the part played by conscious control in favor of spontaneity, we find ourselves in the position where *the very notion of error* . . . disappears." Certainly and so does everything else. For if the work is "an object without meaning," "all events are equally important" or, more accurately, unimportant. Man, alas, tempting as the role may be, cannot play God, not even in his arts.

But now, looking ahead, Professor Meyer rather surprisingly, even as he acknowledges the very different essential nature of the arts, like a good, no-chance-taking, modern critic, speculates on the possibilty that by this very difference "the arts will move in the coming years *not* toward a common, monolithic aesthetic as they seem to be doing today, but toward a plurality of aesthetics, each appropriate to its particular art." Is this new aesthetic after all not so profoundly true then as we had been led to believe? Is it at best a desperate temporary measure? And will the emergence of a plurality of aesthetics spell the end of the Renaissance?

Whatever this speculation may mean, at last Professor Meyer admits, at least by implication, that this new aesthetic is anti-human:

> Man is no longer to be the measure of all things, the center of the universe. He has been measured and found to be an undistinguished bit of matter different in no essential way from bacteria, stones and trees.

I wonder what other bit of matter could so measure itself (need to) and find itself different in no essential way, even as I wonder what tools and rare calculatory, not to say divinatory, faculties— since man is no longer to be the measure—these artists have discovered to dare to reach such a conclusion. Yet they are accurate. Man is clearly not different *if* you strip him of mind, feeling, and imagination—qualities trees, stones, and bacteria do not have and do not need. Men, however, need them more urgently than ever if they are to survive as more than stones and bacteria, as more not only than a distinguished but a distinguishable bit of matter. But if value judgments are to be discarded and each thing—note, word, stone, man—is to be seen newly, excitingly, in and for itself, how can man—or for that matter bacteria, stones, and trees—be called an undistinguished bit of matter? We see what destructive contradictions atomistic thinking can lead to.

One feels compelled to ask, is it that the atom bomb has already gone off for such artists and that they are trying to produce an art for a world without man and, in a sense, not by man or at

least not as we have known him? Is it an acceptance of the bank-
ruptcy and death of the race? On the other hand, this attitude
might be construed as a frantic, touching, impressive attempt of
a small part of mankind to be equal to whatever happens or the
state of the world as they see it now: a disintegrating, if not
shattered affair.   Is not the artist in his sensitivity supposed to
be ahead of his times?   One thinks of the old Yeats with his
exultant embrace of cataclysm in poems like "Lapis Lazuli," preferring to Western reason and hysteria Oriental wisdom and
delight.   Still for him the human emphasis persists, a belief in
gusto, understanding, art.   More and more men seem to think
and act as though they live in a world exhausted, virtually over:
a huge debris of ideas and things strewn round them.   Obviously
the stunning blows that our time has sustained are almost super-
humanly hard to recover from, let alone digest.   But what is
art for if it cannot discover in itself a counter-strength to the
terrible forces released?

Here we collide with a central contradiction.   Even as we
loathe what the Fascists—not to forget our own politicians, tech-
nicians, business men—have done, many of us accept their acts
as true.   Not only because they happened (though for that
reason too: whatever happens, as we saw above, *is*, is real, and
thus in a sense necessary), but because they were so dramatic and
effective, many regard them as revelations of reality.   Hitler's
prophetic boast that his work would go on and on has in its
monstrous fruit proved too accurate.   Anti-humanism has, it
seems, convinced a great number that humanism is not only (as
indeed it is) fallible and vulnerable, but wrong.   So too the
artist, abominating power, mass media, the inertia of the cold
war, the tortures loose in our world and feeling helpless before
them in their vastness and complexity, is immersed, as well as
fascinated and infected, by them.   As he yields, angry, hurt,
resentful of his insignificance beside technology, frustrated by
the dehumanization taking place, is he not, out of revulsion to it,

in danger of joining the enemy, lending his talents to it and, usually without realizing it, serving the worst aspects of the age?

Of course it is a capping irony to realize that it was the Renaissance which released the energies of self-belief and enthusiasm that led to the development of technology and its present great monument to itself (like some of our art, all activity), the atom bomb; even more ironically all the human energy and ingenuity exercised to produce such a machine at this point does little more than dwarf man, fill him and all he does with a sense of insignificance. One can hardly overestimate the oppressiveness of the bomb's worldwide brooding presence or the problem of its meaning. Great spirits indeed are required to cope with it as an idea alone.

A further wry contradiction here. Pursuing the mood of the time, as with technology these artists are ruthlessly committed to experiment and change. In the past, art had meant arriving at something hopefully lasting. Now anything arrived at by that very fact must at once be abandoned. Gladly sacrificing old techniques, such artists frequently if grimly embrace the momentary, the fleeting, real to them because fleeting. Some of them, in their crusading ardor for novelty at any cost, seem to "do away with" rather more than they have. Thus Nathalie Sarraute, probably the ablest spokesman for the anti-novel, in her recent book, *The Age of Suspicion*, exhorts the writer to seek out a reality freed of the "preconceived ideas and ready-made images that encase it" and thereby "attain something that is thus far unknown, which it seems to him he is the first to have seen." By now I hope I have demonstrated that such an urging is not exactly original. But few today would gainsay the young writer's right to try to disentangle himself from his immediate past, especially when it is as overwhelming in attainments as ours. The terms of that disentangling, however, are rather hard to accept, most of all from artists well out of their youth who might be expected to have attained some peace with their great predecessors as with themselves and their parents. But no, Henry James is proscribed for being crude, Proust for being heavyhanded in dealing with our delicate "inner mechanisms." He could not resist people, individuals, irrelevant identities. The new novel, superior to such superficiality, should strive to become as specialized, as abtruse as the most advanced technology. In not a few instances it has. This impatience with characters and audiences means that characters exist merely to convey states of consciousness and unconsciousness, and audiences are at best put up with (like paper or canvas) to try these works out on.

In Mr. Rosenberg's words, ". . . the ceaseless discovery of new techniques is the chief characteristic of *modern work,* which has also left artisanship behind." Out of the notion that content does not matter (in a relativistic time one idea is potentially as good as any other) or out of the abuse of the critical commonplace that in art form is content, technique alone seems important. No wonder for the shallowness of matter one gets quickly bored, one exhausts that technique's possibilities and must move on to new technique. Yet once such new technique gets established, it or the idea behind it tends to become inviolable dogma for its practitioners. Out of revulsion for the conventional and preconceived such hierophants often impose conventions and preconceptions in the name of freedom much more exacting than the old. Heaven help those who innocently question or wonder, the ultimate in betrayal. I am reminded that when the French Revolution's armies were sweeping through Europe as they captured a town they placarded it: "We have emancipated you. Anyone who resists will be shot."

Mr. Rosenberg wisely warns that "a society that does not tolerate outsiders, or which condemns their thought as *ipso facto* void, is an authoritarian community, be it secular or religious, republican, monarchist or totalitarian." Yes, but not also if it is artistic? Much as one may believe in change and moving on, in being sensitive to the always changing world, when change is worshipped for its own sake, a fixed notion and a flood that would sweep all before it, may it not be revolutionary (if by that we mean to go against the tide) to resist such flood?

As Mr. Rosenberg says,

> The *decision to be revolutionary* usually counts for very little. The most radical changes have come from person-alities who were conservative and even conventional—a powerful recoil from the radical present threw them backwards, so to speak, into the future.

In short, in a world furiously changing perhaps one is sometimes most radical and new by being conservative (at least in the sense that most great artists of the past have been: imbued with a desire to preserve precious human qualities, too easily forgotten or ignored for the costly effort their attainment comes to), especially now that every extravagance and aberration has academic sanction, marketplace approval. As though any real artist can be expected to subdue himself, his gifts and needs, to external impositions, taboos, interdictions, abstractions. He can use whatever he needs and wishes to. The proof, as those heeding dogmas literally have often too sadly demonstrated, lies in the work. They do not seem to see that the new must be intrinsic, must come from within, not from without by the arbitrary enforcement of regulations. Experimentation and all that it stood for started in generosity and high spirits; but now as it seems to flag of its own furor, its zest is much in danger of subsiding into simple-minded zealotry, standardized patterns, dogged rigidities of devotion or the most restricted of academicisms.

In fact, I do not care what theories, private or official, ancient or modern, artists develop for themselves as long as they help—or at least do not hinder—the works made. But I am old-fashioned enough to ask what one is to say for theories that lord it over the works. Nevertheless, perhaps for those with little creative gift such concentration on theory is for the best; in their separation of art and theory or replacement of one by the other perhaps they will (some surely have already) happily abandon art altogether. Moreover, if they are as serious and resolute as they believe, should they not leap to the inevitable culmination of their aesthetic—no work at all and the insistence that the world itself (or nature) as it occurs is more than adequate occupation. But happenings and post-happenings may be meant to be examples of a moving into just such occupation.

And yet, for the revolution this aesthetic has ushered in, the questioning of the very foundations of 40,000 years of aesthetic activity, is it not worth it? But has not every age thought itself, proudly and abjectly, the pride in the abjectness, the end and therefore a brand-new beginning? Yet, impressed by such enormous claims, Professor Meyer says that the value of this aesthetic lies, finally, in its challenging us to defend our basic assumptions. "Can we give empirically verifiable reasons for them?" Yes, in our response, endlessly renewed and renewing, to the great works we admire (and *not* in whatever theories or systems thinkers may seek to abstract from them) as against many of the undescribable works being produced.

But perhaps the decisive truth is that the pride of some of us in man (still!) and in his potentialities as well as in his accomplishments much surpasses that of these doubtful artists. I am confident that, even as they dismiss the past and single out one small part of its activity as a substitute for the whole, they are already courting disaster, recommending to the next generation that it, as they are doing to all previous generations, quickly dismiss them for what they are: partial and so untrue. A real belief in one's self involves a fundamental belief in the human past and its continuity, its vitality in us. Just so chance has always been important, the improvisatory, the sudden assertion of luck. At its most rigorous, great art has allowed for it. What is the ancient belief in inspiration if not a recognition of the place of chance, the unexpected? But such art sets up the circumstances that, as it invites, can recognize and accommodate that happy chance, thereby make the most of it. Chance and the random cannot happen without a firm concept of their opposite, choice and the necessary, for them to play against, to discover their natures and their usefulness. The emperor without his clothes is one thing; the clothes without the emperor, quite another. But the most extraordinary act must be the celebration of a performance devoid of emperor and clothes and, of course, since faithful subjects to the two, the audience as well. Yet both Professor Meyer and Mr. Rosenberg in his talk of "dismantling" seem to be promising us such spectral splendor.

III

Franz Kafka
and the Economy of Chaos

A study of the fashions in chaos—that is, its varying dispositions in different times and different societies, might prove extremely revelatory to an understanding of the history of civilization. Applied particularly to the work of one writer, say an artist as tantalizing as Franz Kafka, such a study should help to define his unique quality and his contribution as well as the specific character of chaos in his age. We can at once remark the vast divergences in the pagan, the Jewish and the Christian attitudes toward chaos. In the Judaistic world the invisible was worshipped till the visible nearly disappeared; even bushes went up in smoke. Despite the various beliefs already articulated, we can realize what a splendid moral monolith this tower of Babel was. Chaos was ubiquitous. But it was regarded, with all its multiplicity and by the very oneness of man's inability to translate it, as the single voice of God. Everywhere uttered, this voice the Jews met by falling prostrate before it, to worship what by its inscrutability was terribly superior. Still the ego of man was supreme; in humbling himself, he was elevating and worshiping a part of himself, that which he could not explain.

Among the Greeks, however, the visible, coming into

its own, was enjoyed to the point where the invisible almost emerges. Notwithstanding the idealism of men like Plato, the Greeks generally luxuriated in what they saw; stones became men; the sea was one of their most frequented temples, the passionate home of myriad maidens pure by inconstancy. Even Venus rose. For the Greeks, by embracing their element with gusto, had mastered it. To account for multiplicity, yet to keep it in all its profound particularity, they established their abundant family of gods. Generously graceful, the Greeks even deferred to the unknown god; a stranger in their midst must be welcomed, housed, naturalized. Again, the unknown was a certainty; chaos was accounted for.

As for the first Christians, since they were, largely, converts out of impoverishment and slavery, they were expert at dealing in the invisible, the only element in which they could be free and infinitely wealthy. For poverty and rejection have fierce prides that must also be satisfied. Accordingly, these Christians seized upon the unknown god, and as their company increased, he grew. For even as Christ was the invisible manifested in the shape of man, so the Christian God was the Judaistic deity, also an invisible (the Jews were not to worship idols), embodied, paradoxically, in the unknown god, but stript presumably of human imperfection. The consummation of all wishes, this Christian God nonetheless preserved the slightest nuance of ignorance and fear. The world was still, transparently, the inscrutable word and will of God. As the wealth of worshiping accumulated, however, the church, expanding, adapted an additional Greek practice; it populated itself with the rich embodiments of myriad hopes. Why not employ a host of venerable figures? With the apotheosizing of lowliness, Christianity's power and glory, the hierarchy of the saints came into being. Multiplicity was still maintained; chaos had become a well-mapped city.

So, basically, the acclimations to chaos have expressed themselves. But frequently, in a very short time, an attitude, like chaos itself, undergoes considerable alteration. In fact, occasionally in the same period, one man by his sensitivity to the root impulses of his world can in penetration readily outstrip all his contemporaries. Shakespeare, for example, looked over the shoul-

der of the later Milton far beyond the confines of Milton's world.
In Milton's universe even infinity was tidy. The circle of eternity
was drawn; a sufficiency of faith could, on clear evenings, discern
its rondure. Struck as it was by conflicting beliefs, this universe
stood—stood in the dogma of Milton's wish. For what more could
he request than the architectural order the church prescribed?
A closed world, carefully supervised, with chaos a convenient
supply of building materials for whatever additional wings God
might eventually plan. This was a world to live in—a universe in
which one's esthetic and the world agreed! No wonder Milton
fought so heroically in the crusade of this order.

The tremors in Shakespeare's world, however, were
much mightier. What are Hamlet, Macbeth, Cleopatra and the
rest but quintessentialized human beings questioning their day's
world-picture, questioning, defying, threatening? The picture is
saved, but only after stains and gashes mar its surface. Gradually
other probing fingers enlarged these gashes. Some Renaissance
men, resenting complete projection and a life of promises, began
to study as substance what hitherto had been dismissed as
shadow; humanity itself, as it was, not as it might be or would
like to be, became their occupation, the world too as their senses
knew it. The rent which Shakespeare's plays contain grew until
the distance between the old world and the new became un-
bridgeable for not a few. Still the majority insisted on or passively accepted the old cosmological dispensation.

Perhaps the most ardent champion of this dispensation
in recent times was Dostoyevsky. But an always spreading paradox strikes across the heart of his work for us. Though the world
he envisions is as tormented as a world can be, always, many
miles below, he takes for granted the inexpungable foundation
of faith. The frenzy of life, the changingness of his people, that
he saw as clearly as any eye the world had, he presented mainly
as proof of both the existence of and our need for such a faith.
Of course, within such a stable framework many incidental
chaoses can appear and even prosper. When a deep-sea diver is
confident of the strength and rootedness of his life-line, he can
attempt the blackest, most perilous depths. The paradox and
irony of Dostoyevsky's work is that he has, for the most part,

especially as we seem to come closer and closer to his characters, convinced us of the damnable accuracy of his details; this conviction has strengthened, for an always growing number, doubt of his foundation of belief rather than belief itself. Such a world is as unacceptable to many as Milton's.

Yet even among the most skeptical the nostalgia for the comforts and security of faith clings on. Though he may not be able to accept past mythologies, man is reluctant to abandon them; he is loath to deny his childhood and the proud childhood of his race. Science has battered the door down, exposed us to all the perils of the unknown which space contains. With the womb of wish violated, infinity has become its present self; and the prophecy that we should be as sands on the shore of eternity has been fulfilled. But few have the strength the present demands. Man, it would seem, has not been large enough in himself to support his own visions. Yet, contrarily, he has. For, after all, what is creation but man's creation, his dreams believed in?

But language changes. The dialect of today (language determines our thoughts probably as much as thought the language) for most of its inhabitants poorly contains yesterday's religions. Stuttering at best, this dialect cannot understand the religions or put much conviction in their utterance. The world, moving, has changed shape; the readymade answers can hardly fit. So man must move nakedly through his world (we see, in the album of beliefs, the ridiculousness of ancient costumes or customs) or weave together the pieces of the past. But though man cannot long do without explanations, ours is a time in which most answers are made of such inferior stuff they prove either flimsy or unfashionable even as we try them on. At this juncture the writer perhaps most agonizingly aware of his nakedness is Franz Kafka,* another example that men normally must live in projection; they must push themselves away, open their world before them. Religion or art, these are the principal worlds men try to rear around themselves.

Like Dostoyevsky, completely aware of the confusion

* I wish to thank Professor Paul Weiss for stimulation in talks with him about Kafka.

about him, Kafka in addition was partially taken in by it; he lacked the framework of faith. With a frightening precision he set about to build what he could. And always because perfection was his ambition, he failed. No wonder his books are incomplete. From such a realization, if his art was to be honest, picturing an open world, how could it achieve a conclusion? The inevitable dissatisfaction, however, made his desire that his work be destroyed plain enough. And yet, possessed as he was of a religious temperament, he refused to be victimized by it. He accommodated in his world the very thing modern man has striven to keep out; chaos, the unknown, became a common staple in his work.

As Austin Warren has put it in "Kosmos Kafka," Kafka is "not a moralist and reformer but a man of religion. The problem is one of accepting the universe, of learning, by means of pathos, humor, and irony, to tolerate it. The too painful sense of life as mystery can be transcended by reducing mystery to a kind of pattern. You don't solve the mystery, but you segregate it and give it status, you learn to live with it." This was Kafka's treatment, his economy of chaos. He did not solve chaos; rather he kept it in solution. Yet by the strength of his art, an awareness and so an order appeared. He did not reduce mystery, but by remarking its continuous presence in the most commonplace, eventually the most mysterious might be accepted as rather daily. Kafka captures the dream content of the homely; through him we come awake into the terrible dream of the ordinary that usually comforts us; we see this dream with the impact of clarity and intimacy strangeness alone can insist on, with the wide-awake eyes of the dreamer, for the cul-de-sac the supposed insulation of the ordinary is. It is the feeling of apartness, of being locked out, one occasionally gets in looking, say, at a dog. As it looks through us, we fear it because we do not know what it can do. Now imagine this attitude maintained toward oneself. Such mystery is luminously plain in Kafka's writing. He cannot dispose of it; but, after all, disposal is not his problem or his province; the realization of this mystery is quite enough. Speculation may try to dispose of it; art brings it back furiously alive and thriving. By his realization Kafka's art could not embarrass him. Unlike most economies, it would not suddenly discover that it had not made room for an unexpected, yet terribly important, guest. Generally, in other worlds confronted with such unexpectedness, the entire structure must be leveled and a new one erected. Kafka, on the other hand, does not try to persuade the world to accept his terms. More than that, he does not try to wring meanings (still terms or preconceptions) from the world he sees. That world is enough, almost too much.

Of course Kafka shocks us, for, as we have suggested, he shows us bits of ourselves we thought we had completely concealed, from ourselves as well as from others. Bereft of social conventions and personal habits which normally give us our feeling of immortality, we are plunged into the racing crystal stream of our own core changingness. For the first time we meet our swift, fiery-cold perpetuity. His is the microscope that by the flaw of vision, the bright obliquity, reveals in our daily conventions and convictions the unsuspected horror; our world remains our world, and yet it is terrible, more terrible and strange by this intimacy, this remaining the same. Then can the nightmare be horrified by what is really the daily. What is particularly frightening is the work's relentless logic, its unequivocal accuracy. We are trapped in our logic. And suddenly we understand it. Think of the momentary seen with the terrified eyes of eternity; think also of eternity at the mercy of the transient as, in a sense, it is, of the everlasting able to see itself in the shape of the speedily passing, the human race. We too therefore see ourselves from the outside snared in our vision. But possibly this insight is our only freedom.

There are other logics, that of the insane and of orders we cannot know. Naturally we impugn the existence of such logics. For as men we are doomed to be logical, rational. Perhaps in a universe not made so, that is our fall; for consciousness is chaos. Kafka has described the logic of human chaos, of the very Philadelphia we build around us to hide in, a world that deliberately mirrors only what we externally are. This city is a monument to loneliness, our solitudes made monolith. We need not be surprised that we shudder at the threatening closeness of ourselves. As Kafka demonstrates again and again, whatever we are at a particular moment, that is all we can be. The ape cannot know man as man cannot know the cockroach as the living cannot know the dead. In this exclusive oneness, our clutching of ourselves is hardly surprising. Who cares to surrender what he believes to be all that there is—at least for him as he at that moment is. We are dealing here with the tragedy of being; for whatever one is by the act of being, one surrounds oneself, becomes an infinity of non-being. But the tragedy is not the infinity perhaps so much as the surprises locked up in one's own being, the rack of oneself one is forced to live through. Once we are committed to a shape, we are exposed to the acute ruthlessness of change, of becoming busily acting within us. Little as we experience the outside, we know that we know ourselves less. Despite the urgency of survival, to escape the particular sharp presence of the infinite tightly imprisoned within us, we often yearn for this outside. But for such walls of writing, the externalization of ourselves, we, as Kafka, might be crushed, the weight of the world or ourselves upon us.

Much as we may dislike or gainsay it, for many art has become a surrogate religion: Matthew Arnold saw it as a hopeful prospect; it has proved an inevitable. Instead of accepting an ancient picture, prepared by writers of another world and underwritten by centuries of practice, we turn to the creation of the genius of one. The danger of worship, however, threatens us here also. Certainly it is more understandable than not a few other worships, say that of the state. (Today the world lurches—its own minotaur. What way other than mass-sacrifice, of putting flesh and blood on an abstraction as defiant as the state? Great writers have usually taken account of our carnivorous natures.) Dostoyevsky, for instance, knew the value of blood, realized for some it needed to be spilt; these unregenerates (even as the world bathed in Christ's blood) must experience such transfusion to come alive. But the Dostoyevskies exercise their appetites at second hand; their work is their laboratory of freedom. Art satisfies some; others need murder.

Kafka also could not accept any such absorption in the state; nor could he recommend social panaceas. Not because he did not care about his fellow men; he cared too much to encourage such superficial remedy. No remedy save expression with as much humility and honesty as the human spirit can endure. And the expression, if it is to be honest, meticulous and wise, must take advantage of the normal literary devices practice has established. More than has been appreciated, Kafka was an artist who, in the mirror of his art, did not conquer by cutting off the snake-writhing head of reality, but came to realize it and, never taming, to live with it. Nor did his work turn to stone as other arts and religions have done, a carving of dead monuments and blind edifices against life. For him the living was monument enough, the world his violent vision.

Of course he tried the impossible; with a patience and a care that might have broken the fortitude of a god, he stormed the ever-topless towers of his dream, perfection. He knew that he would fail, knew that the quest was futile, that he could never cross the threshold guarded by his own human flesh. Reality would not yield. He knew; nonetheless with the indefatigability of genius he tried. The quest was futile; yet because it was honest and illuminated by love, the roadway strewn with battle is our triumph; his trial rendered a sentence of knowledge we can enjoy. Ignorance mapped, the unknown delimited, is a kind of knowledge, perhaps the only kind we can expect. Though reality itself may never be seriously threatened, even as the quest turns up importances on the way, it especially endows us with knowledge of the seeker, defines his emotion, perseverence, humanity, and so our own.

Kafka might have attempted the castle by straight siege. But his persistent concern with the village below prevented such directness. This concern is, in good part, his achievement and his worth. Like a Hopkins', Kafka's work is the tension between these two worlds, the fierce longing for both and the further longing to make them one. For the ordinary man there is usually little conflict. In most cases, he sees these two worlds, thinks he occupies them, and keeps them—to him infinitely different—tidily separate. It was their awareness of this distance, smugly advocated by their respective ages, that galled Hopkins and Kafka. So they wandered in the Slough of Despond between. Yet failure, even as it is a fate, applied too diligently, can prove a most splendid occupation. Had they, for instance, made the heavenly world, we might have had nothing. Because of their remembrance of their human responsibility and their love, this world could not be denied; insofar as religion had drawn away from earthly reality, they could not accept it.

But what is it Kafka has done? In simplest terms, he has presented a German subject matter in a style and an exactness that is French. Such a union would be miracle enough. He has given us Job without God or a Job who must discover God or peace within himself, his world, and the fragments of his dream. Not heaven, but the earth, comes first. We shall not try to lasso the loftiest peak with coils of rhapsodic language. In terms of the village, in its sinuous by-ways, in the center of its common pleasures and pangs, the impossible must be grappled with. What more epic conflict when the beginning and the end of the world meet in one heart, when the grappling is so tight we must recognize the opponents as one? Only by clasping ourselves in the myriad shapes we must take can we arrive at grace.

As his clarity admits, unlike other writers of our time, Kafka is not absorbed in style *per se*. Though we must live in our breath, in the world our words construct, these words cannot forget their roots and the quarries they have come from. Kafka's hunger to describe the details of his harried world allowed him small time for ornamentation. In fact because of this desperation, lucidity was a cardinal aim; it was the only way he could survive. Nor did he sit back in the scholarly ivory tower of his work amid a waste land to count over, miserly fashion, the precious fragments of previous greatnesses he has managed to preserve. He was too desperate, and too much in love, to make his work a macaronic skein, say, of quotations lit up at odd angles by their sudden juxtapositions and their presence in a particular mind. Nor had he time or the desire to rival physical builders of cities. Not the naturalistic blueprinting of the brain, heart, and liver; not a listening in on the sputtering dots and dashes of the subconscious; there is another typography here—the hot geometry of anguish, nightmare, and desire immaculately surveyed, manscape. Not only did Kafka achieve the equilibrium that is art, the position midway between the poles of scheme and actuality, system and mindlessness, but he posited the mindlessness, captured the actuality itself into a kind of arithmetic of clarity; with the connotations as infinite and infinitely confusing as they are, he adhered to strict denotation. As the outer world shrinks, the inner must grow; we must live inside. But we must live. The furnishings of the heart and head cannot be changed into wooden pieces, dealt with as prosaically as the contents of a third-floor flat. As precisely as possible, the contents must be examined; yet they must be examined in action.

Indeed Kafka could turn his back to the world nowhere; for he must always see it; he was that world. There is guilt here, but admission that its source (like the god) is unknown. Is it perhaps our unwitting realization that each man makes his world; and, making it, the crime he sees in it, the brutality, the hatred, is his own doing, his own projection? Consciousness is chaos. No wonder, feeling responsible, guilty, man pauses in his making to study the maker. Yet the making ruthlessly continues, another likely reason for the incompleteness of Kafka's work. Possibly too, this incompleteness might suggest, at that point in his books he came too close to himself, look against eye, grasp within hand, too identical to see. The objectification dissolves; the castle, the trial, America, what is the other side of these? Caught in the human condition we cannot possibly break free to basic knowledge. Kafka, however, did not strive to make a god of this ignorance, nor an order to be worshiped. Caught we are, whether country doctor or surveyor, whether ape trying to be a man or man trying to be— Kafka had none of the arrogance of those who would explain God's ways to man; man himself was more than he could explain.

There are few preconceived critical terms we can apply to Kafka's world; they must come out of this world itself, out of the becoming that is art rather than out of the being that is most philosophy and criticism. Such speculation is a finished world, one seen from a distance. Dispassionately participating and detachedly passionate, the artist has one foot out and one in this changingness. To accuse Kafka of allegory is to lose sight of the world he so devotedly built; this world is itself, not a Platonic illustration. To think of Kafka or to try to "explain" him in terms, say, of Kierkegaard is to change Kafka into something he is not—

worse than a poem's paraphrase. We cannot abstract eternal verities or absolutes from his work. In art worthy of the name, the particulars do not exist for the values; rather, the values serve the particulars. Such is the essence of time, of living, and of living—the complexus of it—heightened into art. Then the particulars themselves become a kind of absolute. Let the values, if they are recognized at all, bring us deeper into life, deeper through the compass of clarity art has, not away from life. Kafka knew that feelings, thoughts, appearances, though ephemeral, in their being offshoots of whatever reality there is, are symbols enough. Language itself is a set of symbols. To make these symbols of symbols, in addition, is to attenuate their worth. Kafka surprised change, surprised it in the very act, so kept its pristine, shimmering shape.

But what is it that tinges the atmosphere of Kafka's world with fear and unqualified foreboding? It is precisely this openness, the frozen time yet infinite of solitude, the mesmerized sound of silence and imminence, and the plethoric threat of possibility, a possibility further multiplied in that it is hatching in us. We experience at once the fierce imprisonment of freedom. Jostled by plenitudes of space, we endure the intimacy of measureless distances and the fearful nearness of loneliness. It is not even the world that frightens us as much as our consciousness. Think of the raw, violent meat impatient immediately under our skins; think of the sudden spurt of blood, the hate and the lust and the violence, that blinds our eyes. Then think of what waits, in the ambush of our breath, under the skin of our thinking: the sunken Atlantises in our minds and our veins, the pre-Edens and the primordial slime, the middle-of-the-night remembers. Again, this man who is Hamlet and Hamlet's father one, his own voice and knowledge the poison pouring down his thirsty ear, again this man clings with a frantic genius, with a devotion amounting at times to idolatry, to details. If the problem is infinite, every step is a further expression of prison. But he will not be swept away; he will play secretary to the inner workings of chaos.

It is the grip of Kafka that is particularly precious; whether it be angel or devil he is wrestling with, as long as he can, he does not let go. It is his art that saves him from being devoured. Latter-day versions of chaos rarely share this muscularity. Writers like Kenneth Patchen and Henry Miller, for instance, resenting the hidebound smugness of much of their time, have sought to break through it by encouraging chaos. Satire and diatribe are their major devices. But in their urgency to level hypocrisy, they have lashed out so violently that they have often destroyed the very ground under their feet. Why, a reader can well ask, should we prefer their limited confusion to the vaster chaos they accuse the world of? Satire, to prove effective, must be focused. Unless its employer has solid criteria, clear values, and a larger context he can either readily refer to or take for granted, this satire is doomed to fail.

Chaos, as we saw, can be used only when it achieves some definition, when it can be placed beside something that is patently not chaos. But when the world the writer describes is so baffled, even willfully, that one value cannot be distinguished from another, then what value can any part of it have? Probably, in considerable measure, anti-intellectualism is responsible for the rubble-heaps writers present. Attributing our present miseries erroneously to the failure of intellect, regarding this anguish as irrefutable testimony to the inadequacy of intellect, such writers have heartily jettisoned the intellect's claims. Certainly their books would suggest that they have abandoned whatever rationality they possess.

We can understand such a course; we can even applaud the ambition to recruit other sources of knowledge. With the world increasingly various and rich in grief as well as in culture, we can appreciate a denunciation of superficial harmony through the intellect. Nor would it be wise certainly to emphasize the intellect at the expense of other methods or systems of knowing. Still, to dump the intellect, aside from the fundamental impossibility of such an act, as well as to try to scrap the resources of tradition, is the very ultimate of folly. Sensations for their own sake, exclusive adulation of the ravenous present, rejection of cumulative knowledge, such a course rather than freeing man must kill a good portion of what he is. Art has usually been a catalyst to form and comprehension, not simply a further spice for appetites already living in the midst of explosion.

Perhaps modern writers are trying to discover a new art, a form meet to their day; perhaps, putting on the prophetic robes, they are anticipating the consequences of atomic developments! How absurd, as though they could ever vie with the multifarious frenzies and confusion of living itself. In any event, these writers are correct: intellect has failed, not because it was intellect but because it was not sufficiently so. If the eye, only partially trained, sees distant shapes vaguely, shall we, in a fit of impatience, contemning sight, gouge the eye and trample upon it? Of course the eye, like the body, by its limits is an obstacle— as knowledge itself is; but as long as we are men writing for men, little is to be gained by trying to thrust away what organs we have. Death alone can yield the kind of knowledge many writers seem to desire.

Carlyle, we remember, deplored the growth of consciousness as a symptom of distemper. So perhaps we can diagnose the development of chaos. The Greeks, we saw, had outlawed it. In Milton's world, after the earth was finished, there was little need for it. But we, become more and more scrutinous, increasingly call attention to chaos, so call it into being. Consciousness is chaos. Of course chaos may simply further witness human arrogance; for, as we have observed, chaos is surely of our own making. Earlier man made god out of his ignorance. Now we attribute our ignorance and our notion of chaos to our world. We assume that the perplexity we find in the world, by our finding, must inhere in that world and its objects. Kafka did not shirk the labyrinth; nor, of course, did he ever break through it. For it was his being, the very stuff of his living. But by bringing his best strengths to bear upon it, he peopled it with fearful splendors and the anguished dignity of his love. To suffer, to know that one suffers, and withal to love—that is man's prize heroism. The scientist, for instance, may give his life for the advancement of knowledge; in a moment then, he achieves immortality. The major artist also gives his life, but often in a much more agonizing way—over the protraction of years. He, as an awareness, is the test and witness. We can hardly share Carlyle's animus toward the development of consciousness. But we must be ready to pay the price for the growing burden of riches.

Giacomo Leopardi
Pioneer Among Exiles

THE general ignorance of Leopardi in America among even professional poetry readers and the easy suffrage, not of Italians alone, that his poetry is, after Dante's, the most important in Italy, possibly in the world of his day, in its sophistication and profundity head and shoulders above the work of a Wordsworth or a Shelley, say, as well as a superb precursor in many ways of the achievements of poets like Baudelaire and Rimbaud—all this convinced the QRL editors that they should project a Leopardi number.

Some readers may question the relevancy of Leopardi to us. Convinced that most acts of revivalism remark an age sceptical of its own vitality, the QRL would rather concentrate its special issues on writers discovering themselves now or on major figures of the past who have lacked their first full chance in America. After well over a hundred years of comparative neglect, Leopardi's pertinency becomes increasingly clear. In his grasp of certain basic problems he looks astonishingly like us. Surely not our proudest efforts at gloom can surpass his. Beside him Eliot seems a rather weary don, even as most modern existentialists seem superficial before the essence Leopardi made of many of the qualities we take for granted as unique to existentialism. For with unflagging courage he maintained a steady look at actuality in its most flagrant forms, this with an appealing pride that spurned the comforts not a few of us, bruised and frightened, have succumbed to. His prose as well as poetic matter is usually the sadness of the brevity of youth, its illusions and hopes, and the concomitant horrors of age and decay. At the same time he knew how remote most human desires are from reality; you, "tired heart," he insists in "To Himself,"

> . . . have the right to hate
> Yourself, the world as it is, the brute
> Energy that secretly enjoins the common fate,
> And the immense immeasurable emptiness of things.

Believing life in its common ills as in its end essentially unhappy, he fully understood the common need of consolations. Yet he despised this need (especially as it feeds on the deceits of reason, little more than a form of anesthesia) and the failure of almost all of us to live in denial of it. Eventually he found a kind of fervor and satisfaction, if not contentment, in the acid truth:

> . . . sick or well, I stamp upon the cowardice of mankind, I refuse every consolation, every childish deceit, and I have the courage to bear the deprivation of every hope, to look intrepidly at the desert of life, not to disguise any part of human unhappiness, to accept all the consequences of a philosophy that is painful, but true. Philosophy which, if it is of no other use, gives to strong men the proud satisfaction of seeing every cloak torn from the concealed and mysterious cruelty of human destiny.

Of course one can suspect him, as much as the rest of us, of casting the world in his own image. Dogged by ailments and infirmities—several self-induced by incredible rigors of study—most of his tormented life, incapable for one reason or another of the passionate fulfilment he believed in and devoutly wished, he probably could not help visiting his frustrations on the world he lived in. However, with his wonted uncommon sense plus his veneration for the Greeks, he excoriated the Christian tendency to ignore physical health for "spiritual" reasons. How much our loftiest values and acts depend on it was especially brought home to him by his feeble body; he was hardly one to deny the testimony of his own experience. Describing his feelings of contempt for mankind in its lust for consolations, he can go so far as to admit, "If these feelings arise from sickness, I do not know. . . ."

As thoroughly convinced of the nothingness of this life and the world as anyone, even he for all his clear-headedness could not wash his hands of the whole business, could not go on to conclude logically—no doubt this is one of his principal attractivenesses—that whatever distractions and illusions man seeks out to make life a little more endurable, they must be categorically accepted. For if life is truly meaningless what difference can conduct make? What standards, based as they must be on some first principle, can one allow oneself? Such the contradiction at the heart—and the heart—of his work. On the contrary, since he seems to have put his hope in man's living with man, in the human community against indifferent nature, his sense of outrage at the failure of mankind to be honest, honorable, noble (though at times he admits the emptiness of these qualities too!) was much stronger than most men's. But as we shall discover, perhaps his notion that he saw things as they nakedly, anguishingly, are comprised his final necessary illusion, the nourishment that permitted him to live at least with some ardor. As he said, despair was infinitely preferable to emptiness; though it may have been his disappointments that made him feel the whole world meaningless, at least they made him feel. Believing in youth, its uncompromisingness before evil and weakness till age overtakes it, he clung relentlessly to his own uncompromisingness to the end.

In any case, one can suggest that out of love Leopardi expected too much of man, had too much pride in him and his potentialities to be "tolerant" before his self-indulgences, his deceits. Like Pascal he asked why man, pitiable creature that he is, should be able to rack himself with such gigantic desires and torments. Pound's translation, "Her Monument, the Image Cut Thereon," concludes:

> O mortal nature,
> If thou art
> Frail and so vile in all,
> How canst thou reach so high with thy poor sense;
> Yet if thou art
> Noble in any part
> How is the noblest of thy speech and thought

> So lightly wrought
> Or to such base occasion lit and quenched?

In short, Leopardi adored what he hated, hated what he adored: man's consciousness, that which, separating him from nature and the animals, enables him to recognize the wretchedness (as well thereby to complicate it) and so the superiority of his condition. Envying though he may have the lifelong free fancy of birds, like that of children and the childhood of the race, at the same time Leopardi exercised, enjoyed exercising, his intellect to the full.

Despite his own incapacities he rarely blinked the importance of high-minded aims and mighty efforts; and in his work, as "To Italy" well illustrates, valiantly he sought by direct appeal, by satire, by scathing comment, to rouse his countrymen to noble thinking and noble doing. Entirely aware of the potentialities of depravity (this he saw in nature; in this he saw, alas, the oneness of man and nature), he insisted that we must with utmost resolution bestir ourselves against these potentialities.

Nor did he capitulate to deterministic thinking to the point of relieving us of the responsibilities of our lives. XLV of his *Pensieri* concludes, ". . . the weak live because of the world's will, and the strong because of their own." Yet Leopardi, as his sardonic statements amply attest, was overwhelmingly aware of the hostility of the modern world to art—that is, to sensitivity, distinction, love, meaningful and realized living. No one knew better than he the grimness of the struggle. Steeped in his appetites and his expectations, naked to his surroundings, whether his little desolate native Recanati or pompous, self-infatuated Rome, he experienced it, the smothering of the spirit, with still intolerable, infuriating freshness. Like a Swift before him and a Flaubert after he must rabidly—the price of the artist in him—savor each minute revolting particular.

Animated all his life by the desire for achievement and fame, he realized the folly of this desire, particularly in an apathetic modern world, in a time characterized by him as a "century of boys." What can better convey his scorn than "even mediocrity has become extremely rare!" His age's easy bloated optimism, its naive confidence in progress and the infinite perfectibility of man, convinced him of its hopelessness. He saw through the superficial impressiveness of mass education to its very deep dangers: the thinning, the leveling, and the consequent destruction of real learning. With his customary hawk-like fierceness he pounced on that wonderfully consolatory cliché, "this is a century of transition." It is hard to believe that his denunciation of it was written well over a century ago. How much he would consider us the infants—not to say still-borns—of the children of the 19th century. As he pointed out, it is one thing to remark the absurd in the root of life; it is quite another to elevate absurdities into root principles. How horrified he would be and how grateful for his own poor age could he see the super-fulfilment of his prophecies in the enormous ingenuity we expend to maintain and speed the life of imbecility and to hide from actuality. One can imagine his derision before our egregious efforts to develop a monetary idealism and out of it an interlocking set of ideas to insulate us against the always more vexing "facts of life." Our world seen almost entirely in the abstractions of the newspaper and the blatherskiting of politicians, we are embroiled in arguments, life and death ones, often as real as those of medievalists to us about the permissible congestion of angels on a pinhead, this ironically enough in a country particularly arrogant about its practicality, its realism, its scientific procedures, the latter in many ways the most abstract we have. The atom bomb, that monument of and to abstraction come alive, may at last, in our dedication to it, splitting us from the life that so troubles us, forever abstract us all. Naturally, as a Leopardi would say, as the truth becomes daily more clamorous, daily more unpleasant, so the noise and the rigor of our prejudices must grow.

But such challenge it is that precisely helps to underscore the size of a work of art. What is a major quality of a creative piece if not its ability to exceed its day's limitations. It is the welling up for reasons usually impossible to come by of the magic springs in the desert that makes the genius dear to us, a welling up despite—sometimes it would seem because of—brutality, depravity, destructiveness. It is the ability to feel, to respond, to keep the human reality going in the midst of this destructiveness that compels us to honor and preserve the great works of art. To ignore nothing of human and natural enormity, to meet fate on its own terms, this is the triumph we can hope for, this as well as the heroism of the noble failure persisted in. As Leopardi puts it,

> Works of genius have the peculiarity that, even when they represent the nothingness of things, even when they clearly demonstrate and make us feel the inevitable unhappiness of life, when they express the most terrible mood of despair [it is interesting to compare the despair of a *Hamlet* or a *Macbeth*, say, with that of *The Waste Land*], yet to a great mind even though it may be in a state of extreme depression, disillusionment, blankness, *noia*, and weariness of life, or in the bitterest and most paralysing misfortunes . . . they always serve as a consolation, rekindle enthusiasm; and though they treat and represent no other subject than death, they restore to such a mind at least momentarily that life which it had lost. Consequently that which when seen in the reality of things stabs and kills the soul, when seen in imitation or in any other way in works of genius . . . opens the heart and restores it to life. In any case, just as the author, while describing and feeling so strongly the emptiness of illusions, yet retained all the time a great fund of illusion, and clearly proved that he did by so eagerly describing their emptiness; likewise the reader, however much undeceived both by himself and by what he reads, is yet drawn by the author into that very deceit and illusion latent in the most intimate recesses of the spirit which he was searching. . . . The very contemplation of nothingness is a thing in these works which seems to enlarge the soul of the

reader, to exalt it and to satisfy it with itself and its own despair. . . .
Moreover, the feeling of nothing is the feeling of a dead and death-
inflicting thing. But if this feeling is alive . . . its liveliness prevails
in the mind of the reader over the nothingness of the thing which it
makes him feel, and the soul receives life, if only for a moment, from
the very violence with which it feels the perpetual death of things in
its own death.

It is the *greatness* of the despair that remains with us, the valor of the human
effort: to dare, to persist, to know, as well as to persist in the indefatigable truth
of its deepest, noblest nature: the bracing of truth whatever shape it takes. One
watches a Macbeth in all the agony and negation of the human spirit and one is
deepened as well as vitalized by the magnitude of the struggle, what forces—
superhuman no less than natural—are required to overcome human grandeur.

Nor should we neglect the satisfaction, the independence, it occasionally
affords a man, this salubriousness of wholesale denial, the ability to pierce all
earthly and spiritual vanities. We know how much Leopardi like Flaubert, say,
now and then envied ordinary absorptions; but basically both despised them and
went on to despise all human occupations. In the words of Flaubert:

To be unable to be satisfied by the whole of earthly good, even, so to
speak, by the whole world, to accuse things of insufficiency and nothingness, and to suffer from a perpetual lack and sense of emptiness—
that seems to me to be the chief sign of greatness and nobility to be
found in human nature.

Leopardi in LXVIII of the *Pensieri* is even more explicit about the splendors of
boredom:

In a certain sense boredom is the most sublime of human feelings . . .
that inability to be satisfied by any earthly thing, not even, as it were,
by the whole earth itself, to consider the incalculable breadth of
space, the number, the marvellous mass of worlds—and to find that
all is slight and tiny compared to the capacity of one's own spirit; to
imagine that the number of worlds is infinite, the universe infinite,
and yet to feel that our spirit, our desire would still be greater than
any such universe; to accuse things always of insufficiency and nullity,
to suffer the lack, the void, and therefore boredom—this seems to me
the finest sign of grandeur and nobility that human nature manifests.
And so boredom is little known among men of small importance and
slightly, or not at all, among the other animals.

Man is so constituted that he can plume himself on his capacity for finding
pleasure in nothing in the universe (so he does find pleasure!) and, in the same
breath, in *his* nothingness in the universe. Leopardi can write,

Nothing demonstrates more clearly the power and greatness of the
human intellect, the loftiness and nobility of man, than his power of
knowing and entirely comprehending his smallness. When he, considering the plurality of the worlds, feels himself as the infinitesimal
part of a globe that is the smallest part of one of the infinite systems
that make up the World, and in this consideration he marvels at his

smallness . . . is almost one with nothingness and almost loses himself in the incomprehensible vastness of existence, then with this act and with this thought he gives the greatest proof possible of his nobility, of the strength and immense capacity of his mind, which, enclosed in so small and infinitesimal a being, has attained to the comprehension of things so superior to his nature, and can embrace and contain within his thought this same immensity of existence and of things.

Yet whether it be praise of man for the insatiability of his desire or praise for his magnificent sense of his nothingness (in either case mind, its power of awareness, is at the base of what Leopardi is acclaiming), the unity that runs through both positions is his insistence on nobility. His work is of this order: not a yielding to the waste land and at his maturest not a straining to escape it in cloud-cuckoo-lands, but a declaration for the noble life in the desert, of man's understanding his tragic role in the presence of unqualified knowledge, of maintaining love, friendship, the appetites, great deeds, regardless of the hostility of circumstance and the cost in self: the power men have on occasion of being more than themselves in the moment of extremity—illusions perhaps, yet real by what transpires between these illusions, our feelings, and the world. And the spectacle of such a performance cannot help waking some heroism of response in us. As De Sanctis said,

Leopardi produces the opposite effect to that which he proposes. He does not believe in progress, and he makes you yearn for it; he does not believe in liberty, and he makes you love it. Love, virtue, glory he calls illusions, and he kindles in your breast an inexhaustible passion for them. (De Sanctis translations by Irma Brandeis)

Not that Leopardi lacked his moments of majestic and ecstatic yielding. His perhaps most famous poem, "The Infinite," concludes: "in this immensity my thought is drowned; / and to be wrecked in such a sea is sweet."

Nonetheless, though Leopardi traveled the whole arduous distance of reason, as with many a good Existentialist his heart would not be denied: its truths also require attention, and the primacy of feeling asserts itself again and again, if only in despair. Long ago De Sanctis remarked,

. . . Leopardi, amid the wreckage of principles and with so much scepticism of mind and so much faith of heart, could not and should not have given us anything but a *lyric* work—expression of internal discord, a lament for the death of the poetic world and, indeed, of poetry itself.

This is Leopardi's poetry, the new kind he and his best peers developed. For Leopardi was that oddest, most painful and extraordinary of combinations: a naturalist by intellect and a poet by heart, his poetry the offspring of their violent marriage. A much earlier poet comes to mind here, Lucretius with his passionate avowal to the point of most rigorous dogma of naturalistic doctrine. Like him Leopardi passionately asserts the emptiness, the nullity of life. But whereas

Lucretius exults in this as the source of endless delight and emancipation, Leopardi is most passionate in his belief in the pleasures and passions of life and in his chief objection, not to them, though he sees their only partial satisfyingness, but to their brevity and their loss, their passing in age when we are left with our desires but no power to fulfil them. This objection we must expect to be especially acute in one most nobly endowed with capacity for love and enthusiasm, but physically denied them from the start. Man being mortal attains at best—or, better, recovers—only momentary glimpses of that beauty the hunger for which dogs him all the days of his life; and these glimpses, rare as they are, make the arid times all the worse. Yet a lifetime of agony is not too much to pay for them. Leopardi cannot, like Lucretius, (for Leopardi would have deemed this another lie) persist in depreciating the sweet, any more than he can—except for such moments as the one with boredom' above—call the bitter part of the pill sweet; but he can taste it with manly anger and with a refusal to pretend that it is other than it is.

Such conflict between heart and head in its sharpness makes much of Leopardi's might as well as much of the subject-matter of his writing: his brilliant, tenacious reason going on and on in the midst of his desire and the desire honing, rising, as it sees itself more and more gainsaid; one corroborates and deepens the other even as it gainsays it. It is his poetry, its passion, that defines with painful precision his loss, as it is his comprehension of the loss that sharpens his passion. And at least he still had the splendors of his precise, very precisely realized loss. One of the first to appreciate, for Eden was still freshly behind him, the vastness of the catastrophe of being outcast and therefore the extraordinariness of the wilderness as well as the drama, the fierceness, of one, the wilderness, up against the other, Eden, he constituted the link agonized, crucified, the angel burning, between them. For the 18th century the sense of belonging, if seriously shaken and shrunken, still persisted. But a Leopardi, by the ruthlessness of his reason and the cogency of his feeling of estrangmeent, could find reinforcement in no doctrine, no articulated body of beliefs. With several other early 19th century poets and thinkers, challenging this sense of belonging, contemning its casualness, its passivity and its smugness, believing that it must include all or nothing, Leopardi shattered it. Discovering nothing that could satisfy his longing and the consequent feeling of estrangement, no satisfactory objective correlative for it in the world (as the failure to find an objective correlative is *the* problem and the denial of the world *the* correlative of a Hamlet), at last Leopardi made that irrevocable feeling, the last remnant of Eden, its own objective correlative; and he found unity if only in the completeness of the break through all things, in his lightning-strong, all-things-embracing, all-things-pervading lyrical outcry. (If thoughts and things have forever separated, a separation a William Carlos Williams with his "no thoughts but in things" would heal, at least the separation must permeate all things.)

Intellect is of course at the heart, if not the heart, of this outcry. We know the bittersweet savor of all things, as of that apple tasted and tasting most—most painfully—sweet in the moment of knowledge it produced, paradise seen most vividly in the lightning clap of consciousness (God feared this man "become as one of us, to know good and evil") and therefore of loss. Appropriately Leopardi, employing this consciousness, its powers of memory (already an acknowledgement of loss), most often centered his poems in the image of a lovely young girl out of his youth, as in "To Sylvia," or a mature woman, both as inspiration and absorption. (It was through Eve, we must remember, that Eden attained its happiest, ripest moment as well as its fall.) The young girl, contemplated, summons up the past she occupied, youth in its poignant aura of hope; the woman embodies the possibility of deep love, something Leopardi regarded as the loftiest human emotion, and of a kind of Platonic redemption. But as the girl is finally no more than a bitter mirage, a phantom existing only in the spell of the poem, so the woman he hopes to appeal to, an even crueler image, never responds, never reciprocates his passionate care. As with Poe the muse has become a real woman, but a woman dead to Leopardi who unlike Poe finds nothing but anguish in this death and so one of the several mainsprings of his poetry. As early as *Memoirs of His First Love* Leopardi identifies beauty and a particular lovely woman. At the same time despite his youth, with the scathing objectivity he can apply even to himself, he admits that any other woman might have moved him just as much.

Perhaps as important as woman in his feelings is the moon, an obviously feminine image, feminine too in its influences. For the moon is a softener, an embalmer, a rebuilder in its mildness and dreamlike quality of what time, men, and the harsher seasons mar; like music it is vision's atmosphere, emboldener of the imagination. His eyes often shine with weeping in the moonlight; yet they do shine, shed their glow on things, and see as he remembers. He speaks of "the incredible power music habitually has over me, and . . . the wringing of my heart by certain doggerel songs heard by chance. . . ." A passing singer enchants him as he listens, unseen, from some height, a balcony, a tower, a hill. The human voice, his as well as that overheard, alone in the earth, swelling out, fills all with its lament, charges the world with the poignancy of its being and its gigantic awareness of frailty. That is what one expects of a poet and his poetry, that it will translate the world into human terms and into the breath, alone godly for man, into language where we live and by its loveliness live more freely, gracefully, triumphantly, that he will give us the world according to his heart and ours. For Leopardi music, heights, and delicacy come into their consummate own in that one creature that seems to have remained in Eden—the bird. Its winged way of life, coupled with its light unstable fancy which keeps it a child all its days, permits it a superb, almost mythical harmony with nature. However, in his "The Single Bird," contrasting himself with the bird he addresses, a bird happily solitary according to the dictates of its nature, he must acknowledge the misery of his hermit-like separation from the others and from the joys of youth which he can know only in his deprivation of them.

His glorification of adolescence marks Leopardi out a romantic. He saw youth's anguishes, but thought them delicious ones of hope as against cold indifference and the dying of age; in that he maintained his anguish, he maintained, he believed, some of his passion and youth. He hated society the more for its conspiracy of envy to crush youth out of its children as quickly as possible by its misbegotten forms of education (CIV of the *Pensieri*).

But very much unlike the romantics, at least our general notion of them, he was magnificently capable of incorporating, in an unsurpassed purity of utterance, the complex of feelings summoned forth by an image, event, realization: he was a master of the articulating of these feelings' juxtaposition, interdependence, their working in and through each other, their startling shifts. In his genius for evoking the past in its actual youthful shimmer, simultaneously with an adult intellectual examination of it, memory and realization, and a sense of the prosaic present, Leopardi reminds one of the Joyce of stories like "Araby." Leopardi could achieve a combination of image and idea, statement and situation, these interlacing, one as real as the other, a duet of equal convincing parts very few modern poets have been able to reach (so much so that we hardly have the language or the attitude needed to translate him successfully). This mastery appears in his prose no less than in his poetry and is perhaps for the open play of his extraordinary analytical powers, most clearly displayed in prose of the order of *Memoirs of His First Love* and the "Dialogue of Tristan and a Friend." Such work proves what mordant mind he possessed, how fierce in penetration and psychological insight—all part of his unsparing sense of truth, the rights of observation, particularly striking in a poet marked by solitude; we have had few more devastating commentators on society and its inanities.

Such multiple focus seems especially worth stressing today, for we seem to be moving even in poetry (so strident is the demand for simplification in the political scene) toward didacticism, abstraction, intellection, mere frigid wit-work. Aside from the influence of the academy and the critical assumption that the poet be everywhere proper, Audenesquely superior to his poem, with space of a wide-open, vertiginously-expanding universe pouring in on all sides and simultaneously with the political climate (possibly out of fear of these cosmic blasts) growing daily more insular and rigid, it is not hard to understand why young poets, sensitive as they should be to environment, may feel tongue-tied.

As De Sanctis insisted, there is small point in bewailing the present condition of art, demanding one thing or another of it; science and what it represents has pervaded poetry even as it has the rest of our lives, and it cannot be evicted because its presence corresponds to the current conditions of the human spirit. No matter how much an object's beauty may take us, intellect, criticism and scientific analysis of the object as well as of our response to it, invariably breaks in. Feeling alone no longer satisfies. But as De Sanctis goes on,

> Poetry, since it cannot avoid the encounter with thought must mold it, transfigure it and incorporate it. The only serious esthetic question that remains is that of deciding how far the great have succeeded in so doing. (For the mediocre this is an insurmountable cliff.)

Such incorporating in human terms I would accent.

It is foolish to urge greatness, yet surely one can hope for largeness of effort and for the underscoring of critical standards that do not lose sight of the dimensions of master work, do not allow the confusion of a small thing with a large. Eliot's was a waste land, but at least it was a desert, a desolation, a whimper on a vast scale as Pound's work has been a huge defiance and rage, a dedication to mighty human ends. Now the young seem to have learned their elders' lessons, ironically, too well. Altogether convinced it appears, abjectly, modestly they sit back in the waste land and as modestly, not to say smugly, proceed to claim— if not reclaim—by repetitions some inch of the greyness. And so widespread is this practice that, for the moment at least, not a few critics and poets alike seem tempted to adjudge this practice happy performance, in its way an adequate successor to the courage, the grappling with difficulties and chaos of a Pound, a Williams, a Stevens, still our youngest, most "promising" poets, to applaud what is being done as what should—and must—be done. It is proper perhaps to end with that other great, more recent moral passion Pound who said, ". . . it is well that one man should have a vision of perfection and that he should be sick to the death and disconsolate because he could not attain it." And

> Prince, in this circus of three rings,
> Hell, heaven and earth wherein is nothing clear
> Void, mix'd and loose up to the stratosphere,
> Pity the young who have not known these things.

As the Wind Sits:
The Poetics of
King Lear

Paradox, contradiction, extravagance, outrageous wit loom
large among the ways we have of meeting life and Shakespeare
at their ripest. And never is life more on the stretch than in
King Lear. Blowing from all directions at once, a storm shapes
into magnificent poetry that threatens to rip free of its moor-
ings and to blast the play and its world to pieces. I will try
to show that the storm, as it blows through the play's words,
charging them with maximal power and grandeur, blows thing
and thought apart and leaves those words madly flapping,
tattered husks. Yet the play itself, storm and all, made of
something like adamant, endures. How then exaggerate our
problems with it, the mercuriality, the wonder, and the rigors
we must contend with?

So I begin with an oxymoron as extreme as I can make it:
King Lear is a monument of the stormiest music. For what
help they may be, I recommend two additional paradoxes, the
first formulated by the most balanced Greek tragedian, Soph-
ocles: "Call no man happy until he is dead"; the second, by
the modern poet most enthusiastic for the tragic spirit, Yeats,
from his poem "Crazy Jane Talks to the Bishop," written in
old age when he experienced some of the triumphant irascibility, the sexual ferocity, of Lear: "For nothing can be sole
or whole / That has not been rent." Yeats pursued this in his
"Lapis Lazuli" to an ultimate paradox in which he declared

Shakespeare's tragic heroes gay: "Gaiety transfiguring all that dread."

Armed with these observations, I mean to dare further extravagances, or what would certainly be extravagant for any work other than *King Lear*. A. C. Bradley, exercised like many other critics by the play's "inconsistencies," long ago plausibly compiled them. For me they confirm the play's plausibility. In fact, one might say that *King Lear*, taking on some of the materials of a *Titus Andronicus*, makes them necessary and convincing. But I would be sensible not to be too confident of my response except as I assume, at least as confidently, that it too is bound to be inadequate. Inadequate and, one might almost hope, extravagantly, egregiously, so perhaps germinally wrong. Already fifty years ago, in his "Shakespeare and the Stoicism of Seneca," Eliot suggested, "About any one so great as Shakespeare, it is probable that we can never be right; and if we can never be right, it is better that we should from time to time change our way of being wrong."

King Lear is extraordinary, to begin with, if only for the gamut of response, wrongness and all, it has elicited over its nearly four hundred years of survival. That gamut has gone from laudations of the play as the most sublime work of art ever produced to summary dismissals of it as a fiasco of childish absurdity. We must appeal to a major writer indeed for the best expression of the latter opinion. According to Tolstoy, *King Lear* prompts "aversion and weariness." But like a good, great competitor, Tolstoy never had a kind word for Shakespeare. Tolstoy's towering, stormy life and his dramatic runaway end, giving the lie to his contemptuous words, would seem to attest to the validity of *King Lear*. Even more awesome than Lear's surviving his daughters and his storm is his riding through the assault, favorable and hostile, of his host of critics, directors, actors—an assault revealing something fundamental about the play and also about the ages in which the critics lived as, squinting into its illuminating mirror, each found his own image.

Soon after Shakespeare's lifetime and during the Restoration, the play had little appeal. But in 1681, out of admiration,

Nahum Tate revived it, if with major alterations. As his Dedication says, "Nothing but . . . my Zeal for the Remains of *Shakespear* cou'd have wrought me to so bold an Undertaking." He fully recognized the uniqueness of Shakespeare's "Creating Fancy" and of the play's language and images, "the only Things in the World that ought to be said on those Conditions." Why then did Tate feel obliged to revise it? "I found the Whole . . . a Heap of Jewels, unstrung, and unpolisht; yet so dazling in their Disorder, that I soon perceiv'd I had seiz'd a Treasure." How apt is his description "dazling *in* their Disorder." But it is the unstrung and unpolished, jumbled-about condition of the jewels that obviously distressed him and his age. To make the play palatable for a Restoration audience, he gave it, among other things, a happy ending. As Boileau observed, "Some truths may be too strong to be believed." Or in Eliot's words from "Burnt Norton," "Human kind / Cannot bear very much reality." We are not far from Keats's "negative capability." Shakespeare's sources apart, he was after reality, reality as he knew it in all its relentlessness or, more accurately, in all its indifference, and not the conventions of any one time or society.

But a great change occurred in the nineteenth century. Charles Lamb well expressed the new attitude. Despising Tate's revision, Lamb felt the play "beyond all art" and Lear's "martyrdom" so complete that "a fair dismissal from the stage of life [was] the only decorous thing for him." Lamb was after the decorous and a fair dismissal, one from the stage itself. Like his fellow Romantics Lamb exulted in the sublime, in nature at its most extravagant. The very things about *King Lear* that repelled the eighteenth century delighted the nineteenth. But despite the play's horrors, its physical and other painfulness, or because of them, the Romantics seem to have wanted to exalt it out of existence; it was too good for this world.

Gradually the opinion of the play's inactability changed even though difficulties remained. Bradley, putting it beside works like *Prometheus Bound* and *The Divine Comedy*, calling it "Shakespeare's greatest achievement, but . . . not his best play," still considered it "too huge for the stage." Since then, however, the play has been generally applauded as great theater. We are too well rehearsed in horrors and hideous human behavior to boggle at *King Lear*. In some basic respects we may be closer to it than any age other than Shakespeare's own. And perhaps even closer than his own. Far flung through space as through time, fiercely questioning everything, we have proved outrageous in energy and ruin. But our present condition by that very ruinous energy has also destroyed the possibility of homogeneous response; and though the vast variety of our responses attests to the play's richness, it also attests to our confusion. Inevitably, in a time broken in its beliefs, a multiplicity of views accumulates.

Even so, whatever the time and however subtle and diverse the analyses, *King Lear*, like Lear himself, gaily fleeing, trailing wild flowers and a mad lilt of syllables, refuses to be caught. To land this light-as-air Leviathan, a critic would have to be able to throw out a net as large, as subtle, as complex as the play itself. Understandably critics now seize for dear life on one position or another, even one passage or verse, microscopically attended to, in the hope that it will be the clue to lead them through the tumultuous maze. At their best these concentrations illuminate moments of the play, as the Lilliputians, netting Gulliver, magnified his comb past any normal human capacity. But whatever light they may shed, the illuminations occur often at the expense of other parts and of the play as a whole, certainly of its furious speed, its battering unity; somehow it must be seen and heard all at once, a world experienced in the everywhere resonant round.

In attempting such a response, what immediately strikes me is the huge mélange of materials, a hurly-burly of them, filling the play. Set in a dark abysm of the past, the play seems porous as it lets loose countless fateful if invisible forces. Continuously, with one name or another, the characters strive to fix those forces. In and through these characters, most of all Lear himself, immensely heterogenous elements jostle one another. Like previous Shakespearean plays, *King Lear* is a veritable refuse heap: the wreckage of the ages, shadow-rich ruins, whispering in the wind. Odds and ends of folklore and sundry sources jut through: the Ur-*King Lear*, Sidney's *Arcadia*, Holinshed's *Chronicles*, Florio's translation of Montaigne, and other literary works, myths, cultural history, old songs. Many references, beyond being anachronistic, are thoroughly incongruous, like Edgar's medieval "Child Rowland" or the Fool's self-conscious, mind-jolting "This prophecy Merlin shall make; for I live before his time." Or Lear's calling Edgar a "learnèd Theban" and "good Athenian," as though Lear were an avid student of Plato and the other Greeks.

What a hodgepodge too of gods and supernatural powers is appealed to, from Hecate, Apollo, and Jupiter (rather odd deities, one might think, for ancient Britain); to natural powers, the orbs, the sun, moon, and stars; to nature itself, to Edgar's folk-superstitious fiends, borrowed appropriately from *A Declaration of Egregious Popish Impostures* since Edgar's Tom o' Bedlam is an imposture; to Lear's single God in "God's spies"; to his final gods throwing incense on him and Cordelia as "sacrifices." But, as Sidney and others had loudly complained, Elizabethan theater was always a gallimaufry. It splendidly presented the mind's baggage and often enacted its upheavals—a turmoil of terms and things, drawn higgledy-piggledly from countless times and places.

But this upheaval, further complicated by time's passing, is our basic dilemma: the staggering, if not impossible, effort required of us, first of all, to be accurate about the text itself, the play as it was in its own day. We must acknowledge our fundamental ignorance of that long gone day and the fact that its minds, whatever ambience they shared, were from one moment to the next variable. Second, we must recognize the congeries of buried cities, beyond the ones already there, the play became through the centuries—heaped Troys in ember state, ready, one or another of them, at any breath to flare up again. Finally, we must try to cope with the layer upon layer, in constant upheaval, of our own minds; for all times, as they seem to be in *King Lear*, are indeed contemporaneous in us, leaping at one moment to the nineteenth century, at another to the thirteenth, at the next to the Stone Age and earlier, the lot framed by modernity. All this while each age grapples with its special way of expressing not only its uniqueness but the inexpressible, and strives to capture in words what we always know is there precisely as it eludes us. Wallace Stevens, in his "Notes toward a Supreme Fiction," tells us that "Phoebus was / A name for something that never could be named."

But it is the extraordinary general uprootedness of these words or names in *King Lear*, their welter, that makes a difference and a difficulty even greater than that which we encounter in his other plays. From a not too sympathetic point of view, *King Lear* might be adjudged a ramshackle affair, a thrown-together contrivance that, worst of all, pieces flying, somehow holds together and works. Truly Nahum Tate's unstrung heap of jewels, "dazling in [if not for] their Disorder." So practiced was Shakespeare in the manipulation of diverse intellectual counters (he was fortunate to be born with his gifts when casual jumble was customary) that, by the time he wrote *King Lear*, he could make its miscellany serve, artistically, intellectually, emotionally, his darker purposes. His was, I suggest, an epical ambition to accommodate, as well as reality, the entire mind, its furnishings, its multiple deposits.

Furthermore, *King Lear* is what it is, one might speculate, because of Shakespeare's catch-as-catch-can style, his writing on the run. With an assignment of two, sometimes three, plays a year, he proved himself the genius of adaptability. Working under great pressure and at great speed, he was obliged to use whatever he could lay his hands on. Thus, to fill the play, he threw together the vastly miscellaneous material of his age and the materials lodged in his capacious mind. Writing at great speed, he had a heightened sense of, and could hold in his mind, the whole work at once. Little wonder it echoes and reechoes. He could hope to yoke, by his mind's incandescence and the violence of the play's situation, its immensely heterogeneous materials. Fortunately also, with models like Tamburlaine nearby, Shakespeare found a character, ancient, almost preternaturally powerful, able to confront that tumultuous everything (and nothing) and, with his rampageous spirit, able to justify it if not to pull it all together into one meaningful harmony.

Now I propose that, helter-skelter as the United States has been from its start, a potpourri like *King Lear* is especially congenial to it. Already in the format of the journal, a grab bag of the whole of experience, Emerson and Thoreau were at their best. Can we deny this grab bag, all-inclusive characteristic to Whitman or to Melville in *Moby Dick*, obviously straining after Shakespeare? Moreover, the turbulence of the modern age, the art of Pound, Eliot, Joyce, Picasso, Stravinsky, and others, and our popular media have well developed our capacity for a *King Lear*. Anyone practiced in *The Cantos* or *The Waste Land*, in *Ulysses* and certainly *Finnegans Wake*, each a disgorging of the mind of the writer, a jamboree of materials looted from all times and places, should have a secure purchase on saltancies dizzying enough to require more than Puck-like, jet-propelled mental agility. These modern techniques are not merely a consequence or symptom of technology, the jumbled metropolis, the cheek-by-jowl surrealistic columns of the newspaper, the hither-and-yon of cinema, but a fairly accurate portrait of the feverish activity of the mind, especially of the liveliest examples of it in our time.

Yet, even as one stresses the potpourri aspect of *King Lear*, he may also observe how many things are missing from the play that we hardly think to miss. There is never a reference to Queen Lear or any other relative; nor is there one recollection out of Lear's more than eighty years and his surely tempestuous long reign that is not part of his obsession with his daughters' treatment. Further, beyond the necessary information that Edmund is a bastard (his mother, Gloucester's mistress, must be mentioned to establish Gloucester's character) and has been nine years out and must be nine to come, each time to some place unnamed, there is never a reference to a single memory in the Gloucester world. In short, whatever the remnants of allusions from earlier ages, fossils churned up in the characters' minds and speeches, only the here and now ferociously, overwhelmingly concerns them and us. One could rejoin, What do you expect? This is intensest drama. All such references, particularly domestic or historical ones, would be irrelevant, distracting, diluting. Nonetheless, though *King Lear* impresses us as being vaster than the other major tragedies, they are much richer in their recent past, its active presence.

At the same time *King Lear* is crowded with customs, conventions, and terms that rarely work—various gods, powers, fiends, religious and ethical concepts: kinship, love, marriage, friendship, the law of hospitality, a belief in the truth and its availability, kingship, hierarchy, nobility, the laws, and a plethora of things or objects, usually presented in speeches, hence, no more than words. Far beyond our cognizance, language in all of us is an amazing, mixed-up mosaic, the strata of time itself. But language in this play, more than that of other words, consists of haunting verbal relics from a world largely vanished: words, once possibly effective and satisfying, accepted as identical with reality and the gods, now dilapidated, having little to do with the actual lives of the characters. Ghostlike, the flicker of dead stars, these terms flit about in the wind. Though their sources have long withdrawn, they still hover near, and near perhaps mainly for Lear's and Gloucester's assumption, then Lear's relentless quest, of those sources as energetic realities.

Like its words the play's world itself is a plenitude out of strict economy, vastness and immense bustle out of emptiness; a stage almost as empty as the wind-swept moon encourages a bewilderment that hardly lets us know where, when, who, and what we are. Or in Lear's words, "Who is it can tell me who I am?" Where, beyond the castles of the main characters, never precisely located, does the play take place? In a wood; on a heath, another part of the heath, a hovel, a room in a suddenly present farmhouse somewhere near Gloucester's somewhere castle, and the one specifically named place, Dover, which is not Dover at all, with an altogether muffled battle in a field somewhere presumably near Dover (as later stage directions have it).

The play's landscapes crop up chiefly in speeches. Early on

the whole of Britain appropriately comes under Lear's official hands, but on a map and in most general terms, as he is about to tear Britain apart. Like a god, simultaneously creating a world and giving it away, as though it were his to give, he says to Goneril:

> Of all these bounds, even from this line to this,
> With shadowy forests, and with champains riched,
> With plenteous rivers, and wide-skirted meads,
> We make thee lady.
>
> (1.1.63-66)

And Regan's share?

> To thee and thine hereditary ever
> Remain this ample third of our fair kingdom,
> No less in space, validity, and pleasure
> Than that conferred on Goneril.
>
> (1.1.79-82)

Immediately, his land all gone, rather than crawling toward death, Lear rushes off to hunt. But where and what? Certainly, as far as we can tell, he returns with no spoils. Is it animals he is after, boars, dragons, chimerae, himself? Some brand new realm?

Beyond landscapes and animals, what people at large and their settings help to locate the play in time and place? None beyond Lear's "poor naked wretches" in the third act, in a passionate speech that instantly materializes such a wretch, Edgar feigning Tom o' Bedlam, a splendid anachronism straight out of Shakespeare's day and one of its worst horrors; then Edgar's "Bedlam beggars," never seen, like his never seen, somewhere "happy hollow of a tree" in which he hid from those hunting him, and his verbal "low farms, / Poor pelting villages, sheep-cotes, and mills. . . . "

And what is the play's single most striking scene? It is—like Lear's, words only and even less real than a map, if much more sensuously detailed—Edgar's magnificent, fantastic invention of the cliffs of Dover for the benefit of the blind Gloucester—truly pure poetry! Here, in an extravagant make-

believe like his several roles, Edgar, as magically and effectively as Ariel with his storm and his masque, conjures up a
vast vista in which he gives full play (though his other
speeches, in tune with his roles, are also chockablock with a
madly chaotic lot of creatures, times, phrases) to his imagination and composes a scene that by its contrast intensifies
the bareness and the barrenness we have grown accustomed
to in this play. Though supposed to be about the Dover cliffs,
his speech is description without place, description as place,
description uninfected, unembarrassed by actuality; thus it is
free to fulfill its own gorgeous impulses and desperate needs.
What we increasingly feel everywhere in *King Lear*, the tearing
apart of words and the world, in this speech comes to complete, happy fruition.

Edgar develops a vision as clear and trenchant as a dream,
by its very powerful absurdity all the more cogent and real.
Edgar's "Lest my brain turn and the deficient sight / Topple
down headlong" (4.6.23-24) gives the blind Gloucester his
cue and his action. When Gloucester asks, "But have I fall'n,
or no?" (4.6.56) Edgar, his imagination gaily free, as though
he is urging his father to, instructing him in, the one wholly
emancipating activity, that of the imagination, says, "Look
up a-height; the shrill-gorged lark so far / Cannot be seen or
heard: do but look up" (4.6.58-59). Words doubly effective
for one blind! Edgar gives his imaginative powers an especial
freedom when, at the moment's end, he describes the creature
he pretended he had seen just before Gloucester's fall or his
own pretended role on the summit:

> As I stood here below, methought his eyes
> Were two full moons; he had a thousand noses,
> Horns whelked and waved like the enridgèd sea. . . .

And then the explanation: "It was some fiend" (4.6.69-72).
Gloucester, blind, in turmoil, is a perfect, credulous audience
for such full-blown utterance. But this moment between
Gloucester and his son, one of the several little plays within
the play, no more and no less real than Lear's mock trial of
his daughters, is what we expect of Shakespeare and what this

whole play is: a world most telling in and out of words. Gloucester's incredible leap works as great poetry does, unerringly aimed at nothing but the mind's ear and eye, to their enlargement. Shakespeare had, in the nature of drama, practiced the verbal as reality from the start, but not till now with such audacity and thoroughness.

And the audacity increases the more we consider it. Beyond the storm, what season is it? What grows here? Wild flowers and weeds appear only in Lear's mad wearing of them, mainly in Cordelia's speech. Her description makes Gloucester's earlier words all the more striking:

> Alack, the night comes on, and the high winds
> Do sorely ruffle. For many miles about
> There's scarce a bush.
>
> (2.4.297-299)

So, too, critics have remarked, once Lear pulls up the staples of his world, an abundance of animals runs wild. But, as with Lear's hunting, other than in the speeches of the characters, in metaphor, where are they? The first we meet is, aptly, altogether fabulous and, aptly, out of Lear's rage—a dragon. The next is Gloucester's reference to Edgar: "He cannot be such a monster." Lear, wanting Oswald, exclaims, "How now? Where's that mongrel?" Horses are also frequently present in speech to be saddled somewhere and dashed off on; they image the frantic, helter-skelter quality of the play: "He calls to horse, and will I know not whither. . . . " Rage is especially imaginative at spawning the play's animals: Lear spews up "the sea-monster," "detested kite," "a serpent's tooth," a "wolfish visage." Or animals crowd forth for the measure of men and women. Edgar, claiming to have been a serving man, confesses he was "hog in sloth, fox in greediness, dog in madness, lion in prey." Later, Lear, trying those joint stools, his two daughters, says: "The little dogs and all, / Tray, Blanch, and Sweetheart—see, they bark at me" (3.6.61-62). Why should he not "see" these small, tame, pampered court dogs, see them turn on him, since he mistakenly "saw" his daughters in the first scene, now sees them, these lady braches, as the joint stools? With human creatures like these, "Tigers, not daughters," we scarcely need actual animals.

The condition of the elements and of the heavens in this play, again usually present through the main characters' speeches, also deserves attention. Lear, turning on Cordelia, swears

>   by the sacred radiance of the sun,
> The mysteries of Hecate and the night,
> By all the operation of the orbs
> From whom we do exist and cease to be. . . .
>   (1.1.109-112)

The language and the occasion achieve their solemnity through the series of genitives, which lends the passage an air of permanence and substance by establishing the major functions of heavenly bodies. (This, Lear's initial language of superauthority, will have to be broken.) Gloucester, a good-natured hedonist, seeks to attribute trouble, not to himself, but to external causes. He says,

> These late eclipses in the sun and moon portend no good to us. Though the wisdom of nature can reason it thus and thus, yet nature finds itself scourged by the sequent effects.
>
>   (1.2.106-109)

Edmund, once alone, scoffs at this astrological notion as

> the excellent foppery of the world, that when we are sick in fortune, often the surfeits of our own behavior, we make guilty of our disasters the sun, the moon, and stars; as if we were villains on necessity; fools by heavenly compulsion. . . . An admirable evasion of whoremaster man, to lay his goatish disposition on the charge of a star.
>
>   (1.2.121-131)

We can admire Edmund's vigorous good sense, his hardheaded understanding of weak human nature, even though he fails to see that he is a villain on necessity, one who has "chosen" to be what he is, a bastard, who therefore means to prosper outside the law and the conventions of society. But it is more important to recognize that, like Edmund, the villainous ones in the play, self-insulated, willful creatures, never acknowledge forces, larger than they are and mysterious, at work on them. Utterly practical, busy, rational beings, they are preoccupied with their own material desires, passions, plots. They live in one world only—this one—and have little use for images and imagining. They have successfully suppressed the dialogic, the other voice, in their natures. Only the good-natured in the play admit the existence of, even as they are also available to, mighty powers beyond themselves.

In many a previous Shakespearean play, upheavals in the weather, comets or furious storms, signalize an upheaval in the body politic, usually the deposing or the impending murder of a king; they imply the oneness of, or at least the intrinsic relationship between, man and nature. Gloucester, old-timer that he is, believes "these late eclipses in the sun and moon" ominous. And a great storm does blow up in *King Lear*, but not before or even during the deposing of a king. Instead it is the king himself, deposing himself, and the forces loose in the world that till then he had failed to notice, had been privileged enough to ignore or to think he controlled, that seem to release the storm. An overwhelming corrival presence rather than an omen, it buffets him and presumably those like him exposed, the poor and the mad, not the world he has been plucked out of or those responsible for his expulsion.

Shakespeare's first plays reveal his fondness for storms; and this fondness throughout his career deepened and expanded their significance far beyond their local dramatic effectiveness till a tempest becomes the principal figure or at least the title, initial setting, and impetus of his last play. Frequently these storms in the chaos they produce challenge the authority of a king. Can he, the absolute sovereign of his state, subdue the raging elements, make them, like his subjects, civil? Or is he, like King Alonso in *The Tempest*, powerless before them? It is important and amusing to remember that in that play, through his artistic magic, which controls the very air, another ruler, one deposed mainly because of his absorption in matters other than ruling, is responsible for rousing this tempest, or at'least the illusion of it—a splendid, convincing bit of theatrics, on the order of Edgar's staging and then dispelling of the cliffs of Dover. In *King Lear* a deposed ruler also seems consonant with a storm; but, unlike magical Prospero, as he has no Ariel to make it, so he has no Ariel to curb it.

Lear's magniloquence from the outset, common to Shakespeare and his time, prepares us for Lear's outpourings in the storm. His sky-assaulting speech, something like his normal element, makes Lear and the storm a thunderous duet, two mouths with one air, each inspiring the other. Here Lear's speech goes so far that it tries the very limits of utterance. At first it is almost wholly externalized, that of a dragon or a grandiose man of stone. But forced inward, Lear grows more and more resilient and various in his speech. At last Shakespeare asks all and more of his own seemingly inexhaustible poetic resources by seeking out occasions so extreme that even his eloquence falters and thereby is most telling in such simplicities as Othello's "O!O!O! " and Lear's many-times-repeated "nothing" and "never." But the passions in Shakespeare's work, as in his world, are much more fully expressed than with us. They do seem close to nature in its wildest outbursts. Shaw could say of Othello's words that they are "streaming insignia and tossing branches to make the tempest of passion visible." King Lear's language, echoing the storm, appears to fan it into greater force. By the fiery verbal breaths these figures take they seem to draw the sky, the heavenly bodies, the very cosmos into their orbit.

In recent times, with emphasis on that resonant language, out of our preoccupation with the lyrical and, therefore, with the text itself, we have had the benefit of frequent studies concentrating on individual words and phrases. Caroline Spurgeon and then the New Critics brought resoundingly home to us the astounding echo chamber that is a Shakespearean tragedy. Spurgeon tells us that "only one overpowering and dominating continuous image" pervades *King Lear*, namely, the general 'floating' image kept constantly before us, chiefly by means of the verbs used, but also in metaphor, of a human body in anguished movement, tugged, wrenched, beaten, pierced, stung, scourged, dislocated, flayed, gashed, scalded, tortured and finally broken on the rack.

No wonder Lamb shrank from the play's visualizing or Tolstoy felt "aversion and weariness." "All through the play," Spurgeon continues, "the simplest abstract things are described in similar terms"—that is, violent ones. With the kingdom, the beloved sacred earth, broken by Lear's first act and with his curses and their consequences, wrenching chaos must follow, chiefly in the frenzied thoughts and speeches of the principal characters. Moreover, how can characters so sealed off, none more so than Lear himself, reach out of their emptiness and solitude, their vast empty world, toward each other except through violent deeds and stormy, violating words? Violence and the nothing its destructiveness must produce constitute their principal unity, their almost exclusive community.

The word "nothing" itself, sounded at the first, reverberates throughout the play. Lear, increasingly aware that he is not "everything," is thereafter on the hunt for "something," especially the "something else." Driven by his passionate need to understand the nature of things, to ferret out the truth, he hurtles round. But he does not find it till he sounds "nothing" through and through. Another word, "nature," and its variants, "natural," "unnatural," and "denatured," repeated with hammering insistence at least forty-seven times, accumulates immense significance. The nature of nature, human and otherwise, is crucial to the play. Additional recurrent words, "cause," "serve" and "service," "authority," "patience," "folly," once uttered, also hang in the air, waiting to be recalled. Words are, as I have proposed, the potent ghosts of the play.

Whatever diverse sides and diverse levels of meaning they reveal, these words, live staples, establish among them a del-

icate yet tensile network along whose taut lines the play and
we live. Charged to begin with, enriched in new contexts, they
become their own and the play's memory and energy. Every
word, in a sense a key to the whole, acting as the play's center,
in its moment of utterance bears the play's entire weight. It
is almost the only work I know in which words, achieving
their maximal pitch of resonance as of meaning, seem to be
listening as they speak, fulfilling the Old Testament prophet's
prediction of a time when each word will be simultaneously
a tongue and an ear. Almost by their very ghostliness they
become things in themselves. *King Lear* is that most contra-
dictory thing, a drama of epical power, composed, prose and
all, like a delicate lyric. Here terror, the abyss, nothing grow
substantial with the abrupt shifts, the vaguenesses, the nuances
of a symbolist poem. Most terrifying because of the vagueness.
Dread and awe, usually out of myth, gods, monsters, become
even more awful in *King Lear* for the gods' and monsters'
murmurous, omnipresent absence.

The play opens, cheerfully and ironically, in prose and in
a low key with the commonplace, life as it normally is. Fundamentally attractive, practical characters, Kent and Gloucester, accurately reflect the mundane human condition. Thus
the scene begins, in medias res, with a casual mental error,
a fallacious assumption, that sets the nature of the play. Kent
says, "I thought the King had more affected the Duke of
Albany than Cornwall." (Both Lear and Gloucester will proceed, on the basis of this assumption, to their dooms.) Kent
assumes, therefore, that Lear will give more of the kingdom
to Albany. But despite Lear's desire to be impartial, he will
soon succumb to the favoritism Kent takes for granted in him.
Then, before his bastard son, Gloucester makes much of his
adultery, already something outside the laws of their society.
It is the jocosity of Gloucester, his devil-may-care attitude,
before his own wrongdoing that reveals to us the nature of
the world we are about to enter, its arrogance, its selfishness,
the cruelties arising from its selfishness, and the outrages they
must spawn. It does not occur to Gloucester, talking about
Edmund in the third person yet affectionately, to consider his

son's feelings. Perhaps, since he is a natural child, Gloucester assumes that Edmund accepts such talk as natural. Edmund's first vivacious soliloquy, apostrophizing nature as his goddess, suggests that he does. For his own satisfaction he will, following Gloucester's example, surpass his father's conduct.

In the next scene, the royal auction, matters are reversed. Here official poetry prevails, as far from the first scene's speech as possible. It has nothing to do with daily reality or things as they are. We see at once the two kinds of life that are going on, one, the daily, about to invade and take over the other, the mythical. We had learned from Gloucester that the division of the kingdom had already been settled. This scene is little more than a playlet by Lear, his last official act, his most extreme, to fulfill, he says more profoundly and prophetically than he can know, his "darker purpose." Still he is entirely serious. He at least, if not the others, believes in the ceremony. Imperious, he is full of the pomp and sway of his office at the moment of surrendering it. Yet Lear and Gloucester meet in their unwitting callousness. For what Lear is after is the pleasure of hearing his daughters vie in public for his affection. He expects them to "perform." And he is conducting a bartering contest: the strongest bidder will win the largest prize. Words are to be taken at their face value. The play from the start then is a matter of calculation. The dominating elders set the code: values of love and feeling can, they think, be weighed and equated with property. Gloucester admits that lawful Edgar is "no *dearer* in my *account*." Yet though he says Edmund "the whoreson must be acknowledged," the acknowledgment seems to come to little more than that Edmund "hath been out nine years, and away he shall again." Lear, even as he equates himself with his kingdom, in his distribution of the kingdom blatantly equates love with land or property. How shall Edmund and Goneril and Regan not be the triumphant products of this attitude? In the same way, adultery, set by the first scene, grows into a central focus of the play, into Lear's furious disgust with sex, the source of life, as the poisoning of life.

This court scene has been called (or been accused of being)

a fairy-tale moment. In a deep sense it is, till reality breaks in. The play starts, far more than Lear can realize, at a climax where most plays end. It presents Lear, a veritable Titan, high above the others. He, among the clouds, is about to do what no other mortal can do or at least has the right to do. Having dealt fully with younger kings like Richard II, their being deposed and the havoc that ensues, Shakespeare now undertakes a harder task: depicting an aged king voluntarily about to depose himself and in the act, even as he hopes to establish peace and a tranquil conclusion for the end of his life, speeding anarchy. Richard II, also accustomed to living exclusively in his own highfalutin language as reality, insisted that only he could depose himself; and he also put on a superb spectacle in the act. But however eagerly he rushed to his splendid new role, he soon lost not only the crown but also his life.

At his advanced age Lear would seem, in his first act, to have reached his pinnacle and the end. Most daringly Shakespeare makes him go higher by a plummeting down. For grandeur and natural strength like Lear's this act has to involve a desperate plunge, especially impressive beside Gloucester's pseudoleap. Gloucester believes suicide devoutly to be wished. Lear, never given to such weak thoughts as this, must experience a long, fiercely dramatic day of exuberant dying, a head-on collision with all the elements of doubt and denial. He must be tried, his every inch of king, by pain, by the extremest suffering, that, finally, his kingliness be proved. His inveterate self-deception, the obduracy of it, requires that seemingly endless protraction of his ordeal.

The fairy-tale quality of the first Lear scene brilliantly reflects his condition. For many years he has been able to live in a fictitious world, near his heart's desire. Like Richard, who can hardly think himself anything other than king, Lear assumes his will the will of nature, identical with justice and the gods. Whatever his past conduct, given his personal power, in this respect different from Richard's, one might consider him a Richard who has managed to stay alive. Now, as Lear himself sees, the time has come for him to divest himself of the burden of kingship to "crawl toward death." He expects to relieve himself of kingship's cares but to retain, taking it for granted as his inevitable right, "the name, and all th' addition to a king." It never occurs to him that, with "The sway, / Revènue, execution of the rest," the title and its honors also go, that the name, a mere word, is meaningful only with the sway.

Never balked before, now piqued as a king and a father, Lear is outrageous to Cordelia. He is astonished by her response, ashamed, offended in public and, worst of all, at the moment of what he regards as his most generous deed. Had he not been justified to assume that Cordelia, his dearest love, would be eager to declare her love? Kent, a kind of son to Lear, crossing him immediately after (the second instance of challenge), makes the moment worse. It is as though those Lear most counted on have proved least trustworthy. By the momentum of the ceremony itself Lear is obliged to go on; once started, nothing can stop it. The king of him must suppress the father in him, something not hard to do since that father is also deeply hurt. Here at last Shakespeare's long line of testy old fathers, their wills frustrated by their daughters, but usually little more than bit parts, comes to a climax; the role steps forward to command the center of the stage.

At the outset we find Lear forbidding, even repellent, in the wanton indulgence of his rage. But we are soon drawn into his eruptive passion. If we at first fear him for his age, since it predicts our own and seems destructively infectious, we soon are awed by the strength of his feelings and by his endurance. In fact, we take heart and reassurance from him. Yet terror and pity also thrive in our response—terror that so much can still happen to an ancient king who, living long in a terrestrial paradise, seemed impervious to the trials of the rest of us, and pity that such suffering can be extracted from him. Yet, in the very horror Lear undergoes, Shakespeare shows that hope exists for us all till the day we die. Altogether indurated to being king, Lear must submit to the terrible wrenching that tears him from that role, from the stony shell it has become.

Thrust out of his world, the thinness and fakery of which

he is quickly obliged to see, he is exposed to naked nature and, stripped bit by bit, to his own naked human nature or, finally, as no appeal, no term works, to nothing. When the human world that is built, whatever its artificialities and pretenses, on and out of nature collapses, chaos bursts forth. Lear, a king supposed to establish and maintain order, having released the forces that destroy it, must seek out the center of that chaos, grapple with it to the death. He has the nobility to do so. At the same time he must discover the chaos and the madness of the human world, the savagery lurking under words, manners, clothes. "Nothing," obedient to his early command, comes between this dragon and his wrath; in his own person he must experience all that wrath to discover what treasure, if any, lies buried within and around him.

The loneliness he encounters he now realizes is what he by his insulated kingship has always been immured in. But fortunately his loneliness, oppressive as it is, is not complete. Though we see how long it takes before Lear notices and actually talks with others, he is, pitifully it would seem, companioned by his Fool, a shadow of a man. Yet the Fool in his love for Lear proves efficacious, a guide and teacher, perhaps as that felicitous old ne'er-do-well Falstaff was for Hal. A natural and, as we say, touched, the Fool, aside from being deeply touched by Lear's predicament, is in touch with forces most of us, locked away in our sanity, never know. Earlier times believed naturals sacred, possessed of preternatural powers, yet therefore to be feared, if not shunned. By his broken wits the Fool is out in the open. He has let the world in and to a considerable degree is capable of equaling the hodgepodge I earlier remarked, of seeing things as they are. Like his condition, the Fool introduces into the play a medley of styles, many-sided suddennesses Lear must learn: adages, charms, riddles, songs, obscenity, Mother Goose applied, snatches of nonsense, even a kind of surrealism, and the earthy wisdom that adheres to them.

The fool, the natural, in Lear must be released. If he can not be sole or whole in being rent, at least he must experience all the tatters. Gradually Lear, who has carried on monologues and at best delivered one-way orders to others, overhears, hears, then responds directly. He too is at last in touch. Only Hamlet has anticipated something like the Fool's piercing "madness," the freedom of insight it affords. Falstaff, also outside the confines of society, shares the Fool's rare common sense, his grasp of reality, and his wit, his drollery, his playfulness. Whatever their prudentiality, both see through the world's follies. Though beyond the play's generally oppressive atmosphere there are no ghosts, no witches (Lear does call his two daughters "unnatural hags"), no supernatural beings in *King Lear*, which would seem to invite them at least as much as any other Shakespearean tragedy, the Fool serves his play in a similar capacity as far as his person allows. For the very thing, his being a natural, that enriches the Fool also deprives him. He is wise enough to see the desperateness of his state. "I had rather be any kind o' thing than a fool." Any kind, that is, other than the witless Lear: "thou hast pared thy wits o' both sides and left nothing i' th' middle." Yet, so we have heard, nothing can be sole or whole that has not been rent.

Usually full of songs, the Fool is fuller than ever in his grief, his pining away at Cordelia's banishment and at Lear's as well. To Lear's "When were you wont to be so full of songs, sirrah?" the Fool replies:

> I have used it, nuncle, e'er since thou mad'st thy daughters thy mothers; for when thou gav'st them the rod, and put'st down thine own breeches,
> [*Singing.*]
> > Then they for sudden joy did weep,
> > And I for sorrow sung,
> > That such a king should play bo-peep
> > And go the fools among.
> > (1.4.173-179)

Lear, his grief intensifying his awareness, adopts the Fool's language and something of his demeanor. Inspired by him and then by Edgar as Tom o' Bedlam, Lear emerges as a new kind of king, "crowned" with weeds and wild flowers, "As mad as the vexed sea; singing aloud" (4.4.2) and gamboling about. Close to nature, the freedom of undifferentiated "nothing," Lear has become, after Edgar, a Tom o' Bedlam (it is as though, in his newly sympathetic person, he has taken all beggars into his being), coupled with a Green Man, a Jack-a-Green, and gay; gaiety transfiguring all that dread. Perhaps another term needs to be added to tragedy's classical pair, terror and pity, namely, exultancy. And this play has it, tragical mirth, the violent mixture of emotions, one needed to express the other in its extremity, like Dante's Arnaut Daniel, singing as he weeps, weeping as he sings, groaning as he grows, growing as he groans. So this play is a mighty song out of grief, a jubilant acknowledgment, if not celebration, of our frailty, helplessness, anguish. This much we have as a way, our chief way perhaps, of meeting "the desolation of reality."

Gloucester and Cordelia will also know a mixing of the extremes of feeling. Again we meet an instance of the jostle of elements *King Lear* excels in. Cordelia's emotion is described to Kent by a gentleman who had delivered letters to her on her father's predicament:

> You have seen
> Sunshine and rain at once: her smiles and tears
> Were like a better way: those happy smilets
> That played on her ripe lip seemed not to know
> What guests were in her eyes, which parted thence
> As pearls from diamonds dropped. In brief,
> Sorrow would be a rarity most belovèd,
> If all could so become it.
>
> (4.3.19-26)

Edgar tells of his father's last moment when Edgar at last revealed his identity.

> But his flawed heart—
> Alack, too weak the conflict to support—
> 'Twixt two extremes of passion, joy and grief,
> Burst smilingly.
>
> (5.3.198-201)

Cordelia and Edgar assume the Fool's function once he reaches his limits. Edgar the "Athenian," in some sense Lear's noble "pagan" guide through the worst portion of human hell, and Cordelia, not "a soul in bliss" but a blessed creature, his guide through his purgatory, serve Lear as he becomes available to them. We can see why Tate and others for one hundred and fifty years insisted on arranging their marriage. Edgar, like many of the characters in the comedies, disguised to preserve themselves against an alien world, or fleeing their society to hide in the woods, assumes "the basest and most poorest shape / That ever penury, in contempt of man, / Brought near to beast" (2.3.7-9). He almost envies the poor Tom o' Bedlam he is playing, for little as Tom may be, "That's something yet: Edgar I nothing am" (2.3.21). Play, even as desperate as this, beyond their exigencies a product of their lovely, surplus energies, fulfills Shakespeare's best characters. Edgar has the imagination to play out such a desperate role and, in his quiet, observant youth, imagination enough to learn from it. If *King Lear* has an overseer and commentator, it is he.

The pinnacle of Shakespeare's art is reached when the mad Lear with his semimad Fool engages this feigning madman; together they sing a supreme trio. The vast heath seems empty except for the storm and these forlorn few, refugees, bare survivors, who clutch each other. At Lear's asking "What hast thou been?" Edgar promptly images an additional role for himself, a life crammed with sinful memories.

> A servingman, proud in heart and mind; that curled my hair, wore gloves in my cap; served the lust of my mistress' heart, and did the act of darkness with her; swore as many oaths as I spake words, and broke them in the sweet face of heaven. One that slept in the contriving of lust, and waked to do it. Wine loved I deeply, dice dearly; and in woman out-paramoured the Turk.
>
> (3.4.84-91)

Lear, who will recall Edgar's description of immorality and

improve on it, responds to Edgar's physical condition and to his naked confession:

> Thou wert better in a grave than to answer with thy uncovered body this extremity of the skies. Is man no more than this? . . . Ha! here's three on's are sophisticated. Thou art the thing itself; unaccommodated man is no more but such a poor, bare, forked animal as thou art. Off, off you lendings! Come, unbutton here.
>
> (3.4.100-108)

At last we have man, the thing itself, without any comforts or cushionings, without religion, philosophy, society. The Fool, turning to thoughts of sex this undressing suggests, remonstrates with Lear:

> Prithee, nuncle, be contented, 'tis a naughty night to swim in. Now a little fire in a wild field were like an old lecher's heart—a small spark, all the rest on's body, cold. Look, here comes a walking fire.
>
> (3.4.109-112)

Patly on cue appears the old lecher Gloucester with a torch. Later blind Gloucester and mad Lear, confronting each other, catapult us to a comparable height.

By now this jumble that the storm has produced is at its best, appositely in Lear's mad speeches. His sudden leaps from the mighty and all-powerful to the most minute, the least significant—a lap dog, a wren, a mouse, a fly—are part and parcel of the jostle of elements I have emphasized. These leaps are also a unifying, electric current in the world of the play and a mark of the agile, complete desperation of Lear's mind. To such frenzy an attempt at comprehending, at all-encompassing must come! We have in his words a veritable geyser of things and creatures that the ultimate storm would deliver itself of. Or, in Lamb's words, "the explosions . . . terrible as a volcano . . . turning up and disclosing to the bottom that sea, his mind, with all its vast riches." In *King Lear* the chain of being has indeed been broken, but the links of that cosmic bracelet are still present, dazzling in their disorder as they ricochet off one another.

For moments like those on the heath one must go to the Book of Job or *Don Quixote*. Job would have understood images like Lear's

> Nor rain, wind, thunder, fire are my daughters.
> I tax not you, you elements, with unkindness.
> I never gave you kingdom, called you children. . . .
> . . . .
>
> But yet I call you servile ministers,
> That will with two pernicious daughters join
> Your high-engendered battles 'gainst a head
> So old and white as this.
>
> (3.2.15-24)

Job's situation is even more extreme than Lear's. Despite his virtue, he is stripped, like Lear, first of his wealth, then of his children, and assailed in his own person. His friends insist his sufferings must prove his guilt. Job spurns them. And at last, by a tenacity and outcries like Lear's, he summons forth the Whirlwind. Agreeing to debate with him, It first requires his knowledge of the universe: "Where were you when the world was made, the stars, the animals?" The Voice in the Whirlwind parades the latter in all their splendor before Job. Beaten into new awareness, awed by the mightiness of the bewildering plenitude of creation itself, he realizes how petty, if not irrelevant, his questions and doubts are.

King Lear also puts all into question. Like Job, Lear is sorely tried to rouse this questioning in him. But Lear's day is much later; and though his storm is immense, and as searching in its way as is Job's, it never becomes a voice in dialogue with Lear beyond the harmony of storms I suggested earlier and the myriad voices that break out of Lear's battered self. As with Job, whatever realization Lear achieves, it is expressed, not in things or possessions, but, as he is broken open to a larger world and its creatures, in an expansion of himself, a participating in others beyond that self. At last he too learns,

far past the prudent sense of the Fool's homely adage, to sit
as the wind sits and to make "use of nothing." The Fool puts
it clearly enough:

> He that has and a little tiny wit,
>   With heigh-ho, the wind and the rain,
> Must make content with his fortunes fit,
>   Though the rain it raineth every day.
>   (3.2.74-77)

And Lear replies, "True, my good boy." While force is on our
side, it is delectable. But once it cannot make use of us, it
tosses us aside. Then patience or resignation seems our only
resort. The spectacular tragedy here derives from Lear's endurance and resistance, both so mighty that they summon
forth ultimate force or violence.

At the end, when he seems shattered, it is the touch and
loving presence of Cordelia that restores him, along with the
repose and the music the Doctor, as always in Shakespeare,
prescribes—music, that opposite of the tempest in man and
out, that imaging of order, its model the comportment of the
spheres "from whom," Lear long ago declared, "we do exist
and cease to be." Ears not tuned in, like eyes without feeling,
or light without warmth, must prove inadequate. Feeling and
thought, sight and insight are, briefly at least, brought together
in Lear. For me Shakespeare is saying that, till the day we die,
we may be realized. It is, sardonically, Lear's folly, his assumption of absolute authority, that lets the forces loose to
try him, and so to bring him to his senses and authentic roy-
alty. Truly acting as his mothers, his daughters give him belated birth and the exposure needed to mature him. Kent,
waiting in the stocks for daybreak, can say, "Nothing almost
sees miracles / But misery" (2.2.168-169). And Lear arrives
at a similar sentiment even more extremely: "The art of our
necessities is strange, / That can make vile things precious"
(3.2.70-71).

This exploration of our astounding capacity constitutes the
positive side of the play, its exhilaration, its tragic joy. Also
part of this side is its unblinking expression, the affirmative-

ness that is the play's poetic language, that these things can exist and can be seen and said intensely, precisely, delicately. Positive, too, is Shakespeare's expectation of, his respect for, us, his audience, and our capacity to undergo all the trials of the play. Like Job, Lear experiences the universe at a depth and a height that sweeps away all lesser considerations. "What is the cause of thunder?" (3.4.153) Lear asks, realizing "the thunder would not peace at my bidding" (4.6.101-102). (But it does teach him the truth not only about himself, as he progresses from assuming he was everything to realizing he is one among many, then only a tiny part of the whole, and, finally, nothing, but also about his deceitful daughters: "there I found 'em, there I smelt 'em out.") Much later in another context Cordelia replies, "No cause, no cause." Thunder is resounding cause enough, an answer and an end in itself, as inexplicable and undeniable in its way as Cordelia's irrevocable love for Lear, as irrevocable as her gentle, yet self-possessed loveliness.

No longer believing in easy causality or in the rewards that are guaranteed the good, we must see feeling and goodness as their own rewards, or see nothing. It is how we experience our lives that matters. And when the appetite for whatever happens is courageous and ambitious, even attendant loss becomes a kind of advantage, if not a prize. Shakespeare, at the threshold of the modern world, in *Hamlet* and *King Lear* provides the boldest, most searching examination of that world's fundamental dilemma: the falling apart of thing and thought, thought and feeling. That Shakespeare should situate that dissociation in mythical Britain! But did it not take place in that first place, Eden? What is that outcast man's place—has he any—in the universe? And how, given that universe's composition, establish such a place? The inconsistencies, the mishmash of materials and attitudes, the multilayered, past-echoing present are what Shakespeare is proposing here—what, on this midden of a star, still hot, still eruptive, our world is made of: rocks, tempests, creatures, corpses, ideas in the word-laden air. Each of its own time and place yet jostling one another, they converge on our here and now. This convergence and the storm it releases, the headlong storm of Shakespeare's mastery, supply the play's overpowering unity, its tumultuously driven singleness.

Near the end Lear looks to the peace of a prison for Cordelia and himself. That he should think it the "nursery" he originally sought! Is he not as deluded as ever? For the naive ambition and illusion (one present in Shakespeare's earliest plays) of withdrawal from this world, out of the path of the winds of fortune, never succeeds:

> Come, let's away to prison:
> We two alone will sing like birds i' th' cage:
> When thou dost ask me blessing, I'll kneel down
> And ask of thee forgiveness: so we'll live,
> And pray, and sing, and tell old tales, and laugh
> At gilded butterflies, and hear poor rogues
> Talk of court news; and we'll talk with them too,
> Who loses and who wins, who's in, who's out;
> And take upon's the mystery of things,
> As if we were God's spies: and we'll wear out,
> In a walled prison, packs and sects of great ones
> That ebb and flow by th' moon.
>
> (5.3.8-19)

(The last image seems to have borrowed something from Falstaff. Yet the attitude, with its old tales and laughter, may be closer to Falstaff's than one at first realizes.) We recall Richard II, also in his final prison, attempting to make a world out of his imagination and his bare surroundings, but failing before the death he meets heroically.

Lear, finally, a mighty king once more, every raging inch of him, his last strength upon him, the fierce humanness he has never wholly surrendered, having killed Cordelia's executioner, enters with her in his arms for his last scene; far more awing it is than the first. But now he is a giant howl against the onlooking "men of stone" of whom he once was a prime example. He mourns the intolerable, ungainsayable fact of Cordelia's death: "She's gone for ever. / I know when one is dead and when one lives; / She's dead as earth." But instantly he shies away from this certainty: "Lend me a look-ing-glass [borrowed, one might say, from Richard II]; / If that her breath will mist or stain the stone, / Why, then she lives." Then he resorts to a feather, which he thinks stirs. Suddenly, proving how little we can be sure even of death and of our own senses, even as he says "she's gone for ever," he believes out of the strength of his desire that he hears her:

> Ha,
> What is 't thou say'st? Her voice was ever soft,
> Gentle and low, an excellent thing in woman.
> $\qquad$ (5.3.273-275)

Instantly he follows her gentleness with the ferocity of "I killed the slave that was a-hanging thee." Capping irony this is, for it was this voice of the one dearest to him, a voice so soft and low he failed to hear its true sentiments, that set him off on his disastrous course.

But, starting up again and for the last time, he exclaims at her irreparable death:

> And my poor fool is hanged: no, no, no life?
> Why should a dog, a horse, a rat, have life,
> And thou no breath at all? Thou'lt come no more,
> Never, never, never, never, never.
> $\qquad$ (5.3.307-310)

Just as he had, in the middle of the play, unbuttoned before the beggarly, seminaked Edgar, now before the dead Cordelia he says in heartbreaking simplicity that looks to the final nakedness, "Pray you, undo this button. Thank you, sir." From so little we and the world hang. In the end, by her reticence, Cordelia deceives Lear still. And still to the end he fails the truth. For even as he dies he cries out, "Do you see this? Look on her. Look, her lips, / Look there, look there." However we interpret these words, he has finally found satisfaction. "Call no man happy until he is dead." Such struggle, such suffering out of searching and searching because of suffering, perhaps our liveliest moment, may be our only way, at least briefly, of breaching worlds, holding them together.

The last words properly belong to Kent, "The wonder is he hath endured so long: / He but usurped his life." And to Edgar,

> The weight of this sad time we must obey,
> Speak what we feel, not what we ought to say.
> The oldest hath borne most: we that are young
> Shall never see so much, nor live so long.
>   (5.3.325-328)

Kent's "wonder" is happily ambiguous. So are Edgar's "borne," the amount that Lear has "seen," the life he has most vibrantly, enduringly "lived." The further wonder is that we, like them, have witnessed and survived this wonder.

Lucretius:
The Imagination of the Literal

Several months before I began writing this paper I mentioned to an old friend how, when I was asked to talk about some poet, * Lucretius first of all, like one of his impetuous atoms, leaped into my mind. My friend said, "Knowing your affection for him, I can understand. But you will admit, won't you, that he was an unpoetic writer who somehow wrote a great poem?" "O, no," I replied. "He was a great poet who somehow wrote a triumphant anti-poem." Of course we were both wrong. He was a great poet who wrote a great poem. However, we both were groping for a fundamental fact about him, the tension informing his work even beyond its uniqueness, our sense of his being a kind of Laocoon, grappling with material fiercely intractable. That a materialist, and one so stalwartly dogmatic, should write in poetry at all, let alone write great, sometimes sublime poetry! Yet that struggle, the contradictions at work in it, revealing what it does of him, proves him of an energy consonant with the churning process that is his version of the world. For his materialism was, like him, least of all the dull density of matter we normally identify with materialism. And that struggle, still alive and well in his poem, helped to generate the power that provides the poem, quite apart from its physical magnitude, with its epical character.

Many of us have grown used to thinking of poetry as mainly about itself and often best understood as a conflict between the announced and the covert theme or the poet's essential feeling. Of no poet is this more true perhaps than of the two great Romans, Lucretius and Virgil. With Rome what it was, the emergence of any poetry in it might seem

* This paper was delivered, in an earlier version, at the English Institute at Harvard University in September, 1973.

astonishing. As astonishing, say, as poetry in our own ultra-materialistic age. Yet Roman though Virgil was, if he outwardly supported war, the chief Roman occupation, and emulated his beloved master Homer, internally Virgil's poem is swept by gusts of melancholy and soaked in the weary tears of things. On the other hand, for Lucretius, whom Virgil much admired and possibly envied, those tears were, by the very mortality they signify, exhilirating — at least officially. At the same time, though Lucretius resoundingly sings peace and detachment and opposes Roman power politics, he, Homer's most resembling son, obviously loves a universe basically, incessantly at war. And in conjunction with that universe as well as with his Roman nature, his is the zest of conquest, however mental it may be, an arduous ranging out far past any material exploit, even as it is materialism that enables him to encompass all. More than most poems, *De Rerum Natura* satisfies our notion that a poem is (or should be) a work, like the world it presents, in the making, a discovery; and we ship on with Lucretius in his tremendous voyage of exploration, suffering and enjoying with him the exigencies of the amazing world he dares to undertake.

Indeed Lucretius' ambition is, like his rampart-flaming universe, unbounded. In epic fashion he insists his poem is the greatest. For all other poets, even majestic Homer and the worthy Ennius, were waylaid by particular stories, seduced by the sirens of local events, holocausts superficial as the Trojan War. Lucretius, he assures us, is alone attempting things as they are, the entire actual universe in which stories, myth, history, and the rest shrink to mere contingencies if not illusions. The visible vision and visionary par excellence for him (or at least things as they are, including the underlying, invisible atoms), his is the dream of reality, awaking from all myths and enchantments to that greatest enchantment, nature itself. Against stories and legends, he also opposes those enchantments that defraud the senses and the mind, the spell of Circe, Calypso, the Lotus. *De Rerum Natura* is already, I believe, what Wallace Stevens called for, a poem of earth, if by earth we are willing to mean the heavens surrounding it as well and all that happens in the universe, the excitement of its mighty flux and the prolificacy in the midst of that flux, the wonders briefly composing its waves.

Thus Lucretius is convinced that he alone reveals that universe in all its self-sufficiency; and in the revealing he demonstrates the mind's ability, since a material part of that material universe, to understand, enjoy, draw abundant reassurance from it. Heroically, therefore, he girds himself for his poem's descent into the volcanic core of things. And reading him, one has the sense, so successful is his descent, of being buffeted, struggling like Milton's Satan on his plunge from heaven through chaos. For chaos we would realize, if we had our wits about us, is blissfully everywhere. And chaos, the frenetic workshop of the atoms, is where Lucretius wants himself and us to be. Not simply—though that would be ample reason—because that is where the true action is, but because that chaos, since it is the way things are, is where peace, he clamorously maintains, prevails. Only such awareness, he is positive, battering away at us can set us free.

The excitement of this awareness is directly attributable to Lucretius' temperament, seeking out a theory, a way of looking, that would satisfy it. And he found the way in Epicurus, his hero, who, according to Lucretius, first dared that chaos to wrest illumination and peace from it. The Greek mythical heroes were light-bearers, destroyers of monsters and the dark. But beside Epicurus, Lucretius tells us, how puny they were. What all the labors of Hercules, killing off fabulous yet local beasts, beside the exertions of Epicurus who would rid us, and by enlightened persuasion alone, his understanding's mighty torch, of darkness and the monsters that cave and thrive in the human heart: fear, greed, desire, pride, ambition? Epicurus, in proving via the atomic theory the folly of such feelings, and thereby freeing us from them, became the most venerable of men.

After Homer the pre-Socratics, scrapping the mythical, strove to see things as they are, as the mind reasonably accounts for them (even though their would-be rational explanations often strike us as fabulous). Of the several explanations available, for Lucretius the atomic theory, employed by Epicurus, seemed irresistibly right. Epicurus, we recall, was stoutly anti-poetic. Lucretius' fervent imagination, however, kindled further by the atomic theory, galvanizing it and Epicurus as well, permeated all things. Thus one might say that Lucretius enhanced this secularizing, anti-poetic view into poetry and the sacramental all over again. Did he not *believe* in that view with all his might? With such an example before us, would it be outrageous to propose the possibility that, when our thinkers and critics, phenomenological, structural, matho-logical, and so on, have completed their efforts and relieved our literature and thought, as some time ago religion was relieved, of the sacramental, the loving labor of finding the religious in their position can begin again? All that their assumptions and conclusions will require is a faith ardent as Lucretius'.

The atomic theory and the materialism behind it have of course been with us more than ever and not least in our arts. The practice of Rilke, Eliot, Pound, Williams, H.D., Marianne Moore, Ponge witnesses modern poetry's devotion to things and to energy, the dynamism our day has stressed; thus poetry's devotion to the image, that knot of vitality, and consequently to observation and objectivity: no idea but in things or Pound's "the natural object is always the *adequate* symbol." The emphasis on the natural object rather than on the symbol is crucial here. A number of these poets, certainly in the early part of their careers, were deeply influenced by symbolism. But, on the whole, its hold has been broken for some time. Out of the ambience of science and our media, especially cinema and television, and out of a growing secularization, several of these poets, strikingly Williams and the later Pound, and a host of younger ones, have been eager to attempt things as they are, a kind of literalism, the matter-of-fact. This attempt stems from the notion that things and events and the moment of their happening or emerging are deserving of attention for their own sake.

Thus modern poetry might well consider Lucretius its greatest predecessor if not its founding, godly father. For Lucretius was, one might say, the first imagist, one literally so, thereby surpassing the best our modern poets can do. Not only did he believe in an outside world, but he believed all we see and know are physical films or images shed by that world's things. In fact he needed few similes, Homeric or otherwise, since for him the world itself with its images waited to be luxuriated in. Never merely decorations or poetic adornments, these images constitute the very substance of his poem, a world splendidly illustrated by its own contents. In other words, literalist of the imagination that he was, Lucretius also exploited to the full the imagination of the literal. His poem, like the world he saw, is a mad garden, whatever its laws and boundary-stones, teeming with very literal toads, actual if mind-engendered centaurs and chimerae, absent gods, and a vast medley of atoms. Through this ur-imagism, which concentrated not only on things but on ideas as things, Lucretius enjoyed a most enviable sense of unity. The world is redoubtably other than we, a permanent, multiple assailant; but since we are, like that world, made of atoms, we are fundamentally close kin to it. Moreover, ephemeral though we are, an accident of the atoms' combination, we, consisting of them, for a moment know — share in — their immortality.

And Lucretius exults in them, feels the thrill of their being totally at work, like miniscule Vulcans secretly forging out of their own bodies every good thing — and bad — vibrant around him. It is his own body and the body of the world come altogether alive. In fact, it would seem as though this knowledge of the atom, its workings, and the workings of the universe is a release not only for the knower but for the known, a release of energy and joy, the joy of being discovered, enlarged. And a real communion, an open stream, flows between the known and the knower, something like that among the words of the poem; they throb as the atoms do. Do they not, the atoms themselves and the atoms of their contemplator, once he really exerts himself, begin to attract each other and, most literally, combine?

At first sight Lucretius and Blake might look like opposites to us, the former all materialism, the latter all spirituality. One sees the sun as a host of angels singing; the other, as a bag not of guineas but of whirling atoms. And Blake recommends excess whereas Lucretius exhorts us to reason. Yet a similar godly vehemence drives both; who can deny their imperious stamp, their agreement on Blake's "Energy is eternal delight"? Furthermore, they share a passion for "the enlargement of the individual through his senses" and think the senses a matter of touch. In their well-nigh apostolic passion to penetrate the habitual cover of things they are of a like, resolute make. As they are in their didactic urging, their overwhelming love of mankind, their desire to free it from priest and state-manipulated religion. The paradox obtains here that the fierce if not savage glance of such poets pierces things not only to their inner natures but to abstraction — that of mechanism for Lucretius, that of spirit for Blake; and this abstraction becomes a passionate thing, at least as gripping as the sensuous. But in poets so enormously ambitious paradox, not to say contradiction, is bound to riddle the heart of their work and there to amount to the crossroads where the truth speeds.

And in *De Rerum Natura* the contradictions crop up at the outset. The poem opens with a splendid paean to Venus, the goddess of fertility, or Spring let loose on the world, aswarm as at creation. Since without Venus "nothing emerges into the shining, sunlit world to grow in joy and loveliness," Lucretius naturally seeks her collaboration. Of course, aside from observing the established behavior of epic poems, this paean is intended to supply the honey Lucretius later speaks of as needed to rim the cup of wormwood that is his poem's substance, otherwise obnoxious to the ignorant reader. He must be led into the mysteries by a taste of what he knows and likes. Initiated, he will come to relish, and above all else, the wormwood because it is wormwood.

But now Lucretius begs Venus to end the civil war racking his country. And in a lovely vignette this great painter pictures Mars or war itself "laid low by the irremediable wound of love." A telling if rather odd image one might think, the maker of wounds wounded past his own power to make. Yet locked in the embrace Lucretius desires, would they not, this maker and this breaker of the world, prove ineffectual, and would Venus' victory not end the world altogether? Does the world not depend on their quarreling — one appearing at one moment to prevail, the other at the next — or perhaps on their greatest lovemaking? Lucretius admits, "In this evil hour of my country's history, I cannot pursue my task with a mind at ease. . . ." Since he proposes his poem — the understanding it provides and he already enjoys — as a perfect antidote to turbulence and since he insists that a man's worth is best seen in adversity, we might be puzzled by his plea for peace. But it is primarily the worst turbulence that Lucretius would settle, that in men's minds. Once his reasoning reaches them they must, he is confident, spurn their empty fears and desires, and so of course war will promptly end. Equally paradoxical is Lucretius' declaring that Memmius, the friend for whom he is delivering this poem, "cannot at such a crisis withhold his service from the common weal." We had been given to believe that Lucretius' poem was meant to persuade men to forsake such pointless service. Or are we with sad, pious Aeneas after all?

As though by merely appealing to Venus he had won at least enough peace to proceed, Lucretius urges Memmius to put all aside to heed him undistractedly. And at once, shedding the Roman world of war, Lucretius sheds Venus as well. Yet surely the spirit, the enthusiasm, in his opening paean to her exceeds mere poetic appliqué, mere honeyed bait? He abandons her for his true god, the atom, and for Mars whose poem this actually is, the unceasing, inner strife whereby the world becomes what it is. The other gods, violating reason, have led to "superstition" only, the absurdity of terror before an after-life, employed by priests and the state to reduce men to groveling slavery. Thereon Lucretius works himself into a frenzy of delight as he presents the atom, stripped of all sensuous qualities; a being of no sound, no color, no smell, no taste, no sentience, it is, by Lucretius' lights, the ultimately adorable. With his atoms coupling and wrangling, truly a state of happy, total war (reminiscent, I would suggest, of that moment in the *Agamemnon* when as Helen and Paris are grappling in their boudoir, the Greek and Trojan warriors are grappling on the battlefield), is Lucretius not a poet of sexual fervor, of that consummate moment, beyond memory, that paradise, rather like Blake's at the center of the Prophetic Books, of the permanent now, the moment of complete and naked process, a universe all verb? It is not merely Lucretius' wanting to ensure his poem's being a poem, a dramatic, epical one, nor his Roman nature alone, that prompts him to cram his poem with verbs, nouns, and images of battle.

But here we encounter some of the tension I first remarked. If Lucretius is pre-scientific, able to luxuriate in process itself and in a non-human naturalism as far as physics is concerned, it is pre-scientific humanism that fundamentally motivates him and the pathos, the fragility, the mortality of life that occupies him. He cannot, much as he might have longed to, say yes to the all, aver that whatever is is what should be. For then he would not have composed this poem in the first place, would not have been concerned to free mankind from its fears and hopes, but would rather have applauded all fears, hopes, passions, illusions, fascinating ingredients in the great drama of whatever happens. His god, after all, is not a remote overseer delighting in the total spectacle, however overwhelming its horrors to men, but that being like Epicurus who, suffering for and with his fellowmen, does what he can to alleviate that suffering. So Lucretius can open his second book with

> What a joy it is, when out at sea the stormwinds are lashing the waters, to gaze from the shore at the heavy stress some other man is enduring! . . . What joy, again, to watch opposing hosts marshalled in the field of battle when you have yourself no part in their peril! But this is the greatest joy of all: to stand aloof in a quiet citadel, stoutly fortified by the teaching of the wise, and to gaze down from that elevation on others wandering aimlessly in a vain search for the way of life, . . . O joyless hearts of men! O minds without vision! How dark and dangerous the life in which this tiny span is lived away! Do you not see that nature is clamoring for two things only, a body free from pain, a mind released from worry and fear for the enjoyment of pleasurable sensations?

The whole world here becomes a theater; and as in the theater one of its joys, beyond pity and fear, is our sense that at any moment, should the play become too oppressive, we can withdraw. At first this passage, its honesty and accuracy notwithstanding, may seem cold, a bit smug and self-congratulating, and without feeling for others. But Lucretius is offering us such illustrations out of his profound zeal to teach us the folly of misadventures like war and sea-faring, the joy of those who have, by wisdom, grown superior to them and abandoned their madness.

Like Homer, Lucretius, showing us the vanity of human wishes, would lead us to the peace beyond hope and fear, beyond desire and regret, the peace of things as they are so that we are not deluded by ambitions, superstitions, follies, do not waste what little precious time and life we have in thoughts on the before and after. But, alas, this theater, Lucretius knows too well, is real; no one, regardless of his wisdom or resolution, escapes for more than moments the ceaseless buffets from outside and from within our vulnerable bodies. Even the sturdiest citadels are built on quicksand, the crumbling, volcanic earth (see the conclusion of *De Rerum Natura*). Indeed, "How dark and dangerous the life in which this tiny span is lived away!" In his concentration on the frailty of life, the transiency, the sufferings, despite his protestations of freedom, some critics, Santayana among them, have found Lucretius essentially pessimistic and melancholy, filled with a sense of the futility of life. Such a mood is certainly present at times. But this mood, exclusively stressed, makes us blink his gusto for things, his appetite for "pleasurable sensations," his rapport with the intensity of movement, his absorption in the life of phenomena, his exultation in knowledge, the mind flaming out to and beyond the flaming ramparts of the universe.

But why, for one so in love with fertility, plenitude and pleasurable sensations, does Lucretius turn his back on Venus and later vigorously disparage her? His Fourth Book's famous conclusion makes his attitude clear. By her very splendid allure Venus is little different from the other gods, a seduction, a distraction from the truth, a maker of misery. Sex and its natural involvements are one thing; an all-engrossing single love or passion is quite another. Atoms should snag on to each other and us, but they should not — it is contrary to their true natures — lock forever. One must not be stuck with one image to the oblivion of all other phenomena (including other women). Lucretius appreciates, by its distinctive collocation of atoms, the uniqueness of each object — even possibly the idea that two atoms may beyond all others fit; but he tries with all his might to contemn the Adam in us who thinks there is one and only one Eve and therefore only one woman for him. If for Milton Adam's "idolatry" means that Adam was blinded to the Giver by complete engrossment in only one of His myriad gifts, to Lucretius such possessiveness amounts to forfeiting understanding and the world for one miniscule, soon forever lost, part of it. Loving the uniqueness of things, Lucretius dare not acknowledge (no doubt because of that love and the pain it can produce) their irreparable loss at death. Cries like Lear's over Cordelia,

> Thou'lt come no more,
> Never, never, never, never, never!

Lucretius seeks to deafen for himself and for us with his thunderous denials, his striving to turn such cries into a good. Once dead, we are free forever. Furthermore, new life can arise only out of old death. Thus the most he admits is that "With the voice of mourning mingles that cry that infants raise when their eyes open on the sunlit world." The process of life and death is fundamentally serene and inevitable.

But Lucretius dwells on wasteful lovers:

It is all very well for dainty feet to sparkle with gay slippers of Sicyon; for settings of gold to enclasp huge emeralds aglow with green fire, and sea-tinted garments to suffer the constant wear and stain of Venus. A hard-won patrimony is metamorphosed into bonnets and tiaras or, it may be, into Grecian robes, masterpieces from the looms of Elis or of Ceos. No matter how lavish the décor and the cuisine — drinking parties . . . entertainments, perfumes, garlands, festoons and all — they are still to no purpose.

Dwells too long and too detailedly, even if ostensibly to deplore this folly, not to make us suspect him of more touching humanness than he would care, in his desire to help us, to acknowledge. So he recounts actual love-making rather too precisely not to make us feel that his interest is more than that of the lofty observer. And his wonderful, racy catalog of women, fair to their myopic lovers but seen for what they are by him, in its length and intensity suggest thoroughgoing experience. It is at such moments that one might be tempted to take seriously St. Jerome's statement, in his brief life of Lucretius, that he committed suicide after going mad from an aphrodisiac, that probably of his own appetites. Or the rightful revenge of Venus! Passages like the one concerning the prodigality of lovers remind me of Isaiah who, excoriating the haughty daughters of Zion, must itemize all their disgusting, super-abundant finery, must have it run through his fingers even while casting it away. However great their gusto, Lucretius and Isaiah share a puritanical streak and the entanglements such puritanism seems to ensure. Thus Lucretius' advice to the lover lest he be permanently ensnared: "First, you should concentrate on all the faults of mind or body of her whom you covet and sigh for," leads one to believe that he is more practiced in the ways of love than the purely objective onlooker.

At the same time, though he stresses the fundamental similarity of all women, especially their physical faults, Lucretius does counsel good will: "Then, if the lady is good-hearted and void of malice, it is up to you in turn to accept unpleasant facts and make allowance for human imperfection." So he concludes,

. . . it is by no divine intervention, no prick of Cupid's darts, that a woman deficient in beauty sometimes becomes the object of love. Often the woman herself, by humoring a man's fancies and keeping herself fresh and smart, makes it easy for him to share his life with her. Over and above this, love is built up bit by bit by mere usage. Nothing can resist the continually repeated impact of a blow, however light, as you see drops of water falling on one spot at long last wear through a stone.

An odd analogy that, whatever irony it may imply, not one exactly to inspire enthusiasm! But apparently this advocate of the enjoyments of pleasurable sensations (he does, it is true, intimate that he understands how a woman rich in beauty easily becomes the object of love; some combinations of atoms, for all their delicious anonymity, are more fetching than others) is a Roman moralist after all. Thus he can say,

Certainly wives have no need of lascivious movements. A woman makes conception more difficult by offering a mock resistance and accepting Venus with a wriggling body. . . . These tricks are employed by prostitutes for their own ends, so that they may not conceive too frequently . . . and at the same time may make intercourse more attractive to men. But obviously our wives can have no use for them.

Obviously! Aside from the passionate woman he acknowledged earlier: "Often she is acting from the heart and in longing for a shared delight tempts him to run love's race to the end," one might wonder about such movements' "uses" for the husbands and for vigorous conception as well! Lucretius, it seems, can give assent to such movements among the atoms only. For there he can have his sexuality and enjoy it too, there where it is transformed into something pure, impersonal, strictly functional.

However, basic ambivalence occurs too often in Lucretius for one not to suspect that he was poet artful enough to recognize it as a valuable, accurate poetic resource, one relevant to a purchase on the truth, human and otherwise. We recall Milton's frequent leisurely, not to say luxuriant, rejection of the pagan gods. He lingered on them to have them, at least to enjoy them and their magnificences, in loss; this lingering might be construed as one aspect of paradise lost. Paradise lost, on the other hand, the denial of paradise, seems by what it means paradise enough for Lucretius. Accordingly, he explores ways of embracing, celebrating — almost to the point of appearing to encourage — loss. But ambivalence is at the heart of this attitude. And like Blake's necessary contraries, it is not a contradiction after all but an all-inclusiveness, an and/both rather than an either/or approach, a multiple rather than a simple comprehension of the universe. So, on the one hand, Lucretius speaks of the world's far-off golden age when nature was perfect and man did not need to exert himself; but now, even though nature is running down and man must work harder and harder to survive, Lucretius also points out the recency of new discoveries, the immense improvements in life and art, the civilization that lies ahead. Again, Lucretius deprecates the notion that the gods made the world or made it for us. He must accept the gods as a reality since Epicurus did and since we have the idea of them: but like Epicurus he believes them as remote from and indifferent to us as possible. Ideal Epicureans living in an Edenic state, why should they think of us at all? Rather they are doing that most felicitous thing, conversing as they loll about and, of course, in the one heavenly language, Greek. Here too Lucretius has it both ways. The world is too flawed for gods to have made; at length he describes nature's rigors, often too much for us to deal with. On the other hand, in a superbly Jobean passage, even as he remarks what must be irrationality in the gods did they act the way men think they do, he derides the notion that any god can perform the mighty — as well as arbitrary — workings of the universe.

> ... nature ... runs the universe by itself without the aid of gods. For who can rule the sum total of the measureless? Who can hold in coercive hand the strong reins of the unfathomable? Who can spin all the firmaments alike and foment with the fires of ether all the fruitful earth? Who can be in all places at all times, ready to darken the clear sky with clouds and rock it with a thunderclap — to launch bolts that may often wreck his own temple, or retire and spend his fury letting fly at deserts with that missile which often passes by the guilty and slays the innocent and blameless?

And if such awareness threatens to overwhelm Job, it exhilarates Lucretius. But the Voice out of the Whirlwind uses the universe's inexplicable marvels to awe and convince Job; Lucretius uses them to awe and convince himself and us of the absurdity of gods at work.

Lucretius, we see, is already grappling with the problem of what, how much, can be converted into poetry or rather, since he is not after the "something else" but the something, nature itself, how much of the world can be understood and then absorbed and understood in language. For against the poverty of language, the Latin available to him, much inferior for such matters to Greek, he is struggling to illuminate nature's darkest places. As I said at the outset, for his time and his theme one might wonder at Lucretius' writing a poem in the first place. Why take on the limitations of poetry? But beyond the practice of antiquity to cast most serious matters in poetry, its understanding that poetry made them most memorable, we must recognize Lucretius' pleasure and also belief in poetry. Thus we meet his frequent employment of the letter analogy: letters, few like atoms, shuffled, make up, as the atoms do their things and world, all the different words which constitute the human world. And Lucretius means this analogy more, I would say, than merely metaphorically. Out of his identification with nature, he believes the same impulse works in and through him as in and through the atoms (is he not made of them?). Like the atoms, these letters and their words, lying side by side, combining, engender the world with all its wonders. And Lucretius approves it as he does atomic cohabitation, because though physical (words and letters have an at least minimal substance), a matter of necessary touching, letters are, in all their fecundity, impersonal, entirely given over to what they are doing and not to the doer and his feelings or to the problems outside their act itself. In such contemplation, such vision, whether it be of atoms or letters, there can be nothing personal. Nothing burns in hell, one saint said — one might say nothing is hell — but the self. In his absorptions here Lucretius, beyond his denuciation of desire, greed, and the other human passions, approaches Eastern thought or Christian mysticism, but his is of course a natural or earth mysticism.

And it is the darkest places Lucretius obliges his letters to enter and to enlighten. Think of the least likely, most formidable, most recalcitrant subject, one modern poets generally deplore: the abstract, especially that which is an outgrowth of science, originally anchored in the senses. But Lucretius, bent on the invisible, demonstrates how even such material, and by its invisibility and obduracy, can become most appealing. Thus the pages he devotes to the mechanics of the atom, the inmost workings of the universe, taxing in their way as Dante's doctrinal Purgatorial Cantos, become for Lucretius (and for some of us), by his arduous delight, Pierian, and most of all in the atoms' protean nature. In his view atoms composing an altogether epical world, his poem is, so to say, the Apollonian proving itself by way of the Dionysian, a glance so rapt in the rapture of things it manifests the Dionysian as the essence of life. Certainly his atoms, caught up in a ritualistic pattern, resemble the maenads; in their headlong flight they, anonymous, impersonal, recognize no one, are nothing but all-out frenzy. And they destroy all in their path but like Dionysus create it too; in thought of them we can understand death and rebirth. This, Lucretius' absorption in it, is *amor fati* with a vengeance, wormwood indeed become honey.

Beyond this passionate abstraction but out of it, think of accenting above all an impersonality Eliot might have admired, one of the sweeter fruits of identifying with the processes of nature, yet at the same time producing one of the most personal poems ever written. In attempting to. grasp basic reality, that which continues regardless of superficial changes, one of the things Lucretius did grasp most vividly was himself. The more he tries to dissolve the individual and the ephemeral, to take us into the heart of the charming, iridescent chaos he never tires of describing, the more individual he and his world become. For Lucretius is, like his atoms (and not Blake or Whitman more emphatically), everywhere beating through his words to reach us, touch and move us. But what a universally personal his is. In fact, he might be studied to cure the modern obsession with the opaquely personal, that lust now especially strong for what he would have utterly despised, the gossip of the confessional and complaint.

Epicurean that Lucretius was and faithful to Epicureanism's belief in friendship, we might find it strange that so few friends, so few people, appear in the poem. Beyond Memmius and recollections of earlier great men, usually admirations or opponents — Epicurus, Democritus, Homer, Empedocles — we encounter no mention of actual associates, no sense of family. Living in the midst of a merciless civil war, Lucretius was occupied with deeper matters, the abiding polity of atoms and things, their reassuring relationships. Furthermore, a naturalist need never be lonely. As Thoreau said, "I am no more lonely than a single mullein or dandelion in a pasture . . . or a horse-fly, or a humble-bee." Lucretius, at least in his poem, is too busy even to refute loneliness. Nor can we disregard his missionary zeal. His happiness seems to depend on the happiness of others. His relationship with the universe in no way interferes with or supplants his relation with his fellowmen. Moreover, aside from the fact that in a sense we and all men are present in the immediate appeal the poem makes to us, to help us, to free us — the "tu" addressed throughout the poem is of course Memmius to begin with, but it also surely refers to each one of us — Lucretius focuses on natural phenomena, not to domesticate or subdue them, but to realize them by his loving, learning attention and so to realize and free himself.

Atoms, however, their careers and biographies, are fairly quickly presented; for after all they are of a text no one sensuously knows, with Lucretius' poem a translation of that completely elusive text. Things are another matter or, if of the same matter, by their very tangible, visible, complex nature more exacting. And Lucretius, diving into them in his search for the essential, cannot pull free of their hooked — or is it honeyed? — edges. Flimsy things may be. But so far does he penetrate them that they become vast, intricate landscapes and events as well, quite mythical in their internal machinations. Though the rose, in itself a tiny veritable hurricane, is dissolving as we ponder it, miraculously for a moment, like a lovely woman or a craggy, giant storm, it persists and for that moment holds in equipoise the heaving torrents of summer. Lucretius' vision is happily bifocal, if not multi-ocular. Under his burnishing glance each object becomes an Aladdin's lamp, aglow with itself and at the same time charged with a grandeur, a god, the only one, of energy. And Lucretius serves these objects up to us, plants also, animals, chimerae, events, catastrophes, in the golden net of his poem. At times, especially late in the poem, they come at us as though shot from a cannon. A crazy epic catalog, they threaten to accumulate, for Lucretius' Odyssean appetite, like the world itself and its myriads. Perhaps it is all the countless films flying through the air, accepted in their natural order.

No better instance exists, I think, of mixed forms or genres than *De Rerum Natura*, the most majestic, certainly the most extended, of all monologues, unless it be Pound's *Cantos*. Like that poem Lucretius' is an inexhaustible, brilliant, darting talk, with the universe its province. Like the *Cantos*, a great grab-bag, into it Lucretius has thrown all he has and all there is. A kind of replica world, the poem must contain all things and in the turmoiled way they assault us. Thus Lucretius, in a style rugged and free in its fashion like ours, exercises all modes of discourse and employs all materials: history, fables, legends, conversations, epigrams, mini-dramas, art (paintings), literature, landscapes, etc. Tirelessly he produced a corrival creation, a poem full of all the possible descriptions of nature of his own and of other thinkers, not to contradict one another but out of his enthusiasm for ideas and to exhibit the range and possibility, like the world, of human thought. And he undertook this mammoth assemblage like Pound, and no one more earnestly, to persuade us to change our lives by fundamentally changing our minds. There was no thing and nothing Lucretius would not gladly use for this purpose and, at least as much, for his pleasure in each thing.

A few of his elaborate, laborious and yet, as he insists, "easy" explanations of things, a few of his Rube Goldberg variations, should illustrate his voracity. Here he so easily considers the extraordinary, if not the fabulous, that the commonplace becomes miraculous. He has snakes that, if touched by human spittle, devour themselves; stags that draw snakes from their holes by breathing into them; lions driven off by the mere sight of a cock. However, after accepting things in his terms, marvels that they are, who would be patient with so-called miracles? Each of his complex, schoolmasterly, yet spry explications is as much a tribute to the human mind and his mind as to the object that is the radiant lesson for the day; to the object and especially to the process able to produce it. His genius, it is true, often verges, in its passion for accuracy and thoroughness, on pedantry; at times he showers us with a spate of explanations for one phenomenon. But an ingratiating gaiety accompanies this thoroughness, the agility and the ingenuity with which we feel him wrestling with the object, a mind eagerly on the stretch. And the youth in this work, that of discovery, is almost tantamount to creation itself. However, it is the persistence of things that finally matters, the rational rightness of their character and their kinship to each other. For its laws and its boundary-stones, it is, dynamics and all, a stable, if not a settled, world.

Among my favorite Lucretian objects are the mirror and the magnet. They constitute, like the other objects Lucretius conjures with, happy personae: the magnet as Lucretius; Lucretius the subtle, diligent mirror; the waterfall and the fire hurling out the radiant, perfervid gaze of Lucretius. The private life of things, whether storm or wine or fragrance, he has insinuated himself into like Proteus to make himself always more himself. But what is a mirror? How does it work? (Only in its working is it. Never have the things of the world been more Whiteheadean "events".) In Lucretius' hands it is all done with mirrors. For aside from the mirror's films striking the eye, we must account for the reflected image, its being "seen beyond the mirror — for it certainly does appear to be some distance behind the surface." In Lucretius' words,

It is just as though we really were looking out through a doorway....First we perceive the air within the door posts; then follow the posts themselves to right and left; then the light outside and a second stretch of air brushes through the eyes, followed by the objects that are really seen out of doors. A similar thing happens when a mirrored object projects itself upon our sight. On its way to us the film shoves and drives before it all the air that intervenes between it and the eye, so that we feel all this before perceiving the mirror. When we have perceived the mirror itself, then the film that travels from us to it and is reflected comes back to our eyes, pushing another lot of air in front of it, so that we perceive this before the image, which thus appears to lie at some distance from the mirror. Here then is ample reason why we should not be surprised at this appearance of objects reflected in the surface of a mirror, since they involve a double journey with two lots of air.

Not surprised indeed. We can understand Lucretius' urging that we retire from the distractions of active life; immersed in such strenuous contemplation, who would have time or energy for anything else? Revelation's rituals and revels are more than enough, a voyeurism surpassing any Saturnalia!

And what is the solution of the magnet? After several pages of preliminary explanation Lucretius says, "On this basis it will be easy to elucidate the problem and lay bare the whole cause of the attraction of iron." The drama, truly sexual, begins. Sexual and, as I suggested, warlike. For after initial maneuvers the magnet and the iron undergo an allout tug of war. Like every other thing the magnet stone is a veritable Trojan horse. Like Greek warriors secreted in it and rushing forth unseen, "First, this stone must emit a dense stream or emanation of atoms, which dispels by a process of bombardment all the air that lies between the stone and the iron." Then, like the poured out, sheepish Trojan populace, "atoms of the iron all tangled together immediately . . . tumble into the vacuum." The whole ring, following, "reaches the stone and clings to it by invisible ties." But that, though it might certainly seem to be, is not enough.

> . . . as soon as the air in front of the ring is rarefied and the space fairly well . . . evacuated, it thereupon happens that all the air situated at the back of the ring pushes and shoves it forward from behind. . . . This air . . . creeps nimbly in through the many porosities in the iron and comes up against its tiny particles so as to push and drive it along as sails and ship are driven by the wind.

And of course a similar process works in us. In walking, for instance. Once the mind, moved by an image of walking, jogs the spirit which then jogs the body, bit by bit setting the whole bulk in motion, with the body grown less dense, air rushes in, and through this double effort the body is shoved along "just as a ship is propelled by the constant action of wind and sails."

After such explanations nothing should surprise us, not the workings of the eye, not the more elusive, superfine workings of mind and spirit. For these too, since we think — so have images — of them, must corporeally exist and can therefore be explained. But how do we see? Our eyes, apparently, are magnet-like bull's eyes, attracting images out of the immense welter to strike them. Yet how is it that a mere invisible film becomes an image, the whole image, of its parent object? Lucretius is imperturbable. Analogies are ever at hand. Wind and cold strike us in bits, yet we feel the total effect. More strikingly, "When we hit a stone with our toe, what we actually touch is only the outer surface of the rock, the overlying film of color; but what we feel ourselves touching is not that but the harder inner core of the rock." With one such stone should not Lucretius be able to put those antagonists Berkeley and Johnson forevermore to rest?

As for those subtlest of matters, the mind and the spirit, things they are, but made of the most tenuous, mobile atoms, the spirit particularly and behind it the spirit of spirit or what some might call the soul. Even our feelings and thoughts are corporeal, and the illusions among them; but these latter are simply yokings of images not meant for each other. Hence mythical creatures, satyrs, centaurs, and the rest. One might wonder not only about consciousness but self-consciousness. Is the latter the self emitting atoms that somehow rebound and strike the self? Or are they atoms locked and therefore clashing with each other? Since he believes in reason and its relevancy to, if not oneness with, nature and its atoms, Lucretius has no sense of a conflict, beyond the basic physical one, between objects and subjects, the many and the one. And he is too enamored of the mighty cosmos he is bent on reproducing to have time for a trifle like the self. Furthermore, as we have seen, his poem intends to free us of the fatuous, fiery burden, the curse, of individuation.

However, we know and delight in knowing with Lucretius that the more difficult the task the more doughtily and lovably he undertakes it. For learning, the blessing of knowledge, is all. And this wherever it may take us. Intent on accommodating us to the idea of death, Lucretius, like Achilles over a young warrior he is about to kill, favors us with a rollcall of the noblest dead:

> . . . good king Ancus. . . . Even that King of Kings. . . . Scipio, that thunderbolt of war. . . . the discoverers of truth and beauty. . . . the attendants of the Muses, among them Homer who in solitary glory bore the scepter but has sunk into the same slumber as the rest. Democritus. . . . And the Master himself . . . Epicurus himself . . . . And will you kick and protest against your sentence?

As he reels out in ever increasing crescendo great name after great name, Lucretius gives way to an infectious ecstasy. This ecstasy in the face of the worst, fully grappled with, makes life more exuberantly possible. In addition, does he not, rather as with the extravagances of lovers he dismissed, in disposing of these great by that very act possess and preserve them? They are shining witnesses to his truth and to his unique splendor too. So poetry, even the poetry that denies it, immortalizes. The poem, to some degree at least, disproves the poet's animadversions on immortality. Though we know how close the poem came to being lost, it has stood fast, weathered the batterings of the frantic, indifferent centuries. And it has reached an outlandish time and shore which may be in closer agreement with it than any earlier age.

Finally, in the helterskelter last book, unfinished and happening, in process like the unfinished, happening world, Lucretius with a kind of cosmic rapture delivers a rhapsody of catastrophe piled on catastrophe to prove not only our mortality but that of the universe. I will not say that Lucretius gloats over cataclysms, not more than over their reverse. But he is polemical enough, with a conviction profound and religious enough, to enjoy drawing on the world's worst for proof. This is not an altogether remarkable trait. Each morning my professor of religion would come into class, like a mouse-swallowing cat, with the latest terrible headlines; they delighted as they confirmed him. War, Lucretius is confident, the basic war that keeps the universe going, will finally destroy it. And if Lucretius appropriately starts with Venus and Spring or creation and procreation as the world did, he concludes with Mars and destruction as the world will. If out of Venus and her son Aeneas Lucretius, to begin with, salutes Aeneas' race, that climax of mankind, the Romans, he opens his last book with the true pinnacle of human wisdom and accomplishments, Athens, best of all the mother of Epicurus. And aptly then Lucretius concludes his poem with the destruction through plague of the supreme city. If a rose emerges, but for a moment only, so Athens, that ultimate human flowering, by the law of things must also fall. A clinching demonstration through cataclysm, Athen's end is of the futility of men's efforts, fears, desires. In short, *De Rerum Natura* is one of the strangest consolation books ever written, one celebrating the rugged joys of mortality.

In his redoing of Thucydides' austere record of this plague, of course Lucretius added something of his own impetuosity. He, one is tempted to suggest, heaping anonymous corpses of people many of whom might have been distinguished and noble (no doubt some successful Epicureans among them!), recovers some of the ferocity, not to say exultancy, of Greek tragedy. An energy arising from catastrophe itself crackles in his words. In like manner Tolstoy records how, after a long hideous day working in a plague-ridden town, returning home exhausted and finding himself late at night in a little, moon-lit wood, he filled with an inexplicable rapture. It is something of the aimless joy of Yeats' "Lapis Lazuli." And I still remember with awe listening to Professor Shapley of Harvard also, like Lucretius, explaining the universe. He, drawing himself up to his small, whole, overpeering height, became more and more excited as he reached his climax — namely, what is this earth? A tiny, peripheral, ephemeral planet, he triumphantly exclaimed, in an out-of-the-way corner of a third-rate, running-down galaxy. Man derives as much pleasure, apparently, from considering himself insignificant as from considering himself the universe's prize creation. As much pleasure from singing doom out of apocalypse as from singing creation. Certainly the pleasure out of man's insignificance and the pleasure out of his sense of his worth — the former, the awareness and the certitude of it, producing the latter — pervade *De Rerum Natura.*

Library of Congress Cataloging in Publication Data

Weiss, Theodore Russell, 1916-
  The man from Porlock.

  (Princeton series of collected essays)
  Includes index.
  1. Literature—History and criticism—Addresses,
essays, lectures.   I. Title.   II. Series.
PNPN511.W43   809   82-47622
ISBN 0-691-06518-7   AACR2
ISBN 0-691-01396-9 (pbk.)